Peaceable Kingdom

Peaceable Kingdom

Stability and Change in Modern Britain

by

BRIAN HARRISON

CLARENDON PRESS · OXFORD
1982

306.0941

Oxford University Press, Walton Street, Oxford OX2 6DP
London Glasgow New York Toronto
Delhi Bombay Calcutta Madras Karachi
Kuala Lumpur Singapore Hong Kong Tokyo
Nairobi Dar es Salaam Cape Town
Melbourne Auckland
and associate companies in
Beirut Berlin Ibadan Mexico City

Published in the United States by
Oxford University Press, New York

British Library Cataloguing in Publication Data

Harrison, Brian
   Peaceable kingdom: stability and change in
   modern Britain.
   1. Great Britain—History—George III, 1760–1820
   2. Great Britain—History—19th century
   3. Great Britain—History—20th century
   I. Title
   941.07   DA470
   ISBN 0-19-822603-9

Library of Congress Cataloging in Publication Data

Harrison, Brian Howard.
   Peaceable kingdom.
   Includes bibliographical references and index.
   1. Great Britain—Politics and government—
19th century—Addresses, essays, lectures.
2. Great Britain—Politics and government—20th
century—Addresses, essays, lectures.   3. Great
Britain—Politics and government—1760–1820—
Addresses, essays, lectures.   4. England—Social
conditions—19th century—Addresses, essays, lectures.   5. England—Social conditions—20th century—Addresses, essays, lectures.   6. England—
Social conditions—18th century—Addresses, essays,
lectures.   I. Title.
   DA530.H446   306'.0941   82-6400
   ISBN 0-19-822603-9   AACR2

Typeset by Anne Joshua Associates, Oxford
Printed in Great Britain
at the University Press, Oxford
by Eric Buckley
Printer to the University

'The outstanding and—by contemporary standards —highly original quality of the English is their habit of *not killing one another*. Putting aside the "model" small states, which are in an exceptional position, England is the only European country where internal politics are conducted in a more or less humane and decent manner.'

George Orwell, 'The English People' (1947), in *Collected Essays, Journalism and Letters* (Penguin ed.), iii, p. 47.

Acknowledgements

I most gratefully acknowledge here the generous help I have received from several people whose own pressing commitments did not prevent them from making the time to comment on individual chapters of this book—Brian Farrell on Chapter I; Paul Johnson, Patrick Joyce, and Ross McKibbin on Chapter IV; Lord McGregor of Durris on Chapter VI; Vernon Bogdanor, David Bryan, Ken Morgan, and Philip Williams on Chapter VII. I have frequently adopted their suggestions, though the responsibility for what is published here remains entirely my own. Gill Wigglesworth drew salutary attention to defects of style and presentation in the book as a whole before it was too late.

The editors of the *English Historical Review, Past and Present*, and *Victorian Studies* have allowed me to republish —as Chapters II, III, and V—material which originally appeared as articles in their journals. The Open University allowed me to republish in Chapter VI material drawn from one of their radio programmes. More specific and detailed acknowledgements (including acknowledgements for permission to quote from unpublished interviews and writings) appear in the footnotes for each chapter, but I would like to acknowledge here the fact that the interviews which gave me such help in writing Chapter I were obtained with the aid of a three-year grant from the Social Science Research Council. The Rockefeller Foundation gave me an invaluable opportunity to prepare the first draft of this book at their conference centre in Bellagio in the summer of 1980.

I wish to conclude with a general acknowledgement to the undergraduates I have taught in Oxford since 1961. Two of the eight essays in this book began as lectures which aimed to provide them with guidance in areas where I thought it was needed, but the whole book owes much to the stimulus I have always received from their refreshing willingness to disagree with their tutor in tutorials. Although they may well not realize it at the time, I often learn a great deal from what they say.

Corpus Christi College, Oxford   Brian Harrison
November 1981

Contents

Abbreviations

CD Acts	Contagious Diseases Acts
CND	Campaign for Nuclear Disarmament
COS	Charity Organisation Society
LDOS	Lord's Day Observance Society
LWMA	London Working Men's Association
NUWSS	National Union of Women's Suffrage Societies
NSPCC	National Society for the Prevention of Cruelty to Children
RSPCA	Royal Society for the Prevention of Cruelty to Animals
SDF	Social Democratic Federation
WMLDRA	Working Men's Lord's Day Rest Association
WSPU	Women's Social and Political Union

In each individual footnote, references are first supplied for the sources quoted in the text, in order of appearance, followed by references to other relevant sources. All items cited in footnotes were published in London unless otherwise stated. Full details appear only at the point of first citation; thereafter, abbreviated titles are used. Up to 1803, citations from parliamentary debates come from Cobbett's *Parliamentary History*; from then to 1812 from Cobbett's *Parliamentary Debates*, and thereafter from the several series of *Hansard*. Debates in Lords and Commons were published separately from 1909.

Introduction

The essays published here have been written during the past sixteen years in the course of research on British reforming movements and pressure groups, especially on temperance and feminism. Chapters IV–VII try to meet the need of pupils for adequate secondary literature on an important but neglected theme; they owe less to original research, more to the scattered secondary literature which they seek to integrate. The essays were written at different times for different purposes, but in this edition duplications between them have been eliminated, and they have been arranged so that they can now be read consecutively, though each can be read in isolation if desired. They all concern British history, and fall between about 1780 and the present day. Chapters IV–VII pursue a theme throughout the whole of that period, but Chapter VIII does not go beyond 1914, and Chapters II and III concern only the nineteenth century. Chapter I concerns the narrowest period of all, Edwardian Britain.

The historian who republishes essays already available elsewhere owes his readers an explanation. Chapters II, III, and V have appeared in readily accessible historical journals, but Chapter II has been revised, Chapter III rearranged and amplified, and Chapter V completely rewritten. Five of the essays have not been published before, and all eight are united by an interest in the process of political change and by a preoccupation with the sources of social and political cohesion in Britain since the industrial revolution. For despite all the imperial and commercial exploitation she has witnessed, Britain since the seventeenth century has been a peaceable kingdom, by comparison both with her earlier history and with other nations in a similar situation. The point has been most memorably made by George Orwell, but it repeatedly thrusts itself forward in the historical record. I was not aware of this unifying theme when most of the essays were first drafted, but in retrospect this seems to lend additional justification for gathering together these particular essays rather than others for collective publication. The Victorians viewed the pressures towards social cohesion and political continuity in Britain—particularly the art of compromise and the pursuit of mutual reconciliation through the non-violent reforming movement—as subjects for national pride. Foreigners attending the international philanthropic conference in 1856 were astonished at the vitality of British voluntarism, and were puzzled in 1876 when confronted with the Bulgarian atrocities agitation.[1] Macaulay and Carlyle echoed this Victorian pride, profoundly influenced as they were by the French revolution, the industrial revolution, and Chartism. So did their twentieth-century successors G. M. Trevelyan and Elie Halévy, whose historical writing owed so much to the advent of Socialism, the first world war, and the Russian revolution. Paradoxically the retreat of social polarization since 1945 has enabled British historians to enjoy the luxury of a professional polarization; whereas some choose to focus on fragmenting influences and revolutionary tendencies, others take pleasure in portraying statesmen serenely unruffled by both, but relatively few concern themselves with the interaction between the two.

If only for reasons of historical balance, it is perhaps now time to revive the earlier British preoccupation with the roots of consensus. Such a theme contributes yet another reason— together with Britain's fine historiographical tradition and her precocious industrialization—why the study of British history since 1780 will survive Britain's twentieth-century decline in international status. Political violence in this period was kept to a remarkably low level in relation to comparable societies both at the time and since; this is one reason for the survival of that rich documentation on which modern British historians are able to draw. Many societies today experience difficulties resembling those faced earlier by the United Kingdom; none can face them with quite that sense of venturing into the unknown, nor perhaps with quite that wealth of governmental wisdom and experience which made the whole enterprise less hazardous in the British case. This should not foster complacency—if only because

[1] National Temperance League, *Annual Report. 1856*, p. 16; R. T. Shannon, *Gladstone and the Bulgarian Agitation. 1876* (1963), p. 26.

a large measure of good luck (geographical, historical, economic) attended the process; besides, the social and political challenges presented by industrialization persist into the 1980s, and demand a continuous renewal of our predecessors' resourcefulness and energy, courage and imagination.

The full range of influences producing political continuity cannot possibly be explored in only eight essays. They include those objective conditions that are the speciality of particular types of historian: demographic, economic, climatic, and so on. So serious was the economic threat to social stability in 1839–42 and in the 1880s, for instance, that one historian rightly emphasizes the disjunction between economic dislocation in England and Ireland at those times.[2] There are also given geographical factors; Britain since the industrial revolution cannot be analysed as though it is a closed political and social system. National cohesion owed much to the existence of the English Channel, policed by the British navy, which ensured that—at least till the 1930s—domestic controversy was not exacerbated, as so often elsewhere, by the danger of invasion from an outside enemy which fomented domestic controversy. National cohesion also owed much to the pride in overseas empire taken by subordinate regional or status groups; the Scottish contribution to empire was, for instance, considerable. On the other hand, anti-imperialist groupings in Wales, Scotland, and (somewhat precariously) Ireland found that through supporting the Liberal Party they could simultaneously criticize the empire and integrate themselves more fully into the British political system.

Also relevant to national cohesion are the less objective factors that are susceptible to political influence—patterns of internal disunity, for example. The numerous polarities within British society since the industrial revolution help to integrate society by cutting across one another: London versus the kingdom, town versus country, Englishmen versus the rest—not to mention friction between the generations and the sexes. Then there are the tripartite antagonisms

[2] E. J. Hobsbawm, 'Economic Fluctuations and some Social Movements since 1800', *Economic History Review*, 1952, p. 8; cf. G. M. Young, *Victorian England. Portrait of an Age* (2nd ed., 1953), p. 45.

between Anglicans, Catholics, and nonconformists; or between aristocracy, middle class, and working class (in so far as any of these can be seen as integrated social groupings). Such complex social alignments leave plenty of scope to the politician, who also has at his disposal the institutions which overtly pursue national cohesion: patriotic symbols, jubilees, flags, and ceremonial, together with their less savoury accompaniments—prisons, police, and the army. Such subjects demand the historian's attention.[3] But political stability depends at least as much on the political skill with which objective conditions and political situations are handled as on the conditions and situations themselves.

The eight essays below pay more attention to the political situations than to the objective conditions; they show particular interest in questions of political mechanism and tactics, and in the muting of potentially divisive conflicts between social groups. Chapter I immediately focuses on the territory to be occupied so frequently in later chapters: the point of contact between parliamentary and extra-parliamentary political activity. It seeks to explain the evolution of violent tactics within the women's suffrage movement, and to distinguish between different types of political violence; it highlights the major theme of the book by emphasizing the subtle and equivocal political impact of violence, especially in the British context. Chapters II and III move on to consider groups that tried to lower the incidence of violence by rather direct means—through promoting humanitarian causes. They illustrate how humanitarian movements helped to stabilize the social structure by simultaneously increasing the moral authority of the educated classes while 'civilizing' their inferiors through means that now seem, to say the least, indirect. Chapter II also illustrates in operation a pressure group whose non-violent and cautious methods produced major long-term achievement. Chapter III combines the theme of violence in politics and society with a second theme: the prevalence in nineteenth-century Britain of polarities cutting across class alignment. We are nowadays so alert to class-consciousness

---

[3] I have discussed one aspect of this in 'For Church, Queen and Family: the Girls' Friendly Society 1874–1920', *Past and Present*, no. 61 (Nov. 1973).

as a theme that we easily drift into underestimating the nineteenth-century importance of other social categories— religious, regional, cultural, and occupational—not to mention the categories of generation and gender. Even where class alignments were important, the nature and location of class boundaries were not identical with our own. Chapter III makes all these points at the same time as emphasizing the cross-pressuring which occurred when class alignments at work and at play were not precisely superimposed.

Chapter IV focuses on the politically significant bonds which have arisen at crucial moments between the groups we would now describe as 'middle' and 'working' class, and at the same time emphasizes the importance of humanitarian influences within the British labour movement. Chapter V stresses linkages across social class-barriers from the opposite direction by focusing on those who sought social stability though voluntarily redistributing wealth from rich to poor within a network of personal friendships; philanthropy was also an activity which helped to integrate hitherto excluded groups more fully into the political system. Chapter VI focuses on those whose philanthropic zeal and social conscience carried them into conveying information as well as wealth between the social classes, through systematic inquiry into social conditions. Whether intentionally or not, they were helping to prepare the ground for that major integrative influence of twentieth-century Britain, the welfare state.

Chapter VII carries forward themes developed in Chapters III–VI, but in a different dimension. For at least a century, the British party system has simultaneously split the working class and united sections of it to other classes; it does this by apparently polarizing the nation between two rival political groupings engaged in vigorous mutual criticism and permeated at times even by mutual distaste. Yet if this were the whole story, it would be difficult to see how political cohesion has ever been maintained in modern Britain. Chapter VII tries to show how formal centrist political groupings are by no means necessary for the effective cultivation of centrist attitudes and practices. Chapter VIII analyses the recurring pattern of reforming argument at Westminster before 1914.

It carries forward themes from Chapter VII by emphasizing the importance for political stability of securing political mechanisms that will bring the idealist into regular contact with the pragmatist, by highlighting the contribution parliament has customarily made towards this, and by drawing attention to the importance for the reforming story of the debating situation itself, as distinct from the social pressures which help to mould it and which nowadays tend to receive more attention. But it also develops a theme running through the book as a whole when it emphasizes the difficulty of the politician's role, the complexity of the reforming process, and the distortions which result from viewing political history primarily through the eyes of the vindicated reformer.

The idea that the historian is a God-like figure presiding impartially and without passion over the objective recitation of past events is held by a surprising number of people. It is not a description with which the historian can live comfortably. The decision to write on these topics in the first place, let alone to group them together in this way, reflects a particular political position. My own political outlook is of no intrinsic interest, but the reader has a right to be informed about it because it inevitably influences the interpretations which follow. Its point of departure might have been labelled 'Liberal' if the Liberal Party had survived the 1920s with sufficient energy to inspire its own school of historians; some would now label it 'social democratic'. This does not of course denote the rather narrower alignment marshalled since 1981 by the Social Democratic Party; indeed, Chapter VII recites some reasons why a British social democrat would contemplate forming such a grouping only as a temporary expedient, and would in the long term prefer to align himself with centrists who remain in the Labour or Conservative Parties.

The centrist historian can for the sake of convenience be defined as the historian who sets out on his task with centrist political proclivities without necessarily favouring an institutionalized centre grouping. Such a tripartite categorization of historians is of course crude; it ignores the numerous gradations within all three categories—the important twentieth-century distinction on the left between Marxist and non-Marxist labour historians, for example, and the distinction on the right between Whigs and Tories. Nor are political influences the only important determinants of historical writing; ideally it might be desirable (if somewhat pretentious) to precede any historical work with a brief autobiography, and even if totally honest that would specify only the conscious influences at work. It is important, however, to emphasize the book's centrist standpoint, not because its theme. will be of interest only to centrists (pressures for social cohesion can no more be taken for granted by the conservative than they can be ignored by the radical who aims to be effective), but because its historiographical implications in the modern British context are so great. Brief consideration is given here to four of these implications: for impartiality, for attitudes to political history, for approaches to historical explanation, and for attitudes to the relationship between the study of past and present. Each of these will be discussed in turn.

The centrist historian can no more lay claim to an Olympian objectivity than historians of any other allegiance. It is important here to make a number of distinctions. The influence on him of personal experience and even of inclination or preconception may bring benefits. On the other hand, the influence on him of their uglier sisters bias and prejudice may cause him to betray his profession. The influence on the historian of the weakest among these mental states, recollection of personal experience, is inevitable and potentially salutary. Michael Oakeshott rightly warns us not to confuse the influence of experience with bias; he thinks it quite wrong to suppose 'that what is independent of the particular ideas and prejudices of his own place and time must be what is altogether independent of experience'.[4] Objectivity, in the sense of an interpretation that owes nothing to the personal experience of the interpreter, is impossible. The historian will of course be preoccupied with many things besides current affairs, but he will never be wholly unconcerned about, or uninfluenced by, the fortunes of the society which provides him with his livelihood; hence the vigorous arguments which occur not

---

[4] M. Oakeshott, *Experience and its Modes* (Cambridge, 1933), p. 94.

only among historians at any one time, but also between historians from one generation and the next. Nor will the type of personal experience affecting historical interpretation be confined to political influences. A. J. P. Taylor emphasizes how the most mundane things can influence the grandest of the historian's intellectual perspectives when he says that all the twentieth-century historian's talk of threats to civilization 'means only that university professors used to have domestic servants and now do their own washing-up'.[5]

When we move forward from personal experience to inclination—described by *The Oxford English Dictionary* as 'the condition of being inevitably inclined or disposed towards a particular object; disposition, propensity, leaning' —we are again considering a quality which the historian can turn to advantage. Historical writing that failed in some way to grow out of a particular viewpoint would lack vigour and impact. The historian's inclination is not necessarily a tiresome hurdle to be overcome, a heavy baggage to be shed. Style, choice of topic, range of inquiry, all owe much to the author's conviction and opinion. Inclination and preconception can also develop the historian's imagination in expounding a viewpoint held by others in the past, or his ingenuity at gaining historical comprehension and sympathy. But the potential benefits of inclination go further than this. G. M. Trevelyan describes 'the discovery of the facts' as 'the truly scientific element in the historian's task', and claims that 'the field of facts thus impartially discovered, ought to be common ground for all historians, although they will differ in the interpretations they put on it'. Yet he soon concedes that facts must be selected, and that this can be done 'only on some principle of personal interpretation'.[6] Inclination and preconception will influence the area where the historian looks for his facts, and on which particular facts within the area that he alights; they will also influence the combination of those facts that he later chooses to create. As Oakeshott writes, 'there are no facts which are

    [5] Quot. by J. M. Price in *History and Theory*, vol. 3, no. 1, p. 142.
    [6] G. M. Trevelyan, 'Bias in History', in his *An Autobiography and other Essays* (1949), pp. 68-9.

not ideas'.[7] Even the most austerely professional of the historian's tasks—editing a document or compiling a bibliography—will reflect subjective factors.

Historians on the left are relatively candid about how their political inclinations influence their historical writing; some have even embraced the label, never precisely defined, of 'socialist historian'. If this simply denotes an area of interest, and aims at influencing more than a purely sectarian readership, with no orthodoxy of interpretation, it is a mere synonym for the older label 'labour historian' and is unexceptionable, for its criteria of quality do not diverge from those which apply elsewhere in the political spectrum. No Conservative has yet espoused the label 'Conservative historian', and historians who happen to be Conservatives do not normally dwell upon linkages between their political inclinations and their historical writing. With refreshing honesty, however, Maurice Cowling writes that 'it is rare indeed to find an historian who does not bear on his lips, his pen or his manner, the marks of his time and place, the impress of his education, the evidence of the truths he is trying to express or the power that he has to will by words the creation of a world that is as it should be'.[8] In truth, historians on both right and left offer many instances of fair-minded and penetrating analysis which none the less owe much to their initial political inclination.

But in discussing inclination we hover on the brink of discussing bias. Indeed, *The Oxford English Dictionary*'s definition does not distinguish clearly between the two: 'an inclination, leaning, tendency, bent'. But if bias is interpreted to mean adherence to a commitment more intense than inclination, even that has been seen as in some respects salutary, and by a historian as distinguished as G. M. Trevelyan. He points out that his volumes on Garibaldi 'are reeking with bias. Without bias I should never have written them at all.'[9] He goes on to say that the historian's own enthusiasm may give him insight into the passions which moved men

[7] M. Oakeshott, op. cit., p. 93.

[8] M. Cowling, *Religion and Public Doctrine in Modern England* (Cambridge, 1980), p. 397, cf. preface, p. xxiii.

[9] G. M. Trevelyan, op. cit., pp. 77-8, cf. H. Butterfield, *The Whig Interpretation of History* (1931), p. 93.

in the past: 'I don't deny the dangers of such warmth, but is there not also a danger to truth in a perpetual aloofness that never permits the historian to go down among the men and women of the past as one of themselves?' Trevelyan denies that bias, in the sense of 'any personal interpretation of historical events which is not acceptable to the whole human race' either can or should be avoided by any historian.[10]

Style certainly can come alive when the author discusses subjects and personalities that stir his sympathies. But in such cases the historian has ventured into dangerous territory. The vigour of his prose may merely reflect a reaction against those earlier historical interpretations with which he disagrees, and his writing therefore all too easily ceases to be complete in itself; it becomes parasitic upon earlier writing, or demands subsequent modification. It has reached, so to speak, only the preliminary stage to complete historical digestion. I diverge here from the approach adopted by Robert Skidelsky in his *Oswald Mosley*, a book for whose over-all historiographical aim I have the greatest respect; for there he sets out to occupy a position 'somewhere between that of counsel for the defence and judge', and to make 'the case for Mosley',[11] whereas the historian must surely seek to occupy a more firmly judicial role. True, in a society which allows free public debate, the defects of any one interpretation are exposed to the self-corrective mechanism of reviewing and mutual criticism within the historical profession. That process is rendered the more efficient if in his preface the historian states at least the most relevant among the inclinations that have influenced his writing; 'it is not a sin in a historian to introduce a personal bias that can be recognised and discounted', writes Butterfield: 'the sin in historical composition is the organisation of the story in such a way that bias cannot be recognised'.[12] Ideally, though, the balance the historian aims at should always be internal to his own argument, and should not depend in its over-all emphasis on the existence of complementary and contrary emphases elsewhere.

[10] G. M. Trevelyan, op. cit., p. 69.
[11] R. Skidelsky, *Oswald Mosley* (1975), p. 11; cf. G. M. Trevelyan, op. cit., p. 72.   [12] H. Butterfield, op. cit., p. 105.

If previous experience, inclination, and even bias enter so deeply into historical writing, what is there to distinguish it from a purely imaginative process of creation? Here we come to the distinction between the three mental states so far discussed, often salutary in their effects, and the fourth, prejudice. With its outcrop, propaganda, this is the death of historical writing. *The Oxford English Dictionary* sees prejudice as 'a previous judgement', especially 'a judgement formed before due examination or consideration', whereas the historian is required to respond continuously to new ideas, sensitivities, and sources of information. He must continuously engage in a process of self-questioning, continuously present to himself, in their best possible aspect, ideas and personalities that he finds uncongenial. 'It is a golden rule, which I try to follow', wrote Darwin, 'to put every fact which is opposed to one's preconceived opinion in the strongest light.'[13] The historian can never indulge himself by describing the world as he thinks it should be rather than as it is; his imagination must always be reined in by evidence whose range he is of course in a position to expand, but whose existence he can never create. Furthermore he will always need to provide the safeguard offered by adequate documentation, so as to enable his readers themselves to travel over the factual territory he surveys.

There is, therefore, a clear distinction to be made between the historian's previous experience, his inclination, his bias, and his prejudice; he by no means necessarily travels from the first through the second and third to the last. Of the safeguards against his taking such a journey, apart from the evidence itself, three can conveniently be mentioned here. The first, a sense of proportion, is cultivated not only by the practice of historical writing, and by breadth of knowledge about the society in question, but also by the historian's own experience of life itself; it involves skill in assessing the relative importance within a society or within a single individual of the various factors competing for primacy at any one time. It is a quality essential to political success, involving a sense of balance, a perception of relative significance, and a judgement of human character.

[13] C. Darwin, *More Letters* (ed. F. Darwin and A. C. Seward, 1903), ii, p. 324.

The second safeguard against prejudice, a capacity for comprehension, owes more to intellect, and involves skill at throwing oneself into the mind of a society or individual that is alien either by personality or (for reasons of time and/or location) by culture. It is the quality that enabled John Morley the agnostic brilliantly to recapture the personality and intellect of W. E. Gladstone the High-Churchman, Elie Halévy the twentieth-century Frenchman to evoke the mood of nineteenth-century England, and numerous men and women to write memorably about members of the opposite sex. The complexity of the historian's task is highlighted by the fact that this quality may be nourished sometimes by affinity, real or imagined, between investigator and invesitgated, sometimes by distance between them.

The third safeguard against prejudice—fair-mindedness— is akin to the second, but owes more to temperament, and is more a matter of exertion than of skill. It entails giving a fair hearing to all sides in past controversy, bearing in mind what was possible at the time for each participant to believe and to do; it requires the historian perpetually to conjure up personalities from the past to stand by his elbow as he writes and defend themselves when not given their due. The historian thereby risks bending over backwards to be fair to the side which is unpopular,[14] whether at the historical moment under analysis, or at the time when the historian is himself writing. 'I believe that it is possible to be more objective than most of us are', wrote George Orwell in 1944, attacking nationalistic habits of mind (which for him included Marxist attitudes), 'but . . . it involves a *moral* effort. One cannot get away from one's own subjective feelings, but at least one can know what they are and make allowance for them.'[15] This is a formidable agenda, but it is because historians are professionally bound continuously to attempt it that their unhampered activity is integral to any civilized society—not simply for the type of writing that emerges, but for the type of person

---

[14] For an amusing case-study of how such a position is misrepresented, though, see *The Times*, 23 Sept. 1978, p. 13; 12 Oct. 1978, p. 19.

[15] G. Orwell, *Collected Essays, Journalism and Letters* (ed. S. Orwell and I. Angus), iii (Penguin ed., 1968), pp. 101, 172. Cf. G. M. Trevelyan, op. cit., p. 68.

(whether reader or writer) that such activity, when successful, eventually helps to create.

The adoption of an intermediate political position between
labour and Conservative historians is not the only option
open to the centrist historian who diverges from them. He
could reject their political orientation altogether and operate
on an entirely different plane. But this is not the position
taken in this book, whose centrist outlook fosters the mood
of synthesis which lies behind the three other historiographical consequences of centrism: an intermediate standpoint between social and political history, between particular-
ity and generalization, and between contrasting attitudes
to the relationship between past and present.

There may be some affinity between the mentality which
seeks a centrist political location and the mentality which is
eclectic between historical methods or preoccupations; any
such affinity will certainly be nourished by the experience of
occupying a situation intermediate between Conservative
'political' historians and labour 'social' historians. It is
a historiographical polarity that is artificial and not observed
in this book. For nearly three decades now we have seen
a remarkable flowering in Britain of what is usually called
'labour history'. Pioneered by the Fabians, R. H. Tawney,
and the Hammonds—it 'took off' in the 1950s with the
work of historians now well known and respected within
the profession: Asa Briggs, Eric Hobsbawm, Henry Pelling,
Edward Thompson, John Saville, and several others, together
with the academic journals which published their mono-
graphs: *Past and Present*, the *Bulletin of the Society for the
Study of Labour History*, the *International Review of Social
History*, and so on. The labour historians performed a major
service in rectifying a serious neglect and even distortion of
working-class history. But their concentration on radical and
even revolutionary movements has thrown into the background the factors that have helped to integrate British
society. They sometimes even neglected the integrating role
of the labour movement itself—the trade unions' 'handling'
function, for instance, in moderating industrial conflict;
or the Labour Party's role in gaining wider and continuing
acceptance for British political institutions. The labour

historians have often displayed an almost Marxian lack of
interest in writing about the minutiae of politics; when set
beside the excitements of chronicling millennial hopes
and grand economic transformations, the painstaking business
of co-ordinating disparate groups and personalities behind
viable policies perhaps seems tedious to them as a major
historical concern.

By contrast there is 'the somewhat patrician reluctance of
students of *Hochpolitik* to immerse more than a toe in the
troubled waters of social history', as Patrick Joyce puts it.[16]
The group of Conservative historians associated with Maurice
Cowling at Cambridge displays a meticulous preoccupation
with the intricate rivalries of leading political personalities
which sometimes comes near to presenting the dramatis
personae without the play. During the Home Rule crisis of
1885-6, writes J. R. Vincent, ' "English opinion about
Ireland" was manufactured in England for home consumption, had nothing to do with Ireland, and everything to do
with England.'[17] This group of historians also displays an
obliqueness of approach and a knowing dismissal of the
familiar which gives the impression of deliberately excluding
the multitude not just from the political process being
analysed, but from the capacity effectively to comprehend
it. The veil which conceals the arcana of politics is half drawn
aside only to be quickly replaced before too much is glimpsed.

While showing a subtle appreciation of political realities,
a shrewd perception of the interaction between personality
and policy, and at times a coruscating brilliance of analysis—
historians of this school sometimes give the impression of
inhabiting a different planet from the labour historians. The
two groups seldom operate in the same territory, still less
do they converse. Their mutual disdain can be deduced only
from the directions of their historical effort, for they rarely
refer to one another, let alone attend one another's gatherings; one labour historian reviewing Cowling's *Impact of
Labour* says that even reading the book 'required not only

[16] P. Joyce, *Work, Society and Politics. The Culture of the Factory in Later
Victorian England* (Brighton, 1980), p. 222.
[17] J. Vincent and A. B. Cooke, *The Governing Passion. Cabinet Government
and Party Politics in Britain 1885-86* (Brighton, 1974), p. 18.

unusual effort but also a conscientious suspension of disbelief'.[18] This intellectual gulf reflects a survival at the academic level since 1945 of a polarity which had earlier impinged on society and politics in Britain as a whole.

The Cowling school's distinctly anti-heroic and interactive view of major politicians leads it more naturally to the analytic discussion of political episodes, or at most to group-biography, than to writing the biography of a single individual. But Conservative historians are not all clustered in Cambridge, and many of those elsewhere have concentrated on the writing of biography—whether of their own Party, or of prominent individuals within it: Peel, Disraeli, Salisbury, Curzon, Bonar Law, Balfour, Baldwin, Churchill. This work has brought into historical discussion a wealth of new material, much of it from private archives not hitherto consulted; it has also brought together secondary discussion on common problems that had hitherto been unduly dispersed. But these Conservative biographers resemble the Cowling school in showing little interest in the non-political factors which make for social cohesion, little interest in the outlook, methods, and institutions of Conservatives who operate at lower levels within the community at large. The Conservative historians' high political preoccupations are the more surprising for the fact that Conservatives normally place a relatively low valuation on the political dimension of life. The social history likely to interest the Conservatives, being slanted towards the study of contentment, is admittedly elusive in the historical record. Yet Conservatives know that their Party is by no means the only source of conservative values in British society, and that it promotes the aspirations and even the interests of social groupings far broader than that small élite of the politicians who matter.

Between these two groups of historians—labour and Conservative—advance in one direction seems to entail withdrawal in another. While Conservative historians neglect the history of extra-parliamentary activity, labour historians tend—at least by implication—to dismiss as uninteresting the history of national governmental structures, and sometimes

[18] James Hinton, in *Bulletin of the Society for the Study of Labour History*, Spring 1972, p. 64.

even the institutional structures of the labour movement itself. Yet there are affinities between Conservative and labour historians—affinities which some centrist historians may not share—about the mood in which high politics are conducted, for example. James Hinton, when reviewing Cowling in 1972, expressed distaste for the 'trivial and nasty world of rhetoric and manoeuver' which Cowling's book describes. But emphasis on the careerism and even cynicism of politicians is by no means confined to Conservative historians. Edward Thompson, for instance, reviewing Harold Wilson's *The Labour Government 1964-70* (1971), deplored a government which seemed to stagger from one accident to another, and rose from the book 'with an enhanced contempt for parliamentarians'. Marxist history might have been expected to emphasize structural, long-term, and impersonal factors, yet it has not insulated British labour history from dwelling upon its great 'betrayals' and alleged co-options. 'It is curious that I always attribute these devious motives to other people', wrote George Orwell in August 1940, 'being anything but cunning myself and finding it hard to use indirect methods even when I see the need for them.'[19]

Even on the role of social history, the gulf between Conservative and labour historians is less great than it appears to be on the surface; one is even tempted to say that the distinction between them lies less in the role they allocate to social history than in the degree of fuss they make about the matter. The Cowling school, even when at its most austerely political, is well able to write social history of the highest quality. Emphasizing that the politicians' world in 1885-6 'was closed . . . in that politicians were bound to see more significance in the definite structure of relationships at Westminster, than in their contacts with the world outside', John Vincent points out that 'there was no sharp line dividing what happened at cabinet meetings from a continuous but less formal process of discussion and intrigue from which policy also emerged'. The framework of political debate was established 'not by talking directly to electors,

[19] Hinton, op. cit., p. 65; E. P. Thompson in *New Society*, 29 July 1971, p. 202; G. Orwell, *Collected Essays, Journalism and Letters*, ii, p. 417.

but through the medium of clubs, the lobby, the dinner table, the race meeting, the visit to dine and sleep, the morning call, and the stroll in the park'.[20] Conservative historians know that the social history of the British political élite is a variant of social history at least as important, interesting, and neglected as any other, and in Vincent's *The Formation of the Liberal Party. 1857–1868* (1966) they have produced a brilliant political study which continually crosses the arbitrary boundary between histories of the political and social variety.

Historians of any persuasion will agree that even in the most aristocratic of political systems, popular movements cannot be seen solely through the eyes of those who view them from above, if only because—in Britain, at least— popular movements were never securely within élite control; events during the crises of 1831–2 or 1845–6 spring to mind, in Ireland in the 1880s, or within the labour movement between 1910 and 1931. High politics at such moments consist largely in jockeyings for position in such a way as to re-establish control over potentially dangerous forces. Conversely, no historian can ignore the major implications of decision-making at the high political level for the daily lives of the whole population—a decision-making which is neither predetermined nor predictable. When it comes to the declaration of war, for instance, or to the (less frequently mentioned) avoidance of it, politicians' potential impact on social life is considerable.

A book which contains no more than eight essays on particular topics cannot hope to produce any extensive engagement between Conservative political and labour social historians. The prime concern here is always with the subject-matter, and only incidentally with the historiographical issues raised thereby. But essays concerned with the inter-action between popular movements and the political system inevitably entail some sort of synthesis between political and social history. This book shares the perspective of those historians who emphasize the interest and importance of high politics, particularly in the nineteenth century; it

[20] J. Vincent and A. B. Cooke, *Governing Passion*, pp. 21–2, xi, 5; see also p. 161.

acknowledges the importance of political literacy to a democratic society, and is impressed with the contribution historical writing can make to it. It also proceeds on the assumption
that politics is inherently interesting as a subject of historical
study, and is important not only for its own sake but also for
its revelations about human personality; political activity
subjects human nature to rigorous tests and richly documents
the outcome. But the book combines these attitudes with
the outlook of those historians who felt in the early 1960s
that their immediate predecessors had been rather too
exclusive in their concentration on the intricacies of high
political and diplomatic activity, insufficiently preoccupied
with the social, economic, and intellectual developments to
which politicians must respond, and rather too neglectful
of the wide area of human conduct where the politician's
writ does not run.

This book's centrist perspective is linked to synthesis in
a second area, between the related polarities in historical
writing of narrative and analytic, particular and general,
empirical and theoretical. It is hardly necessary nowadays
to say that Conservatives dislike the very idea of social
science. Not only did Michael Oakeshott long ago dismiss
the idea that 'general laws' analogous to those operating
in the world of science could apply to human relationships;
Conservatives display an almost instinctive distaste for
abstractions—from a knowledge of the crimes that have
been committed in their name, from a preference for experience over intellect, and even from scholarly distaste for
their clumsy over-simplifications.[21] In this they coincide in
their outlook, though partly for different reasons, with
that of the professional historian, who seizes upon generalizations sociological, psychological, or metahistorical with
destructive zeal.

This distaste for abstraction is not to be confused with the
view, distinctly anti-professional, sometimes voiced on right
and left—that documents can be allowed to 'speak for themselves'. Interpretation is inevitably involved even in the
process of selection, and a historian who saw himself as a

[21] M. Oakeshott, *Experience and its Modes*, p. 161; see also the letters in *The
Times Literary Supplement*, 31 July 1981, p. 877; 14 Aug. 1981, p. 934.

mere compiler, collector, or précis-writer would hardly deserve inclusion among the community of scholars. History 'should be argument', Robert Skidelsky rightly points out, and documents 'can too easily become a substitute for judgment—and thought'.[22] The Conservative's very detailed empiricism and pursuit of narrative may well be far from unintelligent. Indeed, it often conceals extensive analysis beneath its narrative exterior, and frequently argues that it is precisely in the narrative sequence that historical explanation is to be found. The Cowling school of historians at its best demonstrates how perceptively such an approach can capture that subtle mixture of motives, that elusive unpredictability of events as experienced by the participants, which all political historians pursue.

Yet it should be possible to recognize the merits of such an approach while at the same time participating in the quest for long-term regularities and patterns in history which is more common at the opposite end of the political spectrum. The centrist historian will bear in mind Butterfield's warning against abridgements of the historical sequence which fail to capture the full complexity of events.[23] He will be reluctant to operate at a level of analysis so abstract as to shed little light on day-to-day human decision-making, and will be wary of detecting patterns in history whose neatness and simplicity jar with his personal experience of how things happen. But he will also gain stimulus from Marx's breath-taking boldness of analysis, and will admire his sense of the interrelatedness of things. He will perhaps also be attracted by those 'theories of the middle range' which R. K. Merton recommended as a goal, and which aim at building up generalization from the sustained analysis of detail—theories which occupy some sort of intermediate position between Conservative empiricism and Marxian generalization.

The centrist historian will seek to straddle a third academic polarity—between involvement with, and distance from, the present. The Conservative rightly fears that the historian too deeply immersed in present-day affairs may be tempted into

---

[22] *Spectator*, 30 Oct. 1976, p. 19.
[23] H. Butterfield, op. cit., p. 102, cf. pp. 7, 21-2, 100.

becoming a mere propagandist for the views of a particular group within his own society, seeking evidence to buttress its preconceptions. 'In history a great volume is unrolled for our instruction', wrote Burke, but if wrongly used 'it may . . . serve for a magazine, furnishing offensive and defensive weapons for parties in church and state, and supplying the means of keeping alive, or reviving dissensions and animosities, and adding fuel to civil fury'.[24] Clearly distinguishing between 'History' and what he calls 'the practical past', which merely serves the current needs of patriotism or religion, Michael Oakeshott insists that 'neither the truth nor the character of history depend, in any way, upon its having some lesson to teach us'.[25] Failure to distinguish between the two has certainly fostered a welter of myth-making and wish-fulfilment, whether in the nostalgic or drum-and-trumpet history sometimes found on the right, or in the inspirational aspects of labour and women's history sometimes found on the left.

The Conservative also recognizes how difficult it is for the historian to convey, even to perceive, the contrasts between past and present. He therefore urges him to take full account of the views even of those (perhaps particularly of those) historical personalities whose attitudes seem to him the least familiar. He knows that the historian who uses historical information as ammunition for current controversy sacrifices all that distinguishes him from (in politics) the political activist, or from (in religion) the theologian—both of whom engage in debates which are in some sense timeless. W. R. Ward rightly distinguishes between the theologian, who uses history as a source of ammunition for use in current theological debate, and the historian who 'cares as much for those past debates which now seem to have been nugatory'.[26] The historian would short-change his generation if he failed to make his distinctive contribution to its understanding, failed to enable his contemporaries to become self-conscious about their values and preoccupations, and failed to help in

---

[24] E. Burke, *Reflections on the Revolution in France* (ed. C. C. O'Brien, Penguin ed., 1969), p. 247.
[25] M. Oakeshott, *Experience and its Modes*, p. 158, cf. p. 103.
[26] W. R. Ward, in *Victorian Studies*, Mar. 1967, p. 312.

emancipating them from parochialism in time just as the social anthropologist and geographer help to emancipate them from parochialism in culture and location. Herbert Butterfield therefore rightly, if somewhat infelicitously, stresses the need for the historian to perform an intellectual 'act of self-emptying' as the preliminary to understanding the past, and describes his profession as involving 'a process of unlearning'.[27]

On the other hand the historian's response to the danger of corruption from the present cannot be a coy seclusion from it, for at the extreme such a position would render his findings incommunicable; a perspective entirely rooted in the past would make it impossible for the historian to acquire a lay readership, and would therefore severely limit his usefulness. The very act of historical writing assumes that the major contrasts between past and present are transcended by characteristics shared by human beings in all ages. 'In reality the historian postulates that the world is in some sense always the same world', Butterfield has himself written, 'and that even the men most dissimilar are never absolutely un-unlike.'[28] Ignorance of recent developments may even harm the historian's perception of the past, for unless he knows the subsequent history of those aspects of the past which he studies, he will be intellectually as hopelessly stranded (though from the opposite direction) as the citizen whose knowledge of his own society is confined to current affairs.

No clear distinction between 'history' and 'contemporary history'—or, in the language of academic departments, between 'history' and 'politics'—can be defended, if only because the frontier between them, always arbitrary, is continuously on the move. In some respects the shortage of adequate documentation converts the study of recent history not into some arcane and distinct discipline, but into a variant of history more akin to medieval or even ancient history, where chains of reasoning and hypotheses are required to bridge gaps in the evidence. Politics and history are intimately related from both directions: in the impact made on historical writing by the political outlook of the historian,

[27] H. Butterfield, *History and Human Relations* (1951), pp. 101, 172.
[28] H. Butterfield, *Whig Interpretation*, p. 9.

and in the profound influence of historical events, and of folk-myths about them, upon the current conduct of politicians. In the full knowledge, therefore, that he lacks any professional expertise on current affairs, and recognizing that unexpected turns in the recent events he analyses may cause his contemporary references to date with alarming speed—the modern historian must repudiate any attempt to interpose some form of cordon sanitaire between past and present, and must tread the delicate path involved in simultaneously trying to shed light on his own society without verging on the propaganda which vitiates the one contribution to its enlightenment that he is qualified to make. The choice does not lie between the writing of contemporary history by professional historians and no contemporary history at all, for where professional historians fear to tread, the territory will be explored by commentators who perhaps lack some of the historian's skills—by sociologists, journalists, political scientists, and laymen of every kind. It would be unfortunate if history were relegated to academic seclusion instead of continuously informing the understanding of our own society; it would be still more regrettable if the mind which is trained to comprehend the unpopular or the unfashionable point of view were somehow barred from illuminating present-day problems.

In some ways, then, the centrist historian's opportunity lies in synthesis. He will not display the labour and Conservative historians' taste for moving only among their own kind. He will of course write about centrists, and with sympathy, but—particularly in the British political system —he will be forced to write about a wider grouping than that. In particular, he will be well placed to acknowledge the immense impact of Liberalism on twentieth-century British political life. The vitality of nineteenth-century Liberalism has hitherto been most readily acknowledged by the Conservative historian, but until recently neither the Conservative nor the labour historian of twentieth-century Britain has given it much attention—if only because both parties were by then keen to emphasize their distinctive credentials while unobtrusively appropriating different aspects of the Liberal legacy. Furthermore if the prime preoccupation is (as here) with the range of opinion represented within the British legislature—the centrist historian may be better placed to comprehend the full spectrum of the opinions operating there than historians on right and left, whose span of comprehension may well move at one end beyond the limits of what is regarded as practicable politics, while failing to encompass the full range of parliamentary opinion on the opposite side.

But the centrist historian faces obstacles as well as opportunities. He may find it difficult to comprehend the fierce passions and firm allegiances which move many human beings. He may, especially in the British context, fail to appreciate the intense loyalty to institutions and political groupings that is felt on right and left. He may mistakenly assume that truth lies in a mere compromise or middle position between two schools of historians, neither of whose views he shares. He will need to remember that antagonists have much in common, though his distance from their quarrels may also enable him to develop perceptions shared by neither (on the motives of politicians, for example). He must shun the temptation to substitute a 'centrist' for a 'left' or 'right' interpretation of modern British history, for to exaggerate the importance, self-consciousness, and self-confidence of centrists in the hope of rectifying what he sees as historiographical distortion would be. to reproduce in his own work the exclusiveness which he finds uncongenial in others.

One asset the centrist historian will, however, enjoy: a harmony between his political inclinations and his professional procedures, for both involve the continuous exercise of judgement about the facts themselves and about how to respond to them. Those who like clear-cut distinctions and black-and-white allegiances will keep their distance from the politics of the centre and perhaps also from the historical profession. 'Those who look for perfection in this world', says Halifax's Trimmer, 'may look as long as the Jews have done for their Messiah.'[29] Centrists know that there are no simple formulas to light the way through the complexities of

---

[29] George Savile, Marquess of Halifax, *Complete Works* (ed. J. P. Kenyon, Penguin Books, 1969), p. 63.

political life—least of all the notion that in any particular political situation the best course lies midway between the extremes. They are the last people to think that they possess a monopoly of the truth—though they also know that others do not. They respect, even envy, the enthusiasm of the committed, but they readily call to mind the tragedies which commitment has sometimes produced. Their expectations of political and social change will be neither millennial nor pervaded by profound conservative gloom. They admire ideals in politics, but they recognize that ideals alone are not sufficient for political achievement, and can even mask self-interest in the subtlest of ways. They will not exaggerate the role of ambition and vanity in the conduct of politicians, but they recognize that the statesman can succeed only through allowing for the prevalence of these human attributes. They know that the art of government is not easily acquired—if only because it demands a rich understanding of human personality, together with the unending patience and sense of timing necessary for the laborious pursuit of agreement between human groups. On the other hand, they will join the critics of authority in seeking to improve on government's present performance, and share their belief that coincidence between political ambition and public interest is by no means automatic, and that therefore the men of government require continuous monitoring from without.

Like their nineteenth-century Whig predecessors, centrists will be wary of subordinating means to ends, for like them they know that the decent society can survive only with the aid of political wisdom operating through agreed procedures for avoiding conflict. They will acknowledge that violent actions can often influence events, but they will labour to ensure that the political outcome diverges markedly from the violent intention, nor will they ever need reminding that violence is in itself an evil. While recognizing the importance of continually adapting political and other institutions in the face of social and economic change, centrists will not thereby feel obliged to welcome every innovation as an improvement, nor will they be tempted to undervalue the benefits which any society enjoys from continuity in its political institutions. Centrists' heroes will perhaps be less well known than those who figure in the pantheons of right and left, for the essence of centrist effectiveness lies in being unobtrusive. Among reformers the heroes of this book include William Wilberforce rather than Thomas Clarkson; Richard Cobden rather than John Bright; John Colam rather than Frances Power Cobbe; James Stansfeld rather than Josephine Butler; Eleanor Rathbone and Mrs Fawcett rather than Christabel and Emmeline Pankhurst. As for the politicians in the centrist pantheon, they can be found in Chapter VII.

Centrism involves far more than mere compromise. It welcomes the participation of many groupings and viewpoints within the British political system, and recognizes the distinctive contribution that each can make. But centrists are well able to defend their own beliefs when necessary, for those beliefs can be held at least as firmly as beliefs on right and left. The need for such defence is perennial, and may even be enhanced by technological changes which in some ways guarantee publicity for the flamboyant and the violent, the impatient and the uncompromising. Yet centrists in Britain have long known that they are more numerous than either the structure and overt mood of political parties or the tone of public comment in Britain make it easy to recognize. They frequently experience simultaneous attack from two political directions; indeed, it is only when this occurs that they suspect they are occupying the right ground. They also know that for three centuries now their impact on British political traditions and social life has been considerable, and not unworthy of respect.

I

The Act of Militancy: Violence and the Suffragettes, 1904 – 1914

The suffragettes have been amply surpassed by subsequent protest movements in the destructiveness and ruthlessness of their acts of militancy. Suffragette leaders explicitly ruled out taking the lives of others; they risked only the health of their own members. Martyrdom, not murder, was their style. Yet their militant acts were extensive and escalating; 1911 saw 176 false fire-alarms and 22 convictions; 1912 saw 425 calls and 27 convictions, and there were still more in 1913. By 9 December 1912, 5,000 letters had already been damaged by arson, though all save thirteen letters and seven postcards had been delivered (in special wrappers indicating the cause of damage); the disruption caused by destroying letters was much more serious before the telephone came to be widely used.[1]

For these and other offences, 116 militants were imprisoned in 1910, 188 in 1911, and 240 in 1912. Attacks on property were unashamedly publicized in the *Suffragette*, which claimed that 150 serious attacks on property had been attributed to the suffragettes during 1912.[2] During the seven months up to and including July 1914 there were 107 suffragette incidents involving arson, eleven involving mutilation of works of art (including the Rokeby *Venus* at the National Gallery in March and Clausen's *Primavera* at the Royal Academy in May), and fourteen other outrages.[3] An insurance-company official attributed £250,000 worth of damage to suffragette incidents in 1913, but some newspapers claimed

---

[1] E. S. Pankhurst, *The Suffragette Movement* (1931), p. 415; Samuel in *H*[ouse] of *C*[ommons] *Deb*[ates], 9 Dec. 1912, cc. 75–6.

[2] *H. C. Deb.*, 7 Apr. 1913, c. 813; *Suffragette*, 26 Dec. 1913, p. 258.

[3] A. E. Metcalfe, *Woman's Effort* (Oxford, 1917), p. 319; *The Times*, 4 June 1914, p. 8.

that twice as much damage was caused by only the most serious attacks on property;[4] at least another £250,000 worth of damage was done in the first seven months of 1914.[5]

So shocking did these events seem at the time that non-militant suffragists tried to protect themselves against the political discredit of being associated with them by frequently repudiating militancy, and by trying to rivet on the public mind a clear distinction (also followed in this chapter) between the militant 'suffragette' and the non-militant 'suffragist'.[6] Yet these acts seem rather less shocking to us, and mild by comparison with political violence since 1914; furthermore, our concept of the conduct proper to women has altered dramatically. We also now know—as contemporaries could not—how circumscribed in time and scope suffragette militancy turned out to be. Besides, everything tends to be forgiven to those who turn out to have been on the right side.

Suffragettes too were shocked; acts of militancy were not committed lightly by respectable Edwardian middle-class women. Even the relatively modest breach of decorum which initiated the escalating militant sequence—Christabel Pankhurst's decision in February 1904 to walk from her seat up to the platform at Winston Churchill's free-trade meeting in the Free Trade Hall, to press her suffragist amendment—was described by her decades later as 'the most difficult thing I have ever done'.[7] Militancy risked not only reputation and professional success, but success in what was then seen as woman's most important trade, marriage. Violent public hostility or clumsiness in the prison-doctor during forcible feeding could destroy woman's greatest asset, her looks. The fizzing fire-bombs and the explosives that suffragettes recalled in old age would be frightening enough in any circumstances, but suffragettes were simultaneously breaching taboos of

---

[4] *Suffragette*, 2 Jan. 1914, p. 270; cf. the lower estimates printed in A. Rosen, *Rise Up Women! The Militant Campaign of the Women's Social and Political Union 1903–1914* (1974), pp. 190, 192, 197, 201, 202, 217, 221 which total sixty-five incidents involving £270,925 damage in 1913.

[5] A. Rosen, *Rise Up Women!*, pp. 222, 229, 231, 238, 242.

[6] On this see *Morning Post*, 21 Apr. 1914, p. 9; *Manchester Guardian*, 25 Apr. 1914, p. 8.

[7] C. Pankhurst, *Unshackled. The Story of How We Won the Vote* (1959), p. 46.

their class and sex. No wonder their ordeal was so vividly remembered in later years.

How can such conduct be explained? The task is difficult, if only because so many unhelpful psychological explanations were offered at the time. Society tries to insulate itself against being influenced by the militant through labelling him as in some way abnormal. The most extreme form of this device is to define him out of the human category altogether, by using such terms as 'bestial', 'inhuman', and 'animal'. This constitutes abuse rather than explanation, but weaker variants of it were applied to the suffragettes. Letters to *The Times* in 1908 seriously drew parallels between suffragette disruption of political meetings and 'the explosive fury of epileptics', or the 'Tarantism' or dancing mania of the Middle Ages.[8] When imprisoned for militancy, the suffragette Mary Richardson narrowly escaped being certified as insane; 'her lack of a sense of proportion', the *Standard* pronounced, 'passes the frontier between eccentricity and mental unsoundness'. The paper attributed the burning of an asylum near Liverpool in 1913 to a 'peculiar form of mental aberration . . . which . . . approximates to criminal lunacy, or at any rate to a form of hysteria of a highly dangerous type, more than to mere imbecility'.[9]

Anti-suffragists even saw militancy as reflecting the instability of the female temperament. Their leader Lord Curzon told their annual meeting in June 1914 that the suffragettes 'have rendered us the service of showing how easily disturbed the mental balance of some women, at any rate, can be'.[10] Anti-suffragist MPs told parliament that enfranchised women would disrupt political life by behaving in like manner; 'they will act in precisely the same manner to obtain any other political object', Arnold Ward declared in 1910, 'whether it be the diminution of public-houses, or Free Trade, or Protection'; suffragettes were proposing 'to

[8] *The Times*, 31 Dec. 1908, p. 13 (T. C. Shaw); 19 Dec. 1908, p. 10 (A. E. Shipley); see also my *Separate Spheres. The Opposition to Women's Suffrage in Britain* (1978), pp. 67, 193.

[9] *Standard*, 13 Mar. 1914, p. 10; 24 Sept. 1913, p. 6; M. Richardson, *Laugh a Defiance* (1953), pp. 154–5.

[10] Curzon, in *Anti-Suffrage Review*, July 1914, p. 108; cf. *H*[ouse] of *L*[ords] *Deb*[ates], 5 May 1914, c. 28.

incorporate that hysterical activity permanently in the life of the nation'.[11] The notion that militancy is somehow peculiarly inappropriate to women has often been voiced since;[12] it shares the anti-suffragist conviction that women are inherently more gentle than men, and that contrasting psychology dictates contrasting social roles.[13] No medical or psychological investigation has so far justified such a view, but it remains widely accepted among laymen.

Historians too have confronted the suffragettes with psychologism. Mary Stocks even claimed that Mrs Pankhurst 'was a born extremist and never well-balanced', and that only the outbreak of war 'saved her from real mental unbalance resulting from the physical and emotional stresses of the militant suffrage movement'.[14] Other historians prefer a form of group-psychologism. R. C. K. Ensor, for example, said that before 1914 'a constant round of excitements, imprisonments, and now hunger-strikes, had brought a great many militants into a psychopathic state, where it was not easy either to save society from them or them from themselves';[15] and in 1957 Marghanita Laski and George Dangerfield complained in their reviews that Roger Fulford's *Votes for Women* gave insufficient attention to psychological motive.[16]

Such explanations would now be thought to attempt either too much or too little. Too much, because the evidence needed to sustain them—on the mental history of individual militants—could not now be obtained. Too little, because even if such evidence were available, such explanations merely attach labels to the conduct which needs to be explained; and they provide no proof that it is the mental instability rather than some other factor which produces the militancy. They can perhaps (given sufficient evidence) show why one militant espouses militancy at a particular

[11] Ward, *H. C. Deb.*, 12 July 1910, cc. 266–7; cf. Harcourt, *H. C. Deb.*, 24 Jan. 1913, c. 896.
[12] *The Times*, 3 July 1978, p. 2 (Mrs Sally Oppenheim's comment on women terrorists).
[13] On these ideas, see my *Separate Spheres*, ch. 4.
[14] M. Stocks, *My Commonplace Book* (1970), p. 78.
[15] R. C. K. Ensor, *England. 1870–1914* (Oxford, 1936), p. 459; cf. H. H. Henson, *Retrospect of an Unimportant Life*, i (1942), p. 123.
[16] Laski, in *News Chronicle*, 17 Apr. 1957, p. 6; Dangerfield in *Victorian Studies*, Dec. 1957, pp. 198–9.

time whereas another does not, and why one individual responds to militancy in this way and another in that. But they cannot explain the emergence of this extraordinary movement, still less its internal dynamic. Militancy came to be seen even as normal within Mrs Pankhurst's Women's Social and Political Union [WSPU], and abruptly ceased for purely political reasons during the 'truce' period between February 1910 and November 1911 (with only a brief interruption) and permanently after August 1914. Militancy did not stem from a psychological type but from what were seen as temporary tactical necessities. It is all too easy to ward off the impact of reformers, whose ideas and even conduct are inevitably disruptive, by accusing them of group-delusion; such argument is the more insidious because pseudo-scientific, and because it widens the distance between the 'normal' and the 'unbalanced'; in reality, the psychologically unstable individual may be more sensitive to, or influenced in his mental state by, serious social evils which require correction in the interests of all.

More help might be expected from the political theorist—continuously preoccupied as he is with the relationship between the state and the individual. Yet his approach is so abstract, academic, and impersonal that it provides little guidance to the dynamics of militancy in any particular grouping—still less to the motives of any individual militant. The historian is therefore left very much on his own—in territory likely to be remote from his personal experience. He is also short of evidence. Authority documents itself carefully, but does not always make its records readily available on such topics; the militant critic of authority must often resort to authoritarian and/or fragmented structures which feel no need to (indeed, perhaps cannot) justify themselves in public. The militant's sudden changes of tactic can remain obscure because explanation cannot be extracted from his leaders through constitutional procedures, annual meetings, or the press. Besides, many militants feel responsibility not to their contemporaries, but only to posterity.

Many suffragettes died without telling their story. At the moment of militancy, militants are often so preoccupied with the world of action that they have little time (and perhaps also little talent or inclination) for sustained writing and thought. It would anyway be dangerous for them to preserve correspondence during the period of militancy itself; the police raided the WSPU headquarters more than once. So fierce a loyalty was generated among militants that Maud Kate Smith concealed the names of her fellow-conspirators over sixty years later, when speaking of them in her room at an old people's home in Solihull. A rather different consideration restrained Connie Lewcock when participating in a Tyne–Tees television programme about her militant career: her fear of encouraging modern imitations of the fire-raising methods she had sponsored nearly sixty years before at Esh Winning railway station. She contented herself with telling the makers of the programme privately about the details.[17] Many years need to elapse before society—or, for that matter, before the militant himself—is likely to feel comfortable at openly discussing the militant methods used to promote a reform, however desirable that reform may subsequently seem. By that time, the militant may have died, or the documents may have been destroyed, or the memory has faded.

Or has it? People do forget much of their experience soon after it occurs, but not events that made a major impact on them at the time. As Mary Richardson put it, when discussing her slashing of the Rokeby *Venus* in the National Gallery in memoirs published half a century later, 'it must all have happened very quickly; but to this day I can remember distinctly every detail of what happened'.[18] Recollection of such events tends to be retained almost intact over a long period, and (as several quotations cited later will show) often evokes description in the present tense. 'Oral history' can therefore fill some of the gaps in the historical sources. Only an interview with Frida Laski in 1975, for instance, could rectify the failure of Kingsley Martin's biography to note the young Harold Laski's attempt to destroy a railway station in 1913 on behalf of the cause. By the 1970s, Connie

---

[17] Author's tape-recorded interviews with Maud Kate Smith, Solihull, 14 Jan. 1975; Connie Lewcock, Blyth, 15 Apr. 1977.

[18] M. Richardson, *Laugh a Defiance*, p. 168; see also P. Thompson, *The Voice of the Past. Oral History* (Oxford, 1978), p. 103.

Lewcock felt able to talk freely and in great detail about what she called 'the perfect crime' that she had helped to commit at Esh Winning.[19]

Interviews can often be used to check one another, and can be supplemented in this area with a wealth of printed material—in suffragette periodicals and archives, suffragette autobiographies (printed and unprinted), and in the many suffragette novels which imaginatively re-created for the Edwardians incidents which the participants did not record directly. In some ways we can discover more about acts of militancy in the past than in the present, though historians have been relatively reticent on the subject. The gestation of the suffragette's act of militancy can be followed through a time-sequence such as might have been experienced by a hypothetical suffragette. There is first the militant's sources of inspiration; then his or her subsequent insulation from the surrounding society; then the organization of militancy, and finally the act itself, with its aftermath.

I

But surely it is impertinent to inquire into the militant's inspiration, for does it not originate in awareness of injustice? True, women's suffering—wife-beating, prostitution, poverty, ignorance, unemployment, indignities of every kind—often features in feminist rhetoric. The suffragism of Vida Levering in Elizabeth Robins's *The Convert* (1907) and of Lady Eversley in Despard and Collins's *Outlawed* (1908) is nourished by their own ill-treatment at the hands of men. In *Ann Veronica*, H. G. Wells's heroine joins the militant suffragettes as a 'last desperate attack upon the universe that would not let her live as she desired to live, that penned her in and controlled her and directed her and disapproved of her'. This is to formulate positively the anti-suffragist's more negative claim that suffragettes are misfits, sour and disappointed people, 'regrettable by-products of our civilisation', as *The Times* put it in 1912, 'out with their hammers and their bags full of stones because

. [19] Author's tape-recorded interviews with Frida Laski, Ealing, 29 Apr. 1975; with Connie Lewcock, Newcastle, 15 Apr. 1976.

of dreary, empty lives and high-strung, over-excitable natures'.[20]

Yet the inspiration cannot lie here, for resentment at personal ill-treatment inspires both militant and non-militant suffragist. The autobiography of Mrs H. M. Swanwick, a key figure in the non-militant organization, conveys a burning sense of personal grievance that is precariously but tightly reined in by her determined rationality. Besides, it is not the most deprived or oppressed who rise in revolt; on the contrary, oppression consists in eagerly embracing one's chains. In reality it was Mrs Pankhurst and Mrs Fawcett, both happily married, relatively affluent and emancipated women, who championed the oppressed. Like Josephine Butler before her, Mrs Pankhurst delighted in publicly giving the lie to anti-feminist claims that 'the happy wife and mother is never passionately concerned about the suffrage'.[21]

Is militancy inspired, then, by male insults of a more public and collective kind? Feminists certainly felt insulted by the Edwardian House of Commons; their Bills were treated as excuses for ribald comment, talked out on several occasions and never taken further, even when they had won a majority at second reading. The talking-out of a women's suffrage bill in 1905 produced a feminist demonstration that marks an important stage in the escalation to militancy.[22] Lady Constance Lytton rightly pointed out in 1908 that an outcry would have resulted if men's claims for the vote had been treated so lightly.[23] Yet 1905 was by no means the first time feminists had been treated so insultingly; as long ago as 1875, Rhoda Garrett had told a suffragist meeting how the insulting parliamentary speeches 'tear the veil from women's eyes, and . . . make them see clearly the true light in which they are regarded by some men';[24] two years later, the women's suffrage bill was talked out for the first time. Non-militants like Mrs Fawcett had in fact been exposed for far

---

[20] H. G. Wells, *Ann Veronica* (George Newnes ed., n.d.), p. 205; *The Times* quot. in R. Fulford, *Votes for Women. The Story of a Struggle* (1958 ed.), p. 229.
[21] Sir A. E. Wright, *The Unexpurgated Case against Women Suffrage* (1913), p. 71.   [22] E. S. Pankhurst, *The Suffragette* (1911), p. 16.
[23] Bodleian Library, Oxford, *Ponsonby Papers*: MS Eng. Hist. C. 658, f. 156: Lady Constance Lytton to Arthur Ponsonby, 28 June 1910.
[24] *Women's Suffrage Journal*, 1 July 1875, p. 97.

longer than the suffragettes to politicians' obstinacy. Seemingly languid politicians kept the non-militant leaders of many other causes waiting for decades. Criticizing suffragette militancy in 1909, H. W. Massingham pointed out how 'nearly all the Chartists and the Radicals of the early nineteenth century died without coming into their kingdom, or after seeing but a very faint vision of it', yet their leaders never embraced militant tactics.[25]

Nor can intensity of feminist inspiration be the answer, for the influence of J. S. Mill or of Charlotte Perkins Gilman was at least as important within Mrs Fawcett's non-militant National Union of Women's Suffrage Societies [NUWSS] as within Mrs Pankhurst's much less numerous WSPU. True, the act of militancy inevitably acquired among some feminists the colour of being more resolute, more courageous, less compromising than constitutional methods. But others saw it as a betrayal of feminist ideals, an unthinking espousal of man's discreditable physical-force methods, a denial of the hope that women's political influence would refine and elevate politics, and a serious hindrance to attaining feminist objectives. Had not J. S. Mill argued that women needed the vote because 'being physically weaker, they are more dependent on law and society for protection'? Non-militants claimed in 1909 that the women's cause 'is fundamentally the opposition of sanity and gentleness, to prejudice, selfishness, and the ideal of brute force'.[26]

We must distinguish between the influences producing commitment to women's suffrage and the influences producing militant conduct on its behalf. Can it then be argued that militants were more profoundly influenced than non-militants by those aspects of the national political culture which justify the challenge to authority? Suffragettes were certainly deeply influenced by such traditions. When defending in court their attempt to 'rush' the House of Commons in 1908, Christabel drew directly upon many of these ideas. 'The whole of our liberties have been won by action such as

---

[25] *Nation*, 25 Sept. 1909, p. 906.
[26] J. S. Mill, *Representative Government* (Everyman ed., 1960), p. 290; *Common Cause*, 12 Aug. 1909, p. 228 (A. M. Allen); cf. Mrs Besant in *The Times*, 5 Oct. 1912, p. 4.

ours', she declared, 'only of a far more violent kind...Magna Carta itself was won by the threat of a breach of the peace.'[27] She also referred to the Star Chamber and to the role of violence in procuring parliamentary reform. She told a meeting in October that the Reform Bills 'were got by hard fighting, and they could have been got in no other way'.[28] Five suffragette protesters at Westminster in 1909 chained themselves to the statues of five men famous for upholding British liberties in the Stuart period. Wat Tyler, the Covenanters, the anti-slavery movement, Peterloo, and the Chartists provided precedents and encouragement; at her trial in 1913 Christabel referred to John Hampden, and described law-breaking as 'right or wrong according to the nature of the law and the authority possessed by the law-giver'.[29]

These libertarian influences were sometimes reinforced by family connection. Through the Gouldens, Mrs Pankhurst was personally linked to the anti-slavery movement and Peterloo; Emmeline Pethick-Lawrence's much-admired father was Harry Pethick, who had elicited a famous judicial vindication of the right of public meeting when defending the Salvation Army against its enemies in 1882. The suffragettes took pleasure in publicizing these libertarian traditions in order to embarrass the Liberal government, and thereby supplied Conservative spectators like Lord Robert Cecil with wry enjoyment.[30] Christabel at her trial in 1908 claimed that the WSPU raid on the House of Commons had followed the precedent set by John Bright in 1867, when he urged a Trafalgar Square crowd to do the same; 'Mr Lloyd-George's whole career has been a series of revolts', she declared.[31]

Yet these influences impinge with equal force on the non-militants, whose campaign originated with that high priest of mid-Victorian libertarian theory J. S. Mill; Magna Carta was

[27] *The Trial of the Suffragette Leaders* (Woman's Press, n.d.), p. 16.
[28] C. Pankhurst, *The Militant Methods of the N.W.S.P.U.* (2nd ed. Woman's Press, n.d.), p. 14 (verbatim report of her speech on 15 Oct. 1908).
[29] *New Statesman*, 1 Nov. 1913 (supplement on 'The Awakening of Women'), p. xi; see also E. S. Pankhurst, *The Suffragette*, pp. 372, 380–1, 468–74.
[30] Cecil, in *Votes for Women*, 10 Mar. 1911, p. 367.
[31] *Daily Telegraph*, 26 Oct. 1908, p. 8; cf. Christabel Pankhurst in *Votes for Women*, 13 Jan. 1911, p. 242.

being cited in favour of the cause long before any advent of militancy.[32] And when dwelling on the precedents for women's suffrage supplied by the nineteenth century's franchise-reform campaigns, non-militants did not confine themselves to emphasizing the arguments which had been used; Leonard Courtney told Manchester suffragists in 1878 that the Reform Bills had been won largely by violent acts,[33] yet militancy did not materialize for thirty years. In reality, the British liberal tradition has always been equivocal on the political role of violence, whether instigated by the enthusiastic reformer or by the soldier and policeman. It justifies militancy as the 'appeal to heaven', as the desperate last resort, but is nervous about going further. The theorists of Victorian Liberalism—Bentham, Paine, Cobden, Mill— feared the use of force as subverting the rationality they wished to cultivate in man, and Irish Home Rule in the 1880s is only the best known among several causes which foundered on the Liberal's overriding distaste for political violence.

Nor does militancy originate in European libertarian traditions. Fred Pethick-Lawrence stressed the influence of Mazzini upon his own outlook, and in 1912 his wife said that she always advised suffragists to read G. M. Trevelyan's books on Garibaldi.[34] But non-militant British feminist pioneers—James Stansfeld, for example, or Josephine Butler —had been influenced by European libertarians, especially by Mazzini. Rebecca West rightly describes Mrs Pankhurst as 'the last popular leader to act on inspiration derived from the principles of the French Revolution',[35] but French radical traditions had impinged on her as a young woman, decades before she became a militant.

Only perhaps from Ireland did libertarian influences impinge more forcibly on militant than on non-militant. Non-militants were of course often sympathetic to Irish nationalism, and made an important contribution to that

[32] e.g. *Women's Suffrage Journal*, 1 May 1871, p. 41.
[33] Ibid., 2 Dec. 1878, p. 201; see also Mrs Fawcett, in ibid., 2 May 1870, p. 23.
[34] F. Pethick-Lawrence, *Fate Has Been Kind* (n.d.), p. 53; M. E. and M. D. Thompson, *They Couldn't Stop Us! Experiences of Two (Usually Law-Abiding) Women in the Years 1909–1913* (Ipswich, 1957), p. 49; *Votes for Women*, 7 June 1912, p. 584.
[35] In her 'Mrs. Pankhurst', in *The Post Victorians* (1933), p. 500.

wave of British liberal opinion which swept away the Black-and-Tan policy of repression in 1921;[36] but Irish nationalism influenced militant suffragette tactics as well as their objectives. There were a few direct suffragette links with Irish nationalism; the libertarianism which inspired Mrs Despard's suffragism, for example, extended also to Irish men. But more important was the fact that Irish history seemed, at least on superficial suffragette investigation, to show that violence produced political results. In 1912 Christabel Pankhurst's periodical, the *Suffragette*, approvingly cited Gladstone's comment on the report of the Parnell commission: 'Sir, is it not the case that in all great movements in human affairs even the just cause is marked and spotted with much that is to be regretted?' Suffragettes often also cited Gladstone's remark of 1884 that 'if no instructions had ever been addressed in political crises to the people of this country except to remember to hate violence, love order, and exercise patience, the liberties of this country would never have been attained'.[37] Christabel quoted this statement at her trial in 1908, and saw Gladstone's espousal of Irish church disestablishment in 1868 as a response to the Fenian outrages and the Clerkenwell explosion which had occurred shortly before. His preoccupation with disestablishment had in fact begun much earlier, partly for reasons unconnected with Ireland.[38] It would also have been difficult to show that Home Rule in the 1880s was assisted by the Phoenix Park murders or by subsequent dynamiting of London; Lloyd George told some suffragists in 1913 that 'the Irish never had a chance of succeeding until Mr Parnell engaged in a constitutional agitation',[39] and we now know that Parnell was far more hostile to political violence than many of his contemporary critics supposed.

Yet mythical history can be at least as powerful as the

---

[36] On this see G. Bussey and M. Tims, *Women's International League for Peace and Freedom, 1915–1965. A Record of Fifty Years' Work* (1965), p. 40; *The Vote*, 27 May 1921, p. 485; 8 July 1921, p. 529.

[37] *Suffragette*, 1 Nov. 1912, p. 31; C. Pankhurst, *The Militant Methods of the N.W.S.P.U.*, p. 15.

[38] J. Vincent, 'Gladstone and Ireland', *Proceedings of the British Academy*, 1977, p. 201.

[39] *The Times*, 8 Nov. 1913, p. 10.

truth when it comes to inspiring political action. Besides, Irish influence on the suffragettes goes further. Whereas the non-militant leader Mrs Fawcett became a Liberal Unionist in 1886, Parnell's ruthless irreverence towards British political parties attracted Christabel and her mother, who imitated it in the very different political situation prevailing twenty years later.[40] This aspect of Irish influence has only limited relevance, however, to the inspiration of militancy. Given women's exclusion from parliament, imitation of Parnell's tactics did of course foster in suffragettes a belligerent mood which easily resulted in confrontation with the government; but suffragette admiration for Parnellite tactics only highlights the movement's overriding preoccupation with parliamentary developments, and is difficult to reconcile with George Dangerfield's portrayal of a generalized Edwardian repudiation of Liberal parliamentarism which linked suffragettes, syndicalists, and Irish nationalists. Considerations of religion and nationality made any formal alliance between Irish nationalists and suffragettes impossible; indeed, by 1912 there was considerable friction between the suffragettes and the Irish nationalist MPs. But if Dangerfield is arguing that there was a subconscious Edwardian repudiation of Liberal parliamentarism, it is difficult to see what kind of evidence could be used to test the idea; besides, the continued vitality of liberal ideals in both Conservative and Labour parties after the Liberal Party's demise renders it scarcely tenable.[41]

In retrospect, British feminism can be assigned an impeccably Liberal ancestry; British feminists employed Liberal rhetoric, oriented their campaigns entirely towards parliament, and held firmly to parliamentarism after 1918. Few indeed were the inter-war links between British Fascism and British feminism, whose main line during the 1930s was always firmly peace-loving and internationalist.[42] Suffragettes may temporarily and tactically have distanced themselves from a Liberal government, but their programme never

[40] On this see the editorial in *Votes for Women*, 7 May 1908, p. 146; and Christabel's article, ibid., 27 Aug. 1908, p. 409; cf. T. Billington-Greig, *The Militant Suffrage Movement. Emancipation in a Hurry* (n.d.), pp. 200-1.

[41] See pp. 325-8.

[42] On this see my *Separate Spheres*, pp. 231, 233.

repudiated Liberalism; indeed, their formal demands were an actual outgrowth of it, building upon that Liberal belief in broadening political participation and in governmental responsiveness to popular pressure which had produced the first three Reform Acts. All four leading WSPU militants— Fred and Emmeline Pethick-Lawrence, Christabel and Emmeline Pankhurst—later became parliamentary candidates, and Fred Pethick-Lawrence eventually became an MP and later Labour's elder statesman in the House of Lords. There was, in the end, a certain appropriateness in locating Mrs Pankhurst's statue so close to the parliament whose proceedings she disrupted, but which in old age she dreamed of entering. Ireland, then, provides the suffragettes with precedents for militancy, but is far more important for its influence on suffragette parliamentarism.

There is in fact little evidence of intellectual inspiration for militancy at all. On the wall of her prison-cell, Lady Constance Lytton inscribed a quotation from Thoreau during 1910, and hunger-striking may have owed something to Russian influence.[43] But the influence of Tolstoy (which was important on some suffragettes) was more likely to foster resistance to violent tactics than support for them. Nor should the historian project on to the suffragettes his own intellectual preoccupations. Sustained thought is difficult in the midst of any public agitation—with its short-term emergencies, its preoccupation with personal loyalties, and its involvement as much with means as with ends. Still more is this so in a militant movement whose conspiracies provoke internal controversy while simultaneously requiring an authoritarian style of leadership which precludes open discussion. Militancy soon antagonized the intelligent woman with a mind of her own; 'I am convinced that the best women concerned in this struggle stand in deadly need of criticism, sympathetic and merciless criticism', wrote Mrs Billington-Greig in 1911.[44] The suffragettes' recurrent scrapes,

---

[43] A. Raeburn, *The Militant Suffragettes* (1973), p. 137; see also *Votes for Women*, 19 Dec. 1913, p. 179 (letter from Lester Smith). E. S. Pankhurst, *The Suffragette*, p. 91 claims that Russian influences were important.

[44] T. Billington-Greig, 'Emancipation in a Hurry', *New Age*, 12 Jan. 1911, p. 246.

passionate loyalties, disputes, and betrayals were incompatible with the perspective and proportion necessary to any effective long-term political strategy and sense of direction. 'This is what I call life', Mrs Pankhurst is reported to have exclaimed to her anxious daughter Sylvia,[45] after heatedly declaiming against women's injustices. She was an impatient, hasty, and unsystematic reader, lacking in a well-rounded education; her inspiration lay elsewhere.[46] The militant is eager for action, and has little time for books.[47]

It is usually a personality, situation, or incident—rather than a book or idea—that makes the initial impact on a militant. For many suffragettes it was the movement which led to the books, rather than the other way round. Lady Rhondda recalled turning to Mill's *Subjection of Women*, Olive Schreiner's *Woman and Labour*, and Cicely Hamilton's *Marriage as a Trade*—none of which could have led her directly into militancy. 'Having made up my mind . . .', she writes, 'I had to discover why I believed what I did . . . My intellectual assent was complete, but it came second, not first.'[48] With writing as with reading, Edwardian suffragists—militant and non-militant—were too preoccupied with campaigning for the vote to spend much time on sketching out the shape of the new society, or on doing more than expose particular abuses and build up a following for the programme that J. S. Mill had laid down half a century before.[49]

In their pragmatic mood and situation, the suffragettes ironically resemble the politicians they fought so bitterly. Today in prison, tomorrow in a nursing-home, and on some bizarre exploit the next day, darting unpredictably about the country—the militant in her life-style caricatures that

[45] E. S. Pankhurst, *The Suffragette Movement*, p. 181; cf. Mrs Despard's anecdote in *The Vote*, 22 June 1928, p. 193.

[46] R. West, loc. cit., pp. 480–1; E. S. Pankhurst, *The Suffragette Movement*, p. 57; D. Mitchell, *The Fighting Pankhursts. A Study in Tenacity* (1967), p. 210; *Votes for Women*, 14 June 1912, p. 601.

[47] Cf. C. C. O'Brien, 'Liberty and Terror', in his *Herod. Reflections on Political Violence* (1978), p. 28.

[48] Lady Rhondda, *This Was My World* (1933), pp. 125–6, 119.

[49] Cf. J. A. and O. Banks, 'Feminism and Social Change—A Case Study of a Social Movement', in G. K. Zollschan and W. Hirsch (eds.), *Explorations in Social Change* (1964), p. 550.

dissipation and fracturing of women's intellect that suffragism aimed to counteract, yet she also apes the hurried, cross-pressured existence that the politician, for quite different reasons, is forced to lead. 'One of the most difficult things in a Suffragette's life', wrote Mary Richardson, '. . . was its variety . . . It was a merciless round. One was an itinerant, abroad in many different worlds.'[50] Both in quality of argument and in its members' intellectual calibre, the WSPU declined in its later years; hence the political obscurity of its most loyal leaders after the vote was won. Reviewing Annie Kenney's autobiography in 1924, Mary Stocks described militancy as a spiritual as well as physical martyrdom. It involved 'the poisoning of mental endurance by those quickly moving years of white-hot excitement, the paralysis of intellectual responsibility by willing subjection to a dominant human will'.[51]

Militancy drew British feminists away from sustained thought about women's over-all situation, and about how they could use the vote once won. As Dr Louisa Garrett Anderson pointed out in 1911, militant tactics 'take too much explanation';[52] public discussion gradually narrowed on to the arguments for and against militant tactics, and by 1913 the subject dominated the *Suffragette*'s editorials. 'The worst of all such appeals to violence as those we have recently witnessed', the non-militant organ complained in March 1912, 'is that they confuse the issue, and only people of strong principles can hold to them in the confusion.'[53] Militancy therefore originated neither in mental delusion nor in intellectual inspiration; such explanations are either inappropriate, or they apply to non-militants and militants alike.

II

The origins of militancy emerge more clearly from analysing the social pressures that build up inside a reforming

[50] M. Richardson, *Laugh a Defiance*, p. 174.
[51] *Woman's Leader*, 31 Oct. 1924, p. 321.
[52] Quot. in A. Rosen, *Rise Up Women!*, p. 156.
[53] *Common Cause*, 14 Mar. 1912, p. 831.

organization. By no means all members succumb to these; many suffragists remained contentedly within the non-militant NUWSS throughout these years. But channelling the like-minded into distinct institutions concentrates the mind and the emotions, and some suffragists moved on into militant suffrage organizations like the WSPU and the Women's Freedom League, and then carried those organizations further down the militant road. The WSPU was not at first a militant organization, and its militancy escalated only slowly after 1904. The decision to join it did not at first seem at all epoch-making, but its members stepped on to an escalator which gradually shifted them towards the more extreme forms of militancy, and provided few moments of transition which required clear decisions of personal strategy.

A militant body inhibits freedom of intellectual discussion and circumscribes political awareness, yet generates emotional pressure and internal rivalry in the display of commitment. Moderates resign or keep silent, and militancy gradually becomes conceivable for members whose initial instincts had been of the most law-abiding kind. Far from constituting a distinct personality-type, the militant is the end-product of a long sequence of events which lead him only half-consciously and sometimes reluctantly forward; analysis of the militant temperament must take account not only of the destination that has been reached, but also of the long journey required to get there. Militancy's origins are more pragmatic than theoretic, more institutional than inspirational. The escalating process of commitment that so often accompanied membership deserves detailed discussion. It is a fourfold process, involving insulation from the surrounding society, growth in internal solidarity, repudiation of society's values, and escalation in the types of militancy that are considered necessary.

Suffragism readily insulated its members from the surrounding society by simultaneous pressures of repulsion and attraction. Militancy's social disadvantages in the wider world soon became apparent. Ostracism, one of respectable society's most potent weapons, was mercilessly deployed against it. When Mrs Cohen of Leeds declared her suffragette allegiance, unpleasant letters began descending through the family letter-box, her son was persecuted at school, her husband was taunted by colleagues, and former friends passed by on the other side. In 1976 she vividly recalled the collapse at least sixty-five years before of her plans to visit the opera with her friends the Aspinalls. When Mrs Cohen announced that she intended going to London for militant work, Mrs Aspinall told her that if she did this she would never speak to her again, 'and I said to her, "well, thank goodness I've found out the depth of your friendship before it's too late", and I walked out. I never went there, and we had booked seats.'[54] When the gay and vivacious Lady Sybil Smith returned from prison in 1913 she found her husband 'all that is kind and affectionate but we do not speak of Suffrage matters. My greatest friends are ominously silent—my mother takes the "high-principled lunatic" line so there we are—Well it might be much worse.'[55]

Society's expulsive power helps consolidate a substitute community among suffragists. Militancy requires no single moment of conversion; casual interest congeals into membership, whose intensity of commitment sharpens at each encounter with the enemy. An exhilarating companionship between women of all classes, temperaments, and political tendencies—often nostalgically recalled in later years— begins to develop. Of her first arrest in 1908, Lady Constance Lytton later recalled that it was at Cannon Row police station that she 'first tasted the delights of that full un-fetter[e]d companionship which is among the greatest immediate rewards of those who work actively in this cause. No drudgery of preliminary acquaintanceship has to be got through, no misdoubting inquiries as to kindred temperaments or interests. The sense of unity and mutual confidence is complete and begins from the first unhesitatingly.'[56]

But with companionship comes the pressure towards orthodoxy, the generation of a loyalty so intense as to stifle independent thought. A tendency towards exclusiveness in opinion is of course present in many types of organization,

[54] Author's tape-recorded interview with Mrs Leonora Cohen, Rhos-on-Sea, 3 Sept. 1976.
[55] Bodleian Library, Oxford, *Evelyn Sharp Papers*: MS Eng. Lett. d. 277, f. 175: Sybil Smith to Evelyn Sharp, 31 July 1913.
[56] Lady C. Lytton, *Prisons and Prisoners* (1914), p. 50.

whether commercial, recreational, political, or academic; but protest movements will be short on members with wider political experience and well stocked with members who lack other outlets for their ambitions. They also lack those major incentives for retaining contact with the wider community: the need to attract votes, customers, readers, or clients. Purity of principle readily comes to seem more important than establishing a broad platform. Disagreeement on tactics or on long-term aims leads not to internal compromise but to schism. Suffragettes ridiculed the anti-suffragist complaint that women's suffrage, by provoking argument between spouses, would fragment the family, but their own substitute-family was riven with numerous group and individual secessions among those who repudiated the official line.

Militant companionship is consolidated by commitment to a faith. The suffragette movement's appeal required response to a 'call' at least as compelling as that of any religious obligation. 'They are fanatical and hysterical women', said the Home Secretary Reginald McKenna, opposing the idea of leaving hunger-striking suffragettes to die without forcible feeding in March 1913: 'who no more fear death in fighting what they believe to be the cause of women, than the natives of the Sudan feared death when fighting the battle of the Mahdi.'[57] Not that Edwardian feminists owed much to denominational attachment; they were far less permeated by nonconformist personnel and culture than their predecessors. Militant dissent was far less central to their inspiration than to that of, say, the anti-slavery movement or the Anti-Corn-Law League. Yet in the secularizing society of Edwardian Britain, feminism resembled Socialism and imperialism in attracting intense dedication from people whose conversion-experience would earlier have taken a religious rather than secular form. The greater the self-sacrifice demanded, the greater the need for an elevated, and perhaps politically impractical, ideal to make it all seem worthwhile. Even a feminist so rationalistic and non-militant as Mrs Fawcett

[57] McKenna, *H. C. Deb.*, 18 Mar. 1913, c.906; cf. Wolmer, *H. C. Deb.*, 2 Apr. 1913, c.457; Lord Robert Cecil, *H. C. Deb.*, 18 Mar. 1913, c.888.

assigned the cause the place in her life that religion had occupied in her mother's.[58]

Many suffragettes were seekers by temperament, moving restlessly between religious and political allegiances; this was their quest for meaning in a world which frequently denied them adequate educational and personal fulfilment. Their links with theosophy and New Thought were extensive; 'militancy and mysticism are closely interwoven', Mrs Swanwick pronounced in 1914, concerned as much with the militant's thought-processes as with her sectarian affiliation.[59] Edwardian feminist enthusiasm had implications for theology, liturgy, and morality, and suffragism seemed an almost holy cause—with its own martyrs, its own semi-religious symbolism, and at times its own almost mystical tone. 'To re-enact the tragedy of Calvary for generations yet unborn', wrote Emily Davison, 'that is the last consummate sacrifice of the Militant!' Women's suffrage, to many of its Edwardian recruits, 'came as a new gospel', writes Ray Strachey, and 'an almost religious fervour entered into their support'.[60]

The militant gradually comes to repudiate society's values, and creates an alternative set of standards and criteria for status. By 1909 Mrs Pethick-Lawrence could describe Holloway prison as 'a graduating university for Suffragettes', urging 'to every one of you who has not yet been I say, go and get your degree'.[61] A full-blown system of honours and distinctions later emerged, whose medals and ribbons enshrine a deliberate inversion of society's official values. Symbolic also of that inversion are those immensely amusing occurrences and situations enthusiastically recalled later at suffragette reunions. Puritans who expect the reformer continuously to display an austere and earnest high-mindedness are usually disappointed; the challenge to convention can often be a highly enjoyable business. Sixty years later, Grace Roe recalled with zest what fun it was making up the middle

[58] R. Strachey, *Millicent Garrett Fawcett* (1931), p. 239.

[59] *Manchester Guardian*, 10 June 1914, p. 6.

[60] Davison quot. in A. Rosen, *Rise Up Women!*, p. 200; R. Strachey, *'The Cause'. A Short History of the Women's Movement in Great Britain* (1928), p. 303.

[61] *Votes for Women*, 23 Apr. 1909, p. 568.

page of the *Suffragette*. As for her Saturday-night meetings with suffragette colleagues in her flat when in hiding in Earl's Court, they resembled the schoolboy's weekly release of energy at a football match: 'we'd sit round the table there and we would be *hilarious*'.[62] Emerging from the pantechnicon for her suffragette raid on parliament, Ann Veronica's doubts and depression 'gave place to the wildest exhilaration'. Looking back over these events, Fred Pethick-Lawrence says that 'many of the women, to my surprise at the time, were singularly debonair and gay . . . they had broken down life-long inhibitions and already achieved a freedom that they had never before known'.[63] This inversion of society's values was by no means complete; it more closely resembles the schoolgirls' surreptitious breaking of the rules when the headmistress is away than the revolutionary's contemptuous and frontal challenge to the established order.

The suffragette's disillusionment with society only carries to a higher pitch the disappointment many altruistic reformers feel at contemporaries who fail to act in the face of such obvious evils. When opponents go on repeating old arguments parrot-fashion, and when so many bystanders show hostility, contempt, and indifference, despite all the reformer's efforts, it is natural for him to move on from resentment to retaliation. Towards the militant organization, society turns its harshest face, and martyrdom raises militant emotion to a peculiar intensity. The WSPU used its martyrs to embarrass a supposedly Liberal government, which was thereby goaded into the harshness of which all governments are capable; male brutality was thereby displayed, allegedly in its true colours, for all to see. Emily Davison's funeral on 14 June 1913 was the most theatrical attempt at exploiting martyr-dom for recruiting purposes, but many lesser-known heroines emerged from militant demonstrations and the hunger-strike. Unfairness and brutality inevitably results from violent incidents, whether intentionally or not, and these tempt

---

[62] Author's tape-recorded interview with Miss Grace Roe, Pembury, 23 Sept. 1974.
[63] H. G. Wells, *Ann Veronica*, p. 209; F. Pethick-Lawrence, *Fate Has Been Kind*, p. 74; cf. E. S. Pankhurst, *The Suffragette Movement*, p. 227.

militants into violent acts which they would once have regarded as inconceivable.

An element of suffragette malice towards opponents is present as early as 1906, when pleasure is taken at disrupting Winston Churchill's election meetings in Manchester; 'there was a spice of poignant satisfaction', Sylvia Pankhurst recalled, 'in spoiling his meeting as a punishment for his insulting attitude towards women and women's claims'. Suffragist activism certainly reinforced any initial sense of personal grievance. Mary Richardson's militancy owed much to the insults she endured while selling suffragette newspapers in the street: 'in a sense I was glad to hit back, to hit out at anything if I could in some way express my detestation of all the filthy remarks I had had to listen to'.[64] Then there were affronts of a more generalized kind—the insulting remarks about women from politicians like Labouchere, the flippant male mood when feminist aims were being discussed, the exasperating male refusal to take women seriously. By June 1910 even the patience of that gentle, courageous, and thoroughly humane suffragette Lady Constance Lytton was wearing thin: 'oh, how I *hate* the respectable world!' she told her sister. 'They are all like a flock of sheep—never can take their stand on their own version of what is right, but must all wait to see how someone else moves first.'[65]

The year 1912 saw a despairing transition from the pursuit of reform to the luxury of retaliating against the society that refused to listen. 'The only way to get at these lazy comfortable people is to hit them in the stomach', said Miss Naylor of the bishops and politicians at a WSPU meeting in December 1912. With equally strange logic, the *Suffragette* announced in the same month, after justifying letter-burning, that 'women will never get the vote except by creating an intolerable situation for all the selfish and apathetic people who stand in their way'.[66] It was but a short distance from here

[64] E. S. Pankhurst, *The Suffragette Movement*, p. 194; M. Richardson, *Laugh a Defiance*, p. 12; cf. Mrs Pankhurst, *Votes for Women*, 24 May 1912, p. 533.

[65] B. Balfour (ed.), *Letters of Constance Lytton* (1925), p. 207.

[66] P[ublic] R[ecord] O[ffice], HO.45/231366 (Box 10695), file 6, p. 4 (report of WSPU meeting on 19 Dec. 1912 at Steinway Hall); *Suffragette*, 13 Dec. 1912, p. 125

to the sex war. The suffragette movement was now making a half-conscious transition from pursuing votes for women towards repudiating woman's subservience to man. The suffragettes 'broke more than windows with their stones', said Lady Rhondda; 'they broke the crust and conventions of a whole era'.[67]

Defiance could be more effective than persuasion in exposing male chivalry (that major plank in the anti-suffragist case) as bogus. 'In the days before militancy women were thought to be the weaker, the clinging, the dependent sex', wrote Christabel in November 1913. 'Now women's determination, courage, fighting spirit, and indomitable purpose have become proverbial.'[68] Her strategy involved projecting women into what were then seen as male roles, creating a gallery of heroines selected for emulating male feats, and relishing the delectable revelation of male stupidity provided by flat-footed detectives; *Votes for Women* launched a series of articles on 'warrior women' during 1911. The non-militant emphasis on the shared humanity of both sexes gave way to assertions of female superiority over men even in the male spheres of war and politics. The chaperon could simultaneously be rendered redundant and the constraints of conventional female respectability cast aside; women could be encouraged (in Christabel's words) to 'grow their own backbone', and woman as 'patient Griselda' could become a historical curiosity at last.[69]

This change of direction was hardly fair to the many suffragettes who had joined what was presented as a short-term political campaign for the vote—even for the vote 'next session'. They were now being marshalled into a campaign which could succeed, if at all, only in the very long term; whose frontal attack on male self-importance was actually counter-productive for winning the vote; and which contained elements of impossibilism. Nor were precise objectives and practicable strategies being devised to guide

[67] Lady Rhondda, *This Was My World*, p. 162.
[68] *Suffragette*, 7 Nov. 1913, p. 78.
[69] B[ritish] L[ibrary], Add. MS 58226 (Harben Papers, f.36: Christabel Pankhurst to H. D. Harben, 7 Aug. 1913; *New Statesman*, 1 Nov. 1913 (supplement on 'The Awakening of Women'), p. x; see also the editorials in *Votes for Women*, 7 June 1912, p. 584; 14 Apr. 1911, p. 460.

the next generation of British feminists; in some ways Christabel's vision gave a foretaste of the future, but the objectives were vague and the strategy minimal in its appreciation of political realities. An idealistic and courageous suffragette rank and file, buffeted by the police, insulted by crowds in the London streets, enduring all the indignities of forcible feeding, dragged away from careers, and divided from family and friends, may well have been victims of the male sex, but they were also the instruments of leaders who were not being entirely honest with their followers. Christabel has often been criticized for remaining safely in Paris and abandoning her mother and followers to the miseries of militancy, prison, hunger-strike, and forcible feeding. But this is to conceal the larger exploitation behind the smaller, and given Christabel's strategy there was a good case for her self-imposed exile. Her real offence was to drive her followers towards intolerable personal sacrifices with no foreseeable end.

As the suffragettes' Parnell, Christabel displays a strange combination of qualities. In campaigning for the vote she could be shrewd on questions of short-term strategy, successful at embarrassing the authorities; but she lacked over-all perspective on the Edwardian power-structure, and so frustrated her formal objective, votes for women. Yet in moving forward into a campaign for women's emancipation on a wider front, she displayed the reverse combination of qualities; there was long-term vision about destinations but vagueness about intermediate ways and means. As feminist star-performer, she entertained her public with a sparkling series of theatrical turns, directed with a ruthless perceptiveness and an exhilarating irreverence, but ultimately with a disastrous obtuseness.

Militancy's escalation now moved forward to its fourth stage: acceleration in the types of law-breaking that were seen as necessary. The traditional Conservative diagnosis of militancy, whereby leaders corrupt their followers, is wide of the mark here, for as *The Times* pointed out on 23 May 1912, ' "the argument of the broken pane" carries those who adopt it very far . . . when once window-breaking and the like are begun, the hotheaded followers are apt to become the leaders'. Prestige within the militant organization is acquired through taking the initiative in some new enterprise of daring which lends its author the appearance of superior toughness and zeal. The militant structure provides a miniature opportunity-society that mimics the relatively open wider society which the movement seeks to create. Members deprived by the wider society of a satisfying social function seize readily upon the relative freedom and glamour of the militant's role, which demands enthusiasm, physical courage, and initiative on practical matters rather than intellect or constructive ability. It may not even be necessary to outwit the police, for except in the higher echelons, what is wanted is martyrdom, 'the only way in which a man can become famous without ability', as a Fabian once put it.[70]

In *The Times* on 5 October 1912, Annie Besant, a keen suffragist, pointed out that 'once crime is entered on it must either become more and more violent until it ends in a revolution, successful or unsuccessful, or it must rouse society against the movement it claims to support, and lead to its suppression. The high-minded, blinded, may begin it; they are soon ousted by the more violent: in such contests the most violent leads.' Suffragette leaders tried to regulate and restrain the pace of militancy, Mrs Pethick-Lawrence recalled, because 'every new step in militancy once taken could not be retraced'.[71] Yet it was difficult for leaders who had themselves engaged in militancy to restrain followers who wished to push it further, especially when those leaders had succumbed to rank-and-file pressure in the past. At her trial in 1912, Mrs Pankhurst emphasized their efforts to prevent the movement 'from going beyond bounds',[72] but her most effective hold over her followers she and Christabel had thrown away: the capacity to deliver governmental concession. This had been the source of Parnell's influence within the Irish nationalist movement; but in bargaining with politicians Christabel could never wield the votes of

[70] B. Shaw *et al.*, *Fabian Essays* (Jubilee ed., 1948), p. xxxii, cited in Shaw's 1908 preface.
[71] Besant, *The Times*, 5 Oct. 1912, p. 4; E. Pethick-Lawrence, *My Part in a Changing World* (1938), p. 238.
[72] *Votes for Women*, 24 May 1912, p. 533.

eighty-five devoted MPs, nor did politicians see suffragette militancy as sufficiently alarming to justify concession. The second of Annie Besant's unattractive alternatives therefore seemed likely, and it was the Pankhursts' devoted followers who paid the penalty for this misleading Irish analogy, this tragic political misjudgement.

Window-breaking began spontaneously at the initiative of Edith New and Mary Leigh in 1908, and on arrest they informed Mrs Pankhurst that, having acted without orders, they would not resent being repudiated by the leadership. 'Far from repudiating them', Mrs Pankhurst recalled, 'I went at once to see them in their cells, and assured them of my approval of their act.'[73] In July 1909, thirteen women took the initiative in systematic window-breaking by hurling stones (wrapped in brown paper with string attached, so as to avoid injuring people inside the buildings) against government-office windows; once again, retrospective approval from the leaders. In the same month, Marion Wallace-Dunlop took a further initiative by hunger-striking in protest against being denied first-division treatment in prison; retrospective justification once more from the leadership. In a letter written soon afterwards, in her curious correspondence with A. J. Balfour, Leader of the Opposition, Christabel testified to the pragmatic, untheoretical way in which militancy escalated: 'we are feeling proud of having destroyed the Government's weapon of coercion. They will never in future be able to keep us in prison more than a few days, for we have now learnt our power to starve ourselves out of prison, and this power we shall use.'[74] Emily Davison's initiative shifted militancy on to a new plane when she fired a pillar-box with incendiaries in December 1911. Neither this, nor Ellen Pitfield's symbolic attempt at burning down the General Post Office in March 1912 received the leadership's approval at first, yet arson—of buildings as well as of letters—soon became official policy.[75] Escalating government repression increased the leaders' difficulties still

[73] E. Pankhurst, *My Own Story* (1914), p. 118; A. Rosen, *Rise Up Women!*, p. 107.
[74] Ibid., p. 121; see also pp. 119–20.
[75] Ibid., pp. 156, 158; E. S. Pankhurst, *The Suffragette Movement*, p. 362.

further by fragmenting their movement.[76] Only a cult of personality could henceforth weld it together.

To the militant rank and file, escalated militancy seems a natural response to injustice and oppression; for the leaders, by contrast, its major merit is publicity. Trading on the existence of a press free from government control, the WSPU's earliest militant acts aimed at breaking into the headlines of newspapers seemingly indifferent to women's suffrage. In June 1914 McKenna regretted press headlines, and even press reporting, of such incidents, in the belief that 'the immediate effect of the denial of all advertisement of militancy would do more to stop their actions than anything the Government can do', yet as Home Secretary he found himself taking up paper after paper and noticing 'that two or three columns are devoted simply to the advertisement of militancy, thereby carrying out for the women one of the main objects which they have in view'. Far from curbing such reports, his remarks merely stoked up the fires of press criticism at his alleged lack of grip; the *Globe* referred to his 'effrontery' in complaining of press reports, and *The Times* pointed out, rather more mildly, that 'the function of newspapers is, after all, to supply news and tell the public what is going on. Regard for ulterior consequences may be carried too far.'[77] McKenna had pinpointed one of the inherent difficulties of democratic society.

Yet the suffragettes paid a heavy price: the headlines could be retained only if militancy was suitably stage-managed. 'Much depended, in militancy . . .', Christabel later recalled, 'upon timing and placing, upon the dramatic arrangement and sequence of acts and events.' The *Observer* in 1913 found one thing worse than the iron entering into the soul—'it is when the limelight enters into the soul'.[78] Two major drawbacks resulted: WSPU demonstrations thereby acquired a factitious appearance, with consequent loss of public sympathy: and it became necessary either to escalate militancy

[76] Cf. F. E. Myers, 'Civil Disobedience and Organizational Change: The British Committee of 100', *Political Science Quarterly*, 1971, p. 104.

[77] *H. C. Deb.*, 11 June 1914, c.522; *Globe*, 12 June 1914, p. 6; *The Times*, 12 June 1914, p. 9; cf. Richard Davy on the press and militancy in the USSR, *The Times*, 14 Oct. 1975, p. 14.

[78] C. Pankhurst, *Unshackled*, p. 153; *Observer*, 23 Feb. 1913, p. 8.

or to refurbish the headline-value of militancy at its existing level by calling periodic 'truces'. Maud Kate Smith recalled the movement's dilemma: ' "Today's Outrage". That put you in a mess, because you've got to see . . . you've got an outrage for the next day, you see, otherwise you don't get the placard.' Retreat is impossible in the game of bluff and counter-bluff with the authorities, for there is an ever-present risk of losing face. By a sort of ratchet effect, each violent innovation is consolidated by *amour propre*; 'even the martyr, not resolute to beware of complacency, may become an egoist', wrote the *Observer* in 1913.[79] Christabel confesses as much in her letter to Balfour of June 1910: unless Asquith reconsiders his decision to refuse government backing for a women's suffrage measure that session, 'we shall be obliged if only for self respect's sake to express our indignation and dissatisfaction by means of militant action'.[80] Yet the politicians could not back down, if only from fear of looking ridiculous. The truce of 1910–11 may have been embarked upon partly for reasons of humanity and reconciliation, but Christabel later recalled that it would also 'give time for familiarity to fade, so that the same methods could be used again with freshness and effect'. Militant methods were used later, though with ever-diminishing impact. In 1911, Cecil Chesterton pointed out that 'now, nothing less than the mutilation of a Cabinet Minister will induce an editor to give sixpence for a paragraph concerning them'.[81]

Mary Stocks later claimed that 'a militant policy cannot stand still—it must either develop more extreme forms and move towards civil war, or cash in on its achievement of publicity, and proceed on more conventional lines'.[82] Yet a retreat from militancy was improbable for three reasons: the leaders could hardly abandon a tactic which still seemed to bring at least an element of success, a retreat would carry

[79] Author's tape-recorded interview with Maud Kate Smith, Solihull 14 Jan. 1975; *Observer*, 23 Feb. 1913, p. 8.
[80] BL Add. MS 49793 (Balfour Papers), f.94: Christabel Pankhurst to A. J. Balfour, 28 June 1910.
[81] C. Pankhurst, *Unshackled*, p. 153; H. Carter (ed.), *Women's Suffrage and Militancy* (1911), p. 10.
[82] M. Stocks, *My Commonplace Book*, p. 68; cf. her review of Annie Kenney's *Memoirs of a Militant* in *Woman's Leader*, 31 Oct. 1924, p. 321.

at least the appearance of indecision and defeat, and it would deprive the WSPU of any reason for its continued existence separately from the non-militant NUWSS. A mere half-retreat from militancy would be externally confusing and internally disruptive, as illustrated by the faltering history of the Women's Freedom League, a democratically structured offshoot of 1907 from the WSPU, rather tentatively militant in policy. Appealing to Mrs Badley for funds in March 1912, its leader Mrs Despard admitted that militancy must for tactical reasons be suspended, yet 'there is . . . a great difficulty to be faced by any militant suffrage society that abstains from militant action for political reasons. Militancy and defiance, while bringing severe criticism, do also bring public interest, enthusiasm, money and members. The cold logic of political facts is not inspiring, and a society which applies such logic does not receive much financial assistance from the ordinary public.' The Votes for Women Fellowship, later the United Suffragists—as an organization which repudiated Pankhurstian extremes of militancy yet which also repudiated mere constitutionalism, and which grouped round the Pethick-Lawrences after they had left the Pankhursts in 1912—came near to falling between two stools. Mrs Pethick-Lawrence saw the problem from the start; the new society was a 'great risk . . . because one cannot say of militancy "We will only go so far" '.[83]

Suffragette history illustrates how militancy can escalate in several dimensions—in the level of propriety it is prepared to breach as well as in the violence it is prepared to promote. And within the violent dimension, there is escalation in the numbers involved and in their co-ordination as well as in the intensity of the violence that is contemplated. In the summer of 1913 Christabel Pankhurst infringed medical taboos with her frank writings on venereal disease, and in the summer of 1914 she flagrantly breached social convention by organizing suffragette disruption of religious services and royal functions. By June 1914 the King was grumbling to Lord Selborne that 'it was most disagreeable to

[83] City of London Polytechnic, Fawcett Library Autograph Collection, vol. 20, part 2: Mrs Despard to Mrs Badley, 13 Mar. 1912; Bodleian Library, MS Eng. Misc. e 618/1 (H. W. Nevinson Diary), entry for 23 Dec. 1913.

have a disturbance always and everywhere they went in public'.[84] As for escalation in violence, we have seen how firmly the road to de-escalation was barred; only the concession of votes for women or the advent of a first world war could bring a sudden end to militancy. The only alternative was a gradual erosion of suffragette strength and numbers due to government repression and the lapse of time. This process was well under way by 1914, and Mrs Pankhurst's prudent disbandment of the WSPU in August characteristically seized a small-scale propaganda victory out of long-term and inevitable defeat.

Yet without the first world war, militancy would probably have ended with a bang, not with a whimper. The bang would not have taken the form of civil war. Mrs Besant rightly pointed out that 'there are not women enough willing to use violence to win success'. Few will risk even the martyrdom that arouses sympathy, let alone the militancy that courts defeat. In challenging the men on their own ground, physical force, the suffragettes were bound to fail. They could not hope for substantial male support—not just because of anti-male suffragette tactics, but because the WSPU campaigned in effect only for removing the sex discrimination from the existing franchise, whereas only adult suffrage could have attracted mass support. By seeking votes for women 'as it is or may be granted to men' (to adopt the WSPU formulation) —suffragettes gained an apparent flexibility of manœuvre only at the price of legislative feasibility.[85] As feminists they could not by definition campaign simultaneously to enfranchise more men, yet it was only from that direction that a Liberal government, aiming to appear progressive and increase its hold on the electorate, could concede women's enfranchisement.

Mrs Pankhurst's youngest daughter Sylvia had the wit to see that a mass campaign explicitly for adult suffrage was the only variant of militancy with a future. In 1914 she based her adult suffragist secession from the WSPU—the East London

---

[84] Bodleian Library, MS Selborne 102, f. 121: Selborne to his wife, 14 June 1914.
[85] *The Times*, 5 Oct. 1912, p. 4 (Besant); WSPU *First Annual Report... 1907*. ('objects' listed on cover).

Federation—on London's East End, and reverted to the mass demonstrations that had produced the WSPU's earlier triumphs, while simultaneously whipping up sympathy through a personal martyrdom at least as rigorous as anything the WSPU could display. She had at last perceived the distinction between tactical or stunt violence (or, in her terminology, 'secret violence'), which has little hope of influencing politicians in a parliamentary system, and the mass violence or civil war (in her terminology, 'open violence'), to the threat of which they are trained to respond, and which they will do their utmost to pre-empt through timely concession. 'Militancy no good unless on a great scale', was Lloyd George's view in February 1913: '—100,000 women in the street w[oul]d mean something. At present a mere handful and greatly declining.'[86]

If civil war could never be the denouement of WSPU militancy, kidnapping was always a possibility, and in February 1913 Lloyd George included rumours of suffragette designs on Asquith's daughter among the factors then damaging the women's suffrage cause at Westminster.[87] But the form of escalated suffragette militancy which the police feared most was assassination. As early as 1909, rumours were flying round London that the suffragettes had decided to assassinate Asquith.[88] Through a Mrs Moore of the Women's Freedom League, the authorities learned that suffragettes were practising shooting with revolvers at London shooting-ranges. In September Edward Troup, permanent under-secretary at the Home Office, thought that there was 'now definite ground for fearing' that one of the suffragette pickets outside the House of Commons would fire at Asquith.[89]

    [86] As cited in BL Add. MS 50901 (C. P. Scott Diary), f. 88: entry for 3 Feb. 1913. See also Sylvia Pankhurst, 'The Women's Movement of Yesterday and Tomorrow' (typescript in the Institute of Social History, Amsterdam, Sylvia Pankhurst MSS).   [87] Scott Diary, f. 88.

    [88] On this see Mrs Berenson's MS autobiography of her daughter Ray Strachey, Chapter VIII, p. 9 (in the care of Mrs Halpern of Oxford, who has kindly allowed me to cite it, together with other extracts from her mother's papers cited later), citing Ray's letter to her mother, 13 Oct. 1909; see also Ray to her mother, 12 Oct. 1909, and Emily Lutyens MSS, Emily Lutyens to Edwin Lutyens, 19 Oct. 1909 (this letter was kindly loaned to me for consultation by her daughter Mrs Links).

    [89] Bodleian Library, MS Asquith 22, f. 224 (Troup's comment on memorandum of George Ridley dated 27 Sept. 1909) dated 27 Sept. 1909.

Forcible feeding later exacerbated feeling still further, and Herbert Gladstone as Home Secretary began receiving threats from aggrieved husbands hinting grimly at reprisals. 'I am in a state of constant anxiety touching the safety of the P.M.', he told Sir Edward Grey in November 1909; 'we know that women have been practising shooting. Some of them are half crazy, or wholly hysterical. The most stringent precautions have to be taken.' The physical attack on Asquith at Lympne showed how easily this could occur, and 'the probability is that if things go on as they are, something very bad will happen'.[90] There were similar attacks on other cabinet ministers—on Winston Churchill and Augustine Birrell in 1910, for example. In October 1909 Mrs Brailsford was arrested while chopping through a protective street barricade with an axe at Newcastle, where Lloyd George was to speak, and in July 1912 Mary Leigh threw a hatchet into Asquith's carriage in Dublin.

We now know that these were intended as only symbolic gestures, but the government did not then possess our knowledge of the personalities involved, nor could it be sure that others would not embark on gestures more than symbolic. Deploring the WSPU's transition from martyrdom to arson, Mrs Besant envisaged 'a danger that women may . . . become second-rate men in their political methods, instead of heroic women'; Russian nihilists had made a similar transition, and 'few know the splendid beginning; all know the violence and the murder which accompanied the end'.[91] In 1913 McKenna told the King that the Cat and Mouse Act would reduce the need for forcible feeding but could not realize his desire for its abolition because some self-starved prisoners might be too dangerous to release; 'for instance, it is quite possible that one of these fanatical women might be convicted of endeavouring to shoot somebody, and she might persist in her intention to shoot if she were released'. In June 1914 the King told Lord Selborne that he was receiving threatening letters every day, and that Simon, Haldane, and Buckmaster shared McKenna's view that suffragettes must not be allowed

[90] BL Add. MS 45992 (Herbert Gladstone Papers), f. 132: Herbert Gladstone to Sir Edward Grey, 10 Nov. 1909; cf. G. P. Gooch, *Under Six Reigns* (1958), p. 150.   [91] *The Times*, 5 Oct. 1912, p. 4.

to die in custody because 'they would take life for life, a Minister's or the King's'. In January 1918 Lord Crewe recalled the Liberal government's mood before war began: 'it is literally true that it would have been no surprise to us, the members of the Government of that day, if any one of our colleagues in the House of Commons who had taken a prominent line either for or against the grant of the vote to women had been assassinated in the street. Nor, I venture to say, would it have been the slightest surprise to Scotland Yard.'[92]

Given the intensity of the passions aroused on both sides by 1914, rank-and-file devotion to the suffragette leaders, and the personal blame suffragettes pinned on Asquith and other leading anti-suffragist politicians, the authorities had reason for their fears. Why, after all, should militancy, which had escalated continuously since 1904, suddenly have stopped short at this particular threshold? The initiative would probably not have come from the suffragette leadership, whose professions of respect for human life were probably sincere; the Irish precedents which so forcibly impressed them did not extend, publicly at least, to the Phoenix Park murders of 1882. Escalation of militancy would once more have thrust itself up from below. And in a situation still further inflamed by hunger-strikes and perhaps also by the death of her mother, or of others in the movement—who will say that Christabel Pankhurst's ruthlessness in pursuit of her cause, amply demonstrated in her personal relationships and during earlier escalations of militancy, would not have extended to condoning even this?

The suffragettes 'do not—they will not and cannot—boldly put on the whole armour of devilry', said the Liberal journalist H. W. Massingham in February 1913, 'and kill some men in order to frighten others into giving them the vote'. His leading article infuriated Massingham's suffragist colleague H. W. Nevinson, who saw it as an incitement to assassination.[93] There is some inside evidence, too, that

[92] Royal Archives, Windsor: RA GV O 459/2: McKenna to Stamfordham, 28 Mar. 1913, quoted by gracious permission of Her Majesty the Queen; Bodleian Library, MS Selborne 102, f. 121: Selborne to his wife, 14 June 1914; Crewe in *H. L. Deb.*, 9 Jan. 1918, c.448.

[93] *Daily News*, 24 Feb. 1913, p. 6; Nevinson, ibid., 26 Feb. 1913, p. 6.

assassination was a possibility. By December 1912, a Miss
Gilliatt was reported by the police as emphasizing the ease of
killing a cabinet minister in a speech at a WSPU meeting on
Wimbledon Common.[94] Olive Malvery in February 1914
claimed that three of Christabel's followers to her own
knowledge possessed revolvers; 'brutality and persecution
have maddened them . . . and one wants to kill the prison
doctor who obscenely insulted and tortured her'.[95] Laurence
Housman, a suffragist with much inside knowledge, later
referred in his memoirs to a devotee of Mrs Pankhurst who,
if Mrs Pankhurst had died in a hunger-strike, 'had made a
vow to do what she regarded as the right and necessary
thing . . . and hang for it'. There can of course be no proof
that an event which did not occur might under other circumstances have taken place; all that can be said is that there was
widespread apprehension at the possibility among informed
people; and, as Huizinga reminds us, the historian (like the
police and the Home Office) 'must constantly put himself at
a point in the past at which the known factors still seem to
permit different outcomes'.[96]

One form of militancy nowhere envisaged is the indiscriminate killing and maiming which has since become
familiar as a militant tactic; suffragette threats to human life
—and they were rare, indirect, and never officially condoned
—always related to specific anti-suffragists. Indeed, by 1914
it was becoming clear to most informed observers that there
was no future in the WSPU's line of tactics. It is often
emphasized that the first world war enabled anti-suffragists
to climb down from an untenable position; it is less frequently stressed that the war performed the same service for
Mrs Pankhurst and her eldest daughter.

III

The move towards the act of militancy itself again involves
four stages: contraction in numbers, elevation of the

[94] A. Rosen, *Rise Up Women!*, p. 185.
[95] *MacKirdy's Weekly*, 7 Feb. 1914, p. 13.
[96] L. Housman, *The Unexpected Years* (1937), p. 295; Huizinga quot. in F.
Stern (ed.), *The Varieties of History from Voltaire to the present* (2nd ed., 1970),
p. 292.

leadership, careful and systematic organization, culminating in the act of militancy itself. Suffragette militancy did not require a large membership free to debate policy but a small army isolated from the general public by its barrack walls, its rigid discipline, and its tight hierarchy. This was but the latest in a succession of contractions in membership and outlook.

In October 1909 the WSPU did not know its own membership even in London, whereas the NUWSS was able to claim 20,000 members. In March 1912 Mrs Fawcett thought WSPU membership in 1909 must have been a little over 8,000, to judge from its annual report; since then her own organization had been recruiting funds and members shed by the militant organization, and in the last fifteen months her subscribing membership had risen from 21,500 to over 30,000.[97] WSPU membership fees suggest that fewer new members were joining in each year between 1909 and 1914; after October 1913, perhaps to avoid advertising this fact, new members' fees were no longer published.[98] Many years later Mary Richardson thought press estimates of 20,000 suffragettes in 1914 exaggerated: 'the actual front-line militants numbered only one thousand odd; and even this figure had dwindled after the "Cat and Mouse" Act had been introduced'.[99] WSPU reticence about membership stems not from inefficiency (the WSPU bureaucracy was extremely efficient), but from recognition that large numbers had by now become irrelevant to the Union's purpose. By February 1914 Mrs Dacre Fox, the WSPU's chief organizer, cheerfully announced three simultaneous sources of contraction when explaining the secession of Sylvia Pankhurst's East London Federation. For reasons of policy, she said, the WSPU did not now saddle itself with a branch structure; it diverged from Sylvia's belief in collaboration between the sexes; and it rejected her strategy of making the campaign for the vote a class movement rather than a women's movement.[1]

[97] *The Times*, 13 Oct. 1909, p. 8; Cumbria County Record Office, Carlisle: Catherine Marshall MSS, Box 8, file 'CEM March 1912', Mrs Fawcett to Mr Lyttelton, 12 Mar. 1912 (carbon copy).
[98] A. Rosen, *Rise Up Women!*, pp. 211–12.
[99] M. Richardson, *Laugh a Defiance*, p. 189.
[1] *Sunday Times*, 8 Feb. 1914, p. 9.

Militancy also required a regional contraction; militant acts needed to be focused primarily on London, the centre of government, which was also a safe hiding-place for conspirators and a good base for co-ordinating and implementing militant forays elsewhere. Although the WSPU originated in Lancashire and at first experienced difficulty in getting launched in London, by 1911 a non-militant could point out that it had 'found a far stronger foothold in London than in the country'. Whereas only a third of the WSPU branches in February 1907 and February 1911 were in the London area, London's proportion had risen to 39 per cent by 1914.[2] London is the source of simultaneous liberation and peril in H. G. Wells's suffragist novel *Ann Veronica* (1909), of a perverted modernity and a breathless rejection of enduring values in an anonymous anti-suffrage novel like *The Home-Breakers* (1913), and of a festering militancy which diverts women from their higher role in Mrs Humphry Ward's antisuffragist *Delia Blanchflower* (1915).

Intense public hostility and systematic government repression now winnowed out from the militants the half-hearted, the independent-minded, the scrupulous, and the timid. Suffragettes were not alone among Edwardians in resorting to violence, which was also employed on this issue by the government and by anti-suffragist mobs—not to mention violence in Ireland and in labour disputes. But whereas the suffragettes were conspiratorial and diffuse in their militancy, anti-suffragist violence was open and concentrated; and whereas suffragette arson, by exasperating those whose livelihood and property it threatened, added recruits to the ranks of the enemy, anti-suffragist violence became so intimidating as seriously to contract the ranks of the friendly.[3] Suffragettes by 1914 were spiralling downwards; accentuated militancy contracted numbers, which in turn accentuated militancy still further.

'Kings will be tyrants from policy', wrote Burke, 'when subjects are rebels from principle.'[4] As early as March 1907

---

[2] *Common Cause*, 6 Apr. 1911, p. 852. Calculations for 1907 and 1911 from NWSPU First and Fifth *Annual Reports*, listing of branches; 1914 figure from R. Fulford, *Votes for Women*, p. 149.

[3] There is a fuller discussion of anti-suffrage violence in my *Separate Spheres*, Ch. 9.   [4] E. Burke, *Reflections on the Revolution in France*, p. 172.

plain-clothes men were shadowing WSPU leaders,[5] and in September 1909 the police increased their staffing in order to protect ministers.[6] By October 1908 suffragette disturbances had excluded women from House of Commons lobbies, a restriction which lasted for several years. In an autobiographical note written much later in life, James Bryce rather nostalgically recalled the 1850s when 'many years before dynamite had been invented, anyone strolling in the Lobby might ask any member for a stranger's Order, and count upon getting one'.[7] By January 1914 Sylvia Pankhurst was aware that her letters were being opened by the police,[8] and the militants had been forced underground. Here as elsewhere with violent protest movements, government's potentially repressive forces were being strengthened—forces which, long after the protesters have faded away, tend to remain.

Towards the end, anti-suffrage violence was directed at suffragettes indiscriminately, and made it difficult for them even to engage in non-violent propaganda. Still more unfairly, it was also directed at the non-militants, whose formal repudiation of militancy could not appease an indignant public which lacked both the time and the inclination to distinguish between feminist sects. By 1913 militancy had therefore terminated that fruitful interaction between militant and non-militant activist which operates in so many reforming campaigns, and which may well have assisted even women's suffrage between 1904 and 1908. Non-militants could no longer adduce militant actions as arguments for governmental concession, for public fury enabled the government to offer frontal resistance in 1913–14, and even to institute the remarkable infringement of individual liberty involved in the Cat and Mouse Act's provisions for rearresting the prisoners released on hunger-strike. Militancy's distractions had to be removed before debates on the substantive

[5] *Daily Mail*, 15 Mar. 1907, p. 8.
[6] PRO Mepol 2/1310 (Suffragette Disturbances): Acting Police Commissioner to Troup, 15 Sept. 1909; Troup to Commissioner of Police of the Metropolis, Sept. 1909.
[7] H. A. L. Fisher, *James Bryce* (1927), i, p. 31.
[8] BL Add. MS 58226 (Harben Papers), f. 95: Sylvia Pankhurst to Harben, 29 Jan. 1914.

issue could once more dominate the scene, and before non-militant suffragists could again hope to get their message across in peace.

The process of contraction was complex, for human beings seldom react uniformly to the same political stimulus; so substantial was the WSPU's overall decline in membership that it masked the small-scale recruitment which resulted from disgust at governmental repression, for some women were actually impelled towards militancy by an outraged sense of injustice at the sight of repression. Ursula Hibbert in Edith Zangwill's *The Call* (1924) had admired the police all her life, but she suddenly realizes that they are capable of brutality when she sees the beautiful suffragette activist Mary Blake arrested, and watches the clothing of a respectable middle-aged suffragette being torn and battered by the hostile crowd during a WSPU deputation at Westminster. She is later shocked by the tortured appearance of Mary Blake after her hunger-strike, and it is not long before she herself takes the militant plunge. It was the sight of a minor martyr thrown to the ground and placed at the mercy of the police during a WSPU demonstration that tempted Grace Alderman, a Preston suffragist, into the WSPU. 'I was baking cakes at the time', she recalled, 'and Mother came into the kitchen with the paper—it was when the Press first began taking photographs—"just look at this!" she said . . . Until then I'd thought England stood for fair play.'[9]

There is also an element of police-created crime in suffragette recruitment. Police and anti-suffragist manhandling of suffragettes made window-breaking seem attractive as a way of ensuring rapid arrest and consequent relative security.[10] Here is an extreme illustration of the general tendency for women's crime-rates to approach more closely to male the greater the freedom and equality for women in the society concerned.[11] Government mishandling of the WSPU, together with police misconduct, provided Mrs Pankhurst with many

[9] P. Hesketh, *My Aunt Edith* (1966), p. 39.
[10] On this see E. Pethick-Lawrence, *My Part in a Changing World*, p. 233; C. Pankhurst, *Unshackled*, pp. 153-4; Lady Rhondda, *This Was My World*, p. 162.
[11] L. Coser, 'Violence and the Social Structure', in J. H. Masserman (ed.), *Violence and War* (New York, 1963), p. 41.

recruits, though with far fewer in the longer term than her militant tactics repelled.

The WSPU's most adaptable and mobile instruments were of course the young, the unmarried, and the unattached.[12] By 1907 it had created a secret youth organization nicknamed the 'Young Hot Bloods', pledged to support their leaders in any militant action. There was always an element of youth versus age about the WSPU, which depreciated the non-militants as old-fashioned and stuffy. 'You know there is something fly and spry about the young ones', Christabel wrote in 1913, 'and they have not often failed us when backed up by superior age and wisdom.'[13] From the beginning, the proportion of those arrested who were young and/or unmarried was high, and the more physically demanding militancy became, the higher the percentage of the unmarried among WSPU subscribers. Mrs Pankhurst was a widow and her three daughters remained unmarried throughout the suffragette period. The young were less likely than the old to sustain injury in the mêlée which militancy often produced, less reluctant to risk the dishevelment and disorder which frequently resulted. By 1913-14, as many as 63 per cent of the WSPU subscribers were listed as 'Miss', and all the WSPU organizers at that time were unmarried.[14] Where family connection did exist, many suffragettes took care to disguise them by adopting assumed names—not simply to protect the family reputation, but to protect their relatives from intimidation.

As an unmarried orphan, solitary by temperament, with no occupation and living outside the country of her upbringing, Mary Richardson was almost the ideal candidate for organizing militancy, as she herself admitted: 'from the first, I had realised I was better able to undertake the more difficult tasks in that I had no family to worry about me and no one I needed to worry over. In the fullest sense I was free to do what was asked.' It was a relief to know that she belonged nowhere. 'I had no home and so there was nobody who

---

[12] Cf. the Committee of 100 in F. E. Myers, art. cit., p. 109.

[13] Schlesinger Library, Harvard University, MC 190 (WSPU Papers): Christabel Pankhurst to 'P', 21 Apr. 1913.

[14] A. Rosen, *Rise Up Women!*, pp. 81, 83, 119, 120, 122, 209-10.

would worry over me and over whom I need worry. From the start it had been this knowledge that had made me feel I must do more than my fair share to make up for the many women who stood back from militancy because of the sorrow their actions would have caused some loved one . . . For anyone who loved me to have suffered on my account would have been an unbearable thing.'[15] Unlike some later variants of militant, the suffragettes had no residential or other social grouping to fall back upon; they were emphatically alone in a male-dominated society, most of whose women readily consorted with the enemy.

The militant élite contracts still further because of its inevitably authoritarian structure. The tightening of bonds within the suffragettes' alternative community proceeds still further at the same time as rank-and-file initiative contracts to preoccupation only with the details of militant strategy. Government repression of the rank and file is therefore reinforced by accentuated emotional and other pressure from the leadership. For unlike Irish intimidation, from which suffragette leaders learned so much, the suffragette militancy which escalated from below was orchestrated from above. Christabel Pankhurst later claimed to have been able to turn it on and off at will.[16] Mary Richardson might dread receiving her militant instructions, but she carried them out. Maud Kate Smith recalled being repelled by letter-burning: 'it made me so ill, because I hated doing it. You can imagine. Fancy destroying a private letter of other people! It *rends* your inside. I'd always feel fearfully ill, I didn't know how to walk away from them [sc. the pillar-boxes], but if it's your job it's your job, you see. I never turned back.'[17]

The leadership required unquestioning obedience on strategy—in Teresa Billington-Greig's words, 'a type of self-subjection, not less objectionable than the more ordinary self-subjection of women to men, to which it bears a close

---

[15] M. Richardson, *Laugh a Defiance*, pp. 54, 174; cf. the Balcombe Street incident, discussed in *Guardian*, 10 Feb. 1977, p. 11.

[16] C. Pankhurst, *Unshackled*, p. 229.

[17] Author's tape-recorded interview with Maud Kate Smith, Solihull, 14 Jan. 1975.

relation'.[18] Political judgement and even moral standards were sometimes abdicated; 'I am no longer an individual', said Ellen Pitfield after forcible feeding in 1909, 'I am an instrument.' Mary Richardson came as near as anyone to the leaders' ideal, and many years later recalled her semi-hypnotic state while travelling on a District Line train to her latest militant exploit. 'I stared vaguely at my fellow passengers and kept muttering to myself. "Green cloak. The plan". It was as if I had become an automaton and was mechanically memorising my instructions.'[19]

Christabel frequently likened the WSPU to an army; since membership was voluntary, expulsion of the undisciplined could be demanded with a clear conscience.[20] An almost clannish solidarity could then build up, with militant acts as the entry permit or first blooding necessary for full acceptance within the group. The WSPU's structure thus strangely parodied the forces of law and order which it opposed. Such intense and unfamiliar suffragette relationships were nostalgically recalled at the numerous suffragette reunions held in later years by old warriors with only their past in common. 'When you have lived with it', Oswald Mosley declared of the spirit of an army, 'you realise it is something unique, one of the wonders of human nature.'[21]

To weld together such a structure, the leaders required not only administrative and executive skill, but the capacity to attract unquestioning allegiance. Here Christabel Pankhurst's uncompromisingly brisk decisiveness and youthful beauty, Emmeline Pethick-Lawrence's fine clothes and intense emotion, Emmeline Pankhurst's dignified presence and magical eloquence, Lady Constance Lytton's aristocratic background and capacity for self-sacrifice, and Annie Kenney's saucy and sprightly Lancashire vim and vigour came into their own; photographs of the leaders were energetically distributed in postcard format. H. W. Nevinson

[18] T. Billington-Greig, *Militant Suffrage Movement*, p. 115.
[19] Pitfield quot. in E. S. Pankhurst, *The Suffragette Movement*, p. 380; M. Richardson, *Laugh a Defiance*, p. 179.
[20] e.g. E. S. Pankhurst, *The Suffragette Movement*, pp. 316, 517; C. Pankhurst, *Unshackled*, p. 83; *Suffragette*, 25 Oct. 1912, p. 14.
[21] Sir O. Mosley, *My Life* (1970 ed.), p. 48.

in December 1911 found Annie Kenney doubtful about WSPU militancy, yet his demands for reason made no impact on a young woman who said she 'would go through fire for Christabel'.[22] Among the bitterest press criticisms she and her mother faced was the accusation that they led young girls astray; yet they needed to provide a warm substitute-community which could furnish all the reassurance that the wider society had once provided. Substitute parents, idealized elder sisters, and sympathetic friends were needed by those who had forsaken all for the cause. Asked in 1974 why she admired Mrs Pankhurst so much, Mrs Leonora Cohen replied that 'she was a lovely, motherly woman. After my own mother, in my eyes, she had a heart; she was typical to me of a lovely woman.'[23]

Mary Richardson's almost personal fealty to Mrs Pankhurst led her to see it as a real favour when she was granted a personal interview to receive instructions about blowing up a railway station in the Birmingham area. Her subsequent slashing of the Rokeby *Venus*, 'the most beautiful woman in mythological history', was by her own account a symbolic protest against government injury to 'the most beautiful character in modern history', Mrs Pankhurst, who was being 'slowly murdered' by the process of arrest, hunger-strike, and release.[24] Audrey Moze, heroine of Arnold Bennett's *The Lion's Share* (1916), succumbs to the magnetism of 'Rosamund', the suffragette leader; to the hero-worship of the working-class suffragette Jane Foley; and to the romantic gesture of renunciation involved in forsaking Parisian wealth and comfort for London's militant hazards. Mrs Billington-Greig in 1911 described this process of seduction with the cold analysis that springs from disillusioned familiarity: 'the yoke is imposed by a mingling of elements of deliberately worked up emotion, by the exercise of affectional and personal charm, by an all-pervading system of mutual

[22] Bodleian Library, Oxford, MS Eng. Misc., e 617/1 (Nevinson's Diary), entry for 7 Dec. 1911.

[23] Author's tape-recorded interview with Mrs Leonora Cohen, Rhos-on-Sea, 26 Oct. 1974; cf. Lady C. Lytton, *Prisons and Prisoners*, pp. 26, 29.

[24] Quoted from Mary Richardson's statement after slashing the Rokeby *Venus*, printed in *Suffragette*, 13 Mar. 1914, p. 491; see also M. Richardson, *Laugh a Defiance*, p. 137.

glorification in which each of the three leaders by turn sounds the praises of the others'.[25]

Once enmeshed in the WSPU's law-breaking, it was difficult for the militant to draw out; she knew too much about the organization, and they knew too much about her. She did not wish to betray loyal friends, and if she risked betrayal their revenge could be more terrible than anything governments could do; the painfulness of the withdrawal symptoms outweighed any punishment the authorities could devise. It sometimes took more courage to repudiate militancy than to engage in it—so insulated from the surrounding community had suffragettes become by 1912. Within this *imperium in imperio* the liberties of the independent-minded suffragette were curtailed even more completely than within the formal structure of male-dominated authority.

What was gained in militant effectiveness was lost in political perception. Suffragettes captive within so authoritarian and insulated a structure could hardly grasp the realities of Edwardian political power or perceive militancy's major drawbacks. The unpredictable incidence of the militant act may terrorize out of all proportion to its physical result, but indiscriminate also is the hostility it generates. So small and authoritarian a militant body could not possibily generate the continuous and coherent planning needed even for militancy to be seriously disruptive, let alone for wider political understanding to grow. Buildings were destroyed, letters were burned, windows were smashed, but on no systematic over-all plan, and with no hope of extracting governmental concession, yet at the cost of rank-and-file suffering sometimes so great as almost to pass the limits of what can humanly be endured.

Still, in a society as complex as Edwardian Britain, never could so much damage be done to so many by so few. Suffragettes exploded the anti-suffragists' 'physical-force argument' by showing that relative physical weakness could be counterbalanced by brains, organization, courage, and ingenuity; these could work wonders of destruction. 'Civilisation was so complicated', Mrs Pankhurst declared at Ipswich

[25] T. Billington-Greig, 'Emancipation in a Hurry', *New Age*, 12 Jan. 1911, p. 247.

in 1913, 'that a very little thing could put everything out of working order.'[26] WSPU efficiency, here as elsewhere, was impressive; 'you need not worry, as everything has been foreseen', ran the WSPU's characteristic instructions for its demonstration of 21 November 1911.[27] The mass window-breakings of 1911–12 co-ordinated tactical violence so as to lend it the appearance of a mass violence which would seize the headlines. For this and other militant purposes, key figures of authority from Christabel Pankhurst down-wards needed to be preserved from authority's clutches; WSPU organizers were usually told to avoid direct implica-tion in militancy themselves, or at least to avoid getting caught.

Rank-and-file militants volunteered (sometimes on invita-tion) and supplied their names. They were given precise instructions on what to do and where; weapons, missiles, and explosives were assembled at the right place at the right time; well-to-do sympathizers put up the militants in their homes in preparation for the larger London demonstrations of militancy; non-militants, or would-be militants restrained by family or professional considerations, were strategically placed around the country to receive the hunger-strike's exhausted victims. 'I just got a letter', said Hazel Inglis of her window-smashing over sixty-four years before, 'and inside it, it just had the date and underneath "Lower Regent Street Post Office, six o'clock"; so I knew what I had to do, you see, the time and everything.' Jessie Stephen's letter-burning in Glasgow 'was organised . . . with military precision. We met in this place, and we were all handed our tools . . . and we covered the whole of Glasgow in that way and nobody was ever caught, because the thing was done at different times, you see.'[28]

The act of militancy itself is perhaps the least interesting phase in the sequence under discussion. Accustomed as

[26] *East Anglian Times*, 12 Feb. 1913, p. 5.

[27] B. L. Arncliffe-Sennett Collection, vol. 15, p. 71: note signed A. B. Ham-bling, headed 'Final Instructions to Members of Demonstration, November 21st. 1911'.

[28] Author's tape-recorded interviews with Miss Hazel Inglis, Coulsden, 16 Mar. 1976, and with Miss Jessie Stephen, Bristol, 1 July 1977. See also Lady Rhondda, *This Was My World*, p. 153.

we are to relative freedom of movement for women, and
emancipated as we have become from the rigours of middle-
class convention, we appreciate only with difficulty the scale
of the physical and moral courage militancy then required.
Unlike some later types of militant, suffragettes were rebel-
ling against the contemporary stereotype for their sex with
their tough, single-minded, almost ruthless role as woman of
action. 'You little know how we women have to screw up
and screw up our courage to acting point', Miss Pleasance
Pendred, twenty-five years a London schoolteacher, told the
court after being arrested for damaging property in 1913.[29]
The act of militancy transcended mere politics and became
a moment of irrevocable commitment, a symbolic break with
the past, and a personal statement about one's relationship
with parents, husbands, relatives, and society at large; that
is why decades later it was recalled with such stark clarity
and precision.

For these women were not natural militants, and the anti-
suffrage vision of them as wild, unkempt maenads seeking
all whom they could devour was libellous; Mrs Pankhurst
can be taken at her own valuation when she described herself as 'by nature a law-abiding person, as one hating violence,
hating disorder'.[30] Many suffragettes were gentle and beautiful women whose unresting conscience responded to the
suffering they saw all round them and which they had
perhaps personally experienced; spurred on by colleagues
within a militant structure, their desperation readily assumed
violent forms. Their often simplistic, non-political, non-
party standpoint was dry tinder which readily took fire
when the political situation was misrepresented to them by
their leaders, and when the politicians' response seemed to
conform to the picture thus painted.

The suffragettes never glorified the act of militancy as
such. For them it was never more than a weapon in what
was seen as a predominantly parliamentary campaign; it
never became a proto-Fascist assertion of physical strength,
if only because it usually took conspiratorial and surreptitious forms which required ingenuity and courage rather

[29] *Suffragette*, 28 Feb. 1913, p. 306.
[30] Ibid., 14 Nov. 1913, p. 99 (speech at New York, 21 Oct. 1913).

than brute force. Nor was it ever seen as procuring the syndicalist's mystical moment of collective liberation. Most militants felt no enthusiasm whatever for the act in itself. 'When I had to do any militancy, I nearly died with fright', Mrs Cohen recalled, 'because I *hated* anything . . . whatever to do with confrontation or disturbance of any sort.'[31] The fear of looking foolish, the danger of arrest, and the threat of physical assault were the least of it; far more daunting was the fear of letting down much-loved suffragette leaders and colleagues, and the torture involved in upsetting uncomprehending parents and incredulous relatives. Worst of all was the internal battle involved, steeling oneself to break with upbringing and convention for the cause. As Mary Richardson explained, it was a battle which had to be fought out in silence while pretending to play the part 'of a normal, quiet individual when one is thoroughly involved in the most abnormal activities'.[32]

The minutes and seconds before the moment of militancy often seemed an agony. Amber Blanco-White could not bring herself to destroy a window that had taken so much skill and work to manufacture: 'the contents of the window did not seem to matter, but look at that lovely glass . . .', she recalled, 'it glitters, it shines . . . and I simply couldn't bring myself to do it'. Hazel Inglis recalled wandering about in a semi-daze immediately before smashing her window: 'what's difficult to do is to get through the ten minutes before you do it; that's the awful time. When you have come to do it, it's nothing at all.'[33] Mrs Cohen was so terrified when embarking on her self-chosen mission to smash open a jewel-case in the Tower of London that she forgot to alight at Mark Lane underground station and had to go all round the Circle Line again before she could nerve herself to get out.[34] The act of militancy itself was a positive relief

[31] Author's tape-recorded interview with Mrs Leonora Cohen, Rhos-on-Sea, 26 Oct. 1974.

[32] M. Richardson, *Laugh a Defiance*, p. 139.

[33] Author's interview with Mrs Amber Blanco-White, Hampstead, 11 Feb. 1977, from which she kindly allowed me to quote; and tape-recorded interview with Miss Hazel Inglis, Coulsden, 16 Mar. 1976.

[34] Author's tape-recorded interview with Mrs Leonora Cohen, Rhos-on-Sea, 26 Oct. 1974; cf. Lady Rhondda, *This Was My World*, p. 154.

by comparison. 'I'm doing it! I'm doing it!' cried one terrified suffragette in Bond Street, whose colleague's accusations of disloyalty to Mrs Pankhurst had goaded her into smashing her window. 'It was very frightening because you had to do all these strange things alone', Maud Kate Smith recalled, 'and there was always the awful dread that you'd mess it up, you see, suppose it wasn't a really good protest when you'd done it, and you were always alone.'[35]

IV

Militancy's impact on women's suffrage as a political issue is too large a theme to embark upon here. Nor is it even possible systematically to survey its impact upon the life of the individual; no comprehensive sampling of its role in suffragettes' later careers is now possible. But a few concluding suggestions can be made about the range of responses it could evoke over the long term. Its overt impact could be nil; Hazel Inglis, when interviewed in 1976, was keener to talk about her later career as a music-teacher than about her window-breaking episode. Aged suffragettes in the 1970s were often so forward-looking and questing in outlook that the present and future interested them more than the past. Militancy often led nowhere—not even into feminist activity, for the women's suffrage campaign imposed a temporary unity on feminist crusaders which could not be maintained once the vote was won.

But for some suffragettes the act of militancy left at the very least the most striking of memories behind; it was an adventure, described to generations of awestruck listeners in later years. When Birmingham's Maud Kate Smith went to London for a militant act, she needed help from the WSPU organizer; 'you see, that was one thing that made it so frightening, because we didn't know *where* we were, and we didn't *know* London, and we didn't know London members, and we were all alone in the world, once we'd stepped off the train, unless the organiser came with us'.[36] In *The Lion's*

[35] L. Housman, *Unexpected Years*, p. 271; author's tape-recorded interview with Maud Kate Smith, Solihull, 14 Jan. 1975.

[36] Ibid.; cf. M. E. and M. D. Thompson, *They Couldn't Stop Us*, pp. 22, 34.

Share, women's suffrage whirls Audrey Moze out of her staid Essex countryside milieu into an exhilarating world of advanced women and international conspiracy based on Paris and London. When she helps break up a meeting at Birmingham she feels 'as if she had stepped straight into romance' and, says Bennett, 'she was right—she had stepped into the most vivid romance of the modern age, into a world of disguises, flights, pursuits, chicane, inconceivable adventures, ideals, martyrs and conquerors'. At the end of the novel she embarks on militancy because, as the modern emancipated woman of the day, she wants 'all the sensations there are'.[37]

It is hardly surprising that for many suffragettes their militant years seemed a culmination or apogee. 'Can one never pin down on paper the joy and emotion of 1906–14?', asked Isobel Seymour many years later.[38] For Mary Richardson, as for so many others, all that went before was a mere preparation, all that followed was a mere anticlimax; her autobiography is almost entirely concerned with her brief suffragette moment. Leonora Cohen at the age of 102 could look back over a long, varied, and interesting public career, yet when preparing herself for an interview in 1974 she assumed that it would be her half-hour's militancy at the Tower of London that would be the subject of interest. The sheer range of activity required in a militant organization offered brief self-realization to many women who never regained it afterwards; perhaps Christabel Pankhurst was herself one of these.

The career of the relatively little-known Aeta Lamb can perhaps stand for the many suffragettes who subsequently never really found a role. She was a passionately keen feminist who suffered acutely over the sufferings of women, but could never communicate at public meetings with the working wives and mothers and young women she most wished to influence; her sensitive but anonymous obituarist says that 'somehow her melancholy appearance and her somewhat timid manner excited these women to ridicule her—and very often to laugh at her'. She was active within the suffragette

[37] A. Bennett, *The Lion's Share* (1916), pp. 166, 333.
[38] Quot. in E. S. Pankhurst, *The Suffragette Movement*, p. 312.

machine, was arrested three times, and was twice imprisoned in Holloway. Intelligent, sensitive, and retiring, she was impractical in small things and somehow never found a niche in life after the vote was won. 'When applying for work—, she would hold herself prim and stiff and look so melancholy and weary—that a possible employer—especially if he were a man—would have no possible hint of the great intellectual powers which lay within that frail and silent woman.' Her pride made her difficult to help, and during her last years she occupied a small room alone in Hampstead, incapable of cooking for herself; she lived on 22/6 a week, 17/6 of which went on rent. When the obituarist last saw her, she was 'emaciated to an appalling degree', but was troubled only by the thought that she had wasted her life in not doing enough for women. When reassured on this count she managed to murmur 'I am so glad you think so', and seemed pleased. She died of cancer at the age of forty-one.[39]

The suffragette's destination was by no means always so bleak. The notion of suffragette mental derangement has already been dismissed; suffragettes acted rationally within a subgroup whose irrationalities were collective and structural rather than individual and personal. None the less the determination to defy opinion, tried and tested by the process of steeling themselves to commit their acts of militancy and their subsequent hunger-strikes, may well have caused some suffragettes to move from independence to eccentricity— Grace Chappelow, Mary Leigh, Lilian Lenton, and Edith Rigby, for example. In other cases, the commitment to one crusade developed a taste for participating in many others. A taste for 'causes' no doubt led many women into the feminist movement in the first place; their experience as militants merely reinforced the willingness to dissent which is nourished in most protest movements. Mrs Phoebe Pole sees a direct connection between her suffragette career and the causes, both feminist and non-feminist, which she later espoused; in her windows, as in those of Connie Lewcock, posters for nuclear disarmament and other causes greet the interviewer from a later generation as he approaches the

[39] Museum of London, Suffragette Collection, 57.70/3: Notes on Aeta Davis Lamb; cf. P. Hesketh, *My Aunt Edith*, p. 90.

front door. Christabel Pankhurst's later career, whose religious evangelism removed her entirely from the forefront of the British political stage, is often seen as a strange discontinuity; yet it called for many of the crusading qualities in which the WSPU had schooled her. There are many lesser examples, for whom Mrs Malvin Side must do duty. A one-time follower of Sylvia Pankhurst, she was found by a reporter in comfortable shoes and thick football socks on the Aldermaston march of 1972. She had participated in all eight Aldermaston marches organized by the Campaign for Nuclear Disarmament [CND], and according to the reporter wore 'a string of protest badges displayed like medals across her chest'.[40]

Suffragettes were poorly equipped by militancy to generate in their maturity the new political institutions and approaches the enfranchised woman required. Their lawbreaking record sometimes held back their careers, but more important was the militants' difficulty in adjusting to party politics and the working of parliamentary institutions. Between the wars the suffragettes contributed to public life no single woman to compare in political effectiveness with the non-militants Eleanor Rathbone, Maud Royden, Ellen Wilkinson, Kathleen Courtney, or Mary Stocks—or even with the anti-suffragists Violet Markham, Violet Bonham-Carter, and the Duchess of Atholl; as a non-militant suffragist shrewdly remarked in 1909, 'it is in great measure how we have fought which will determine what we shall win'.[41] Even the non-militants found themselves in a strange world after 1918; 'most of our reforms today require difficult re-adjustments of a complicated, antiquated structure of case law and Statute law', said Eleanor Rathbone, president of the non-militants' successor-organization, the National Union of Societies for Equal Citizenship in 1926: 'we were backwoodsmen in pre-war days; now we need to be skilled artisans'.[42] The equal franchise was most skilfully effected in 1928 by non-militants with no suggestion of militancy.

Christabel never saw it as her business to educate her

---

[40] *The Times*, 4 Apr. 1972, p. 2; author's tape-recorded interview with Mrs Phoebe Pole, on 23 Feb. 1980.
[41] A. M. Allen, in *Common Cause*, 12 Aug. 1909, p. 228.
[42] E. F. Rathbone, *Milestones* (Liverpool, 1929), p. 32.

followers in the democratic process. 'We are not playing experiments with representative Government', declared a WSPU internal memorandum, resisting the pressures for internal democratic participation which caused the Women's Freedom League to break off in 1907; 'we are not a school for teaching women how to use the vote'. The suffragette contempt for politics extended beyond rejection of the male politicians; it lay at the heart of their own organization. As Christabel later recalled, 'by instinct and reason, I was apprehensive of the entrance of "politics" into our Union'.[43] A body which responded to disagreement with schism or expulsion could provide experience neither of that continuous collaboration between the sexes, nor of that continuous compromise between divergent opinions, which democratic politics entail. Evan Durbin was perhaps correct in arguing that 'democracy is the epiphenomenon of a certain emotional balance in the individuals composing a nation'.[44] Perhaps it requires, at least in its leading opinion-formers, certain qualities of tolerance and compromise which the WSPU was not well fitted to encourage.

Why did the linkage between militancy, sectarianism, and the authoritarian political structures so far discussed affect suffragism only in Britain? Because no other country offered Edwardian Britain's peculiarly conducive mix of institutions, traditions, personalities, attitudes, and situations—the Pankhursts' remarkable amalgam of efficiency, self-sacrifice, and theatre; national libertarian traditions that nourished earlier in Britain than elsewhere a pressure for women's emancipation which Britain's relatively advanced service sector could stimulate but not yet adequately satisfy; the peculiarly entrenched position of anti-suffragists in a unitary state with imperial responsibilities and long-established political procedures; and a relatively settled social structure which— unlike society in Australia, New Zealand, and on the American frontier—would cause women numerically to dominate

[43] City of London Polytechnic, Fawcett Library Collection; File Labelled 'W.S.P.U. 1908-1912', cyclostyled 'Letter sent to Inquirers from 4, Clement's Inn'; C. Pankhurst, *Unshackled*, p. 81.

[44] E. Durbin, *The Politics of Democratic Socialism. An Essay on Social Policy* (1954 ed.), p. 241, cf. p. 257.

the electorate if universal adult suffrage were conceded, a fear which the still greater political dangers unleashed by the first world war only partially removed. In an Edwardian situation of apparent political stalemate women became, in Mrs Pankhurst's words (though never in Mrs Fawcett's) 'rebels, because there is no other way open to us to obtain redress for the grievances, the grave grievances, which women have'.[45]

Nor does the story end there, for the suffragettes' expertise in self-projection did not desert them in later life. Their second career in British history involved promoting a gradually mounting, though indirect, historiographical challenge to the non-militants. Pankhurstian patriotism in the first world war soon spirited away the discredit stemming from pre-war suffragette militancy. The electoral needs of the Conservative Party in the 1920s and the enthusiasm of Lady Astor presented the suffragettes with Stanley Baldwin's unveiling of Mrs Pankhurst's statue at Westminster in 1930 and with Christabel's DBE in 1936; Sylvia Pankhurst's *Suffragette Movement* (1931) added scholarly weight. Feminist colour was provided by the Suffragette Fellowship, founded to advance women's emancipation and 'to perpetuate the memory of the pioneers and outstanding events connected with women's emancipation and especially with the militant suffrage campaign'.[46] The Fellowship became a sort of old girls' association, the small circulation of whose little periodical *Calling All Women* belied its title. Its contents—primarily obituaries, reminiscences (often heavily self-censored), and unveilings of plaques—show that the second of its two roles took priority. In 1945 it was preoccupied with raising funds for a reading-room that could house suffragette records, and for replenishing the flowers in front of Mrs Pankhurst's statue. By 1955 it was compiling a roll of honour for suffragette prisoners and had fallen into a routine of placing flowers before Mrs Pankhurst's statue on her birthday (14 July) and of holding a social function on 'Prisoner's Day' (13 October).

[45] PRO HO 45/236973 (Box 10701), file 71, p. 2 (P. C. O'Connor's short-hand notes of WSPU meeting, Pavilion music-hall, 14 July 1913).

[46] Suffragette Fellowship, *News Letter for 1945*, statement of objects.

Its activities did not go uncriticized even from within the feminist ranks. 'Just to hear the speeches at the Suffragette Fellowship meetings, and to read the various volumes dealing with the movement shows how utterly they lack what is needed', Teresa Billington-Greig told Christabel in 1956. 'The purely personal story on "I-went-to-prison" lines is re-told *ad nauseam* without historical or political background, philosophy or principle.' The suffragettes' second career had no immediate bearing on British feminist effort after 1918, for suffragettes' public appearances were usually made only in commemorative contexts. 'All that is left of what was once a vital movement', wrote Adela Pankhurst in 1961 of the Suffragette Fellowship, 'is now nothing more than a coterie worshipping a sort of "Sacred Cow".'[47]

Yet such depreciation was to ignore the major long-term political importance of myth. By now the camera shutters were clicking and the journalists' pens were poised to record events such as the unveiling of the Fellowship's commemorative plaques at Manchester and London in 1961.[48] And as the suffragettes passed into old age, their militancy so obviously failed to pose a threat, their respectability seemed so patent that admiring journalists, authors, broadcasters, and media people (like them, pre-eminently communicators) —helped them to merge fully at last into the mainstream of British life. The suffragettes' crude assaults on the politicians stemmed from an impatience with politics which continuously bubbles beneath the surface of even a democratic society, and which became fashionable even among some intellectuals as the suffragettes entered the 1960s. The militant campaign became transformed into a combat between darkness and light, leaving no place for the non-militant.

Why, then, did the non-militants fail to retaliate? Partly because—pragmatic, rationalistic, and politically prudent to the end—they felt that British women had nothing to gain from reopening old feminist wounds; even at the height of

---

[47] City of London Polytechnic, Fawcett Library Autograph Collection, vol 20, part 1: Teresa Billington-Greig to Christabel Pankhurst, 26 Oct. 1956; H. Moyes, *A Woman in a Man's World* (Sydney, 1971), p. 37.

[48] *Calling All Women*, July 1961, p. 7.

the suffragette crusade their loyalty to women made them reluctant publicly to condemn militancy, despite the damage they knew it was doing. Once the vote was won, it seemed more important for feminists to unite behind campaigns for women's further advance, for unlike the militants, the non-militants remained at the centre of the feminist stage after 1918. Their outlook fitted well with a more widely felt desire in post-war Britain to forget old quarrels; indeed, this mood had itself helped to push through the first instalment of women's suffrage in 1917-18. An interesting exchange between Hensley Henson and the Bishop of Chester during the Lambeth Conference's debate on the position of women in the Church in 1920 illustrates the mood. Combatively rationalistic as usual, Henson raised the standard anti-suffrage objections against the type of woman who yearned for broader opportunities, and cited the suffragettes, who 'immediately lost their heads and became fanatical and absurd, and . . . showed that they had moved out of their proper sphere'. The Bishop of Chester regretted Henson's reference to 'a thing of the past', and thought it ungenerous 'if, after this lapse of time we are to be reminded of the extravagances of that most disastrous period'; Henson lost his motion.[49]

The non-militants confined their self-defence to the balanced and judicious historical analyses that can be found in books like Ray Strachey's *'The Cause'* (1928) and Mary Stocks's *My Commonplace Book* (1970). But these lacked dramatic appeal, and in old age the non-militants could not tempt the media with the *frisson* of a prison record; indeed, they sometimes even themselves felt guilty at the lack of it. Nor were suffragette leaders entirely mistaken in their historical excursions. Sylvia Pankhurst's historical works are of major scholarly importance, and suffragettes rightly condemned other historians for inaccuracy in historical detail (though they themselves did not always practise what they preached) as well as for facetiousness of tone. Yet the indignant letters fired off by Christabel and Sylvia at their

[49] Lambeth Palace Library, London, LC 107: typescript proceedings, 28 July 1920, ff. 161, 168.

long-suffering champion Fred Pethick-Lawrence in 1957, in response to Roger Fulford's *Votes for Women*, contain more than hints of a Pankhurstian desire to domineer which might secure temporary successes in practical affairs but which—even when reinforced by restricted access to documents and threats of legal action—had no hope of moulding historical interpretation in the longer term.[50]

But the Pankhursts' apologia in old age was not in itself responsible for increased public sympathy with the suffragettes; the relevant factors there were primarily the sentimental attractions of a rewarding of the brave and a vindication of the underdog, together with the need felt by a busy public for a simplified, readily digestible interpretation of events which would simultaneously inspire further feminist effort. So powerful were these influences that nowadays if anyone is asked who won the vote for British women, the name of Pankhurst is more likely to be voiced than any other. Furthermore in their second career the suffragettes provided a romantic and resolute inspiration to women that was probably more important as an aid to British feminism than their earlier role had been in getting the vote. It was all very unfair on the non-militants, whose long-term contribution to women's emancipation had been so very much more important; they were left to grumble privately to one another in their seventies and eighties about how the true sequence of events had become distorted in the public mind.

But in one respect, at least, the suffragettes fully deserved their fame. The courage with which so many of them faced the difficulties of extreme old age became proverbial; they seemed to epitomize the resourcefulness and determination of the British middle-class woman, and offered to the whole of British society a standing demonstration of the psychological factors that make for vigour and usefulness in later life. Yet it was their final tragedy that in some cases the determination and independence they had earlier developed as militants transformed their very last days into a sad and

---

[50] Trinity College Library, Cambridge, Pethick-Lawrence MSS, Box 9/44–5, 71–3.

humiliating battle against an enemy they could not overcome. As Donald Munro-Ashman said of his mother's struggle to prevent deafness from forcing her to abandon the public stage she had mounted as a young suffragist so many years before, 'she'd never give up, you see, she was a real fighter'.[51]

[51] Author's tape-recorded interview with Dr Donald Munro-Ashman, Bucklebury, 30 July 1975.

Animals and the State
in Nineteenth-Century England[1]

'I suppose that there is hardly anyone nowadays who would not be disgusted by the thought of deliberate cruelty to animals.'[2] Lord Devlin could hardly have written that in 1800 because sensibility is blunted in a predominantly rural society whose inhabitants are continuously aware of their dependence on the slaughter of animals, and of animals' cruelty to each other. Besides, with nature only precariously tamed, nineteenth-century England had every reason to be wary of animals. Students of Victoriana will recall what happened to Emily Brontë when giving water to a stray dog, and how she branded the wound with a red-hot iron without telling anyone; an annual average of forty-eight people in England died from hydrophobia in the 1870s.[3] Cruelty to animals also resulted from long-standing cultural attitudes. 'Their cruelty to . . . animals was due to an utter lack of imagination, not to bad-heartedness', wrote Flora Thompson of the boys in Late-Victorian Lark Rise; 'a boy's instincts with regard to animals are nearly always of tyranny', wrote Miss Loane, discussing London's working class in 1907: 'babies unable to walk alone will clutch up sticks and stones and try to use them against perfectly unoffending dogs and cats'. Even between the wars Suffolk adults showed brutality to animals by the standards of the 1960s. 'The men all did it', a Suffolk man recalled, 'ferreting, breaking necks,

[1] This is a revised version of the article published in the *English Historical Review*, Oct. 1973. Since this article was published I have become aware of J. E. G. De Montmorency's valuable article, 'State Protection of Animals at Home and Abroad', *Law Quarterly Review*, xviii (1902), pp. 31–48, and have made some modifications as a result. To avoid confusion, I have referred to the Society throughout by its initials 'RSPCA', but strictly speaking this is incorrect for the years before 1840, when it first acquired the prefix 'Royal'.

[2] P. Devlin, *The Enforcement of Morals* (1968), p. 17.

[3] *Parl*[iamentary] *Papers*, 1892 (C.6841), XXIV, p. xliv; W. Gérin, *Emily Brontë. A Biography* (paperback ed., 1979), p. 155.

stoning . . . But not now. And there were all the gin traps.
The early morning was full of little screams—very exciting
and strange.'[4]

In the 1800s humanitarian attitudes were so unfamiliar
that legislation had to be recommended on other grounds;
bull-baiting, for instance, was condemned less for its cruelty
than because it demoralized the people or unfitted them for
work. A disgusted Wilberforce complained that the leading
parliamentary opponent of bull-baiting in 1800, Sir William
Pulteney, 'argued it like a parish officer, and never once
mentioned the cruelty'.[5] In the predominantly urban society
at the end of the nineteenth century, however, animals'
claims seemed less in need of such oblique justification. This
important transition deserves attention for its own sake.
Textbooks on nineteenth-century Britain hardly remind
us that in 1870 England, Wales, and Scotland contained
1,064,621 licensed dogs and that in 1871 Great Britain contained over two million horses; by 1880 Great Britain supported twenty-seven million sheep, six million cattle, and two
million pigs.[6] Nor do we always acknowledge the centrality
of animals in nineteenth-century commerce, recreation, and
transport.

The subject is also important for pressure-group history,
for the RSPCA was among the most successful continuous
influences on nineteenth-century opinion. Furthermore it
was a 'cause group' which, unlike most of the better-known
groups which fall into this category, consistently collaborated
with the authorities. The nineteenth-century RSPCA, like
the Howard League in the 1950s, was often 'caught between
the opinions of its own members and the opinions of the

---

[4] F. Thompson, *Lark Rise to Candleford*, p. 143; M. Loane, *The Next Street But One* (1907), p. 78; cf. J. Lawson, *Progress in Pudsey* (Caliban ed., Firle, 1978), p. 76; R. Blythe, *Akenfield. Portrait of an English Village* (Penguin ed., 1972), p. 103.

[5] R. I. and S. Wilberforce, *The Life of William Wilberforce* (1838), ii. p. 366.

[6] For dogs, see *Parl. Papers*, 1877 (163), XLIX, p. 1; there were of course many unlicensed dogs in England at the time. For horses, see F. M. L. Thompson, 'Nineteenth-Century Horse Sense', *Economic History Review*, Feb. 1976, p. 80; railways temporarily increased the demand for horse transport, on which see H. J. Dyos and D. H. Aldcroft, *British Transport* (Leicester, 1969), p. 213. For the other animals see B. R. Mitchell, *European Historical Statistics 1750–1970* (1975), p. 306.

government department with which it must work'.[7] There is
also light to be shed here on the dynamics of state intervention, whose historians usually focus on the conflicts
between nineteenth-century voluntarism and problems of
public health, factory hours, education, and emigration. Yet
far from curtailing the work of voluntary bodies, legislation
on animal cruelty reflected and enhanced their influence.
'In other countries the intervention of the State would be
invoked', said a supporter in 1870, 'and an organisation of
public prosecutors and overseers would be established, but
in England it was their pride to do these things themselves,
and to trust to the State nothing they could accomplish by
local efforts.'[8] Here, as so often elsewhere, we witness the
pragmatism of Victorian attitudes to the state and the
internal dynamic attending certain types of state intervention, together with the importance of moral and religious
purposes in inspiring it. Four questions will be asked about
the nineteenth-century movement to protect animals: what
is the chronology of legislation? How was it enforced? What
techniques were used in winning support for it? And how was
it defended in argument?

I

The nineteenth-century protection of animals was promoted
in two broad ways: through progressively widening the scope
of legislation, and through extending the number and geographical range of the agencies for enforcing it. Factory
legislation begins with 'a vaguely benevolent and general type
of enactment' but becomes 'constantly more particular, more
detailed, and more scientifically directed as time goes on'.[9]
The parallels with legislation on animal cruelty are considerable, but not complete. It initially protects only a small
group of animals, but steadily extends in range, and its provisions and enforcement are gradually tightened up as time

[7] J. B. Christoph, *Capital Punishment and British Politics* (1962), p. 28.

[8] S. Laing, at a public meeting inaugurating the Sussex branch of the RSPCA
reported in *A[nimal] W[orld]*, 1 Feb. 1870, p. 96; cf. Lord Aberdare, in RSPCA,
68th A[nnual] R[eport], p. 145.

[9] B. L. Hutchins and A. Harrison, *A History of Factory Legislation* (3rd ed.,
1926), p. 201.

passes. It is not belittling 'the rôle of men and of ideas' or obscuring 'the fact that decisions are ultimately made by people' to say that here, as with legislation on factory hours and emigrant ships, the nature of the problem and the mechanism for law-enforcement made it very likely that legislation would steadily increase in quantity. and complexity.[10] With legislation on animal cruelty, this process occurred in five broad phases.

Up to the 1830s humanitarians were primarily concerned with horses and cattle. During the late eighteenth century, a powerful combination of evangelical piety, romantic poetry, and rational humanitarianism gradually advertised the plight of animals; legislation regulating cattle slaughterers was passed in 1785, and the RSPCA (founded largely by evangelical humanitarians in 1824) concentrated at first on cruelty in London's meat-markets. The first attempt at legislation against bull-baiting, in 1800, faced the type of ridicule that greeted every nineteenth-century assault on animal cruelty, including Lord Erskine's famous speech defending animals in 1809. In 1822, however, Richard Martin's measure to prevent cruelty to cattle established the principle of legislatively protecting animals against cruelty; hitherto the law, in its concern for animals, had been exclusively preoccupied, not with preventing cruelty, but with protecting property. Subsequent amendments to Martin's Act were consolidated by an Act of 1835. This phase of RSPCA activity culminated in its first dramatic success: its attack on Stamford's bull-running in 1838, when it braved highly placed local hostility, and brought in government troops. Bull-running received its quietus in 1870; when a troupe of Spanish bullfighters began throwing darts at animals in the Agricultural Hall, Islington, the RSPCA's secretary John Colam jumped into the ring and stopped the show.[11]

[10] J. Hart, 'Nineteenth Century Social Reform: a Tory Interpretation of History', *Past and Present*, No. 31 (July 1965), pp. 61, 59; see also D. H. Blelloch, 'A Historical Survey of Factory Inspection in Great Britain', *International Labour Review*, Nov. 1938, pp. 628 ff.

[11] On this incident, see RSPCA *1870 A.R.*, p. 22; RSPCA Executive Committee Minute Book No. 11 [henceforth cited as *Minutes No. 11*], p. 330 (14 Mar. 1870); the minutes are kept in the Society's archive, and I am most grateful

By then the RSPCA had already launched into the less dramatic but more widespread cruel sports involving dogs and cockerels. In 1835 Martin's Act was extended to cover 'wanton' cruelty, and enacted fines for those who kept, places for 'running, baiting, or fighting any bull, bear, badger, dog, or other animal (whether of domestic or wild nature or kind), or for cock-fighting'. Here as with restraints on drinking hours, the earliest battles were fought out in London. The Metropolitan Police Act of 1833 forbade such exhibitions within five miles of Temple Bar. The RSPCA claimed that when its constables burst into an upstairs room at Euston in 1838, 'some of the persons present were fashionably attired; but the major part consisted of the lowest characters in the Metropolis'. Henry Mayhew later noted the popularity of organized dogfights among London costermongers, and this second phase of RSPCA legislation seemed hostile to the pleasures and even the livelihood of the very poor.[12] This impression was reinforced when the Act of 1835 forbade dog-cropping, when the Metropolitan Police Act of 1839 prevented the use of dog-carts in London (extended to the whole country by an Act of 1854), and when RSPCA officers in the 1840s concerned themselves with horses and donkeys at London fairs.[13] Legislation to protect animals against commercial exploitation was refined and extended in later years. An Act in 1849 removed ambiguities in the law, and another in 1854 extended protection to animals previously at risk. Later in the century, the RSPCA's major concern shifted to protecting animals during transit, with important legislation in 1878 and 1894.

Its concurrent attack on cock-fighting, like its attack on bull-baiting, involved less a contest between social classes than between urban and rural styles of life. The Society came up against rural magistrates and prosperous residents

to the Society's executive director for allowing me to consult them. There is a vivid description of bull-baiting, which brings out all its brutality, in *Morning Chronicle*, 3 Mar. 1851, p. 5.

[12] De Montmorency, art. cit., p. 35; RSPCA *13th A.R.*, pp. 65–6; Mayhew, *London Labour [and the London Poor]* (Cass ed., 1967), i, p. 15. For drinking hours, see my *Drink and the Victorians. The Temperance Question in England 1815–1872* (1971), pp. 327–9.

[13] For London fairs, see RSPCA *16th A.R.*, p. 12; *18th A.R.*, p. 14.

who resented metropolitan meddling. A Hanworth cock-fight of 1838 saw an RSPCA constable named Piper killed in the subsequent mêlée; and when the RSPCA constable went to Orton in Cumberland during 1849, he found 200 people assembled for the fight, and was driven off by missiles. Evidence could not be obtained against the offenders 'owing to the strong local prejudices and popular passion which exist in favor of the Cock-fighting'. This sport remained popular in Cumberland in the early 1950s, reinforced in its popularity 'by the fact that it is done surreptitiously in defiance of laws to which the local community has never given its assent'.[14] Still more recently, a Conservative MP has pronounced it 'nature's way that animals were cruel to each other', and has defended traditional country sports against interference by town-dwellers whose keeping of pets remains unmolested by country people.[15]

Whereas the RSPCA began with urban attacks on rural culture, its third phase—the defence of wild birds—involved defending the countryside against urban desecration. But this also involved subordinating the countryside's growing of food to its provision of recreation for an increasingly urban population. Naturally the earliest legislation to protect animals could succeed only if the animals were domestic and if their protection did not threaten the food supply. The defence of rural animal life owes much to the nineteenth-century scientist's extended understanding of nature. 'He must be a dull man', wrote Darwin, 'who can examine the exquisite structure of a [honey] comb, so beautifully adapted to its end, without enthusiastic admiration'; Darwin not only subscribed regularly to the RSPCA, but offered it many suggestions on policy. Charles Dixon's *Rural Bird Life* (1880) did much to encourage sporting men to get out their field-glasses and observe birds instead of shooting them; and in moving forward to defend wild birds in the 1860s and 1870s, the RSPCA was assisted both by

[14] RSPCA *1850 A.R.*, p. 17; W. M. Williams, *The Sociology of an English Village. Gosforth* (1956), p. 134. For Hanworth, see the excellent account in RSPCA *Minutes No. 2*, pp. 296–8; E. G. Fairholme and W. Pain, *A Century of Work for Animals* (2nd ed., 1934), p. 81. See also RSPCA *14th A.R.*, p. 16; *15th A.R.*, pp. 15, 129; *25th A.R.*, p. 11.

[15] *The Times*, 25 Oct. 1975, p. 5.

naturalists in the British Association and by precedents from overseas.[16]

The question was first raised at the Association's Dundee meeting by Canon Tristram in 1867. He argued that when birds of prey were slaughtered indiscriminately, disease among grouse could not be effectively checked. In 1868 the Association heard Professor Newton complain of the sporting men from London and Lancashire who were wiping out Yorkshire's sea-birds.[17] A committee was appointed to consider enacting a 'close' season for shooting sea-birds, and the first legislation passed (in 1868) was founded upon its report. This Act was to wild birds what Martin's Act of 1822 was to animals in general, and inspired much corrective and supplementary legislation. Here, as elsewhere, scientific research and state intervention march together, for the defence of wild birds rested largely on evidence about their diet; the select committee of 1873 on the protection of wild birds was almost exclusively preoccupied with this topic. Further reinforcement came from the knowledge that legislation was more advanced in America, Norway, Switzerland, and elsewhere. The RSPCA first recognized American precociousness here when Mr Angell of Massachusetts addressed its executive committee in 1869; Colam told the select committee of 1873 that he would like England to imitate the USA and ensure that all animals were protected by statute.[18]

In relation to legislation on wild birds, the RSPCA was as usual discreet; it mobilized the experts and lent them the support they needed for winning over the public. In 1872 the British Association's close-time committee tried to

[16] C. Darwin, *On the Origin of Species* (Penguin ed., 1968), p. 248, cf. pp. 82, 114–15, 170–1, 421. See also D. E. Allen's excellent *The Naturalist in Britain. A Social History* (Penguin ed., 1978), pp. 229–31. For Darwin and the RSPCA, see *A.W.*, 1 May 1882, p. 66.

[17] See the useful anonymous article, 'Protection of Wild Birds', *Quarterly Review*, Jan. 1881, pp. 104–8; H. B. Tristram, 'On the Zoological Aspects of the Grouse-disease', *Report of the 37th Meeting of the British Association for the Advancement of Science* (Notes and Abstracts section), p. 97; A. Newton, 'On the Zoological Aspects of Game Laws', *Report of the 38th Meeting . . .* (Notes and Abstracts section), p. 108.

[18] For Angell, see *Minutes No. 11*, p. 212 (14 June 1869); for Colam, see S[elect] C[ommittee] of the H[ouse] of C[ommons] on Wild Birds Protection, *Parl. Papers*, 1873 (338), XIII, QQ.3408, 3415.

extend the legislation of 1868 to cover declining species, but foundered on the quixotic widening parliamentary amendments of the radical MP Auberon Herbert; the committee felt that the amended bill attempted 'to do too much, and not to provide effectual means of doing it'. It knew it must not run too far ahead of public opinion, and in 1874 resisted Earl de la Warr's proposal to legislate against birds' nesting. Its original intentions were implemented by legislation in 1876, and the law to protect wild birds was further extended and clarified in 1880, 1881, 1888, 1894, 1896, and 1900. Contemporary marine life was also vulnerable; the rock-pools Edmund Gosse had known in childhood 'exist no longer', he recalled in 1907, 'they are all profaned, and emptied, and vulgarised. An army of "collectors" has passed over them, and ravaged every corner of them.'[19] The RSPCA's preoccupation with cruelty involved it less deeply in defending fish; the extensive nineteenth-century protective legislation for them was more concerned with property and with preserving food supplies, though these preoccupations were eminently compatible with preserving endangered species.

Not until 1876 did animal-cruelty legislation move forward, in its fourth phase, to cruelty committed exclusively by educated people—that is, to vivisection. In the 1820s and again in the 1860s, the RSPCA showed concern about such experiments, especially in France. In England it was theoretically possible to prosecute scientists under the terms of Martin's Act, but in practice it was difficult; 'if a Machiavelli was putting forward a plan to promote the suffering of animals', Samuel Haughton told the royal commission in 1876, 'he could not suggest a better one than extending Martin's Act, and leaving the troublesome machinery to work'.[20] Disraeli had appointed the commission at the Queen's instigation, and no doubt this lent zest to Robert Lowe's denunciation of the proposed laboratory inspection

---

[19] British Association, *1872 Report*, p. 321; E. Gosse, *Father and Son. A Study of Two Temperaments* (Penguin ed., 1949), p. 111. For RSPCA attitudes to wild birds, see *Minutes No. 12*, pp. 138, 140 (9 Jan. 1872); *A.W.*, 1 Oct. 1880, pp. 146-7.

[20] R[oyal] C[ommission] on the Practice of Subjecting Live Animals to Experiments for Scientific Purposes [henceforth cited as *R. C. Vivisection*], *Parl. Papers*, 1876 (C.1397), XLI, Q.1891.

as 'to the last degree an insult to an educated and scientific body of men'. Sir William Gull told the royal commission that laws against animal cruelty were intended 'for the ignorant, and not for the best people in the country', and Sir John Simon ridiculed proposals for a licensing system that would treat scientists like publicans and prostitutes. With royal and religious sympathy the RSPCA had no need to cultivate democratic support, and suggested the prohibition of all painful experiments but that all necessary experiments should be allowed if performed under anaesthetic. As events turned out, the Act of 1876 resembled the Anatomy Act in its enforcement provisions; an inspector was appointed to supervise scientists licensed to experiment on animals under anaesthetic, and restrictions (closely resembling the RSPCA's recommendations) were imposed on the number and types of experiment. The Society determined to operate the new legislation despite its imperfections, and in 1881 encouraged the Home Secretary in refusing licences under the Act to three leading physiologists.[21]

Nineteenth-century protection was extended to animals in a fifth and final way when legislation was passed to defend wild animals. Here too the RSPCA had to tread carefully, for it could not afford to alienate aristocratic lovers of field sports. Bitter disputes at twentieth-century RSPCA meetings reflect the Society's continuing failure to satisfy radical demands for an attack on coursing, steeplechasing, and all blood sports.[22] The Society's policy was to intervene in such sports only to restrain deliberately cruel acts. But by the 1870s radical criticism pressed it into considering ways of restricting some types of aristocratic sport. In 1871 it inspected pigeon-shooting matches at Hurlingham and the Gun Club. In 1883 Lord Randolph Churchill pronounced pigeon-shootings 'the most horrible and repulsive sight possible to imagine';[23] but Churchill faced much parliamentary

[21] Lowe, *H. C. Deb.*, 9 Aug. 1876, c.916. Gull, in *R. C. Vivisection*, Q.5482; see also Simon, Q.1491. For the 3 physiologists, see *Minutes No. 14*, p. 302, cp. *A.W.*, 1 Feb. 1877, p. 18. On the whole subject see R. D. French, *Antivivisection and Medical Science in Victorian Society* (Princeton, 1975).
[22] See e.g. *Sunday Times*, 21 June 1970, p. 1.
[23] *H. C. Deb.*, 7 Mar. 1883, c.1684. For the RSPCA intervening at a steeplechase, see *Minutes No. 14*, p. 68 (8 Apr. 1879). For the RSPCA and pigeon

hostility, and the Society (urged on by the more radical Humanitarian League) was still trying to curb the sport in the 1890s, together with stag-hunting and rabbit-coursing. Here it was probably hindered rather than helped by its links with the monarchy, for stag-hunting was patronized by the Queen herself. A close time for hares was enacted in 1892, and in 1900 a general measure was obtained to protect wild animals in captivity (including birds, fish, and reptiles). But plenty of territory remained for the twentieth century to occupy, both here and in the area that the Society described at the end of the century as 'the modern method of preparing domestic fowls for the poulterers' markets by a mechanical means of feeding them'; for the moment, the Society found no cruelty in the system.[24]

II

The RSPCA did more than merely legislate; at an annual meeting in 1844, R. E. Broughton described it as 'the hand-maid—the support—the carriers into effect of the acts of the legislature'. The law needed to be publicized and enforced, and during 1836, for instance, the Society circulated 25,000 abstracts of the Act passed in the previous year; its annual reports explained in detail how cruelty could be prosecuted. By 1873 the Society had issued applicants with 100,000 copies of the legislation to protect wild birds. The police were among these applicants, for the Society always sought their full and informed co-operation.[25]

Yet the RSPCA did not rely solely on the police. It supplemented legislation by creating a sort of private police force with a strictly limited area of concern. Its prosecutions

shooting, see *Minutes No. 12*, p. 50 (11 Apr. 1871); p. 64 (9 May 1871); and *A.W.*, 1 Aug. 1873, p. 117.

[24] RSPCA *74th A.R.*, p. 121. See also *68th A.R.*, pp. 124–5; *70th A.R.*, p. 162; *A.W.*, 1 Feb. 1896, p. 19. For the Queen's buckhounds, see H. S. Salt, *Seventy Years among Savages* (1921), pp. 152, 160, 203.

[25] Broughton, in RSPCA *18th A.R.*, p. 37; cf. his comments in *17th A.R.*, p. 38; for Colam, see SCHC on Wild Birds Protection, *Parl. Papers*, 1873 (338), XIII, Q.3408. For the RSPCA publicizing legislation, see *11th A.R.*, p. 14; *Minutes No. 8*, p. 180 (10 Nov. 1856); *Minutes No. 7*, p. 79 (6 Aug. 1849); p. 85 (8 Oct. 1849); *Minutes No. 13*, p. 288 (9 Jan. 1877).

roughly doubled in every decade between 1830 and 1900, so that during the 1890s it conducted 71,657 prosecutions. This formidable total was secured through co-operation between two distinct elements in the Society, the paid constables and the unpaid subscribers. In 1832 there were only two paid constables, who supplemented their weekly pay of 10s. with rewards for successful prosecution. The system was disliked by London magistrates, and was discontinued for a short time. But by 1855 the number of constables had risen to 8, by 1878 to 48, and by 1897 to 120.[26] These men never feature in the RSPCA periodical *Animal World*, and appear in the executive committee's minute-books only when they make wage claims or misbehave. Yet their contacts with the public were central to the Society's social role.

Rules of 1856 show that they were full-timers working nine hours per day (or, when their turn came, per night). Superintendent Whitehead was given a fortnight's notice in June 1887 when discovered combining his employment with another occupation. RSPCA constables (or inspectors, as they later came to be called) were forbidden to take money from any other source without permission. Inspector Plant was discharged in April 1873 for accepting a bribe to conceal a cruelty case, though he was reinstated on explaining 'that he was a young officer and had been seized by a sudden temptation offered him when off his guard'. The inspectors were assigned their daily duties by the superintendent, and were occasionally sent into the country if the Society wished to respond to requests from a provincial subscriber. They had to submit a written report of each day's activities to the superintendent, and were not allowed to leave their assigned beat without giving good reason.[27]

For an inspector to gain public respect, he required good qualifications. RSPCA inspectors apparently had little veterinary skill or experience with animals. Colam at the

[26] See p. 131.
[27] RSPCA *Minutes No. 12*, p. 322 (28 Apr. 1873); cf. *Minutes No. 8*, p. 168 (8 Sept. 1856). For Whitehead, see *Minutes No. 16*, p. 87 (8 June 1887). For the inspectors' duties, see *Minutes No. 8*, pp. 173–5 (13 Oct. 1856); *Minutes No. 7*, p. 257 (10 Nov. 1851); RSPCA *73rd. A.R.*, p. 68.

annual meeting of 1901 referred to their initial 'special training as regards the structure and ailments of animals', but he said more about their training in 'the provisions of the law protecting animals, the law of evidence, the theory and practice of detective work, and kindred subjects'.[28] As employees of a purely voluntary body the inspectors, both then and now, needed to conciliate the public, avoiding tactless or unsuccessful prosecutions.[29] When advertising for a new constable in 1856, the Society wanted a man 'conversant with the practice of Police Courts' with 'ability for conducting prosecutions'; it gave preference to 'those Candidates who have already served in the police'. RSPCA inspectors did not immediately shake off their police connections on appointment. In 1881 the Wigan police required an RSPCA inspector and former policeman to help in suppressing riots; and in 1884 Yarmouth police successfully requested help from an RSPCA constable. The inspector's task throughout the century was dangerous, and RSPCA literature made nothing of the benevolent and friendly inspector who now features so prominently in its publications. At Ringmer steeplechases in 1879, Inspector Maidment was 'maltreated by a mob', at Manchester in 1884 Inspector Harper was 'violently assaulted by some "Roughs" ', and in November 1899 a doctor attended Superintendent Harper 'who had been assaulted, and was still suffering from a bad scalp wound'.[30]

The Society maintained strict discipline among its inspectors. In 1838 they were given badges; in 1853, armlets. In 1856 the executive committee resolved to supply them 'with a frock coat and trowsers of dark green, a hat and Cape similar to those in use by the Police. The Coat to have the letters P.C. and a number worked in white on

---

[28] RSPCA *77th A.R. 1901*, p. 157; cf. *72nd A.R.*, p. 273.

[29] Cf. R. D. Lee, 'Cruelty to the R.S.P.C.A.?', *New Statesman*, 4 July 1969, p. 12.

[30] For the 1856 advert see *Minutes No. 8*, p. 161 (4 Aug. 1856). For Wigan, see *Minutes No. 14*, p. 250 (21 Feb. 1881); for Yarmouth, *Minutes No. 15*, p. 154 (14 July 1884). Maidment, in RSPCA *Minutes No. 14*, p. 68 (8 Apr. 1879); Harper, in *Minutes No. 15*, p. 90 (5 Feb. 1884), *Minutes No. 18*, p. 26 (27 Nov. 1899); cf. A. W. Moss, *Valiant Crusade. The History of the R.S.P.C.A* (1961), pp. 63–4.

the Collar.' During the 1840s the executive committee inspected a journal of constables' proceedings monthly; in 1850 constables had to explain in person why they had obtained so few convictions, and in December 1851 the constable with fewest was dismissed. There was further trouble in 1853, and in 1877 there were several dismissals for inefficiency. The terms of employment in 1856 were very strict; according to executive-committee minutes, each constable was 'liable to immediate dismissal for unfitness, neglect of duty, or Misconduct', the committee being free, if it thought fit, to dismiss him 'without assigning any reason'.[31]

Drunkenness was a major difficulty here, as with the police at the time, and constables in 1856 were liable to instant dismissal for 'the slightest intoxication while on duty'. Several were dismissed for this offence, but when the police reported James Rutherford in the following year for being drunk on duty he was given a second chance. In 1888 Inspector Parker was reinstated on taking the teetotal pledge; by 1889 twenty inspectors (about a quarter of the whole) were teetotallers, and according to Colam 'had formed themselves into a Society as a bond of union among themselves and to encourage others to join them'. There seems to have been less friction towards the end of the century; there were isolated cases of bribery, insubordination, inefficiency, and absenteeism, but here as elsewhere Colam's skilful management had greatly improved matters. Summoning him into the meeting on 23 February 1880, the executive committee's chairman Colonel Burdett praised him for this among other things: 'though you rule them with a strong hand it is with a kind heart at the same time (suaviter in modo, fortiter in re)'.[32]

[31] RSPCA *Minutes No. 8*, pp. 173–4 (13 Oct. 1856); uniforms are also discussed in ibid., p. 3 (8 Aug. 1853); p. 179 (10 Nov. 1856); and in A. W. Moss, *Valiant Crusade*, pp. 61–2. For discipline, see *Minutes No. 7*, p. 108 (10 Dec. 1849); p. 282 (9 Feb. 1852); p. 374 (10 Jan. 1853); *Minutes No. 13*, p. 296 (13 Feb. 1877); cf. *Minutes No. 5*, pp. 105–6 (5 June 1843).

[32] *Minutes No. 8*, p. 174 (13 Oct. 1856); *Minutes No. 16*, p. 213 (5 Mar. 1889), Colam; *Minutes No. 14*, p. 147 (23 Feb. 1880), Burdett. For Rutherford, see *Minutes No. 8*, p. 204 (13 Apr. 1857); for drunkenness dismissals, see *Minutes No. 6*, p. 267 (9 Aug. 1847); *Minutes No. 13*, p. 112 (9 Mar. 1875); *Minutes No. 16*, p. 114 (6 Dec. 1887); *Minutes No. 18*, p. 39 (12 Feb. 1900). For Parker, see

The policeman analogy should not be overstressed. Like the temperance agent, the RSPCA inspector and his employers were joint participants in an inspiring crusade; formal discipline was therefore seldom necessary and even inappropriate. In the unfortunate letter which Colam wrote in 1905 to members of the committee while they were discussing who should succeed him, he criticized the favourite candidate Captain Derriman (who was in fact chosen) for being a martinet, 'for there is no style so objectionable in teaching and guiding our men as the autocratic military style'. The inspectors did not come from the lowest levels of society, and there usually seems to have been adequate competition for the posts advertised. Of four applicants in 1843-4, the two successful candidates were a former army sergeant whose wife kept a shop and a man who had been a policeman and coachman; the two unsuccessful candidates were a warden of Cold Bath Fields prison, and a porter/surgeryman at St. George's Hospital. It is impossible to say how typical these appointments were.[33]

The Society aimed only to recruit the respectable, and to ensure that they remained so. When it found its chief constable 'living in a wretched apartment, in an obscure Court', in 1843, it pronounced this 'a most disgraceful state and place for a person holding a respectable situation', and insisted on a move. It disliked its inspectors piling up debts, and dismissals sometimes followed, though loans were occasionally made.[34] The chief constable was relatively well paid, with £150 a year throughout most of the century, but the inspectors were paid much less. In 1842 it was decided that their salaries should rise from 21s. to 22s. per week after two years' service 'to encourage good behaviour, and steadiness of conduct'. During the Crimean War they were

---

Minutes No. 16, p. 152 (19 Mar. 1888), cp. Turner, in *Minutes No. 17*, p. 49 (12 June 1893).
[33] Colam letter in *Minutes No. 18*, p. 356 (13 Feb. 1905); cf. *New Statesman*, 4 July 1969, p. 12. See also *Minutes No. 5*, pp. 123, 212, 230.
[34] *Minutes No. 5*, p. 105 (5 June 1843). For dismissals and reprimands, see *Minutes No. 10*, p. 129 (9 June 1868); *Minutes No. 15*, p. 268 (20 July 1885); *Minutes No. 17*, p. 101 (23 July 1894). For loans, *Minutes No. 15*, p. 174 (4 Nov. 1884); *Minutes No. 16*, p. 21 (7 Dec. 1886); p. 168 (5 June 1888); p. 223 (15 Apr. 1889).

temporarily given an extra 2*s*. 6*d.* per week 'on the ground of the present high prices of necessaries', and their memorial of 1872, referring to the high food prices, produced an over-all increase of fifteen per cent. By 1893 market influences were operating between charities, for the NSPCC was cream-ing off the best applicants for the post of inspector; this produced a rise of more than ten per cent. Wage differentials in those days were formidable; the secretary was receiving £1,000 a year at this time.[35]

Wages are not the whole story; inspectors were rewarded for energy, especially in the Society's early years. But there were dangers in this, and in 1876 it was made clear that inspectors must not benefit from fines imposed as a result of successful prosecutions; during the 1870s inspectors were also forbidden to accept subscribers' gifts.[36] Interest was increasingly shown in the inspectors' widows and in pension schemes. People normally made their own pension arrange-ments at this time, and the periodic grants made to widows were apparently seen only as concessions. The Society paid £10 in 1867 and 1883 for inspectors' funeral expenses, and made grants of £30 in 1871, £25 in 1872, and £15 in 1885 to the widows of long-serving inspectors. These grants were intended—if the case of Mrs Love in 1868 is any guide —merely to facilitate 'self-help; Mrs Love was given £15 'to assist her in an undertaking by which she hoped to be able to maintain herself'. The same ideals of self-help lie behind the pension scheme first discussed in 1872, when the executive committee unanimously agreed 'that a scheme of superannuation be devised for worn-out officers to which the officers of the society be requested to subscribe'. It is not clear whether any action resulted, but an 'Officers' Provident Fund Committee' certainly existed by 1892, for in that year the executive committee agreed to supplement one of its grants.[37]

---

[35] *Minutes No. 5*, p. 34; *Minutes No. 8*, p. 65. See also *Minutes No. 12*, p. 238 (23 July 1872); p. 392 (22 Dec. 1873); *Minutes No. 17*, p. 20 (9 Jan. 1893).

[36] For a reward, see Robert Reed's case, in *Minutes No. 8*, p. 65 (13 Nov. 1854). For fines, see *Minutes No. 13*, p. 258 (20 June 1876), cf. *Minutes No 14* p. 106 (28 July 1879). For gifts, see *Minutes No. 14*, p. 238 (24 Jan. 1881); *Minutes No. 15*, p. 82 (14 Jan. 1884); p. 366 (19 July 1886).

[37] *Minutes No. 11*, p. 42 (7 July 1868); *Minutes No. 12*, p. 138 (9 Jan. 1872);

Like the Gladstonian treasury, the Society's managers knew they were distributing moneys not their own, but on several occasions money was given to sick inspectors. In 1865 the chief constable Mr Love, whose health was failing, was given £20 owing to 'his long energetic service'; again, in 1895 Chief Inspector Peet—now unfit after twenty-five years' service—was allowed a guinea a week. The Society gave protection of another type—declining, for example, to accept the Earl of Cawdor's complaint of Inspector Fair in 1880, whose conduct 'appeared to have been moderate and praiseworthy'.[38]

Inspectors fill only half the enforcement picture, because many subscribers gave time and effort, as well as money; they intervened directly against cruelty, provided the information or resources for others to intervene, and made suggestions (often backed with money) for eliminating cruelty in specific areas. The Society often responded. Direct personal intervention against cruelty was dangerous; according to the pioneer humanitarian Lewis Gompertz in 1852, a knowledge of pugilism would be useful in such cases. Lord Erskine, Samuel Gurney, and Richard Martin all intervened directly to prevent cruelty in the London streets, but Martin admitted in parliament that when he saw a man ill-using a horse on Ludgate Hill, he preferred not to intervene personally, but 'offered five shillings to two men for chastising him'. One aspect of the Society's role was simply to organize, systematize and foster vicarious chastisement of this kind; one set of working men were being paid to police another. As George Pritchard said of the Vice Society in 1817, 'individuals are deterred from coming forward ... by personal timidity, and the expenses attendant on prosecutions', whereas through the Society 'the moral feelings of the country can with irresistible power be brought to bear'.[39]

Minutes No. 16, p. 394 (25 Apr. 1892). For grants, see *Minutes No. 10*, p. 68 (14 May 1867); *Minutes No. 12*, p. 118 (28 Nov. 1871); p. 182 (26 Mar. 1872); *Minutes No. 15*, p. 42 (3 July 1883); p. 232 (7 Apr. 1885).

[38] Love, in *Minutes No. 9*, p. 322 (10 June 1865); Peet, in *Minutes No. 17*, p. 119 (14 Jan. 1895); Fair, in *Minutes No. 14*, p. 166 (13 Apr. 1880).

[39] Martin, *The Times*, 2 June 1821, p. 3, cf. ibid., 16 June 1821, p. 3; Pritchard, in SCHC on the Police of the Metropolis, Second Report, *Parl. Papers*, 1817 (484), VII, p. 481. See also L. Gompertz, *Fragments in Defence of Animals* (1852), p. 86; Erskine, *H*[ouse of] *L*[ords] *Deb*[ates], 2 June 1809, c.852. For

It was easier simply to content oneself with informing, perhaps supplementing this with a donation for an inspector to be sent down. Depending on circumstances and on one's perspective, such payments could be seen as a mere brushing under the carpet of the ugliness on which the over-delicate informant's very livelihood often depended; or they could be regarded as courageously and selflessly helping to eliminate the long-established cruelties which in the modern situation had become superfluous or inconvenient. Unless some particularly flagrant cruelty was at issue, the Society usually insisted on local subscriptions to cover the cost of suppressing local cruelty.[40] The Early-Victorian campaign against bull-running and cock-fighting owed much to information provided by country clergyman eager for anonymity; and without the information provided by the local magistrate Richard Newcomb, it is doubtful whether Stamford could ever have been prised away from its bull-running in the 1830s. It could be dangerous even to provide information; the local chief of police noted that by 1840 vengeance had descended on a Mr Ratcliffe, who kept the RSPCA posted on Ramsgate donkey-drivers' cruelties; they had assaulted his son 'twice within the last three weeks'.[41]

The subscribers also contributed ideas. The suggestion from Miss Wemyss in 1870 that the Society should test the law on ratting prompted Colam into prosecuting successfully at Coventry; and in January 1872 it congratulated Mr Brewin of Cirencester for getting the law clarified on the watering of cattle. J. H. Buckeridge of Sonning specialized in offers of financial backing for his suggestions; in 1854 he contributed £25 on condition that legislation against dog-carts be introduced 'during the present session', and in 1860 he contributed £50 to encourage the Society into

---

Gurney, see SCHC on the state of Smithfield Market, *Parl. Papers*, 1828 (551), VIII, p. 35.

[40] e.g. RSPCA *1852 A.R.*, p. 179; RSPCA *Minutes No. 8*, p. 339 (14 Dec. 1858); *Minutes No. 16*, p. 264 (7 Jan. 1890).

[41] Letter dated 21 Sept. 1840, in RSPCA *Minutes No. 4*, p. 32, cf. p. 149. For clergyman-informers, see *Minutes No. 3*, pp. 114–15 (letter from the Revd A. F. Taylor, 25 Apr. 1839); p. 231 (letter from the Revd R. Kemp, dated 25 Feb. 1840); *Minutes No. 5*, p. 261 (1 July 1844). For Newcomb, see *Minutes No. 2*, p. 201; *Minutes No. 3*, pp. 39–40.

extra effort against vivisection. Likewise Miss Gordon in 1848 agreed to subscribe annually if the Society would reward donkey-drivers 'whose kind treatment of them and respectability of conduct should appear to deserve notice and approval'.[42]

The RSPCA always encouraged humanitarian inventions, but to modern eyes it seems indifferent to the offenders' motive and situation. It never asked itself whether violence, if repressed in this sphere, might not break out more dangerously elsewhere; indeed, it adopted the contrary view— that restraint in small things cultivated restraint in large. It did not distinguish between cruelty which has pathological origins, cruelty which springs from traditional or agricultural thoughtlessness, and cruelty stemming from industrial competition. 'You got frightened and frustrated', an old miner recently recalled of his dealings with pit ponies, 'and you had to take it out of somebody.' Original sin sufficed for the Revd Richard Burgess at the annual meeting of 1844; he described 'the exercise of dominion' as 'congenial to the natural disposition of man—and where it cannot be exercised over man, it falls, often in tyranny and cruelty, upon the inferior creation'.[43] Pit ponies interested the RSPCA only from the early 1870s. Its president Lord Aberdare, a South Wales magistrate for a generation and drawing much of his income from local mines, told the annual meeting in 1878 that until recently he 'was not at all aware of the extent of .the cruelty inflicted in mines'. There were about 25,000 pit ponies in 1881, but animals working underground were not protected until the Coal Mines Act of 1911, and cruelty to animals employed in

[42] Wemyss, RSPCA *Minutes No. 11*, p. 286 (24 Jan. 1870); p. 334 (11 Apr. 1870). Brewin, *Minutes No. 12*, p. 136 (9 Jan. 1872). Buckeridge, *Minutes No. 7*, p. 263 (8 Dec. 1851); *Minutes No. 8*, p. 33 (8 May 1854); *Minutes No. 9*, p. 36 (11 Dec. 1860); but see *Minutes No. 10*, p. 123 (26 May 1868). Gordon, *Minutes No. 7*, p. 7 (14 Aug. 1848). Cp. Mr Marland, *Minutes No. 11*, p. 96 (12 Oct. 1868).

[43] For the miner, see C. Storm-Clark, 'The Miners, 1870-1970: A Test-Case for Oral History', *Victorian Studies*, Sept. 1971, p. 72; Burgess in RSPCA *18th A.R. 1844*, p. 20, cf. Hon. W. F. Cowper, in *19th A.R. 1845*, p. 40. For a controversial argument on the relationship between industrialism and humanitarianism, see James Turner, *Reckoning with the Beast. Animals, Pain and Humanity in the Victorian Mind* (Baltimore, 1980).

transport was eliminated only by the railway and the internal combustion engine.[44]

But the Society grew more imaginative as time went on. During its first decade, the policies of prosecution and education were seen by some as mutually exclusive; even in the 1850s there was much argument on their relative importance. But pressure from William Adams Smith and others procured a subcommittee on education in 1857, and there were loud cheers at the annual meeting in 1858 when Smith argued that 'if we keep pace with society education for the future must be *our* means—at any rate our first means'. Education and prosecution were eventually seen as mutually reinforcing. In the 1860s education made further strides when an intelligent new secretary, Colam, was appointed, and when a special ladies' committee under Baroness Burdett-Coutts was formed. Detailed reports of court cases, once prominent in the annual reports, gradually disappeared.[45]

The RSPCA began as a London organization; of its 219 prosecutions in 1844, no less than 181 concerned cruelty there.[46] Its earliest provincial efforts focused on the spa and seaside towns where rich Londoners holidayed. During the 1830s inspectors were sent to other parts of southern England; by 1844 they had virtually become travelling agents for the Society. During that year individual inspectors spent time at Coventry (at Lady Cave's request), a month at Brighton in June, a week at Maidstone, a month in the Birmingham area, three weeks in Essex, at least a week at Bristol, some time at Ramsgate, another week at Brighton in September, a fortnight in Uxbridge, and some time on a tour of the north-east. As the Society grew, its centralized and London-based version of self-help impinged on longer-established and decentralized rural traditions of self-government. When the inspectors told the local magistrate the Revd Hildyard which local people had participated in a cock-fight at Deeping St. James, Lincolnshire, in 1840,

[44] Aberdare, RSPCA *54th A.R., 1878*, p. 82; cf. *72nd A.R.*, pp. 148-9; Fairholme and Pain, op. cit., p. 152. For pit pony numbers, F. M. L. Thompson, 'Horse Sense', *Economic History Review*, Feb. 1976, p. 80.

[45] RSPCA *1858 A.R.*, p. 29; cf. *1852 A.R.*, pp. 42-3; RSPCA *Minutes No. 7*, p. 356 (8 Nov. 1852). See also p. 147.

[46] RSPCA *18th A.R., 1844*, p. 52.

he said the Act 'did not authorize them to go through the country as Informers or Spies'.[47]

Under Colam, the Society spread wider still, taking a pride in 1868 that almost twice as many convictions had been secured outside London as inside; there were ten times as many by 1888.[48] Between 1868 and 1872 Colam made several tours to stimulate provincial branches. By 1875 there were 77 branches in the United Kingdom, 254 by 1901. The list for 1875 includes resort towns—Cheltenham, Bath, Malvern, Tunbridge Wells, Scarborough, Weston super Mare, Torquay, Leamington; country towns like Colchester, Exeter, Gloucester, Keswick, Norwich, and Oxford; but also several industrial and commercial towns, notably Birmingham, Bradford, Hull, Leeds, Liverpool, Manchester, and Newcastle. By 1901 there were also over 750 'bands of mercy'. — organizations educating children in kindness to animals—for the Late-Victorian RSPCA expanded its scope generationally as well as geographically. But it made slow progress in major cities like Birmingham and Manchester. A branch in Birmingham was formed with difficulty in 1862, and had to be disaffiliated seven years later; and by 1879 the Manchester branch had become 'supine'. Perhaps provincials suspected a London-based society which enjoyed aristocratic support, but a related problem was the Society's relative failure with dissenters; Colam complained at Wakefield in 1872 that they 'generally throughout England were not alive to the importance of this question'.[49]

The RSPCA's ambitions did not stop short at national boundaries. Humanitarians were keen to purge Britain's national image of its association with cruel sports; Lord Stratford de Redcliffe told the annual meeting of 1862 that the barbarous Turks were more humane than the Christians, and J. S. Buckingham at the annual meeting of 1842 described Arab gentleness as 'an anticipation of the Millennium, when the lamb and the lion will be seen lying

[47] Hildyard, in RSPCA, *Minutes No. 3*, p. 245, cf. p. 146.
[48] RSPCA *1868 A.R.*, p. 39; *65th A.R., 1889*, p. 127.
[49] *A.W.*, 1 May 1872, p. 124; cf. RSPCA *Minutes No. 14*, p. 76 (13 May 1879). For Birmingham, see *Minutes No. 9*, p. 125 (11 Mar. 1862); *Minutes No. 11*, p. 214 (14 June 1869); there was more trouble in 1883, see *Minutes No. 15*, p. 28 (16 May 1883). For Manchester, see *Minutes No. 14*, p. 98 (8 July 1879).

down together'. None of this deterred the RSPCA from attacking cruelty overseas long before the Society had gained national coverage at home, and as early as 1836 W. A. Mackinnon preened himself at the annual meeting on the fact that 'to Englishmen alone is the credit due, of having been the first—(as in all other humane propositions) to take up the cause of the suffering dumb creation'.[50]

So short was the Society's memory that cruelty to animals began to seem peculiarly Latin and Catholic, and early attention was given to French vivisection, Spanish bullfights and Italian brutalities. Lord Shaftesbury, touring Italy in 1833, detested the ill-treatment of a horse on the road to Loretto: 'never did I see such a fiend as the postillion', he wrote; 'blood and hell were in every line of his face'. William Adams Smith, feminist champion of oppressed nationalities, virtually acted as the RSPCA's chief agent in Naples. In 1854 he used his RSPCA connections to exert pressure on the King of Naples against local animal cruelty. When he urged the Society in October 1860 to sponsor the anti-Catholic lecturer Father Gavazzi in exposing cruelty in Naples, the executive committee thought the time unsuitable, as the public 'could not be induced to attend to any subject except the one which so completely engrosses their thoughts'; but in the following month the new situation in Italy induced them to contribute £10 for the purpose.[51] In 1858 RSPCA representatives attended the annual meeting of the Société Protectrice des Animaux in Paris, thus reciprocating the Vicomte de Valmer's attendance at their Society's annual meeting of 1852; and in 1862 the Society launched a special fund for European operations. The Late-Victorian RSPCA took a pride in establishing offshoots in South American seaports, and prevented the Prince of Wales from attending bullfights while visiting Lisbon and Madrid in 1876.[52]

[50] De Redcliffe, in RSPCA *A.R., 1861-2*, p. 37; Buckingham, in *16th A.R., 1842*, p. 22; Mackinnon in *10th A.R., 1836*, p. 23, cf. *15th A.R., 1841*, p. 42.

[51] E. Hodder, *Shaftesbury*, i, p. 180. cf. C. Buxton, *Memoirs of Sir Thomas Fowell Buxton, Baronet* (1848), p. 494. For Adams Smith, see RSPCA *Minutes No. 8*, p. 18 (13 Feb. 1854); p. 37 (15 May 1854); *Minutes No. 9*, p. 28 (9 Oct. 1860); p. 31 (13 Nov. 1860); see also ibid., p. 44 (12 Feb. 1861); p. 60 (23 Apr. 1861). For a memoir of Smith, see *A.W.*, 1 Feb. 1871, p. 72.

[52] South America in RSPCA *Minutes No. 17*, p. 106 (8 Oct. 1894); bull-

Kindness to animals came to seem peculiarly British. As Mocatta told one annual meeting, 'the Society in Naples, unfortunately, like nearly every society out of England, America and one or two continental cities excepted, is very badly supported'. The Mid-Victorian Society established closer contacts with America. In 1858 Mr Rarey, an American, received its gold medal for humane ways of training horses, and in 1869–70 visiting American humanitarians accentuated the Society's shift towards humane education.[53] Protestant prejudices were reinforced in the early 1880s when Irish Catholics began maiming cattle; the Society (spurred on by the Queen) organized itself to expose these 'horrible mutilations' in December 1881. Yet an editorial in the first number of *Animal World* stressed that 'humanity is unsectarian. We shall introduce neither theology nor politics into our columns.' The Society never became a mere vehicle for anti-Catholicism; it never singled out Irish immigrants for special attention, though it was keen to attract Catholic support. In 1879 it arranged a special interview with Archbishop Manning, a prominent antivivisectionist, to discuss ways of attracting Catholic support, and in 1886 it used Manning as intermediary in trying to influence the Pope.[54] In 1900 the Society appropriately concluded the century by trying to get the president of the Swiss Republic to incorporate the destruction of wounded war-horses into the Geneva Convention.[55]

III

Legislation and enforcement were consolidated by a skilful handling of public opinion; prudence and professionalism

fights in *Minutes No. 13*, p. 224 (8 Feb. 1876); p. 248 (22 May 1876); *Minutes No. 14*, p. 110 (11 Nov. 1879).

[53] Mocatta in RSPCA *66th A.R.*, p. 121. Rarey, in RSPCA *Minutes No. 8*, p. 294 (24 May 1858). See also *Minutes No. 11*, p. 210 (14 June 1869); p. 375 (27 June 1870); *Minutes No. 14*, p. 366 (17 July 1882).

[54] Quotations from RSPCA *Minutes No. 14*, pp. 312–14 (22 Dec. 1881); *A.W.*, 1 Oct. 1869, p. 8; see also *A.W.*, 1 Feb. 1882, p. 18. For Manning, see *Minutes No. 14*, p. 86 (10 June 1879); *Minutes No. 15*, p. 116 (1 Apr. 1884); p. 356 (1 June 1886).

[55] RSPCA *Minutes No. 18*, p. 81 (12 Nov. 1900).

were the hallmarks of RSPCA strategy. 'I have felt all my life
an irresistible impulse to rush in whereve'r anyone is "oppressed" and try to "deliver" him, her, or *it*', wrote the antivivisectionist Frances Power Cobbe. Fortunately for the
animals, the RSPCA was less breathless; its approach to vivisection in 1875-6, for instance, is instructive. 'I look upon
this as a moral question, and therefore one that does not
admit of compromise', said antivivisectionist J. M. Holt in
the parliamentary debate; vivisection must be banned, not
regulated.[56] The evidence given to the royal commission by
G. R. Jesse, hon. secretary of the Society for the Abolition
of Vivisection, was hardly designed to win support for his
cause; nor did he conceal his regret that anyone had thought
it necessary to appoint an inquiry into so obvious an evil.
Colam said the RSPCA did not want vivisection totally
abolished, and disclaimed responsibility for 'the rash literature which has been printed on this subject'. Unlike the
antivivisectionists, the Society saw the inquiry as a necessary
preliminary to legislation, and presented the commission
with nearly 800 pages of foolscap manuscript.[57] Though
regretting government concessions to the physiologists,
the RSPCA remained in continuous contact with the government during 1876 and abstained from the luxury of repudiation: 'let us rather endeavour to enforce the Act, by which
means its defects will be advertised, and an efficient law be
ultimately enacted'. Its attitude to the wild birds' legislation
of 1880 was identical. Whereas antivivisectionists after
1876 moved increasingly towards abolitionism, the RSPCA
adopted the alternative and characteristic strategy of pressing
for stricter regulation.[58]

The Society's prudence reflects its political awareness, its
recognition that a non-specialist humanitarian body might
need to moderate its opposition to the powerful on one issue
in the hope of attracting their support on another. The
RSPCA was to the antivivisectionists in the 1870s what the

[56] F. P. Cobbe, *The Life of Frances Power Cobbe by Herself* (3rd ed., 1894),
ii, p. 244; Holt, *H. C. Deb.*, 9 Aug. 1876, c.903.
[57] Colam, in *R. C. Vivisection, Parl. Papers*, 1876 (C.1397), XLI, Q.1567; see
also RSPCA *Minutes No. 13*, p. 184 (25 Oct. 1875).
[58] *A.W.*, 1 Feb. 1877, p. 18; see also *A.W.*, 1 Apr. 1875, p. 50; 1 Oct. 1880,
p. 146.

Howard League was to the opponents of capital punishment in the 1950s; both the Society and the League were forced by their very nature into discretion, and were compelled to risk hostility from their zealots. John Colam was the epitome of prudence; 'wily he certainly was . . .', the humanitarian H. S. Salt recalled; 'he was a veritable Proteus in the skill with which he gave the slip to any one who tried to commit him to any course but the safest'.[59] But the Society had been prudent from the start, and Prebendary Jackson told its annual meeting in 1867 that the Society must aim to steer a middle course between brutality and sentimentalism.[60]

Prudence could avoid alienating the zealots by encouraging them to form distinct organizations for specific purposes: dogs' homes, societies for protecting birds, retreats for horses, organizations for bee-keepers, anti-hunting and anti-vivisection groups, and even the NSPCC. The successful reformer captures the energy, imagination, and resourcefulness of the enthusiast but sifts out his tactical errors and political innocence. The RSPCA's preoccupation with seeking out the sources of power has caused restiveness among radicals for generations.[61] From its earliest years it cultivated support among monarchs and aristocrats, perhaps the best route even to popular support at this time. Faced with a problem, its almost instinctive response was to approach the powerful. Concerned in 1862 about animal cruelty in Ceylon, it contacted the Colonial Secretary and had a law passed against it; worried in 1868 about the harmful effects of muzzling on dogs, it immediately turned to the police and the Home Office; anxious in 1899 for horses injured in the Boer War, it tried to alert the Secretary for War to the evil. Before attempting legislation on any matter it consulted its legal experts and its leading officers (usually politicians), and prepared the ground carefully. If private pressure seemed

[59] H. S. Salt, *Seventy Years*, p. 161; see also J. B. Christoph, *Capital Punishment*, p. 30.

[60] Jackson, RSPCA *1867 A.R.*, p. 44; cf. Hope, *1860 A.R.*, p. 42.

[61] RSPCA *Minutes No. 11*, p. 178 (20 Apr. 1869); p. 344 (9 May 1870); *Minutes No. 14*, p. 150 (23 Feb. 1880); *A.W.*, 1 June 1886, p. 87; *67th A.R.*, p. 107. For the NSPCC see *A.W.*, 1 Sept. 1884, p. 132; *Minutes No. 15*, p. 152 (14 July 1884); p. 308 (18 Jan. 1886); cf. Lee, *New Statesman*, 4 July 1969, p. 12.

more likely than publicity to attain the desired end, then it opted for discretion. Its attitude to the bullfights planned at Lisbon to celebrate the Prince of Wales's arrival there is characteristic; the secretary was instructed to call on Disraeli's private secretary privately 'to ascertain the truth of the reports thereon, and if so whether any step could be taken by this Society by Memorial or otherwise for the purpose of appealing against such proceedings'. Again, before it published its memorial on vivisection in the same year, Colam was instructed to ask the Home Secretary 'whether or not it will embarrass the Government'.[62]

Prudence demanded centralized authority, for it was essential to avoid embarrassments in parliament and in the courts. In 1860 when cruelty legislation was unexpectedly introduced into the House of Lords, the Society got it withdrawn. Caution was still more necessary when the law needed testing in the courts; control was maintained over inspectors while employed by a local branch, and the management of local branches was investigated before affiliation. For similar reasons, factory inspectors standardized procedure in the 1840s and the National Vigilance Association supervised all prosecutions in the 1890s.[63] Late-Victorian affiliated branches had to contribute adequately towards the cost of inspectors, and could prosecute offenders only on instruction from headquarters. Independent branches could always get advice, but were forbidden to use the Society's name. When the Liverpool branch embarked on a lawsuit in 1868 contrary to headquarters advice, and incurred a debt of about £250, the Society refused to help. The branch was urged to rely only on trained inspectors in future, and 'in all cases of doubt or difficulty to apply to their secretary, whence they would obtain the advantages of the experience of the Parent Society'. The ultimate

---

[62] RSPCA *Minutes No. 13*, p. 224 (8 Feb. 1876); *Minutes No. 13*, p. 288 (9 Jan. 1877); cf. *Minutes No. 18*, p. 45 (12 Mar. 1900).
[63] House of Lords incident in RSPCA *Minutes No. 9*, p. 3 (26 June 1860). For centralization, see M. W. Thomas, *The Early Factory Legislation. A Study in Legislative and Administrative Evolution* (Leigh-on-Sea, 1948), pp. 259–61; O. MacDonagh, 'The Nineteenth-Century Revolution in Government: A Reappraisal', *Historical Journal*, 1958, p. 60; W. A. Coote (ed.), *A Romance of Philanthropy* (1916), pp. 121–2.

sanction (threatened at Birmingham in 1883) was to dis-affiliate, and form an official branch in the area. The cold shoulder was also initially given to the ill-organized Bands of Mercy founded by the American Revd J. Timmins in the 1880s.[64]

The Society was equally cautious when delegating powers to its agents. For some years it made grants to a Miss Hicks, who seems to have been a freelance detector of animal-cruelty offences. In 1868, however, a railway carrier com-plained of her 'abusive language and vexatious conduct', and the RSPCA connection with her ended not long after-wards. The Society preferred prosecution only on the basis of evidence provided by its own inspectors. A close watch was maintained over them, and when Inspector Dobie, 'induced a man to bait a badger and afterwards prosecuted him for such offence' in 1871, he was 'severely censured and cautioned never to repeat such improper conduct'. Difficult or important cases were conducted by Colam personally, usually with success; in 1893 he received a writ for malicious prosecution for the first time in his career. 'If he had selected the Bar as his profession', Dr Fleming told him in 1886, 'he would have risen to the top of the tree.' Not surprisingly, when he retired in 1905 he wanted a former solicitor to succeed him.[65]

Even in 1849 the RSPCA could pride itself on having a much lower failure rate in the courts than the police. Occasionally of course it had to test the law where it was ambiguous, or alert the Home Secretary to magistrates ignorant of the law. But it was wary of encouraging sympa-thetic magistrates to impose severe sentences; these might be expedient occasionally, but they risked arousing public sympathy for the defendant.[66] The RSPCA never ran too far

---

[64] For Liverpool, see RSPCA *Minutes No. 10*, pp. 109-10 (17 Mar. 1868). For Birmingham, see *Minutes No. 15*, p. 28 (16 May 1883). For Timmins, see *Minutes No. 15*, p. 254 (2 June 1885); RSPCA *65th A.R., 1889*, pp. 84-5, 131. The RSPCA's regulations on branches are clearly outlined in *Minutes No. 11*, p. 260 (13 Dec. 1869).

[65] Hicks, in RSPCA *Minutes No. 9*, p. 106 (Nov. 1861); p. 218 (8 Dec. 1863). Dobie, *Minutes No. 12*, p. 44 (28 Mar. 1871); cf. R. D. Lee, *New Statesman*, 4 July 1969, p. 12. Fleming, *Minutes No. 15*, p. 378 (19 July 1886), cf. *Minutes No. 18*, p. 356 (13 Feb. 1905). See also *Minutes No. 17*, p. 48 (12 June 1893).

[66] For the police failure rate, see RSPCA *23rd A.R., 1849*, p. 40. For

ahead of public opinion—not (as its radical critics alleged) because its humanitarianism was lukewarm, but because it wished its humanitarianism to be effective. The zealots— E. A. Freeman versus field sports in 1870, Miss Cobbe versus vivisection in the 1880s, H. S. Salt versus stag-hunting in the 1890s—were restive.[67] Yet a division of labour gave them free rein without weakening the general campaign for protecting animals. The RSPCA could not lightly risk its funds on lost causes, and its critics did not always perceive the courage and self-discipline often required from those who seek moderate policies as the best on offer, and who daily reckon with the problems posed by a pressure group's delicate relationship with the public.

Prudence was complemented by professionalism. Then, as now, the Society was a lay body, which specialized in mobilizing the general public's enthusiasm and even, on occasion, its sentimentality in defence of animals. But by the 1880s in its attitude to fund-raising, manipulating opinion, and enacting legislation, it had become distinctly professional. It was professional also in a second sense: it steadily accumulated knowledge on animal questions, particularly in their legal aspects. By the 1860s its expertise was frequently being drawn upon by public, police, and politicians. Entertainers asked permission for their proposed animal displays, inventors and authors sought the Society's public approval, humanitarians overseas asked Colam for advice, civil servants requested information. In August 1868 the Home Office asked Colam for suggestions about amending the law on the protection of animals; in May 1873 the London School Board sought examiners in kindness to animals for its pupil-teachers; in June 1894 the Home Office wanted information on the cab traffic; in 1896 the Society sent Colam off on a European tour to collect information for the Board of Agriculture on Continental methods of controlling

unsympathetic magistrates, see RSPCA *Minutes No. 8*, p. 68 (11 Dec. 1854); *Minutes No. 7*, p. 73 (9 July 1849); p. 82 (6 Aug. 1849). For oversympathetic magistrates, see the case discussed in *Minutes No. 11*, p. 208 (14 June 1869). See also *The Patriot*, 17 June 1844, p. 4.

[67] E. A. Freeman, 'The Controversy on Field Sports', *Fortnightly Review*, 1870, p. 687; F. P. Cobbe, *Life*, ii, p. 262. See also R. D. Lee, *New Statesman*, 4 July 1969, p. 12; L. Gompertz, *Fragments*, p. 276.

dogs.[68] 'The Society has gained the high position of a Public Institution', Charles Darwin told the annual meeting of 1882; '. . . hence, calls upon it are made regardless of its actual means.' Pressure groups of this sort were warding off that dangerous concentration of 'intelligence and talent' inside nineteenth-century government, that starvation of talent outside it, which J. S. Mill so dreaded.[69]

Expertise was not accumulated through the RSPCA inspectorate; animal cruelty diverged here from factory hours, public health, and education. Non-governmental inspectors lacked the education and status for such a role. Legislation owed more to the Society's skilful channelling of public indignation behind sympathetic legal and scientific experts. Throughout the century, it encouraged the professionalization of groups concerned with animal welfare. It consistently upheld the veterinary surgeon's status, which needed 'to be raised higher for his own good, and for the better treatment of animals'; *Animal World* in 1878 therefore recommended government aid to veterinary science. The Mid-Victorian RSPCA depended heavily on Professor Spooner for advice on vivisection and inventions. The Late-Victorian RSPCA depended equally heavily on Dr Fleming, President of the Royal College of Veterinary Surgeons, and in 1880 supported his attempts to improve his profession's educational standards.[70] It also encouraged the professionalization of the farrier; in 1889 it supported the Farriers' Company scheme for providing the trade with a proper examination and training, and in 1896 gave the Company £50 towards its expenses.[71]

---

[68] *Minutes No. 11*, p. 74 (18 July 1868); *Minutes No. 12*, p. 330 (13 May 1873); *Minutes No. 17*, p. 92 (25 June 1894); *Minutes No. 17*, p. 232 (7 July 1896); cf. J. B. Christoph, *Capital Punishment*, p. 29.

[69] Darwin, in RSPCA *58th A.R., 1882*, p. 81; J. S. Mill, *Principles of Political Economy* (ed. W. J. Ashley, 1917), p. 949.

[70] *A.W.*, 2 Sept. 1878, p. 131; see also RSPCA *1853 A.R.*, p. 47; *1867 A.R.*, p. 48; *A.W.*, 1 Apr. 1882, pp. 58-9. For Fleming, see RSPCA *Minutes No. 14*, pp. 218, 220 (22 Nov. 1880); p. 338 (11 Apr. 1882). For a biography of Spooner, see *A.W.*, 1 Feb. 1872, pp. 69-70.

[71] RSPCA *Minutes No. 16*, p. 261 (16 Dec. 1889); *A.W.*, 1 July 1890, p. 110; *Minutes No. 17*, p. 228 (22 June 1896); *Minutes No. 14*, p. 126 (9 Dec. 1879).

IV

RSPCA voluntarism never excluded co-operation with public authorities. By 1855 the Society was preparing a textbook, and its circular urged clergy and masters of national schools to include kindness to animals in 'the system of education among the poorer classes'. Two government school-inspectors were elected to the executive committee as honorary members in July 1857, with power to vote on all educational questions. W. H. Bowyer made helpful suggestions when he attended the committee on 28 June 1858, and the inspectors helped distribute RSPCA literature; but they do not seem to have attended the committee on any other occasion.[72] The Society cultivated government inspectors of mines in the 1870s as an entrée to mines whose owners refused voluntary co-operation. RSPCA inspectors were reluctant to go down mines, and in 1875 were deprived of two weeks' pay for refusing to enter pits in South Wales. But in 1877 the Society apparently failed to secure full co-operation from the Home Office; 'inspection is practicable enough', it complained in 1878, 'and requires only the will of Government to make it compulsory'. Only government could override the rights of private property; 'because we are powerless, we press the Government; because powers have been given to it to override private rights and establish inspection, we say our Government is responsible for the absence of supervision in mines, and for the cruelty which prevails there'.[73] In 1886 it tried to insert into the Mines Regulation Bill a clause which would enable its officials to accompany the government inspectors on their visits. By this time, some mines inspectors were co-operating with the Society and reporting cases of cruelty; but in 1896 it still wanted the Home Secretary to appoint RSPCA constables as unpaid assistant inspectors of mines.[74] It was equally eager to extend public inspectors' powers over vivisection, often complaining that

[72] RSPCA *Minutes No. 8*, p. 113 (25 June 1855). See also ibid., p. 183 (8 Dec. 1856); p. 187 (12 Jan. 1857); p. 267 (8 Feb. 1858).
[73] *A.W.*, Jan. 1878, pp. 7–8. See also RSPCA *Minutes No. 13*, p. 112 (9 Mar. 1875); p. 124 (23 Mar. 1875).
[74] RSPCA *Minutes No. 15*, p. 322 (2 Mar. 1886), cf. *A.W.*, 1 Mar. 1890, p. 34; *Minutes No. 14*, p. 60 (24 Mar. 1879); *Minutes No 17*, p. 173 (28 Oct. 1895); p. 239 (12 Oct. 1896).

the 1876 Act's inspector did no more than register information, and never visited laboratories.

The Society also cultivated the police, whose initial jealousy of its inspectors was overcome; the police were eventually asked to swear in some of the inspectors. It tried to educate the police into taking action against animal cruelty by regularly rewarding sympathetic policemen; 150 rewards were ordered to be sent out to chief constables as late as 1873.[75] Many of the convictions for animal cruelty nominally secured by the police, always far more numerous than the Society's own convictions, were therefore indirectly obtained by the RSPCA.[76] Sir Richard Mayne, the metropolitan police commissioner, was invited to undertake the management of the Society's inspectors in 1852-3, but the RSPCA felt unable to accept his conditions. Yet Sir Richard was sympathetic; 'there are few old policemen', *Animal World* recalled on 2 May 1887, 'who have forgotten the sharp earwigging he was in the habit of giving an officer whom he discovered guilty of any neglect in stopping a gross act of cruelty on his beat'. Mayne's successor, Sir Edmund Henderson, continued this tradition; on retirement he gave £10 to the Society and joined its executive committee.[77] The annual report for 1901 said cruelty convictions were increasing partly because of the Society's increased activity, but also because attitudes among magistrates and the police had improved. Police energies were inevitably restrained, though, by fears that the public would lose confidence in a police force which devoted more time to rescuing animals than to repressing crime.[78]

On Smithfield market, the Society combined enthusiasm

[75] For jealousy, see SCHC on Smithfield Market, *Parl. Papers*, 1847 (640), VIII, Q.5364. For swearing in, see RSPCA *Minutes No. 7*, p. 164 (5 Aug. 1850); p. 170 (11 Nov. 1850); p. 177 (9 Dec. 1850). For rewards see *Minutes No. 12*, p. 300 (24 Feb. 1873).

[76] For figures, see p. 131.

[77] For Mayne, see RSPCA *Minutes No. 7*, p. 329 (22 June 1852); p. 334 (12 July 1852); p. 337 (9 Aug. 1852); *Minutes No. 8*, p. 3 (8 Aug. 1853); p. 8 (14 Nov. 1853). For Henderson, see *A.W.*, 2 May 1887, p. 73; *Minutes No. 15*, p. 328 (15 Mar. 1886); p. 366 (19 July 1886); *Minutes No. 16*, p. 141 (7 Feb. 1888).

[78] RSPCA *77th A.R., 1901*, p. 112; but see Lyall's comments in ibid., p. 156. For public confidence, see *A.W.*, 2 May 1887, p. 73.

for public inspection with a humanitarian justification for public management; cruelty seemed endemic in an increasingly overcrowded, insanitary, and largely private meat-market. 'No person of humane mind can pass through Smithfield on a Monday or Friday morning . . . without the greatest violence being done to his feelings', wrote James Grant in 1842. In such circumstances, humanitarian and police patrolling could achieve little. The RSPCA soon realized that the Smithfield cattle-drovers were, as Samuel Gurney argued in 1828, 'placed under circumstances that necessarily excite their temper', and that permanent improvement could be attained only by moving the market and reforming its management. In 1847 an RSPCA inspector told the select committee that cruelty was so inevitable in the market that he 'often and often and often' made no charge against drovers whose cruelties he witnessed.[79]

Smithfield market is therefore an early instance of undoubted evils driving philanthropists into the arms of the state. Humanitarians like Charles Dickens soon came to favour stringent public inspection and the adoption in London of publicly controlled abattoirs like those in Paris. Samuel Gurney, Sir Henry Parnell, and James Mills gave glowing reports of them to the select committee of 1828: 'I would beg leave, though not an admirer of the French, to borrow and take an example from them', said Mills, a civil engineer. But vested interests here were very strong, and were championed powerfully by London MPs; when reinforced by the traditional prejudice against the French, they were irresistible. Admitting the 'manifest advantage to the community' from the public slaughterhouses in almost every Continental city, the select committee of 1828 felt that compulsory superintendence by public inspectors 'would be repugnant to the feelings of Englishmen'. The RSPCA none the less resolved in April 1829 to urge on sympathetic MPs 'the establishment of cattle markets in the suburbs with

---

[79] J. Grant, *Lights and Shadows of London Life* (1842), ii, p. 182; Gurney in SCHC on the state of Smithfield Market, *Parl. Papers*, 1828 (551), VIII, p. 38; for the inspector see SCHC on Smithfield Market, *Parl. Papers*, 1847 (640), VIII, Q.5326. See also SCHC on Smithfield Market, *Parl. Papers*, 1849 (420), XIX, Q.697.

contiguous Abattoirs and a resident inspector to prevent the dreadful cruelties in slaughtering animals'.[80]

Here the Society's repudiation of libertarianism persisted throughout the century. Libertarian objections were again raised in 1847 when Lord Robert Grosvenor defended the Paris scheme before the select committee, but his rejoinder was robust: 'I consider that every law that is made interferes with the right of private action ... It is in this country, I think, more than in any other country, merely a question of that which would be most to the advantage of the public in general.' In 1855 the Society tried to ensure that the new Public Health Bill would require all slaughterhouses to be licensed, and not merely new slaughterhouses. The public slaughterhouse was again championed in 1869, when a subcommittee was appointed to promote the scheme; and the Society strenuously resisted the butchers (who wished to preserve private slaughterhouses) during the parliamentary debates on Smithfield in 1873, but in vain.[81] It felt that public control, by reducing the number of slaughterhouses, would reduce animals' sufferings by increasing both publicity and expertise. But it was difficult to overcome the Mid-Victorian loathing of all things French. 'It was useless to compare London with Paris on a subject of this kind', Mr Locke declared in the debates of 1873; '. . . what was Paris in comparison with London, and what was a Frenchman in comparison with an Englishman? The thing was absurd.'[82]

In promoting legislation on animal cruelty, as on factory legislation, theoretical influences were less directly important than practical difficulties; 'each successive statute aimed at remedying a single ascertained evil'.[83] The RSPCA was a

---

[80] SCHC on the state of Smithfield Market, *Parl. Papers*, 1828 (551), VIII, pp. 134, 6; RSPCA *Minutes 1824-32*, p. 93 (6 Apr. 1829)—this first volume of minutes has no number. For Dickens, see his *Uncollected Writings* (Penguin Press, 1969), i, pp. 101-11; and his *Reprinted Pieces* (Oxford, 1958), pp. 589-600.

[81] Grosvenor, in SCHC on Smithfield Market, *Parl. Papers*, 1847 (640), VIII, Q.5826. See also RSPCA *Minutes No. 8*, p. 83 (26 Feb. 1855); *Minutes No. 11*, p. 160 (19 Mar. 1869); *Minutes No. 12*, p. 306 (11 Mar. 1873); p. 312 (24 Mar. 1873).

[82] *H. C. Deb.*, 2 Apr. 1873, c.499.

[83] Sidney Webb's preface to B. L. Hutchins and A. Harrison, *Factory Legislation*, p. ix.

businesslike body; no political theorist was ever cited at its annual meetings. Nor would one expect any frontal critique of *laissez-faire* from a body so firmly based on the Mid-Victorian voluntarist ideal of the active citizen. But certain patterns of more abstract argument did recur in discussions elsewhere on animal cruelty. RSPCA historians see their Society as obviously enjoying access to correct principle, and as progressing steadily in a direct line to the present, triumphing *en route* over 'derision and contempt . . . pre-judice, ignorance, and selfishness'. It may indeed be true that 'our ancestors were blind to the sufferings of animals because they had never been taught to see them', but the reformer's achievement is paradoxically minimized when described in such Whiggish terms; his reputation demands that full justice be done to the RSPCA's opponents.[84]

Critics did not confine their arguments to the substance of the humanitarian case; they predictably seized upon questions of personality and tactics. In 1824 Hume complained of humanitarian inconsistency, for instance; why did not Martin also campaign against brutal flogging in the army? Some wondered how Martin could reconcile his enthusiasm for animals with his penchant for duels. Peel thought that more injury was done to Martin's cause 'by the manner in which he brought forward the subject, than by any other circumstance'.[85] But more interesting are the three sub-stantive arguments used against the humanitarians: that legislation was unnecessary, that legislation if attempted would fail, or that it could succeed only by unduly infringing individual liberty.

Critics who used the first of these arguments claimed that cruelty was already declining. 'Laws never ought to be called in but where other powers fail', said Windham in the debate of 1809. Bull-baiting, he argued in 1800, 'is already so much fallen into disuse, that it seems as if the bill has been brought in now lest it should be quite abolished before it could be passed'. He was correct about bull-baiting, which had already

[84] From the dedication to Fairholme and Pain, *Century of Work*, and from ibid., p. 2; cf. A. W. Moss, *Valiant Crusade*, dedication.

[85] Hume, *H. C. Deb.*, 9 Mar. 1824, c.866; Peel, *H. C. Deb.*, 20 Apr. 1826, c.530.

begun to decline by the early nineteenth century without legislative aid.[86] The RSPCA's tactics of the 1830s may even sometimes have reinforced traditionalism by stirring up the locality's distaste for compulsion from London. The very emergence of the Society was a symptom as well as a cause of humanitarian progress. A variant of the first argument was to question the humanitarian's priorities. In an ideal world, said Windham in 1800, legislation against cruelty might be required; but in practice parliament's time was too precious 'in times like the present, when questions of vital importance are hourly pressing on our attention'. The argument often reappeared: 'they were legislating for pigeons', said Earl Fortescue in 1884, during a debate on trap-shooting, 'when affairs at home and abroad were calling urgently for attention'.[87]

Humanitarians could retaliate here only by stimulating public concern about animals, for at no time does any objective rank-order exist to register the relative importance of reforming causes. Someone must do for animals what Clarkson did for slaves, or what Shaftesbury did for climbing-boys—convince the politicians that here were creatures worthy of their attention, and so counter Joseph Hume's objection in 1843 that 'it was much more important to legislate for men than for dogs'. Some early humanitarians even shared their opponents' ranking of reforms, but as good evangelicals felt with Wilberforce that the Christian 'watches himself also on small as well as on great occasions', because the latter 'can hardly ever be expected to occur, whereas the former are continually presenting themselves'.[88] RSPCA meetings often referred to the boy who 'not awakened to a sense of his wickedness, when he is tormenting a poor fly

[86] W. Windham, *Speeches* (1812), iii, p. 315; i. p. 339. See also R. W. Malcolmson, *Popular Recreations in English Society. 1700–1850* (Cambridge, 1973), pp. 122 and ff.

[87] W. Windham, *Speeches*, i. p. 332, cf. p. 341; Fortescue, *H. L. Deb.*, 9 May 1884, c. 1823; cf. Clare Read in the wild birds' debate, *H. C. Deb.*, 29 Apr. 1873, c. 1188.

[88] Hume, *H. C. Deb.*, 15 Mar. 1843, c. 973; W. Wilberforce, *A Practical View of the Prevailing Religious System of Professed Christians* (6th ed., 1798), p. 247; cf. D. Newsome, *The Parting of Friends. A Study of the Wilberforces and Henry Manning* (1966), p. 52.

with a pin . . . will grow up a hard hearted, selfish, and cruel man'.[89]

But here the libertarians were given a prize opportunity, for they could expose as bogus the humanitarians' claim to be concerned primarily for the national welfare, and reveal their objective as sectarian. In 1809 Windham thought pioneers of new eras in legislation should meet 'a reasonable distrust . . . lest they should be a little led away by an object of such splendid ambition, and be thinking more of themselves than of the credit of the laws or the interests of the community'. There was certainly much self-congratulation at RSPCA annual meetings, and nineteenth-century philanthropy did bring social and sectarian advantages, especially to the evangelicals. 'What shall we abolish next?', Wilberforce asked Henry Thornton in 1807, after the bill abolishing the slave-trade had passed its second reading.[90] Evangelicals took up many causes; outsiders' sympathy with any one of them could be eroded by distaste for the rest. Some early champions of animals, for instance, simultaneously attacked popular recreation through the sabbatarian and temperance movements.

Evangelical priorities must be judged in the context of their fierce (and now unfashionable) pursuit of personal self-discipline. The RSPCA's pioneers were not only defending animals; they saw themselves as civilizing the lower orders, and contested Hume's dichotomy between concern for dogs and men. The Bishop of St. David's told the annual meeting of 1846 that the uneducated man 'is after all but a child in the maturity of his physical powers . . . a savage in the midst of all the refinement of our civilization'; governments concerned for the citizen's moral growth must curb animal cruelty.[91] The early RSPCA concentrated unashamedly on cruelty committed at the lower end of society, and asserted openly that cruelty was more common there than elsewhere.[92]

[89] Bishop Lonsdale of Lichfield, in RSPCA *1860 A.R.*, p. 20.

[90] W. Windham, *Speeches*, iii, p. 304; cf. the personal ambitions of T. F. Buxton in C. Buxton, *T. F. Buxton*, p. 84. For Wilberforce, see F. K. Brown, *Fathers of the Victorians* (Cambridge, 1961), pp. 107-8, 257. See also p. 423.

[91] Connop Thirlwall, in RSPCA *20th A.R.*, *1846*, p. 20; cf. p. 127.

[92] See W. A. Mackinnon, in RSPCA *13th A.R.*, *1839*, pp. 30-1; *14th A.R. 1840*, p. 41; and Lord Dudley Stuart, in *16th A.R.*, *1842*, p. 30.

This made it easy for critics to harp on the dangers of class legislation. In 1809 Windham thought the proposed legislation should rather be entitled 'A Bill for harrassing and oppressing certain Classes among the lower Orders of His Majesty's Subjects'; in 1802 he feared that 'if to poverty were to be added a privation of amusements' the poor would become desperate and would embrace 'that dangerous enthusiasm which is analogous to Jacobinism'. He doubted whether a single bull-baiter could be found 'out of the whole number of the disaffected', or whether a single sportsman 'had distinguished himself' in the London Corresponding Society.[93]

Although cruel sports were never patronized as exclusively by the poor as their defenders alleged, the early RSPCA was certainly timid in its approach to aristocratic sports like steeplechasing and hunting. And it was as inaccurate as its critics in founding its early case against humbler sports like badger-baiting, bull-running, and cock-fighting on the claim that their patrons 'were the lowest and most wretched description of people'. Attacking dog-carts in the House of Lords during 1854, the Earl of Chichester claimed that 'the men who used these carts were men of bad character, and they employed this mode of conveyance, not on account of its expedition, but of its cheapness'; Grantley Berkeley rejoined that the Earl had fallen 'into a worldly mistake, too common as well as manifestly unjust', that bad characters were usually poor. 'When legislative humanity desires to make a public appearance', he complained, 'rags and poverty are sure to afford a means for its introduction.'[94] The libertarians claimed to fear the consequences of such legislation as long as the poor were not directly represented in parliament.[95]

Yet the Society had to begin somewhere. As Martin explained in 1824, 'he wished to stop cruelty as far as he was able: he wished to prohibit those cruelties which public

---

[93] W. Windham, *Speeches*, iii, p. 315; i, p. 353; i, p. 346.

[94] Martin, *H. C. Deb.*, 26 Feb. 1824, c.487, cf. Burdett, *H. C. Deb.*, 11 Mar. 1825, c.1013; Chichester, *H. L. Deb.*, 4 July 1854, c.1079; Berkeley in *The Times*, 10 July 1854, p. 10.

[95] e.g. S. Herbert, *H. C. Deb.*, 24 Mar. 1843, c.1478; W. Windham, *Speeches*, iii, pp. 320-1.

opinion would follow him in saying ought to be prohibited'.[96] The early RSPCA certainly aroused resentment among working people; but further experience broadened its perception. Furthermore, its opponents' arguments were often linked to a patronizing view of the working man's role; William Smith claimed in 1826 that those who defended their recreations did so 'rather from a contempt for the lower class of people. It was as much as to say, "poor creatures, let them alone" . . .'. Lord Erskine claimed in 1809 that revolutions occurred only in nations which neglected 'the cultivation of the moral sense, the best security of states, and the greatest consolation of the world'.[97]

Nevertheless humanitarians attracted many skilful opinion-formers who diverged on other issues, and were therefore able to penetrate many different groups. Windham referred contemptuously in 1802 to 'this union of the Methodists and Jacobins'. The movement attracted Christians like the Revd Richard Burgess, who argued at the annual meeting of 1846 that man is 'deceitful above all things, and desperately wicked', and therefore required 'to be restrained from an undue exercise of power'—but also radical humanitarians like Lord Dudley Stuart, who at the same meeting found it 'difficult to believe that man is cruel by nature'.[98] A. V. Dicey's humanitarian alliance between evangelicals and utilitarian radicals can be seen in operation here, but espousing state intervention in a period which Dicey labels 'the age of individualism' with the aid of Benthamites whose individualism Dicey exaggerates.[99] The RSPCA could attract money from T. F. Buxton and Lord Shaftesbury (in 1844), but also from Jeremy Bentham (in 1831) and from Mr and Mrs J. S. Mill (in 1856), and a life membership from Edwin Chadwick (in 1863). Furthermore, although the Society did not publicly cite them, the writings of Bentham and J. S. Mill

[96] *H. C. Deb.*, 11 Feb. 1824, c.133; cf. Erskine, *H. L. Deb.*, 15 May 1809, c.570.

[97] Smith, *H. C. Deb.*, 21 Feb. 1826, c.649; Erskine, *H. L. Deb.*, 15 May 1809, c.570.

[98] W. Windham, *Speeches*, i, p. 346; Burgess, in RSPCA *20th A.R., 1846*, p. 42; Stuart, in ibid., p. 59.

[99] A. V. Dicey, *Lectures on the Relation between Law and Public Opinion in England during the Nineteenth Century* (1905), p. 219; see also pp. 107-8, 187-8.

contained several passages justifying state interference in this sphere.[1]

The opposition's second major line of argument—that legislation would fail—sometimes simply enlarged upon the novelty of the reform. Windham emphasized (in 1802) the antiquity of the sports under attack, and (in 1809) the fact that 'we ought to take care . . . how we begin new eras of legislation';[2] laws enforceable only through public support must of course take account of such factors, otherwise attempts at prosecution may simply arouse sympathy for the oppressor, or even cause him to seek revenge. 'A £5 fine', said Mr Escott in a parliamentary debate on slaughter-houses in 1844, 'was only calculated to make a man who had paid it, vent his spite in a more virulent degree when he had an opportunity. We ought to trust to education.'[3]

If, on the other hand, humanitarian legislation was to succeed, opponents claimed (in the third major branch of their case) that the price of success would be too high; an intolerable sacrifice of liberty and domestic privacy would be required, and in the British context this meant failure in practice. Legislation in such a 'petty, meddling . . . spirit' would merely 'furnish mankind with additional means of vexing and harassing one another', said Windham in 1800. In 1810 and 1816 the humanitarians faced hostility from the Earl of Lauderdale, a devotee of political economy who operated from the House of Lords. Likewise in 1824, 1826, 1843, and 1849 a leading opponent in the House of Commons was Joseph Hume. Lauderdale and Hume were doing more than apply their principles blindly; there was good sense in Hume's argument of 1849 that 'the multiplication of Acts might render the matter difficult instead of simple'.[4] Government was inefficient and corrupt, illiteracy was widespread, and reliance on prosecuting working people seemed inferior as a remedy to the popular education that he and

---

[1] See pp. 153–4.

[2] W. Windham, *Speeches*, iii, p. 304; cf. i, p. 354.

[3] Escott, *H. C. Deb.*, 24 July 1844, c.1336.

[4] W. Windham, *Speeches*, i, p. 333; *H. C. Deb.*, 13 June 1849, c.125; cf. Fairholme and Pain, *Century of Work*, p. 39. For Lauderdale, see *H. L. Deb.*, 8 May 1810, c.882; 26 June 1816, c.1265. For Hume, see *H. C. Deb.*, 9 Mar. 1824, c.866; 20 Apr. 1826, c.530; 22 Mar. 1843, c.1287.

other political economists energetically promoted. The
RSPCA's opponents in the 1820s included an administrator
as experienced as Robert Peel, who claimed in 1824 that such
matters were 'too minute—too much the property of local
custom and regulation—to be fit matters for legislation'; in
1826 Peel urged Martin to 'let public opinion and the acts of
individuals remedy the evil complained of'.[5] In the 1840s
T. S. Duncombe, radical champion of Finsbury's working
men, specialized in the libertarian line of attack. 'No encouragement ought to be given to societies for meddling with
everybody's business but their own', he declared, opposing
a bill to regulate slaughtering in 1844.[6] Assaults on 'grand-
motherly legislation' became a commonplace of Victorian
parliamentary debate.

Yet the RSPCA recognized that much cruelty (even vivisection) occurred on private premises or inside the family,
and wisely did not attempt the impossible. It also knew how
much can be achieved even in influencing private conduct by
regulating conduct which is public. Lord Mahon told the
annual meeting of 1835 that dogs were not protected
'because we wish to avoid an inquisition into private life . . .
legislation can however prevent our streets from being the
scenes of cruelty', and as the Bishop of St. David's argued at
the annual meeting of 1846 the public spectacle 'communi-
cates an immoral contagion of the worst and most virulent
kind among those who witness it'.[7] There is some evidence,
necessarily impressionistic, that the Society had already
influenced standards of public conduct by the 1840s.[8] The
price of such improvement might be an element of hypocrisy,
but this is an aspect of Victorianism on which historians
now look more kindly, recognizing that secure humanitarian
advance is inevitably slow.[9] A similar debate now occurs in

---

[5] *H. C. Deb.*, 26 Feb. 1824, c.493; 20 Apr. 1826, c.530.
[6] *H. C. Deb.*, 24 July 1844, c.1334. See also pp. 147–8.
[7] Mahon, in RSPCA *9th A.R., 1835*, p. 29; cf. the Vice Society, in SCHC on
Police of the Metropolis, Second Report, *Parl. Papers*, 1817 (484), VII, p. 482.
Connop Thirlwall, in RSPCA *20th A.R., 1846*, p. 24.
[8] Mackinnon, in RSPCA *1850 A.R.*, p. 31; Ewart, in *19th A.R., 1845*, p. 20.
[9] Cf. G. Kitson Clark, *The Making of Victorian England* (1962), p. 64; S. Mar-
cus, *The Other Victorians* (New York, 1966), p. 146; H. Perkin, *The Origins of
Modern English Society, 1780–1880* (1969), p. 288.

the area of film censorship, where libertarians once again compete with interventionists for the humanitarian label.

In the nineteenth-century political climate, the RSPCA could not offer too robust a challenge to libertarianism, but at the annual meeting of 1837 the Earl of Carnarvon ridiculed the idea that 'liberty of crime could be conducive to the happiness of any one'. Frustrated in its efforts to get mines, slaughterhouses, and laboratories inspected, the Late-Victorian RSPCA attacked 'the doctrine of the sacredness of alleged rights of the citizen, the domicile, and of private property' as 'a British fetish'. In this it would have enjoyed J. S. Mill's support, for he described 'the domestic life of domestic tyrants' as 'one of the things which it is the most imperative on the law to interfere with'.[10] Complaints that it was impossible to make men moral by act of parliament encountered the humanitarian rejoinder that 'whatever is morally bad cannot be politically right'; there was also educational and symbolic value in getting kindness to animals incorporated into the law.[11]

The Society's most prominent members sometimes challenged *laissez-faire* views in other areas. For eighteen years Samuel Gurney was president of the Anti-Slavery Society, a body which diverged significantly from free traders; W. A. Mackinnon helped legislate for public health and clean air; Lord Aberdare promoted temperance legislation; Lord Shaftesbury championed intervention on factory hours and public health. When Shaftesbury died in 1885, *Animal World* published a two-page memoir, complete with illustrations; in 1893 it printed a full-page engraving of him together with a long article on his work, for the Society. By contrast, John Bright's death in 1889 encountered greater reserve. Though personally kind to animals, Bright never subscribed to the Society or gave it legislative aid; furthermore he twice

[10] Carnarvon, in RSPCA *11th A.R., 1837*, p. 17; *72nd A.R.*, p. 147; J. S. Mill, *Principles of Political Economy*, p. 958. See also *A.W.*, 1 Apr. 1896, p. 51; Jan. 1878, pp. 7–8.

[11] *Gentleman's Magazine*, July 1809, p. 645, citing Dr Edward Barry's sermon on brutal sports (1801). See also Mackinnon in RSPCA *10th A.R., 1836*, p. 23, and my 'State Intervention and Moral Reform in Nineteenth-Century England', in P. Hollis (ed.), *Pressure from Without in Early Victorian England* (1974), p. 310.

'declined to attend the meetings of the parent Society in London, though he was urged to do so by intimate friends'.[12] The Society's quiet but cumulative persistence ensured eventual interventionist success, but the size of its task can be grasped only by fully recognizing the strength and contemporary plausibility of its opponents. The RSPCA was run with patience, skill, tact, and perseverance; but its case was never cut and dried, nor were its structure and personalities ever beyond reproach. When viewed in this light, its achievement seems a remarkable nineteenth-century exercise in the art of the possible.

    [12] *A.W.*, 1 May 1889, p. 67. For Shaftesbury, *A.W.*, 2 Nov. 1885, pp. 168-9; 1 Sept. 1893, p. 131.

III

Religion and Recreation
in Nineteenth-Century England[1]

'Religion and recreation', said the Revd H. R. Haweis, attacking the sabbatarians in 1877, '. . . meant to a certain extent the same thing—both meant to be born again'.[2] These two worlds often conflicted sharply before 1914, if only because they competed for the same public. Each sought victory by purloining the attractions of the other. Their conflict aroused immense interest at both local and national levels, yet it is now sufficiently remote from our concerns to provide a revealing window into Victorian souls. Would Birmingham today brim with controversy, as in 1880, on whether the town hall should accommodate Sunday evening lectures? Do modern Banbury's leading citizens clarify their mutual relationships (amid great drama) through debating whether to petition parliament against Sunday postal deliveries?[3] The conflict between religion and recreation was exciting if only because recreational trends were not yet clear. Would extended leisure and the decay of older rural sports produce a more sober and serious public? Or would new and equally frivolous, even brutal, recreations take their place? A great deal seemed to hang on the outcome.

If Bristol's census of recreation in 1881-2 is any guide, excitement also prevailed here because of the near stalemate between the two sides. 104,557 people in a total population of 206,513 entered drinking places on the first Saturday night in 1882, whereas total religious attendance (morning and evening) on 30 October 1881 was 116,148.[4] Competition

---

[1] This chapter originated in a contribution to the Past and Present Conference in London on popular religion on 7 July 1966. A shortened version of it was published in *Past and Present*, no. 38 (Dec. 1967), which provides the basis of this chapter. But there have been substantial additions to it, as well as alterations in style and arrangement.   [2] LDOS *Occasional Paper*, Mar. 1877, p. 562.
[3] A. W. W. Dale, *Life of R. W. Dale of Birmingham* (2nd ed., 1899), pp. 406-9, 413; *Banbury Guardian*, 20 Dec. 1849, p. 2.
[4] *Nonconformist and Independent*, 2 Feb. 1882, pp. 106, 108.

was heightened by the fact that nineteenth-century churches and chapels were very much involved in the recreation business. Not only was the sheer joy of religious activity relished by some for its own sake; religious institutions sponsored many recreations that would now be seen as purely secular in nature—libraries, youth clubs, women's meetings, thrift clubs, athletic functions, holiday outings, Sunday schools, and choirs. So central to the singing world were Late-Victorian Lancashire chapels that operatic impresarios toured them in their search for talent.[5]

Recalling his youth as the son of a Victorian minister, E. E. Kellett in 1936 describes how the chapel 'took, by itself, the place now hardly filled by theatre, concert-hall, cinema, ball-room, and circulating-library put together. Here were all things required for social intercourse: recitals, songs, lectures with or without the lantern, authorized games, and talk. It was a liberal education.'[6] The attractions held out by pubs and chapels grew so vigorously that they split off from the parent body and diversified into distinct institutions— the chapels generating separate choirs, schools, sports clubs, and youth organizations just as the pubs generated distinct music-halls, debating clubs, political organizations, and pleasure-grounds. But in the Mid-Victorian period, this outcome could hardly have been predicted.

Such vigorous competition inevitably brought to the surface those deep-rooted polarities in British life associated with Anglican versus nonconformist, rough versus respectable, provincial versus Londoner, town-dweller versus countryman, puritan versus pleasure-lover—not to mention the more universal polarities of male versus female, old versus young, intellectual versus the mass. Experience at work of course nourished class polarities reflecting access to control. over the means of production, but social alignments at work and play were by no means exactly superimposed. As one historian has pointed out, popular radicalism 'was the product of the leisure of Saturday night and Sunday morning, the

---

[5] City of London Polytechnic: Teresa Billington-Greig MSS, file labelled 'Schooldays—Family Life—Her Parents', mentions an impresario's approach to her father, chief tenor in his church.

[6] E. E. Kellett, *As I Remember* (1936), p. 121.

pothouse and the chapel, not of the working week'.[7] The relationship between recreation and social class is discussed here partly to illustrate how an abundance of conflicts within a society may actually help to integrate it; the members of any one social class were cross-pressured in such a way as to ensure that nineteenth-century Britain was 'sewn together by its inner conflicts'.[8] This theme can be elaborated through discussing three humanitarian movements: the Lord's Day Observance Society [LDOS], the temperance movement, and the RSPCA. Selected aspects of each of these campaigns will be analysed in this order.[9]

Two subsidiary themes intrude themselves. Historical debate on nineteenth-century state intervention tends to focus on social rather than moral reform, and so neglects areas where *laissez-faire* was a genuinely popular cause; it therefore becomes difficult to see how the Conservative and Liberal parties before the advent of the welfare state ever acquired a popular following. The answer of course partly lies in argument over foreign affairs, but also in the fact that sections of both parties could often mobilize a popular following against the moral interventionism of the other. A second theme is the relationship between nineteenth-century humanitarianism and popular religion. Church historians often look out at the masses through the deanery window, yet here we encounter religion at the levels of mass conduct and belief. By espousing restrictions which alienated the masses from religion, and by causing the churches to diversify their activities in the pursuit of recruits, the churches' recreational pretensions probably contributed towards that secularizing trend which lies behind any discussion about

[7] J. R. Vincent, *The Formation of the Liberal Party 1857–1868* (1966), p. 79.

[8] E. A. Ross, quot. in L. Coser, *Functions of Social Conflict* (1956), p. 77.

[9] The discussion which follows is based on the annual reports of the LDOS and RSPCA, together with their publications, and on my *Drink and the Victorians. The Temperance Question in England, 1815–1872* (1971). For sabbatarianism, see J. Wigley, *The Rise and Fall of the Victorian Sunday* (Manchester, 1980), though on pp. 111, 183, it makes criticisms of this essay's earlier published version which either attribute to me views which I do not recognize, or which are unsupported by any evidence or argument marshalled there. There are two somewhat unsatisfactory books on the RSPCA—E. G. Fairholme and W. Pain, *A Century of Work for Animals* (2nd ed., 1934) and A. W. Moss, *Valiant Crusade* (1961).

leisure patterns. Religion and recreation had begun to compete not just for time, but in values; and we now know that
the values associated with secularized mass entertainment
eventually triumphed. An initial description of the three
movements under discussion will be followed by analysis of
their class basis of support, then of the class basis of their
opponents, and then some conclusions will be drawn.

I

The attacks on sabbath-breaking, intemperance, and animal
cruelty all feature in the Vice Society's *Address to the Public*
of 1803, but they were soon taken up by distinct movements
—by the LDOS, founded in London in 1831; by the temperance movement, originating after 1829 in American influence
over English philanthropists; and by the RSPCA, founded in
London in 1824. All three movements were predominantly
evangelical in origin and aim. The LDOS was run entirely
by Anglicans; with Lord Shaftesbury as its most prominent
supporter, it held firmly to the Bible amid the perilous forces
of infidelity and popery, hoping that if Sunday were preserved for religion, the old Protestantism would survive into
a vastly changed world.

The other two movements were more progressive in outlook. The first national temperance organization, the British
and Foreign Temperance Society, attacked only spirit-
drinking, and was supported in the 1830s by bishops,
admirals, philanthropists, aristocrats, and nonconformists.
It was soon ousted by the more radical Preston-based teetotallers like Joseph Barker or John Finch, and the 1860s
whose radical working-class following alienated many early
evangelical sympathizers. But the temperance movement at
no stage officially encouraged self-confessed infidel teetotalers like Joseph Barker or John Finch, and the 1860s
saw the return of an upper-class respectability which had
departed in the late 1830s. This new move—led by Dean
Close, Frederick Temple, and Henry Manning--ensured the
Late-Victorian prosperity of denominational temperance
organizations like the Church of England Temperance
Society. The temperance society therefore eventually became

a valued adjunct of church and chapel, and was condemned by secularists accordingly. Yet the temperance movement's capacity for uniting all denominations behind an exhilarating moral crusade involved a tendency, dangerous to religion in the longer term, to push into the background alarming intellectual and theological doubts. Its Mid- and Late-Victorian meliorism in effect appropriated the outlook of its many Early-Victorian freelance secularist fellow-travellers, but by then, of course, the radical working man had begun to move on further.

The RSPCA was likewise supported by Christians partly for Christian purposes. Its founders included penal reformers and opponents of slavery; it thrived on information supplied by rural clergymen, and bishops held forth at its annual meetings. Here too the ultimate aim was, among others, to convert the masses, however indirectly. 'It is not merely for animals that this Society is instituted', said Bishop Lonsdale of Lichfield at the annual meeting of 1866: 'but it is for ourselves.'[10] The Society hoped eventually to civilize manners, and hence incline the masses towards religion.

These movements used similar methods of agitation. All three regarded example-setting by the rich as at least their initial ideal. The LDOS was bitterly disappointed when the Queen encouraged Sunday bands at Windsor; Henry Solly, Samuel Morley, and Dean Close all became teetotallers to help their weaker brethren; and 1862 saw the Earl of Essex realizing in Bond Street the RSPCA's ideal by intervening personally to defend a horse against cruel whipping. All three educated the public through their periodicals, tracts, and petitions, but the role of the branch differed in each case. Sabbatarian enthusiasm was worked up by the LDOS travelling clerical secretary, but local branches were little more than *ad hoc* groups mobilized for petitioning and fundraising purposes by rural clergymen when required. In the temperance movement the itinerant lecturer was of more central importance, founding local temperance societies which produced petitions when necessary, but which also assumed the continuous role of providing supporters with wholesome recreation. Central control was stronger within

[10] RSPCA *A.R., 1866*, p. 33; cf. *20th A.R., 1846*, pp. 23–4.

the RSPCA, whose branches emerged more slowly and never acquired the temperance society's continuous recreational role.

The three movements diverged somewhat in their attitude to legislation. Prosecution was vigorously pursued by the sabbatarians only in the few disastrous months during 1870-1 when the Revd Bee Wright was active in London. Private conduct was unmolested, however—public desecration of the Sabbath being the sabbatarian bugbear. Effort concentrated on getting divine commandments embodied in national legislation. Temperance reformers repudiated the Vice Society's policy of prosecuting the sinner; instead they encouraged the individual to reclaim himself, and pitied the drunkard as victim of a society which surrounded him with temptations. The contest between educators and prosecutors therefore took a different form here, centring on attitudes to the drink trade. Whereas the 'moral suasionists' wanted to destroy the trade by recruiting the number of abstainers and so syphoning off its custom, the prohibitionists—mobilized from 1853 in the United Kingdom Alliance—formed local auxiliaries which did not require abstinence from their members and which frequently supplanted the older, and abstaining, temperance society. Like the sabbatarians, prohibitionists sought to embody their values in symbolic national legislation which would in itself be educational in its effect; but neither group gave much thought to questions of practical enforcement. Both were accused of seeking merely to evade complicity in the evils they attacked, but both were groping towards a more sophisticated view of the relationship between personal conduct and environmental pressure.

The prohibitionists campaigned for the 'Permissive Bill', which would have gradually introduced their reform by ratepayer majorities. But as they never got the bill through parliament, ratepayers never had a chance of implementing it, and prohibitionists were never therefore required to outlaw the drink manufacturer and retailer, though through vigilance committees and influence in local government they could often harass the trade on details. By contrast the RSPCA was faced with enforcement problems from the start.

At first it concentrated on prosecution, but during the 1850s its educationists prevailed over its prosecutors. By merely prosecuting, said one educationist, 'you punish the individual, but you do not take care of the animal'. At the annual meeting of 1876, Ruskin could still complain that 'our action has been a little too much in duty in the police court and not enough in the cottage', and prosecution remained important in the Society's work.[11] But by the late 1860s, educational effort absorbed more and more of its energies. The purely educational periodical *Animal World* was launched in 1869, and Baroness Burdett-Coutts's Ladies' Committee began distributing prizes and literature in 1870. Prize-givings gradually supplanted the speeches at annual meetings, and were watched by thousands of children. By 1901 as many as 195,796 essays were being submitted, and by 1892 800 'Bands of Mercy' had been set up—aiming, like the temperance movement's 'Bands of Hope' (launched in 1847), to recruit the younger generation for humanity.

All three movements sought at least the appearance of national coverage, but contrasted somewhat in their regional basis. Sabbatarianism was particularly strong in rural Wales and Scotland, though the LDOS was based on London and depended primarily on English support, especially south of a line from Boston to Gloucester. Of its 196 English branches in 1870, 124 were south of this line, and of these 38 were in the Greater London area. Distribution was somewhat random, several branches being located in small villages, but the south-coast resorts were well represented. Thirty-eight of its fifty branches in 1901 were south of the Boston–Gloucester line.

By contrast, temperance zeal flourished best in the north of England, which supported two organizations with national pretensions after 1853—the prohibitionist United Kingdom Alliance at Manchester, and the moral-suasionist British Temperance League, based for thirty-four years at Bolton, and after 1880 at Sheffield. The movement was also relatively strong in Wales and Scotland. The only large national temperance organization based on London after the demise of the (anti-spirits) British and Foreign Temperance Society in

[11] Danieli, in RSPCA *28th A.R., 1854*, p. 62; Ruskin, in *53rd A.R., 1877*, p. 38.

1848 was the Quaker-dominated and somewhat timid National Temperance League. Teetotalism had originally been forced on London by Lancashire orators, and in 1834 when there were 83,763 temperance-society members in England, Lancashire and Yorkshire alone accounted for 34,612. The Alliance always had difficulty in rousing Londoners. Based much more firmly on nonconformist support than either the RSPCA or the LDOS, it was strong in relation to population in Cornwall and north of the Trent. In absolute terms, the Alliance was overwhelmingly dependent on the north; in 1873–4, Manchester contributed more than three times as much to its funds as London.

Until the 1860s the RSPCA was preoccupied primarily with London, but under the energetic John Colam (secretary from 1862) it expanded rapidly, so that in 1868 twice as many of its convictions came from outside London as from inside. Of its 61 English branches in 1875, 26 were south of the Boston–Gloucester line; and of its 379 English branches in 1900, 230 were south of this line. The RSPCA thus eventually succeeded in gaining a national coverage more uniform in relation to population than either sabbatarians or temperance reformers.

The collaborative impact made by the three movements amounted to more than the sum of its parts, for all three combined to attack that recreational network which embraced gambling, adultery, drinking, cruel sports, sabbath-breaking, and blasphemy. All these sins were rife at the racecourse, the pub, the theatre, the 'feast', and the fair, and religious conversion often entailed a simultaneous abandonment of them all. Hippolyte Taine, when returning to London from the Derby in the 1860s, saw 'drunks in the road the whole way back; at eight that night they were still to be seen at Hyde Park Corner, reeling about and being sick'.[12] Sabbatarians frequently attacked cruel sports and drunkenness, especially on Sunday; indeed the Sunday-closing movement grew out of their collaboration with temperance reformers. Again, early teetotallers strongly attacked the cruel sports so often promoted by drinksellers. Two early teetotal societies met in converted cockpits; and as

---

[12] H. Taine, *Notes on England* (ed. and tr. E. Hyams, 1957), p. 36.

humanitarians, prominent teetotallers naturally defended animals too.

The arrest statistics for England and Wales reveal the major impact these movements were making, though they were not responsible for all these arrests, and the temperance movement directly for none.

Table of Arrests for Three Types of Moral Offence: 1866-1906[13]

Offences against	Sentence	1866	1876	1886	1896	1906
Lord's Day	Fine	374	458	2,083	3,516	5,263
Observance Act	Prison	6	3	3	–	–
	Discharge	71	73	37	56	65
	Other	35	22	9	21	5
	Total	486	556	2,132	3,593	5,333
Animal Cruelty	Fine	3,226	5,698	5,648	9,325	9,651
Acts	Prison	224	326	184	225	215
	Discharge	1,082	1,875	1,764	3,353	3,259
	Other	97	261	275	16	38
	Total	4,629	8,160	7,871	12,919	13,163
Licensing Acts	Fine	61,658	158,987	135,937	155,042	184,152
(drunkenness	Prison	9,341	23,665	8,017	7,148	7,258
clauses)	Discharge	29,209	19,730	17,591	24,562	19,012
	Other	4,160	3,185	3,594	506	1,071
	Total	104,368	205,567	165,139	187,258	211,493

Alone of the three, the RSPCA boosted the total with its own system of enforcement, with inspectors mounting from three in 1837 to 120 in 1897. Its prosecutions mounted dramatically with each decade.[14]

1830-9	1,357
1840-9	2,177
1850-9	3,862
1860-9	8,846

[13] Judicial Statistics, sample years, *Parl. Papers*, 1867 (3919), LXVI, p. 32; 1877 (C.1871), LXXXVI, p. 32; 1887 (C.5155), XC, p. 32; 1898 (C.8755), CIV, pp. 76-7; 1908 (Cd.3929), CXXIII, pp. 72-3. Figures under 'prison' include reformatory detention.

[14] RSPCA *77th A.R., 1901*, p. 166.

1870-9	23,767
1880-9	46,430
1890-9	71,657

Politicians soon became responsive to such co-ordinated pressure.

II

Narrowing the focus to the class basis of these three movements, the LDOS attracted very few aristocrats, and was not among Exeter Hall's more popular causes. Its local secretaries were usually clergymen, and in 1840 its members had to subscribe at least 10s. a year. Its local impact often relied on support from interested parties among the well-to-do. Its petitions could mobilize rural religious opinion and swamp the antisabbatarianism of London and the provincial towns. Yet sabbatarians attracted some genuine working-class support, not only from the status considerations affecting the 'respectable poor',[15] but from sheer self-interest; working men feared that a 'free Sunday' would eventually cause only six days' wages to be given for seven days' work. The former Chartist Robert Lowery in 1856 urged working men to guard their Sunday as 'the "Magna Charta" of all your rights and liberties'.[16] Cabmen, postmen, railway workers, and hairdressers had everything to gain from sabbatarian restriction. With LDOS encouragement, 2,344 out of 6,211 London cabs held six-day licences by 1865. Here was a firm basis for alliance between evangelicals and working men, consolidated by sabbatarian support for the Saturday half-holiday. The LDOS saw itself as defending employees' leisure-time against employers' rapacity, and in the 1840s it scorned that political economy 'which it is the disgrace of the present age to view as coincident with political morality'.[17] Its contest after 1855 with the antisabbatarian

---

[15] M. E. Loane, *Neighbours and Friends* (1910), p. 90.

[16] *Robert Lowery. Radical and Chartist* (ed. B. Harrison and P. Hollis, 1979), p. 46, cf. p. 169; Lowery's attack on the 1855 Sunday Trading riots is in *Proceedings at the Annual Conference of the . . . London Temperance League* (1855), p. 17 (British Library shelf-mark, PP 1047 o).

[17] LDOS, *12th A.R., 1843*, p. 16; cf. *7th A.R., 1838*, pp. 62-3; *10th A.R., 1841*, p. 20.

National Sunday League—many of whose members had been Anti-Corn-Law Leaguers—involved a struggle between protection and free trade. There was always a strain of social paternalism in the LDOS, whose secretary in 1883 said that housing reform and the Sunday closing of public houses would do more to elevate the masses than the Sunday opening of museums.[18]

The LDOS always made much of its popular support, distributing prizes in 1852 to working men for essays on the Sunday question. Speakers at its annual meeting of 1857 included a potter, and the platform of an Exeter Hall sabbatarian meeting in 1866 sported a former soldier, a butcher, a scavenger, and a sewer-flusher. When Sunday postal services were withdrawn in June 1850, about eighty postmen attended the Revd Canon Stowell's church to return thanks for their freedom; their example was followed by sixty-five Liverpool letter-carriers. Parliament soon recanted, however, and sabbatarians in 1866 were still lingering over the frequent illness and death of overworked postmen; Post Office profits were, they insisted, 'the price of blood'.[19] By 1851 several towns had formed working men's sabbatarian associations, and these eventually united into the Working Men's Lord Day Rest Association [WMLDRA]. Its membership was open to all who could subscribe a shilling a year. By 1866 it had several London branches, and outposts in Bristol, Newcastle, and among postmen in Birmingham, Liverpool, Coventry, Worcester, and Manchester; in that year it distributed nearly half a million publications. Anti-sabbatarians denied that it contained genuine working men. Its secretary in 1895 had to admit that of 1,648 subscriptions in 1894, 592 came from ladies and 156 from clergymen, but he claimed that working men contributed many of the 940 subscriptions between 1*s.* and 5*s.* Pressed further, he confessed that 'the working people are not accustomed to give much money to objects of this sort, and although they value the Sunday, yet we could not carry on our work

[18] *Sunday Review*, Oct. 1883, p. 12.
[19] W[orking] M[en's] L[ord's] D[ay] R[est] A[ssociation], *9th A.R., 1866*, p. 4.

vigorously unless we had got the support of others'.[20]
Clearly the Association depended on subscriptions and
leadership from above, like the Operative Anti-Corn-Law
Associations and the many other working-class bodies mobilized by predominantly middle-class reforming movements.

Yet there was a genuine coincidence of interest between
sabbatarians and working men who feared exploitation, as
several labour leaders testified; George Potter in 1872, for
instance, and Henry Broadhurst, who in a parliamentary
debate on Sunday opening in 1882 'implored the House not
to deprive the working man of the sublime satisfaction and
advantage of having rest one day in the week, but to let him
feel that for 24 hours in the week all men were equal'.[21] In
the evangelical periodical *The Rock*, Broadhurst ridiculed
many of the arguments for Sunday opening. 'I have some
religious feeling in the matter', he said; 'the first condition
of spiritual welfare must be some kind of decent material
life and leisure'. He pointed out that Lord Dunraven, the
National Sunday League's champion in the House of Lords,
was also a member of the Liberty and Property Defence
League, a body which detested the trade-union movement;[22]
the antisabbatarians did not recover from Broadhurst's attack
till the 1890s. In 1899 another labour leader, John Burns, in
a deputation against Sunday newspapers, urged the Home
Secretary 'to stand between the boys and the girls, and the
newsagents, and two or three greedy men who, in their
desire to compete with each other, were prepared to
introduce a system which was the beginning of industrial
barbarism'.[23]

Popular sabbatarianism did not necessarily spring from
religious zeal. Broadhurst held liberal religious views on the
Sunday question, and in 1883 stressed that he did not
personally support any sabbatarian organizations. Again,
John Burns was a freethinker, and in 1896 publicly supported

[20] S[elect] C[ommittee] of the H[ouse] of L[ords] on the Lord's Day Act,
Parl. Papers, 1895 (H.L.178), VI, QQ.2269–75; cf. *Free Sunday Advocate.* Aug.
1895, p. 14.
    [21] Potter, in LDOS *Quarterly Publication*, Mar. 1873, p. 277; Broadhurst, in
Free Sunday Advocate, July 1882, p. 6.
    [22] *The Rock*, 30 Mar. 1883, p. 200.
    [23] LDOS, *68th A.R.*, appendix, pp. 5–6.

the Sunday opening of museums and art galleries. Lord Shaftesbury was a deeply religious sabbatarian who acknowledged the movement's dependence on secular motive at the LDOS's annual meeting of 1871; 'we have not to deal with Christian people', he said, 'we have to deal with millions of un-Christian people'. At the annual meeting of 1880 he regretted that the Sabbath was now defended only by secular arguments; of the 30,000 working people who petitioned against the Sunday opening of Bethnal Green Museum, he thought that 'not more than 5,000 were actuated by any other feeling than that, if Sunday were lost as a day of rest, it would soon be thrown into the category of working days'.[24] As soon as the work-free Sunday could be safely defended by secular argument alone, popular support for the LDOS was likely to die away. Much of it probably stemmed from a desire to ensure that if Sunday work was required, it should be compensated by higher pay or by week-day leisure.

Like the LDOS, the temperance movement enjoyed much popular support. It began as a highly respectable anti-spirits movement designed to retain the moral initiative for the upper crust, but the 1830s saw a series of schisms in which working men declared for teetotalism, and the anti-spirits movement eventually died in 1848. The 'Seven Men of Preston', among the first publicly to sign the teetotal pledge, were of humble origin—cheesemonger, carder, clogger, roller-maker, plasterer, shoemaker, and tailor. The very word 'teetotal' was first applied to total abstinence from all intoxicants by a reformed plasterer. Teetotallers transformed temperance meetings from occasional gatherings of influential local worthies, summoned to discuss ways of elevating their inferiors, into counter-attractive functions which enabled working men to insulate themselves from public-house temptation. Teetotallers prided themselves on being able to reclaim the reprobate; Father Mathew in Ireland after 1839 enrolled teetotallers in hundred of thousands.

The movement's founders were alarmed by this moral initiative rising from below, particularly when it was joined

[24] LDOS, *Quarterly Publication*, Oct. 1871, p. 164; Oct. 1880, p. 813; cf. *Free Sunday Advocate*, Apr. 1881, supplement, p. 7.

with political radicalism in Henry Vincent's Teetotal Chartist movement of 1840-1.[25] The teetotal movement appealed strongly to the working-class desire for self-dependence, self-education, and respectability; it attracted such ardent self-helpers as John Cassell, Robert Lowery, George Howell, Thomas Burt, John Burns, Benjamin Lucraft, and Keir Hardie. The Early-Victorian teetotaller was not George Orwell's contemptible 'cap-touching type—the type who tells you oilily that he is "Temperance" and votes Conservative'.[26] He was often a rugged self-reliant, and progressive individualist, genuinely attached like so many working men to Gladstonian Liberalism. The former Chartists Patrick Brewster, John Fraser, and William Lovett all supported the United Kingdom Alliance from the start, and Lovett in 1870 defended prohibition in a series of articles for the *Alliance News* as 'the greatest and most needed of all reforms'.[27] Here was one of the popular pressure groups which joined nonconformists to labour leaders, and whose faith in popular moral idealism led it to champion franchise extension in the 1860s. Its leaders made crucially important gifts to the Reform League; 'let there be any extension of the franchise', it declared in 1859, 'that shall make the registration spoon dip low enough to take up the cream of the working classes, and we shall sweep all before us in the House of Commons'.[28]

Yet the growth of Garibaldian teetotal lifeboat crews in the 1860s was one of the last occasions in the temperance movement when working men took the initiative. Late-Victorian temperance drifted into providing nonconformists with a mere substitute for a social policy, and Catholics with an agency for improving the image of Irish labourers; Manning believed that his temperance activities had given him the hold over the London dockers which enabled him to end the Dock Strike of 1889,[29] but the former Chartists

---

[25] On this see my 'Teetotal Chartism', *History*, June 1973.

[26] G. Orwell, *The Road to Wigan Pier* (Penguin ed., 1962), pp. 74-5.

[27] *Alliance News*, 16 Apr. 1870, p. 124.

[28] *Alliance Weekly News*, 7 May 1859, p. 781.

[29] St. Mary of the Angels, Bayswater, Manning Papers: 1890 Memoranda, p. 100. For a general discussion, see A. E. Dingle and B. H. Harrison, 'Cardinal Manning as Temperance Reformer', *Historical Journal*, 1969, pp. 485-510.

who toasted Gladstone in lemonade[30] were beginning to look antique. The 1890s saw several public controversies between Socialists and teetotallers, and Harry Quelch unravelled the false economics of prohibitionism in damaging newspaper articles.[31] Victor Grayson twice interrupted debates on the Licensing Bill in 1908 to demand that parliament deal with the unemployment problem; 'there are thousands of people dying in the streets while you are trifling with this Bill', he told an angry House. Yet many Labour Party pioneers recommended temperance, if only as an aid to their movement, and fully supported the bill in 1908; Grayson seems to have been addressing them when leaving the House after his first interruption: 'you are traitors to your class. You will not stand up for your class. You traitors.'[32]

The RSPCA was relatively popular with the rich, relatively weak with the poor. Respectable working men intensely disliked brutal sports, but they also disliked the meddling image and aristocratic flavour of the RSPCA; they wanted to elevate working men, not prosecute them. The Society owed little to popular radicalism, much to the sentimental love for animals prevalent among the rich, particularly among women, who supplied 470 of its 739 nineteenth-century legacies.[33] By 1832 the Society's patrons already included seven Earls, one Marquess, and six other peers; in 1867 Dr Bradford found a hundred aristocrats among RSPCA subscribers.[34] The desire to hob-nob with aristocrats and royalty packed RSPCA annual meetings, and full-page photographs of aristocrats graced its annual reports in the

[30] E. P. Thompson, 'Homage to Tom Maguire', in J. Saville and A. Briggs (eds.), *Essays in Labour History* (1960), p. 288.

[31] e.g. E. Evans and J. M. Skinner, *Official Report of a Public Debate on the Direct Veto Bill . . . 1893* (Chatham, n.d.); H. Hibbert and H. Quelch, *Would Universal Teetotalism Tend to Lower Wages? A Public Debate . . . Lincoln . . . 1897* (n.d.). For Quelch's articles, see his 'Socialism and Temperance Reform', in his *Literary Remains* (ed. E. Belfort Bax, 1914); also his 'Boots or Beer? and the Economic Necessity of Waste', in *Social–Democrat*, 15 June 1908. See also my *Drink and the Victorians*, pp. 391–405, and pp. 201, 203–4 below.

[32] *H. C. Deb.*, 16 Oct. 1908, c.631; 15 Oct. 1890, c.497; cf. *Justice*, 21 Mar. 1908, p. 6.

[33] All legacies listed in RSPCA *77th A.R., 1901*, pp. 35 ff. See also J. Obel-kevich, *Religion and Rural Society: South Lindsey 1825–1875* (Oxford, 1976), p. 41.

[34] Bradford, in RSPCA *A.R., 1867*, p. 50.

1890s, when one could neither become a member for less than 10/6 per year, nor a life member for less than ten guineas. With such ample support higher up, the Society never needed to adjust its tactics so as to mobilize its full potential lower down.

III

While some working men openly supported two of these movements, and sympathized with the over-all objective of the third, others opposed all three. Some working men felt that the LDOS was depriving them of their traditional recreations without providing any alternative beyond church-going. Sabbatarian restriction seemed irrelevant to the most urgent needs of contemporary society, and G. J. Harney, breaking up a sabbatarian meeting at Carlisle in 1839, claimed that the sabbatarian religion was 'fear God, honour the Queen, and work for your tyrants'. The coal-dealer William Pritchard at Banbury's meeting on the Sunday question in 1849 hinted that sabbatarian attacks on Sunday postal deliveries would deprive the working man of his Sunday newspaper 'whereby he learns what a slave he is made'.[35] Sunday newspapers were major organs of working-class opinion at the time.

Sabbatarian restrictions weighed particularly heavily on the poor because, in contrast to their superiors, they spent much of their lives in public. While their clubs and homes gave the rich independent facilities for recreation, food-preparation, and travel, the poor relied on public facilities which were subject to legislative restriction. Radicals on the watch for hypocrisy and self-righteousness spotlighted the bellringers, coachmen, and servants whose Sunday labours enabled the middle and upper classes to attend church. And while the rich could store up their week-end food supplies on Saturday, the London poor were not paid till Saturday night and could not keep food fresh in their insanitary homes; hence the flourishing Sunday trade of small food shops and stalls. Resentment at the class bias inherent in

[35] Harney, *Carlisle Journal*, 21 Dec. 1839, p. 3; Pritchard, *Banbury Guardian*, 20 Dec. 1849.

mounting sabbatarian legislation showed itself forcibly when crowds gathered in Hyde Park to shout 'Go to Church' at Sunday promenaders in June and July 1855.[36]

The respectable working man shared the sabbatarian's ideal of a work-free Sunday, but he did not normally favour legislating to ensure that the free time was devoted to religion. On the contrary, as an enthusiast for self-education he often recommended the Sunday opening of art galleries and museums. According to circumstances, he therefore features in both sabbatarian and antisabbatarian camps, and is more often motivated by secular expediency than by religious principle. The first petition for the Sunday opening of museums, drafted by Lovett, was presented in 1829. The *Poor Man's Guardian* whipped up antisabbatarian zeal in 1833-4 against Sir Andrew Agnew's Bills; the campaign was pressed by Hume and Molesworth, and Sunday lectures were given in London by Lovett and W. J. Fox. The anti-sabbatarian National Sunday League was formed in 1855 by London goldsmiths, wood-carvers, jewellers, and other craftsmen. Its founder was R. M. Morrell, a jeweller, and his League attracted support from Lovett, J. S. Mill, George Combe, and many writers, intellectuals, and artists.

By 1870 the League was strong enough to capitalize upon a second burst of popular antisabbatarian indignation. In that year, London sabbatarians encouraged a semi-literate nonconformist preacher the Revd J. Bee Wright, to prosecute several small traders of offending against an Act of Charles II. The policy of prosecuting small men while allowing the rich to retain their Sunday servants seemed unjust, and when four men were brought before a Hammersmith court for crying fish, muffins, and crumpets on a Sunday, one of the accused linked sabbatarian injustice with wider social grievances by claiming that he could not maintain his large family without working on Sundays. Furthermore, he said, the Act was antiquated: 'they were not living in the times of Adam and Eve, but of civilization'.[37] *Reynolds News*, always eager to expose 'one law for the rich, another for the poor',

---

[36] These incidents are discussed in my article, 'The Sunday Trading Riots of 1855', *Historical Journal*, 1965.

[37] LDOS, *Quarterly Publication*, Jan. 1870, pp. 108-9.

took up the matter in several editorials during 1871, and the National Sunday League tried unsuccessfully to prosecute the Lord Mayor's coachman for driving the Mayor to church on Sunday. Eventually the Home Secretary warned the LDOS against relying on prosecution, and Shaftesbury at its annual meeting of 1871 warned the Society that its policy might cause hostile mobs to gather in Hyde Park or Trafalgar Square. Bee Wright's retirement from sabbatarian crusading was hastened in June 1871 by the conviction of Mr Jackson, his witness, for being publicly drunk and incapable. Public meetings on the Sunday question in the early 1870s resulted in furious passion and sometimes in physical violence. The secretary of the LDOS, rising in 1873 to address a Sunday League meeting in Islington, was greeted by derisive shouts of 'Parson', 'Bee Wright', and 'You're not a working man', and the riotous debate in 1873 between the evangelical Revd H. S. Cooke and Mr Lloyd Jones reveals the exasperation evoked in popular audiences by evangelical phraseology and bizarre sabbatarian arguments.[38]

To many working men, the sabbatarian outlook seemed antique, a Jewish shibboleth originating in an alien environment. 'The Jews knew nothing of railways or of our circumstances', argued Lloyd Jones in 1873, 'and the attempt to bind us by their regulations was a superstitious attempt.'[39] Such arguments attracted a most important group of working men, the secularists. Although a few liberal clergymen like Stewart Headlam, Septimus Hansard, H. R. Haweis, and Dean Stanley lent their support, the National Sunday League owed much to secularists, and embraced Bradlaugh's maxim 'a free Church in a free State, and a free Sunday for a free people'. In campaigning for the Sunday opening of art ' galleries, it was aiming to secularize both recreation and culture. Its faith in self-improvement blinded it to modern trends almost as completely as evangelicalism blinkered the LDOS; mass popular entertainment would frustrate the purposive, improving objectives of both, for the League never favoured Sunday theatres. Sabbatarians were running

---

[38] LDOS, *Quarterly Publication*, Mar. 1873, p. 279; *Free Sunday Advocate* Mar. 1873, p. 91.
[39] *Free Sunday Advocate*, Mar. 1873, p. 90.

up against socio-economic change in yet another respect by insisting on simultaneous weekly rest for all citizens, for urbanization, increased leisure, and cheaper travel were creating a mass recreational market which could be exploited only by people whose weekly work-rhythm, like that of the clergy, pulsated out of phase with that of their clientele. The trend has since gone further, with the continuous shift-working demanded by the increased cost and complexity of modern industrial processes.

The National Sunday League secured several parliamentary divisions on Sunday opening before gaining victory in 1896. This long delay owed something to the partial breakdown on this issue of the traditional Liberal alliance between non-conformists and free traders; free-trade principles might attract nonconformists in many spheres, but they seemed less attractive here. Nonconformist voluntarists could avoid having to choose between their free-trade and sabbatarian enthusiasms only by recommending Sunday observance on a voluntary basis. Yet here, as with the curbing of factory hours, legislative compulsion was arguably required to bring collective practice into accord with individual aspiration. This did not prevent the National Sunday League from being popular with many Liberal working men. George Odger, G. J. Holyoake, William Lovett, and George Howell were all Sunday openers; Thomas Burt became president of the Sunday Society in 1881; and both Will Crooks and John Burns defended Sunday opening in 1896. Nor were anti-sabbatarian numbers unimpressive. On 7 May 1876 a procession composed of 'the *élite* of mechanics' approached the British Museum to deliver a Sunday-opening petition; the procession stretched down Oxford Street from Oxford Circus almost to Hyde Park.[40] Neither side in the dispute, however, could rest its case on majority support, for as Holyoake pointed out, only a minority among working men would enter a museum on Sundays; it was 'a question of conscience to be decided, not by numbers, but by principle'.[41]

The League also promoted 'Sunday Evenings for the People' which in 1873 attracted over 24,000. The Sunday

[40] Ibid., 1 June 1876, p. 145.
[41] Ibid., Aug. 1884, p. 14.

Lecture Society was founded in 1869, F. J. Furnivall's Sunday Shakspere Society in 1873, and in 1875 the Sunday Society, designed to campaign among the well-to-do for the Sunday opening of art galleries. The League's Sunday excursions were patronized by 21,000 in 1869, and by 31,000 in 1890. The League's Sunday activities were inspired by that same defiance of superstition which motivated the London radicals of 1832 when they obtrusively feasted on the fast day ordained by the government to ward off cholera. Sabbatarians liked to think that excursionists were disreputable, yet such travels required both forethought and thrift. When the Banbury sabbatarian minister Joseph Parker accused Sunday excursionists in the 1850s of being 'the laziest, dirtyest, poorest and silliest of the working classes', ridicule from local secularist working men made his life intolerable.[42]

Pubs were so central to the life of the working man that temperance reformers inevitably faced formidable opposition. Mobs often broke up the meetings of pioneer teetotal lecturers, and the Hyde Park riots of 1855 forced a relaxation of licensing restriction and thereby furnished opponents of the temperance movement with an argument which they used with effect for decades. The *Daily Telegraph* warned H. A. Bruce in 1871 that unless he relaxed his proposed restrictions on London's opening hours 'we shall have street riots of the most formidable kind'.[43] 'I am just off to the Permissive Bill meeting', wrote H. J. Wilson to his sister in the same year, 'very doubtful if I shall get home with my skin complete.'[44] He had already been knocked on the head at an earlier temperance meeting in Sheffield. There were hostile riots against the Licensing Act of 1872 in several towns, and a prohibitionist meeting in Exeter in the same year culminated with the bursting of a flour-bag on the chest of the prohibitionist Bishop Temple.[45]

The Alliance denied that this was genuine working-class opinion; it came from 'rather the unworking classes . . . a

---

[42] B. S. Trinder, 'Joseph Parker, Sabbatarianism and the Parson's Street Infidels', *Cake and Cockhorse* (Banbury Historical Society), i, no. 3 (Jan. 1960).
[43] *Daily Telegraph*, 10 May 1871, p. 4; cf. ibid., 20 Apr. 1871 p. 5.
[44] W. S. Fowler, *A Study in Radicalism and Dissent* (1961) p. 26.
[45] E. G. Sandford (ed.), *Memoirs of Archbishop Temple* (1906), i p. 481.

crowd of roughs—a congregation of scamps'.[46] An unthinking traditionalism and even publicans' drink bribes certainly played a part; yet educated working men were also worried by temperance restriction, and raised several arguments against even its moral-suasionist phase. Francis Place and J. B. Leno thought the temperance movement had the effect of advertising working-class frailty. Place denounced the report of the parliamentary committee on drunkenness, chaired in 1834 by the pioneer temperance reformer J. S. Buckingham, as 'an attempt to stigmatise and debase the whole body of the working people'.[47] Unlike the committee, he believed that working people had become more sober during his lifetime. J. B. Leno despised the reformed drunkards who postured on teetotal platforms; he thought that their foolish speeches discredited their class.[48] Suspicion was heightened by observing the movement's scepticism towards Teetotal Chartism, in which working men sought sobriety on their own initiative; the official teetotal movement wanted teetotalism adopted only on physiological or moral grounds, not to embarrass the government by depriving it of revenue. Some working men saw teetotal pledge-signing as a confession of weakness; a real man should be capable of abstaining without surrendering his liberty. This ideal of the self-reliant individual, fearless of diverging from mass opinion, pervades Mill's *Liberty*.[49]

Secularists disliked the temperance movement's religious leadership; they wanted a sober working class, but without religious proselytism. National Sunday Leaguers claimed that genuine opponents of drunkenness would help them in getting Sunday counter-attractions to the drinking place.[50] Teetotal Chartists recruited several seceding working men who deplored the snobbery and restrictions on opinion they found in official temperance societies. The modern critique of temperance, founded on recognizing the importance of

[46] *Alliance News*, 13 June 1863, p. 188.
[47] BL Add. MS 27829, f.82 (Place Papers); the committee is discussed in my 'Two Roads to Social Reform. Francis Place and the "Drunken Committee" of 1834', *Historical Journal*, 1968.
[48] J. B. Leno, *The Aftermath* (1892), p. 38.
[49] e.g. *Odd-Fellow*, 12 Mar. 1842, p. 2.
[50] *Free Sunday Advocate*, 1 May 1876, p. 133.

environment as an influence on conduct, was rarely voiced. Whatever Owenites or Labour Party pioneers might feel privately about the aetiology of drunkenness, the need for sobriety in their own ranks was too urgent for them to denounce temperance advocates. Robert Owen supported Buckingham in 1834; Ernest Jones was among the many Chartists who often advocated abstinence and even prohibition; and Philip Snowden, despite powerfully criticizing the temperance movement at the outset of his career, preserved a lifelong loyalty to teetotalism. The most effective environmentalist critique came from a radical secularist G. J. Holyoake. Prefacing his attack with a key quotation from Comte—'nothing is destroyed until it is replaced'— he maintained that temperance reformers could not succeed till they provided improved non-alcoholic drinks and better recreations than the publican.[51]

Prohibition encountered a different set of objections. Working men's objections to H. A. Bruce's two restrictive Licensing Bills of 1871-2 applied more to prohibition. Sheffield's working-class hostility to the Permissive Bill, which Roebuck had mobilized in the 1860s, was revived in 1871-2 by J. W. Burns; two meetings on the question held in Paradise Square in April 1871 and August 1872 each attracted over 10,000. Sheffield's teetotal working men were outnumbered; when a local temperance advocate tried to address a meeting in 1872, 'a tremendous shout of derision arose from all parts of the square'.[52] London's working-class leaders were divided—Applegarth defending the 1871 Bill, and Robert Hartwell opposing it through the public-house meeting of a 'Public Rights Defence Committee' which threatened a hostile demonstration in Hyde Park.[53] Rival groups of working men interrupted each other's meetings in Manchester in 1871-2;[54] and whereas 10,170 Liverpool mechanics and 7,023 labourers had signed the local petition for the Permissive Bill in 1871, in 1872 working men gathered

[51] G. J. Holyoake, *The Social Means of Promoting Temperance* (1859).
[52] *Sheffield Daily Telegraph*, 27 Aug. 1872, p. 3.
[53] *Daily News*, 20 Jan. 1872, p. 6; *Alliance News*, 8 July 1871, p. 434.
[54] *Manchester Guardian*, 9 Apr. and 2 July 1872; *Morning Advertiser*, 5 July 1872, p. 3.

ominously at local anti-temperance public meetings.[55] At Maidstone in 1872, as in Hyde Park in 1855, a libertarian mob collaborated with the soldiery.[56]

Both 'class legislation' and 'liberty' arguments were brought against restriction. The *Bee-Hive*, organ of London trade unions in the 1860s, opposed prohibition because it seemed undemocratic to withdraw drink facilities from an area simply on a vote of householders; propertyless working men depended more than others on the drinking place. Besides, under a prohibition regime, householders would store intoxicants in their cellars, whereas working men would have to go without.[57] Liverpool publicans in placards against the Act of 1872 raised the cry 'one law for the rich . . .', as did a speaker at an Ipswich working men's meeting hostile to the new Act. Again, upper-class clubs were exempt from licensing regulations, and in 1872 anti-restrictionist crowds at Coventry, Cheltenham, and Exeter demonstrated outside them.[58] Furthermore the huge number of arrests for drunkenness, though not directly promoted by the temperance movement, owed something to the impatience with drunkenness encouraged by its propaganda, and seemed yet another example of upper-class hypocrisy. For as the Chartist Feargus O'Connor pointed out in 1838, the well-to-do either drank in private or were quietly shepherded home by the police and therefore seldom appeared in court at all.[59]

As for the proposal of 1871 to reinforce restriction with government public-house inspectors, this was to arouse traditionalist fears of spies or placemen among working people who were not yet conscious of the gains they might make through increased intervention by the state. A popular form of *laissez-faire* hindered all three of the movements

---

[55] *Liverpool Daily Post*, 15 May 1871, p. 7.

[56] *Licensed Victuallers Guardian*, 24 and 31 Aug. 1872; *Morning Advertiser*, 20 Aug. 1872, p. 2.

[57] *Bee-Hive*, 12 Mar. 1864, p. 4; 4 June 1864, p. 4; 20 May 1871, p. 9.

[58] *Liverpool Daily Courier*, 28 Oct. 1872, p. 5; J. T. Read at Ipswich, *Licensed Victuallers Guardian*, 21 Dec. 1872, p. 421; the demonstrations outside clubs are noted in *Licensed Victuallers Guardian*, 24 and 31 Aug. 1872, and *Licensed Victuallers Gazette*, 24 Aug. 1872, p. 140.

[59] *Northern Star*, 21 Apr. 1838, p. 6; cf. ibid., 24 Feb. 1838, p. 6; 31 Aug. 1839, p. 6; 30 Nov. 1839, p. 1.

under consideration. The more sophisticated objection, that licensing restriction promoted monopoly, was less frequently heard in 1871-2 than a blind distaste for state intervention in any form. Working men at Coventry and Ashton in autumn 1872, and at the Ipswich meeting, sang 'Britons never shall be Slaves'—as in Hyde Park in 1855.[60] The Tory radical populist J. R. Stephens effectively voiced these popular prejudices; he had attacked the temperance movement in all its phases—teetotalism in 1847 and 1848, Sunday closing in 1867, and Bruce's Licensing Bill in April 1871—in extraordinary rambling speeches full of colloquialisms, jokes, irrelevances, dialect terms, and local allusions. Bruce's proposal for inspectors in 1871 seemed to him a centralizing, meddling proposal; as he pointed out in 1867, the public house was 'every Englishman's freehold', 'as old as the hills, and . . . one of the institutions of the country'.[61] The proposed inspectors also angered working men in Bristol and Sheffield. 'Has free old England come to this', asked J. W. Burns, 'that the working classes must have their footsteps dogged by a continental system of spies?'[62] Stephens returned to the attack in October 1872 with a two-and-three-quarter-hour speech in Stalybridge town hall against the new Act. He exposed the fallacies of teetotalism and defended the popular right to hold trade-union meetings and to enjoy company in public houses.[63] During the next month an Ashton mob showed its teeth and besieged the home of the leading local temperance reformer Hugh Mason.

Of the three movements, perhaps the RSPCA was the least popular with working men. Between 1838 and 1841 it prosecuted 243 offenders; all but one of the 159 whose occupations are known were working men.[64] Full details of court cases were published as a long appendix to each

[60] *Licensed Victuallers Guardian*, 21 Dec. 1872, p. 421; *Ashton Reporter*, 9 Nov. 1872, p. 3.

[61] *Ashton Reporter*, 13 Apr. 1867, pp. 6-7; see also ibid., 30 Mar. 1867, p. 7; 29 Apr. 1871, p. 7; *National Temperance Advocate*, iv (1848), pp. 29, 38-42.

[62] *Sheffield and Rotherham Independent*, 2 May 1871, p. 7; *Western Daily Press*, 29 Apr. 1871, p. 3.

[63] *Ashton Reporter*, 26 Oct. 1872, p. 3.

[64] These figures are calculated from the lists of prosecutions in RSPCA *13th, 14th,* and *15th Annual Reports*.

annual report; these took up 41 of the 1842 report's 114 pages, for example, 43 of the 1860–1 report's 186. Although isolated middle-class offences were described, the general impression conveyed is one of widespread working-class brutality, though admittedly the most brutal of all the cases reported was committed by a prosperous merchant. These summaries show no curiosity about the accused, who is described in hostile terms as 'a brutal-looking fellow', 'a rough, dirty, brutal-looking fellow', or 'an extremely ill-looking fellow'—phrases culled at random from the reports for 1839 and 1857. Attempts to arrest working men for cruelty were often violently resisted.[65]

Gompertz urged London's animal lovers to avoid rebuking 'any offender before numerous others of his class,—a hackney-coachman before a stand of coachmen, or a drover in Smithfield, or even one of one class before numbers of the others, as they usually combine together'.[66] John Mansfield, the dog fancier, convicted in the 1840s for promoting a dog-fight in the Seven Dials, paid his £5 fine 'and, in less than five minutes, he was proceeding homeward, accompanied by a large fierce dog . . . and followed by hundreds of the lowest characters'.[67] When spectators at a Mile End dog-pit in the 1850s were eventually forced out into the street, the police were 'assailed by a shower of stones and brickbats, hurled at them by the mob, who had collected in great numbers'.[68]

RSPCA prosecutions caused working men to be punished for long-established practices. When Richard Pedrick, accused at Brixton of ill-treating a dog, heard the sentence of 20s. fine or fourteen days' hard labour, he 'cried and bellowed most outrageously'.[69] He and other working men were suffering for the humanitarian notions being pioneered by other social classes. Charles Escritt, accused of organizing a dogfight, said when arrested, 'there's always some busy devil in a town'.[70] The radical MP T. S. Duncombe, always

[65] e.g. RSPCA *Minutes No. 4*, pp. 31–2.
[66] L. Gompertz, *Fragments in Defence of Animals*, p. 87.
[67] RSPCA *20th A.R., 1846*, p. 79; cf. Hanworth, RSPCA *Minutes No. 2*, pp. 296–8; *The Times*, 18 Apr. 1838, p. 7.
[68] RSPCA *A.R. 1852*, pp. 73–4; A. W. Moss, *Valiant Crusade*, pp. 63–4.
[69] RSPCA *13th A.R., 1839*, p. 61.
[70] RSPCA *25th A.R., 1851*, p. 75.

well informed on working-class views, voiced Escritt's fears in parliament, and saw RSPCA support for the Slaughtering of Horses Bill of 1844 as 'alone . . . a sufficient reason for opposing it, as no encouragement ought to be given to societies for meddling with everybody's business but their own'. Radical working men at this time pinned their humanitarian hopes on education, not on prosecution, and were less preoccupied with animals than with the brutal flogging of human beings.[71]

The complaint of 'one law for the rich . . .' once more appears; the RSPCA was criticized for attacking the dog-fights and cock-fights of the poor, while ignoring the fox-hunting and game-shooting of the rich.[72] An interruptor pleaded unsuccessfully at the annual meeting of 1840 for horses ridden to death in steeplechases and for stags hunted to death in Windsor Park,[73] yet both sports were sometimes even publicly defended by RSPCA spokesmen;[74] T. F. Buxton's RSPCA connection did not intrude upon his game-shooting.[75] The Society did not protest when the Queen patronized stag and otter hunts;[76] even the LDOS showed greater moral courage than this. Still, the RSPCA could not move too far ahead of public opinion, which naturally extended its sympathy first to tame animals, and only later to animals in general. Furthermore by the 1860s the Society took pride in the fact that the decision to prosecute was not affected by the offender's social class,[77] and in 1863 it prosecuted the Marquess of Hastings for promoting cock-fights at Donington Hall. At all times the Society was prepared to prosecute in particularly brutal cases of hunting and steeplechasing.[78]

In reality the accusation of class bias ignores the classless

---

[71] Duncombe, *H. C. Deb.*, 24 July 1844, c.1334; cf. RSPCA *6th A.R., 1832*, p. 16 (interruption at the annual meeting); BL Add. MS 37775, p. 53; 37776, p. 72 (LWMA, 'Minute Books, Nos. 3 and 4').

[72] *Patriot*, 3 June 1844, p. 391; 17 June 1844, p. 423.

[73] RSPCA *14th A.R., 1840*, p. 40.

[74] e.g. RSPCA *A.R. 1867*, p. 40.

[75] C. Buxton, *T. F. Buxton*, p. 162.

[76] RSPCA *Minutes No. 5*, p. 299 (4 Nov. 1844); see also p. 91.

[77] RSPCA *A.R. 1866*, p. 33; cf. *52nd A.R.*, p. 24.

[78] e.g. RSPCA *A.R. 1870*, p. 22; *A.R. 1859*, p. 12.

nature of so many brutal sports at this time. The Local magistrates and police obstructed RSPCA attempts to suppress the Stamford bull-running in the 1830s; Londoners' interference with an ancient local festival was bitterly resented, and the Society had to rely on government troops.[79] Many Early-Victorian cock-fights were carefully and expensively organized, with county and even international matches. When RSPCA inspectors broke into them, wealthy individuals, farmers, and army officers were often found participating; for example, at a cock-fight in a Haymarket pub during 1865, they came upon a Captain Augustus Berkeley acting as chairman and referee.[80]

A more fundamental reason for working-class hostility to the RSPCA remains. James Deratt, accused of driving a horse in very poor condition, said 'he was very vexed to be obliged to drive the horse, but he had a large family, and if he had refused to drive it he should have been immediately discharged'.[81] The immediate responsibility for the animal was usually the working man's, but it was the owner whose conditions of employment and demands on his employee often made cruelty inevitable. Furthermore, working-class recreational cruelty, like working-class drunkenness, was far more likely to take place in the public places subject to regulation. Like most reforming organizations, the RSPCA naturally began by seizing upon the most obvious and immediate causes of the evil under attack—the drover with his stick, the coachman with his whip; time alone could reveal the more complex causes of cruelty. RSPCA supporters usually assumed that cruelty sprang from ignorance,[82] but R. Batson, at the annual meeting of 1836, showed more insight when he fixed upon the prevailing competitive spirit. 'Owing to this competition', he said, 'poor people are driven to make greater exertions to earn a subsistence, and these exertions are principally obtained from the animals under their charge.'[83]

The Society was very slow to adopt the remedies suggested

[79] There are excellent reports from Stamford in RSPCA, *Minutes No. 2* pp. 23, 201, 216-18.
[80] RSPCA, *A.R. 1865*, p. 132.
[81] RSPCA, *15th A.R., 1841*, p. 86.
[82] e.g. Bishop Lonsdale in RSPCA, *20th A.R., 1846*, p. 20.
[83] RSPCA, *10th A.R., 1836*, p. 40.

—state regulation of the number of passengers in horse-buses, special medical aid for the animals of the poor. Still, it eventually saw that employers must sometimes be punished for the cruelty of their employees, and in 1887 it noted proudly that 813 owners had been convicted for causing their servants to commit cruel acts.[84] The Society suffered from the fact that its critics were always moving on. Socialist humanitarians in the 1890s, for instance, claimed that 'so long as pecuniary profit and self-interest are accepted as the guiding principles of trade, it will remain impossible to secure a right treatment for animals' because 'economic necessity leaves no scope for humaneness'.[85] Edward Carpenter even saw vivisection as the capitalists' irrelevant and cruel way of grappling with the diseases which resulted from their own firms' pollution and disruption of the environment. Working men, he insisted, must stand by their fellow-victims of capitalism, the animals.[86]

IV

Karl Marx could hardly contain his contempt for these three movements. For him, 'members of societies for the prevention of cruelty to animals, temperance fanatics, hole-and-corner reformers of every imaginable kind' were diverting working people from their true interests and 'redressing social grievances in order to secure the continued existence of bourgeois society'.[87] Attempts at sabbatarian legislation in the 1850s constituted 'a conspiracy of the Church with monopoly capital'; the struggle against clericalism 'assumes the same character in England as every other serious struggle there—the character of a *class struggle* waged by the poor against the rich'.[88] No critique of Marx could rest securely on three brief and incidental remarks, but they are incisive enough to call for comment.

[84] RSPCA, *63rd A.R., 1887*, p. 132; cf. *76th A.R.*, p. 103.

[85] Anon., 'The Animal Question and the Social Question', *Hunanity*, Oct. 1898, p. 75.

[86] E. Carpenter, 'Vivisection and the Labour Movement', *Humanity*, Nov. 1895, p. 68.

[87] K. Marx, *Communist Manifesto* (ed. Laski, 1948), p. 154.

[88] *Marx and Engels on Britain* (Moscow, 1953), pp. 415, 417.

Humanitarian and sabbatarian reforms threatened the livelihood of only a few propertied people. They therefore flourished, whereas reforms directed at more central evils of industrialism—the weavers' proposal for a minimum wage, Robert Owen's evidence before poor-law inquiries, Prince Albert's advocacy of relieving unemployment through public works—were all rejected.[89] Humanitarians could hardly attack the very foundations of their subscribers' prosperity. The existence of a major evil does not, of course, justify the abandonment of campaigns against minor evils, especially if the latter are less closely related to the former than Marx supposed. But nineteenth-century humanitarian campaigns—peripheral in their concerns by twentieth-century materialist standards—certainly had the effect of diverting attention away from worse evils, while simultaneously lending property the appearance of virtue.

Yet it is dangerously exhilarating to attribute all society's evils to a single cause. Cruelty to animals stemmed partly from ancient rural customs and attitudes which were removable only through education, and which the industrialists themselves frequently repudiated; humanitarian values would have required deliberate propagation in nineteenth-century England even had Marx's utopia been realized there. Furthermore, humanitarians gradually began to relate their problem to wider considerations of social structure, or stimulated others into doing so. And the twentieth-century retreat of mass poverty has demonstrated the complexity of the relation between drunkenness, cruelty, and social structure; although improved social conditions have eliminated much drunkenness and cruelty, sadism and escapism persist not only in Western affluent societies but also in the Soviet Russia which once blamed alcoholism on Tsarist exploitation.[90]

Finally, these three movements appear 'hole-and-corner' only when viewed from Marx's peculiar perspective. He

[89] E. P. Thompson, *The Making of the English Working Class* (2nd ed., 1968), pp. 331, 333; Robert Owen, *Life* (1857), i, p. 133; F. C. Mather, in A. Briggs (ed.), *Chartist Studies* (1962, paperback ed.), p. 404.

[90] M. G. Field, 'Alcoholism, Crime and Delinquency in Soviet Society', in S. M. Lipset and N. J. Smelser (eds.), *Sociology. The Progress of a Decade* (New Jersey, 1961), p. 577.

rightly saw that they were blurring class divisions; but because he foresaw an era of mounting class conflict, he underestimated their historical significance. Furthermore, the alliance between sabbatarians, temperance reformers, and some groups of nineteenth-century working men was one among several factors preventing the struggle of poor against rich from ever assuming a uniformly anticlerical guise. And because Marx was primarily interested in the working-class critique of the nineteenth-century economic order, he failed to grasp the distinctly anti-industrial and traditionalist outlook of sabbatarian paternalism. Few movements have been more continuously out of sympathy with their times than the LDOS since its foundation; in so far as industrialists were interested in this question at all, they tended rather to support the Free Sunday.

All three movements had the effect of complicating class alignments by forcing the working men who opposed them into an alliance with other social classes. They divided the working class at several points—between nonconformists and secularists, radicals and traditionalists, autodidacts and illiterates, puritans and *bon viveurs*. The nineteenth-century attack on traditional recreations is perhaps better understood in terms of culture-conflict. Banded together in opposition to the humanitarians and the philanthropists were working men anxious to preserve their traditional entertainments and hostile to the cult of respectability; free traders opposed to state regulation; rural magistrates hostile to new-fangled and soft-headed humanitarian ideas exported from the Great Wen or Cottonopolis; drinksellers with all their local prestige; *bon viveurs* and traditionalists from every social class; army officers for whom manliness, drinking, and cruel sports went together; urban magistrates suspicious of private informers; aristocrats nostalgic for shared recreation between all social classes; sportsmen, racing men, and aristocrats seduced by 'low life'; people in all groups irritated at the righteous indignation displayed by nonconformist shopkeepers and sentimentalists from Exeter Hall. Recreational conflict was never precisely superimposed upon the conflict of interest between employer and employee. Besides, nineteenth-century class alignments were always complicated by the persistence of controversy over aristocratic values; these were particularly relevant to the humanitarian issue. *The Communist Manifesto* did not perhaps appreciate the full force—in the British context, at least—of its own analysis, whereby in the earlier stages of capitalism 'the proletarians do not fight their enemies, but the enemies of their enemies, the remnants of absolute monarchy, the land-owners, the non-industrial bourgeois, the petty bourgeoisie'.[91]

These were by no means the only nineteenth-century reforming movements to diversify class relationships. When militant puritanism erected screens between the theatre and the bar at the Empire Theatre, Leicester Square, in 1894, the London labour movement was divided on the issue and a young military cadet of good family, Winston Churchill, led an assault on the innovation. Sylvia Pankhurst, discussing women's suffrage, recalled that 'from first to last, its oppon-ents were mainly the professional Party politicians . . . the brewing interests, the wealthy unoccupied "men about town", and the naval and military officer class, all of whom feared that . . . the enfranchisement of women would really intro-duce a new era in politics'.[92] Her personal standpoint perhaps caused her to omit working-class anti-feminist pub-goers and trade unionists from her list. Class jealousies of course occasionally embarrassed these movements and even frag-mented them internally—dividing teetotal from anti-spirits societies, Teetotal Chartists from teetotallers, Sunday Society from National Sunday League. Nevertheless such divisions were either ephemeral or insignificant when seen against the long-term co-operation between members of all social classes which these movements inspired, both in opponents and sympathizers.

As for the two subsidiary themes illuminated by the nineteenth-century debate on religion and recreation, all three movements repudiated libertarian attitudes. 'The time will come', wrote Bentham, 'when humanity will extend

---

[91] *Communist Manifesto*, p. 130; cf. D. A. Hamer, *Liberal Politics in the Age of Gladstone and Rosebery. A Study in Leadership and Policy* (Oxford, 1972), p. 14.

[92] S. Pankhurst, *The Life of Emmeline Pankhurst* (1935), p. 25; see also R. S. Churchill, *Winston S. Churchill*, i (1966), pp. 232-4.

its mantle over every thing which breathes'; 'it is by the
grossest misunderstanding of the principles of Liberty', wrote
J. S. Mill, 'that the infliction of exemplary punishment on
ruffianism practised towards these defenceless beings has
been treated as a meddling by Government with things
beyond its province'.[93] In 1875, to the delight of prohibitionists, the *Examiner* cited the success of state intervention
against cock-fighting in refutation of Herbert Spencer's
minimal concept of the state.[94] In the recreational sphere,
radicals, free traders, Liberals, nonconformists, and working
men could all be found championing state intervention. Yet
in the same area *laissez-faire* prejudices enjoyed a popular
following which they did not always receive elsewhere.
J. S. Mill's regulationist approach to cruelty did not apply
over the whole range of moral conduct, which he thought
could best be fostered through leaving the citizen free to
manage his own affairs. To the publicans' delight, he parted
company with Liberal moralistic interventionism; when listing unjust infringements of individual liberty, he began with
sabbatarian and temperance legislation.[95] This brought him
—together with individualist radicals like Roebuck and a
few Liberationist nonconformists—into an incongruous
political alliance with traditionalist Conservatives and
working men. Recreational issues thus cut across political-
party as well as social-class alignments.

Finally, all three movements probably achieved the reverse
of their intention by losing the churches more recruits than
they gained. They accentuated the suspicion, widespread
among working people, that religious activity was a cloak
for upper-class self-interest, by creating an appearance of
'one law for the rich and another for the poor'. Thomas
Wright found this the greatest of the 'grievance ideas' prevailing among working people, and cited Sunday-trading
legislation as his first example.[96] In 1866 Samuel Pope,
a leading prohibitionist, gave a lame answer to this type of

---

[93] Both quoted in H. S. Salt, *Animals' Rights. Considered in Relation to Social Progress* (1892), pp. 6, 126.
[94] *Alliance News*, 8 May 1875, p. 296, citing *Examiner*, 24 Apr. 1875.
[95] J. S. Mill, *Liberty* (Everyman ed., 1960), pp. 144–6.
[96] T. Wright, *Our New Masters* (1873), pp. 153 ff.

objection; admitting that prohibition would inconvenience the poor more than the rich, he was content to assert that 'the truth was the law was not unequal. It was the social condition that was unequal.'[97] Yet in a society where living conditions contrasted so markedly from class to class, justice could not be done simply be applying the same law right across the board. The attempt to moralize recreation also made nineteenth-century religion seem negative and pharisaical,[98] and nourished secularist prejudice. Too rarely were alternative recreations provided which were as attractive as those under attack; humanitarians often disapproved of light-hearted recreation altogether. It was the sporting aristocrat and the publican-entrepreneur, not the humanitarian, who filled the recreational gap created by the decline of the old leisure patterns. If the nineteenth-century churches failed to attract the majority of working men, paradoxically this was at least partly because of their attempts to win them. In a democratizing society, this was a dangerous failure.

But these movements accentuated secularization in other ways too, by helping to secularize the very content of religion. The nineteenth century's assault on pain was itself nourished by increased doubts on whether earthly suffering would be compensated for by heavenly bliss; with no after-life to redress the unfairness and injustice of existence here below, humanitarian reforms became urgent. This could not of course be the standpoint taken by the humanitarians' Christian allies; yet they too were threatened in their beliefs by humanitarian activity, for all three movements encouraged Mid- and Late-Victorian Christians to subordinate considerations of theology to the hope of capturing a moral crusade—a change which early nineteenth-century atheists had always wished them to undertake. A Unitarian like M. D. Hill of Birmingham had very little difficulty in co-operating with evangelicals in promoting temperance; as he told Frances Power Cobbe, 'I cannot afford to part with the Evangelicals, who are my best helpers. Thus though I wholly disagree with

[97] *Alliance News*, 6 Jan. 1866, p. 3, speech at Ashton.
[98] Cf. E. R. Wickham, *Church and People in an Industrial City* (Lutterworth, 1957), pp. 194–8.

them about Sunday I never publish my difference.'[99] If twentieth-century humanitarianism owes much to nineteenth-century religion, twentieth-century religion owes little to nineteenth-century humanitarianism.

By the 1860s, many Christians had already begun to seek salvation in the largely earth-bound preoccupations which concern so many of them today. Indeed, it is largely because of the churches' subsequent retreat from the centre of the political stage that the twentieth century tends to view the nineteenth-century moralist's concerns as peripheral; for the Victorians, moral questions were of central importance, and carried important implications for material welfare. Manning was in the forefront here, throwing himself heart and soul into prohibitionism. But J. H. Newman always kept aloof—not because he was unconcerned about drunkenness, but because he feared that prohibitionism was one of many contemporary movements which withdrew matters of conduct from religious jurisdiction. He complained in 1878 that men were now expected to be virtuous on purely secular grounds; 'we are having a wedge thrust into us which tends to the destruction of religion altogether'.[1] In Newman's eyes, therefore, Manning with all his enthusiastic crusading was achieving precisely the reverse of his original objective; and over the perspective of a hundred years, who can say that Newman was wrong?

---

[99] F. P. Cobbe, *Life*, i. p. 346. See also J. Turner, *Reckoning with the Beast*, p. 80.

[1] T. Kenny, *The Political Thought of John Henry Newman* (1957), pp. 171–2.

IV

Traditions of Respectability
in British Labour History

The term 'respectable' is defined by *The Oxford English Dictionary* as 'worthy of respect, deserving to be respected, by reason of moral excellence' (first citation, 1755), or as 'of good or fair social standing, and having the moral qualities naturally appropriate to this' (first citation, 1758); the second of these usages was employed later to indicate 'honest and decent in character or conduct, without reference to social position, or in spite of being in humble circumstances'. Whereas respectability at first denoted a position of established social standing, reinforced by the appropriate amount of property, its implications for morality assumed increasing significance, and eventually came to describe a life-style which could be observed at all social levels.[1]

Historians agree that the concept of respectability deeply influenced nineteenth-century working people, but disagree about its social location and time-span. Eric Hobsbawm focuses on the situation at work, and gives special attention to the artisan, whom *The Oxford English Dictionary* defines as 'one who is employed in any of the industrial arts'. Respectability certainly did influence him, but its impact was far broader. Furthermore, family life and recreation were as relevant as the work-situation for determining respectability, and Seebohm Rowntree's invention of the phrase 'secondary poverty'—to denote the poverty that springs from unwise expenditure as distinct from inadequate income—highlights the significance of expenditure by comparison with income. A work-centred approach to respectability ignores the crucial importance of both housewife and cultural context. The working-class autobiographer, inevitably

[1] For useful discussions of the concept, see H. McLeod, *Class and Religion in the Late Victorian City* (1974), pp. 13, 21; G. F. A. Best, *Mid-Victorian Britain* (New York ed., 1972), pp. x, 199, 260; G. M. Young, *Victorian Essays* (ed. W. D. Handcock, 1962), p. 122.

untypical even of his own segment within his class, articulated respectable values that were much more widely diffused; his works helped to recruit respectability's ranks, and deserve more prominence in the discussion than they often receive; they spontaneously corroborate one another on details, and they evoke a common philosophy of life.

It is still more misleading to circumscribe respectability's influence in time and social location by discussing it only in the context of the growth of a 'labour aristocracy', as an intruding event which can conveniently explain why predictions of class polarization made in the 1840s fail to materialize. The phrase was occasionally used in the Mid-Victorian period, but if it is assigned so central an explanatory role, respectability's so-called 'classical period' needs to be hedged in by artificial discontinuities located in the 1840s and 1890s for which there is little evidence in the contemporary record.[2] In reality, although the term 'respectability', with its connotations of political and economic 'independence', had only recently come to be applied to working people, some of its essential cultural constituents go back at least to the seventeenth century and in some respects as far back as the division of function between craftsman and labourer, with its associated concept of apprenticeship. Nor does respectability's influence cease with the 1890s; the institutional forms, and even the political formulations, through which it impinged on working people did of course change in the early twentieth century, when the decline in aristocratic values made it less necessary to cultivate respectable values so energetically, and when new economic structures required working-class dignity to be upheld in new ways. But as a political influence, respectability lived on.

It is also misleading to discuss respectability solely in the context of an élite group that is 'conservative' in outlook,[3] because this introduces a jarring note of exclusiveness. Respectability did of course closely scrutinize its aspirant

[2] A. E. Musson, 'Class Struggle and the Labour Aristocracy, 1830-60', *Social History*, Oct. 1976, p. 355.

[3] E. J. Hobsbawm, 'The Labour Aristocracy in Nineteenth-century Britain', in his *Labouring Men* (1964), p. 302.

recruits, but—in the nineteenth century at least—its institutions and culture were highly evangelical in mood, and extended respectability's influence far beyond its paid-up membership. Pelling rightly stresses the continuously changing recruitment to Hobsbawm's alleged labour aristocracy and its close contacts with the groups immediately below it;[4] but after undermining Hobsbawm's argument, he does not go on to reveal the full scope and span of respectability's impact on British labour history. Furthermore the respectable artisan's conservatism is too narrowly circumscribed. Three political categories of respectable working man need to be distinguished: first, the Conservative working man, who was in some circumstances deeply influenced by respectable values both during the nineteenth century and since, yet who tends to get brushed aside in this strangely compartmentalized discussion. Then there is the nineteenth-century radical artisan who (as Pelling rightly points out) was often far from Conservative in the formal sense,[5] and who can be seen as conservative only when viewed from a more Marxian twentieth-century perspective. In a predominantly aristocratic political culture he championed an opportunity-society where social standing was acquired through skill, enterprise, and hard work rather than through birth or inherited wealth; he sought recruits at the humblest social levels, in a sequence of assertive movements which tried to consolidate the territory gained through legislatively adjusting the moral and social environment. Finally, there is respectability within the Labour Party, a variant of conservatism whch is perhaps the subtlest and longest-lasting of them all.

The intention here is not at all to dissent from Hobsbawm's emphasis on the political and social importance of respectability. As Thomas Wright pointed out in 1873, the working classes 'are not a single-acting, single-idea'd body. They are practically and plurally *classes*, distinct classes, classes between which there are as decisively marked differences as there are between any one of them and the upper or

---

[4] H. Pelling, *Popular Politics and Society in Late Victorian Britain* (1968), pp. 46–54.

[5] Ibid., p. 56; Hobsbawm, *Labouring Men*, p. 274, is of course aware of the 'radical artisan'.

middle classes.'[6] The aim is' rather to free Hobsbawm's emphasis from undue constriction in numbers, time-scale, and range of political impact. With this in view, a threefold discussion will be conducted. First, the life cycle or career pattern associated with respectability will be clarified; second, the institutions which flowed naturally from that life-cycle; finally, the party-political ideas and strategies that flowed from them.

I

The respectable life cycle now to be discussed is a composite account built up from the many autobiographies produced by its practitioners. Its raw material comes overwhelmingly from nineteenth-century sources because this was the century when the respectable working man first developed the capacity and resources necessary for articulating his ideals, and found in radical movements and in the Gladstonian Liberal Party a powerful vehicle for his assault on feudalism. But the essential constituents of the respectable life-style reappear during the twentieth century in different forms and in different political contexts, as will be shown later. The model can rest only partially on statistical evidence, for it is largely concerned with cultural influences that ramified through working-class institutions in subtle ways.

The complexity of respectability's impact can perhaps best be emphasized through distinguishing between the seven 'positions' that the respectable working man can occupy on social class. Position one assumes contentment with the over-all standing of his class in society, and with the location of himself and the likely location of his children inside his class. Position two entails satisfaction with his own location but desire to advance his children within his class. If dissatisfied with his own situation within his class, he can take up position three, seeking (together with his children) to move within it. But he may abandon class loyalty and aim either to move himself up and out of the working class (position four), or to ensure that his children

[6] T. Wright, *Our New Masters* (1873), pp. 2–3; cf. [T. Wright], *The Great Unwashed* (1868), p. 5.

do so (position five). The working man dissatisfied with the over-all standing of his class occupies position six—whereby he seeks greater recognition for it within the existing political and economic system—or position seven, whereby he seeks to change the system so as to improve the over-all position of his class, or even to abolish the others.

The range of choices would widen further if allowance were made for downward as well as upward movement, and for divergence (often important) between the social aspirations of husband and wife. Furthermore, the choices relate only to horizontal status-divisions of a class nature, whereas other subdivisions, horizontal or vertical, were relevant for many working men. And in practice any one individual could move between these positions in the course of a lifetime, or could even adhere to more than one of them simultaneously through failing to distinguish clearly between them. During the nineteenth century, the respectable life cycle was largely concerned with positions three, four, and six, but respectability as a political influence in Britain since the industrial revolution has embraced all seven positions at different times and in different circumstances. In the discussion which follows, all seven options therefore need to be borne in mind.

The respectable life cycle provides no more than a hypothesis when any individual working man is under consideration—a set of questions to ask about him, rather than a formula that can be indiscriminately applied, still less an exclusive social category. Some working men may have appropriated aspects of the respectable life-style purely instrumentally, for particular purposes or at specified moments, in lives not consistently permeated by respectable values at all. Respectability was always a process, a dialogue with oneself and with one's fellows, never a fixed position, and many may well have been influenced only partially or temporarily by it. Yet to say this is not to dismiss its social and political importance; on the contrary, the widely felt need to advertise one's respectability, however hypocritically, testifies to the power of the ideal.[7]

---

[7] Cf. P. Bailey, ' "Will the Real Bill Banks Please Stand Up?" Towards a Role

The respectable life cycle can be broken into at more than one point; it does not necessarily begin with childhood, because one of nineteenth-century respectability's greatest strengths was that it was continuously recruited through converting adults. Experience at work was, however, of central importance to respectability, and it is best to begin there. The importance of craft skills within the nineteenth-century work-situation, and the centrality of the small-scale workshop, make it impossible to separate the discussion of work from that of self-education. The educational mechanism for syphoning intellectual ability upwards was much less efficient in nineteenth-century society than it is now; many educated and talented working people before the 1920s were trapped within their class. Resentment did not necessarily result; an autodidact did not necessarily want to move up socially when he could so easily acquire respect within his own sphere. Position three (personal social mobility within one's class) could be realized from several directions—by excelling in one's craft, by rising within working-class organizations, or by self-education; none of these routes to success necessarily entailed moving on to position four (mobility out of one's class). The working man's self-education was as likely to be acquired in home and workplace as in school. By the mid-nineteenth century, a wealth of literature was available for self-education: *The Pursuit of Knowledge Under Difficulties*, Cassell's *Popular Educator*, Chambers's readers, and the newspaper press. In the 1850s George Howell wrote to *The British Controversialist* for guidance on reading, and Joseph Arch articulated the beliefs which grew out of his personal experience through reading the speeches of Gladstone and Bright in the newspapers.

Given the distractions rife both at home and in the workplace, character was at least as important as intellect for academic success; the legend of Bruce and the spider often recurs in the literature of respectability. Francis Place noted his own ability to 'dismiss a train of thought at pleasure and take up another', but the young Thomas Burt found study difficult in the absence of privacy, except in the summer when the warm weather made it possible for him to work in an attic.[8] The possession of a watch or clock became the mark of respectability, for a book like Hugh Miller's *My Schools and Schoolmasters* taught the young Ramsay Mac-Donald and others like him 'that time and life were precious';[9] the young Thomas Cooper cut his food into pieces so that he could eat it with a spoon and read at the same time.[10]

The English classics, and especially the Bible, Shakespeare, Milton, and Bunyan were the staple diet, so that a common cultural background joined Gladstone and Bright to their working-class audiences. Instruction could be taken in by ear as well as by eye—at the many lectures on cultural and literary topics then available, not to mention sermons. Thomas Hudson the temperance pioneer bought himself a dictionary so as to profit fully from sermons, and working men thirsty for knowledge made tours of the London preachers on a Sunday.[11] Nor was chapel-going confined to sermon-tasting, given the many week-night mutual improvement and educational opportunities chapels offered. Serious-mindedness was the hallmark of respectability, and therefore an interest in religion—whether sympathetic (in chapels) or hostile (in secularist societies).

Much of this self-improvement took place during leisure time, but it was not impossible at the sort of workplace (then common) where a small work-group conducted continuous conversation undistracted by noisy machinery. The future Chartist R. G. Gammage, working as a young man in a Northampton coach-trimming workshop, found that its debates gradually dissolved his inherited Tory beliefs.[12] The

[8] F. Place, *Autobiography*, p. 218; see also T. Burt, *Autobiography* (1924), p. 122; J. F. C. Harrison, 'The Victorian Gospel of Success', *Victorian Studies*, Dec. 1957, p. 161.

[9] L. M. Weir, *The Tragedy of Ramsay MacDonald. A Political Biography* (1938), p. 12.

[10] *The Life of Thomas Cooper; Written by Himself* (1872), p. 59; cf. W. Lovett, *The Life and Struggles of William Lovett* (1876), pp. 35–6; *Robert Lowery. Radical and Chartist*, p. 63.

[11] T. Hudson, *Temperance Pioneers of the West* (1887), pp. 11–12; cf. Cooper, *Life*, p. 127.

[12] *Newcastle Weekly Chronicle*, 29 Mar. 1884; see also *Robert Lowery*, pp. 59–60; F. Peel, *The Risings of the Luddites, Chartists and Plug Drawers* (4th ed., 1968), p. 53; C. Kingsley, *Alton Locke. Tailor and Poet* (Everyman ed., 1970), p. 37.

factory presented greater difficulties: noise, weaker links
with the employer, attenuated respectable traditions. Alfred
Williams's *Life in a Railway Factory* (1915) is a monument
to what a perservering working man could achieve in such
places, but his employer's suspicions, the distractions of the
heavy machinery, and the practical jokes of workmates
almost broke him, and eventually caused him to leave.

Self-improvement at work was not necessarily academic in
nature; a *cursus honorum* in craftsmanship or in levels of
responsibility opened out from the apprentice's first workshop which amply catered for ambition. 'To-day he who is
born a worker must remain a worker for the rest of his life',
wrote Engels in the 1840s, for whom revolutionary consciousness would result from such blocked social opportunity; yet increased size of firm and complexity of processes
could open out a long chain of promotion. In nineteenth-
century railway companies, for example, a railwayman could
spend a lifetime moving up the uniformed hierarchy.[13]
Occupational ascent often required a geographical move as
well—for Somerset's George Howell and Cornwall's William
Lovett, to London. This was not only psychologically difficult, it was materially risky, because it involved forsaking
the security of nearby friends and relatives. With migration
of person came a questioning of belief about religion and
politics, as well as alertness to regional contrasts in wages
or conditions, both invaluable in a labour leader.[14]

A working man's trade embedded itself deeply into his
mental outlook. Nineteenth-century craftsmen were often
photographed holding the equipment associated with their
trade and wearing occupational clothes. Joseph Arch on
entering parliament in 1885 proudly refused to wear a
black coat; 'I aped nobody—I wore my rough tweed jacket
and billy-cock hat; the same I generally wore at my country

[13] F. Engels, *The Condition of the Working Class in England* (Tr. and Ed.
W. O. Henderson and W. H. Chaloner, Oxford, 1958), p. 25. See also F. McKenna,
'Victorian Railway Workers', *History Workshop Journal*, Spring 1976, p. 33;
R. Q. Gray, *The Labour Aristocracy in Victorian Edinburgh* (Oxford, 1976),
pp. 89, 129-30.

[14] J. Arch, *The Story of his Life* (ed. Countess of Warwick, 3rd ed., n.d.),
p. 40. See also S. Budd, 'The Loss of Faith. Reasons for Unbelief among members
of the Secular Movement in England, 1850-1950', *Past and Present*, Apr. 1967,
pp. 121-2.

meetings. As I was, so I wished to be.' Thirty years after ceasing to work as a stonemason, Henry Broadhurst was still dreaming about working at his trade,[15] and long after George Howell had ceased bricklaying he was thrown into a depression by bad weather. Trade skills were worth acquiring, if only because the craftsman's income was relatively regular, and roughly double that of the labourer; during the Mid-Victorian period, this differential actually widened, and began to contract only after the first world war.[16] The proportion of any one occupation who enjoyed such high wages varied between trades, but the widespread incidence of such differentials helps to explain the vitality of the respectable culture under discussion. It is hardly surprising that a skilled working man often preferred long periods of unemployment or of underpaid work at his trade, rather than take a labouring job. Restrictions on recruitment to a trade, or legislative attempts at enforcing respectable values, could cause sections of the working class to be locked in bitter conflict with one another.[17]

Subcontracting lent additional elaboration to a hierarchy which did not terminate with the foreman, and the transition to employer was but a short (if often temporary) step for craftsmen whose capital requirements were limited to buying a stock of tools and paying the rent on a small workshop. The census regarded this move as so unimportant that it often went unrecorded. The proportion of employers in the national work-force as a whole was high; during the twentieth century, the proportion has fallen from 13 per cent in 1911 to 10 per cent in 1921 to 7 per cent in 1951, and firms have been growing in size and contracting in number.[18] The proportion was much higher in particular trades and localities —in shoemaking, for example, where the distinction between

[15] J. Arch, *Life*, p. 358; see also H. Broadhurst, *The Story of his Life* (1901), p. 2.

[16] Hobsbawm, *Labouring Men*, pp. 291-3; P. Thompson, *The Edwardians. The Remaking of British Society* (1975), pp. 14, 311, shows a narrower, but still substantial, differential for 1913-14.

[17] [T. Wright], *Some Habits and Customs of the Working Classes by a Journeyman Engineer* (1867), p. 258; see also J. Vincent, *Pollbooks. How Victorians Voted* (Cambridge, 1967), p. 17.

[18] P. Deane and W. A. Cole, *British Economic Growth. 1688-1959. Trends and Structure* (2nd ed., Cambridge, 1967), p. 247, cf. pp. 248, 258.

craftsman and shopkeeper hardly existed,[19] and in cities of small workshops like Sheffield and Birmingham. Lancashire poll-books reveal an identity of voting habits between employer and employee that suggests the persistence of such affinities even among groups fully exposed, at whatever level in the hierarchy, to experience of the large factory.[20]

Marx and Engels fully recognized the role of foremen and skilled mechanics in upholding discipline and maintaining machinery within the factory, but Marx in the 1860s dismissed maintenance men as 'numerically unimportant' (thus setting aside the crucial question of their influence) and Engels engaged in wish-fulfilment by defining foremen and master-craftsmen out of the working class altogether— as renegades who had 'been tempted by increased pay to enter the service of the middle classes', men who were 'no longer genuine workers' and 'not genuine members of the proletariat'. Both Marx and Engels thereby condemned themselves in later life to exchanges of mutual lamentation at the 'bourgeois infection' which sent the working classes in unsuitable political directions.[21]

But what of respectability in domestic life? It certainly affected patterns of courtship. Charles Booth regarded premarital sexual intercourse as 'one of the clearest lines of demarcation between upper and lower in the working class'.[22] Seebohm Rowntree's figures show that in 1899, 58 per cent of the labourers married under the age of twenty-six, but only 49 per cent of the skilled workers. Rowntree deduced that 'the exercise of prudence and of forethought increases as you advance in the social scale', and displayed an even greater differential in 1936.[23] Late marriage may partly reflect the skilled craftsman's marked tendency to marry

[19] Cf. R. Q. Gray, *Labour Aristocracy*, p. 131.

[20] P. Joyce, *Work, Society and Politics*, pp. 205, 210–11.

[21] K. Marx, *Capital. A Critique of Political Economy* (Tr. S. Moore and E. Aveling, New York paperback ed., 1967), i, p. 420, cf. i, p. 423; F. Engels, *Working Class,* pp. 141, 193, 225; Marx and Engels, *Correspondence 1846–1895* (1934), p. 147 (Marx to Engels, 9 Apr. 1863); cf. pp. 115–16, 461.

[22] Quot. in P. Thompson, *The Edwardians*, p. 70.

[23] B. S. Rowntree, *Poverty. A Study of Town Life* (2nd ed., 1902), pp. 173–4; B. S. Rowntree's *Poverty and Progress. A Second Social Survey of York* (1941), p. 527 shows the equivalent figures for 1936 as 53 per cent and 33 per cent, respectively.

among his own kind; a Mid-Victorian artisan in Kentish London was 60–70 per cent likely to marry into the skilled artisan or non-manual categories.[24]

In choosing a home, the respectable working man kept a wary eye open for the subtle gradations of status which existed between houses even in the same street, let alone in different streets or in different parts of the town. The Mid-Victorian housing estate at Shaftesbury Park (Wandsworth) — with its restrictions on drinking facilities and its high standards of maintenance—was not alone in being aimed at the respectable working man from the start. On signing the pledge in the 1830s, Thomas Whittaker at once moved out of his shilling-a-week rented accommodation; 'the home that had satisfied my wants as a drinker', he later recalled, 'was not in harmony with my self-respect as a teetotaler, and I soon put myself in possession of a house rented at twelve pounds a year.'[25]

Respectability usually required the Mid-Victorian working man to support his family without sending his wife out to work. Women's employment was conventionally assigned to the unmarried or the widowed, and was associated with the twin misfortunes of having failed to find, or having lost, a husband. In every age-group in 1911, the percentage of the widowed and unmarried women who were in employment far exceeded the percentage of the married women who were at work.[26] Like mother, like daughter; as late as 1912, despite the good working conditions at Oxford's factories, 'the superior artisan or clerk would not dream of letting his girl go to a factory'.[27] Trade-union regulations and factory legislation were used by men like Broadhurst and Burt to exclude groups like the pit-brow women from the work-force. As Joseph Livesey the teetotal pioneer pointed out in the 1830s, a married woman 'ought to employ her time in

[24] G. Crossick, *An Artisan Élite in Victorian Society. Kentish London 1840–1880* (1978), pp. 119–26.
[25] T. Whittaker, *Life's Battles in Temperance Armour* (1884), p. 66; cf. *Alliance News*, 2 Oct. 1875, p. 636.
[26] 1911 Census, General Report: *Parl. Papers*, 1917–18 (Cd.8491), XXXV, p. 161.
[27] C. V. Butler, *Social Conditions in Oxford* (1912), p. 65; cf. William Lovett's poem, *Woman's Mission* (1856), p. 16.

making and mending garments for the family, washing, cleaning, and cooking, and in superintending the children',[28] and she was particularly praised for her educational role within the family.

But what of life within the home? *The Communist Manifesto* predicts that in the later stages of capitalism the proletarian's relation to his family will have 'no longer anything in common with the bourgeois family relations' and that to him law, morality, and religion would be 'so many bourgeois prejudices, behind which lurk in ambush just as many bourgeois interests'.[29] Yet if a single word were required to describe the ideal of the respectable working man's home life, a middle-class privacy would capture most of what was important; 'with advance in the social scale, family life becomes more private', wrote Rowntree in 1901.[30] Domesticity, 'keeping yourself to yourself', home-centredness— these were the values inculcated by teetotalism from the start. The respectable Edwardian working-class wife would no more stand gossiping at the street door than her husband would idle his time away at the pub.[31]

Her pride in good housekeeping bound her closely to women higher up in the social scale—from whom (in her younger days perhaps, as a domestic servant) she often learned most of what she knew. These were the women who enabled Edwardian poverty surveys to analyse patterns of working-class family expenditure. Through her skills at 'making do', the respectable housewife could stave off poverty; through pride in her home, she could consolidate that achievement by keeping her husband out of the pub. In Edwardian Salford her social status rose the earlier in the week that she did her washing, and a bad display on the line sacrificed status.[32] In Edwardian Middlesbrough an impressive proportion of her slender resources went on 'Globe Polish' for the brass, 'Zebra Polish' for the grates, and 'Gold Dust' for the

[28] J. Livesey (ed.), *The Moral Reformer*, 6 Jan. 1838, p. 33.

[29] K. Marx, *The Communist Manifesto* (ed. H. J. Laski, 1948), p. 133.

[30] B. S. Rowntree, *Poverty*, pp. 108–9.

[31] B. Webb, *My Apprenticeship* (2nd ed., n.d.), pp. 237–8; Lady H. Bell, *At the Works. A Study of a Manufacturing Town* (Nelson ed., 1911), p. 318.

[32] R. Roberts, *A Ragged Schooling. Growing Up in the Classic Slum* (Fontana ed., 1978), p. 85; R. Roberts, *Classic Slum* (Pelican ed., 1973), p. 32.

clothes.[33] Everywhere the quantity and upkeep of property influenced social rating, a fact regularly harped upon by the nineteenth-century temperance tract. The distinction between the housewife who does or does not whiten her front doorstep (crucial for Robert Roberts in Edwardian Salford), or between the careful and the careless council-house tenant (important for Rowntree at York in the 1930s)—remains a live issue in many parts of the country to this day.[34] The mirrored, ornamented, and bracketed overmantel symbolized social success, and was displayed with other symbols in the front parlour where it would be safe from daily use and visible from the street through a carefully laundered aperture. Even the piano must have adorned some Edwardian working-class homes, for in 1910 there were between two and four million new and second-hand pianos in Britain.[35] Both at home and at work, the respectable working man sought independence, but it was perhaps the demanding nature of his public life that led him to seek a certain tranquillity at home as well; here, at least, he would call no man master.

The home enshrined companionship between the sexes— J. S. Mill's 'silent domestic revolution' whereby 'women and men are, for the first time in history, really each other's companions'.[36] Unlike the labourer, the respectable working man did not accumulate prestige by prowess in fighting or drinking; wife-beating, like drunkenness, was the mark of the unregenerate. 'A man may be the friend of another man, a *woman* alone can be his *companion*', Francis Place pronounced.[37] Recreational self-sufficiency at home was formally propagated by the London Working Men's Association [LWMA], whose address of 1836 urged members to 'read . . . talk, and politically and morally instruct your wives and

---

[33] Lady Bell, *At the Works*, pp. 101, 103.

[34] R. Roberts, *Classic Slum*, p. 37; B. S. Rowntree, *Poverty and Progress*, p. 242.

[35] R. Roberts, *Classic Slum*, pp. 33–4; C. B. Hawkins, *Norwich. A Social Study* (1910), p. 89; C. Ehrlich, *Social Emulation and Industrial Progress— The Victorian Piano* (Belfast, 1975), p. 7.

[36] *H. C. Deb.*, 20 May 1867, c.821.

[37] F. Place, *Autobiography*, p. 256, cf. pp. 224, 254–5; cf. W. Lovett, *Life and Struggles*, p. 442; T. Cooper, *Life*, pp. 378–9; *Robert Lowery. Radical and Chartist*, pp. 62–3; Mrs Vincent's preface to W. Dorling, *Henry Vincent. A Biographical Sketch* (1879), p. ix.

children' and 'let them, as far as possible, share in your pleasures'.[38] Respectable working men might resist women's economic emancipation, but they regularly recommended her education and enfranchisement.

The life of the respectable working-class housewife should not be idealized; for her there was loss as well as gain. With husband at work during the day, deprived of the vitality and stimulus of street life but required to display considerable housekeeping skills on a tight budget—her role was in some ways more testing than that of the woman at work. A degree of commitment to his public life was required from the respectable working man that often distanced him physically, emotionally, and even culturally from his wife, whatever the respectable ideal might inculcate; perhaps this was partly why George Howell's wife became an alcoholic, and why John Burns's wife worried so much.[39] Furthermore, if the ever present danger of poverty actually materialized, there was none of the psychological or even material comfort of neighbourliness to fall back upon; then, as now, poverty hid itself away. Place when unemployed visited nobody but his parents, and received visits only from his brother. Respectable parents did not let their children out of the house on Sunday without shoes or respectable clothes.[40] 'I have tried to keep things respectable', wrote George Howell in 1877, begging for financial help, 'and never allowed anyone to know how severe the struggle has been.'[41]

Respectability's life cycle begins anew with the attempt to propagate respectable values; this was done not only through didactic writing but through the careful rearing of children. Late marriage made families small, and birth-control made them still smaller. Birth-control was a semi-medical form of self-help that held out the same promise of simultaneous progress in health and wealth as did vegetarianism and

---

[38] Quot. in D. Jones, *Chartism and the Chartists* (1975), p. 193.

[39] F. Leventhal, *Respectable Radical. George Howell and Victorian Working Class Politics* (1971), pp. 25, 212; for Burns see my *Separate Spheres. The Opposition to Women's Suffrage in Britain* (1978), p. 41. See also F. Place, *Autobiography*, p. 255; J. Arch, *Life*, p. 47.

[40] F. Place, *Autobiography*, p. 115; L. Heren, *Growing Up Poor in London* (1973), p. 100; R. Roberts, *Classic Slum*, p. 39.

[41] F. Leventhal, *Respectable Radical*, p. 195.

teetotalism; all three movements aimed their propaganda at the respectable working man, and within the working class birth-control seems to have spread from the skilled artisan downwards; by 1911 the biggest families were found among outdoor labourers, whereas some working-class families were as small as those of the middle class.[42] Status was becoming associated with the smaller family. By the late 1950s large working-class families reaped unfavourable comment in middle-class Woodford; 'if you take a walk up Greenacres Estate, they look at you and say, "Oh, look at all those children"'. Mid-Victorian respectability's fear of the labourer's large family helps explain the shrill tone of radical attacks on improvident marriage. J. S. Mill in 1859 even favoured a state ban on marriage by partners unable to show that they can support a family, and Lovett grumbled about 'the swarms of half-starved, neglected, and ignorant children' whom 'the industrious and frugal' would be required to support as criminals and paupers.[43] A rather similar middle-class fear nourished eugenic zeal half a century later.

Child-rearing is one of the great unknowns in nineteenth-century British social history, but the privacy of the respect-able home and the presence of the mother within it probably ensured more meticulous, adult-supervised, and home-centred child-rearing than lower down in society. A 'character' had to be cultivated in the child which could brave the anonymity of the big city, where neighbours could no longer monitor conduct; hence the need for an internal regulator, still more stringent than neighbours in its demands. The struggle to keep clean—continuously fought out in school, meeting-hall, and church as well as in the home—was a battle so continuous and instinctive that it leaves few traces in the literature. Buttressed by punctuality, it would preserve the children 'from corrupting influences'.[44] A

---

[42] E. H. Phelps Brown, *The Growth of British Industrial Relations* (1965 ed.), p. 6.

[43] P. Willmott and M. Young, *Family and Class in a London Suburb* (1960), p. 120; [W. Lovett], in *Bee-Hive*, 18 July 1868, p. 1. See also J. S. Mill, *Liberty* (Everyman ed., 1960), p. 163.

[44] W. Lovett and J. Collins, *Chartism. A New Organisation of the People* (Leicester ed. 1969), p. 38; R. Roberts, *Classic Slum*, p. 46; LWMA *Address from the Working Men's Association to the Working Classes, on the Subject of National*

continuous self-segregation from lower grades began in child-hood, with consequent painful encounters whenever respect-able children found themselves at the mercy of the unclean or when young trainee craftsmen were exposed to the bad language of workmates.[45] Like the middle-class child of the 1930s, the offspring of the Victorian respectable working man feared the rough children 'who threw words like stones and who wore torn clothes', longing to forgive them though they never smiled.[46]

Ridicule greeted the attempt to abandon dialect speech, then a sign of low status, and the child was driven into nursing his ambitions in the company of the women in the family—another root of respectability's feminism, however incomplete. Thomas Burt, for instance, found an ally in 'my mother, a model housewife', who 'kept everything tidy, and did her best to protect me';[47] and despite the tough ruthlessness of her determination to survive, it is his mother who is the heroine of Robert Roberts's *Ragged Schooling*. For there was all too little encouragement from the sur-rounding community. 'Class patriotism' guaranteed that the working man who tried to 'better himself' would meet resentment; respect for book-learning was by no means universal within the working-class community.[48]

Yet it was impossible to quit the 'scenes of revelry and riot, of debauchery and vice, filthy language, ribaldry, and coarse oaths'[49] until respectability had become entrenched and adequate funds accumulated for a move. Chapel and temperance hall, havens of respectability within the slum, might suffice for the adults, but as for the children, 'seduc-tions and temptations await them in every corner'.[50] In 1872

Education, p. 7 (bound with LWMA Miscellaneous Pamphlets and Addresses in BL, shelf-mark 8138 a 55).

[45] R. Roberts, *Ragged Schooling*, p. 161; H. Broadhurst, *Story of his Life*, p. 9; A. Williams, *Life in a Railway Factory* (1915), p. 282.

[46] S. Spender, *Poems* (1933), p. 23; I owe this reference to Dr Henry Kamen, University of Warwick.

[47] T. Burt, *Autobiography*, p. 122; cf. R. Hoggart, *The Uses of Literacy* (Pelican ed., 1960), p. 245; F. Place, *Autobiography*, p. 21.

[48] Hon. G. C. Brodrick *et al.*, *Essays on Reform* (1867), p. 39 (essay by R. H. Hutton).

[49] Howell, quot. in F. Leventhal, *Respectable Radical*, p. 6.

[50] W. Lovett and J. Collins, *Chartism*, p. 70.

Archbishop Manning described respectable families beset by the pub, 'this moral pestilence on their threshold'; the walls of the home were sometimes 'so thin that the noise of revelry and the words, it may be, of impurity and blasphemy are heard in the chambers where they rest'.[51] Jealous neighbours, to whom respectability's every triumph seemed a reproach, narrowly scrutinized the effort socially to rise, or at least not to fall, and were quick to find fault. The stakes were high, for failure could produce a last state that was worse than the first. The decision during prosperity to move to a better house often caused great financial loss to the family which in adversity could not afford the extra expense.[52] So much was sacrificed in the hope of a success which often turned out to be elusive.

'For one who comes safe through the furnace, there are a hundred who crack in the burning', Charles Kingsley's Chartist Crossthwaite declares. Henry Vincent saw life as 'a stern, sturdy battle', and the noblest youth as bracing himself up 'to fight this battle in a noble, erect, and independent way'.[53] Respectability's triumphs were often private, and the rewards distant, if only because so much of the battle involved a long-term triumph of one half of the personality over the other. Observers called up images suggesting cruel alternatives; Lady Bell saw the ironworker's narrow path between streams of fire on one side and a sheer drop on the other as symbolizing a life which brooked no error.[54] Working men of any grade were required to display an intense self-discipline the demands of which became wellnigh intolerable when reinforced by personal ambition. Poverty was an ever present possibility, far more widely experienced within a lifetime than would be guessed at from its national prevalence at any one time; young children, illness, and old age in a society with minimal public provision frequently pushed a family under; George Howell's persistent search for security, for instance, reflects a continuing fear that

[51] *Alliance News*, 5 Oct. 1872, p. 707; cf. H. McLeod, *Class and Religion*, pp. 45–7.
[52] Lady Bell, *At the Works*, p. 108.
[53] C. Kingsley, *Alton Locke*, p. 61; *Banbury Advertiser*, 27 Oct. 1859, p. 4.
[54] Lady Bell, *At the Works*, p. 375.

the poverty vividly experienced during childhood would return.[55]

Respectable hopes were often disappointed. Some occupations set up an entrance qualification which self-education alone could never overcome; and if the self-help ideal had been universally accepted, the few posts open to the socially mobile—nonconformist minister, radical politician, journalist, labour leader, schoolteacher—would have been rapidly oversubscribed.[56] Nor did thrift and hard work always bring the security which might have been expected. Despite all Lovett's self-denial, his autobiography sadly admits his inability to provide for himself in old age.[57] Nor was it perhaps as easy to learn from mistakes as the Smilesean myth implied. Thomas Hardy once cited Roger Ascham's dictum that 'by experience we find out a short way by a long wandering', to which Hardy added that 'not seldom that long wandering unfits us for further travel, and of what use is our experience to us then?'[58]

It is hardly surprising that when success was gained, so many working men rushed into print. So completely have Marx and Freud eroded the notion that the world is our oyster, to be opened at will—so conscious are we of the psychological and even physiological price we pay in making the attempt (even when successful)—that this autobiographical tradition has now run dry, and needs briefly to be discussed. Nowhere are the continuities between seventeenth-century Puritanism and nineteenth-century working-class respectability more evident; the ancestry of these works goes back to the spiritual autobiography, though their purpose had now become entirely secular. Their authors wished to warn fellow working men of the psychological strain involved in social ascent, but also to spur them on by showing that others had preceded them on the road. Men like Thomas Cooper, who had themselves been spurred on by reading self-help autobiographies, wished to add to the

[55] F. Leventhal, *Respectable Radical*, pp. 2–5; cf. F. Place, *Autobiography*, pp. 205, 218.

[56] T. Wright, *Our New Masters*, p. 115; see also J. F. C. Harrison, *Underground Education in the Nineteenth Century* (Leeds, 1971), p. 6.

[57] W. Lovett, *Life and Struggles*, p. 400; cf. T. Cooper, *Life*, p. 390.

[58] T. Hardy, *Tess of the D'Urbervilles* (1965, paperback ed.), p. 118.

common stock. The Chartist Robert Lowery, for instance, hoped that his experiences might 'serve as suggestions—helps to young men in such circumstances as mine were'.[59] Now that working men could read, the self-help tradition could be handed down in writing as well as by word of mouth. The autobiographies may occasionally, as with Place, strike a note of self-satisfaction that life's battles have been survived unscarred; but they also reveal a consciousness of insecurity which, in Broadhurst at least, is moving. His unpretentious life story describes how as a prominent public figure he none the less kept his tools by him even in old age, least set-backs should send him back to his trade as a stonemason.[60]

The autobiographies performed a second function; they aimed to cut through the misunderstandings of working-class leaders fostered by journalists and interested parties, and to reveal them to their superiors in their true colours. Explaining one class to another came naturally to working men in an intermediate social situation who shared much of their superiors' outlook and much of their inferiors' experience. Oh that the rich could see how identically they would themselves behave if placed in the same situation as the poor![61] Working people are displayed in a good or bad light according to the angling of the autobiographical mirror—an ambiguity of analysis and tone that reflects an ambiguity of social experience. There is sympathy, of course, with working-class sufferings, but there is also an impatience, and even a disgust, at obscurantism, brutality, and traditionalism which is sharpened by the personal experience of working-class jealousy and obstructiveness. Joseph Arch recalled the jealousy he encountered when first elected to parliament and the 'dreadful ignorance' of trade-union colleagues when he struggled to organize the agricultural labourers; 'being president of a Union was not all sunshine and honey'. The lifelong struggle to keep one's distance could no more be shaken off by an Arch or a Howell than by the early elementary

[59] *Robert Lowery. Radical and Chartist*, p. 40; cf. W. Lovett, *Life and Struggles*, p. 1; T. Cooper, *Life*, p. 278; F. Place, *Autobiography*, p. 12.
[60] H. Broadhurst, *Story of his Life*, p. 2.
[61] Ibid., p. 54; *Robert Lowery. Radical and Chartist*, p. 30.

schoolteachers observed by Miss Loane, who 'neither from early personal experience nor by sympathetic study . . . know the principal class with which they have to deal'.[62]

Even a Christ-like pose is sometimes assumed, the auto-biographer being martyred by the many Judases the labour movement contains. An ageing Henry Broadhurst told Beatrice Potter in 1889 that in youth one might perhaps surmount malign attack (in his case from Keir Hardie within the TUC, of which Broadhurst was secretary from 1875 to 1890), but in old age a respite was required.[63] Labour leaders feared corruption and incompetence among followers too sorely tempted by want and insecurity, too seriously hindered by ignorance and inexperience; the rank and file feared that leaders disillusioned with their weaker brethren would succumb to the many temptations offered from above. For though it is entirely misleading to see working-class respect-ability simply as involving emulation of conduct prevalent within another class (respectability was too deeply rooted within the working class, and too precarious within the middle class, for that) respectability often required the work-ing man to express disgust with members of his own order. Respectability was never cramped within any clearly distinct status-group or occupation; it was an attitude of mind which deeply influenced those who rose, remained stationary, or fell. It impinged on groups of working men of every political opinion and religious denomination, in every region, and at every status-grade within their class, at whatever stage they had reached in their progress towards self-improvement. It was an anxious state of mind, rendered tolerable only by the companionship available in respectability's institutional framework. It is a structure that has now either vanished or decayed, and if only for that reason it deserves to be discussed.

---

[62] J. Arch, *Life*, pp. 247, 385, cf. p. 272; M. Loane, *From their Point of View* (1908), p. 297 (I owe this reference to Dr McKibbin). See also F. Leventhal, *Respectable Radical*, pp. 79, 81.

[63] B. Webb, *Diary*, 14 Feb. 1890 (typescript copy in the London School of Economics Library).

II

Education, thrift, prudent expenditure, religious idealism, and secular crusading were all dimensions of working-class respectability that created their own institutions; each will now be briefly considered. In the absence of public libraries, the second-hand bookseller was a key figure for nineteenth-century labour organizations, not merely for displaying the riches available, but for providing guidance on their contents.[64] The self-improving working man did not usually dominate chapels, mechanics' institutes, Sunday schools, debating societies, and early athletic and football clubs, but he was prominent within them. Schools were at first rather thin on the ground, but with the Mid-Victorian creation of a nation-wide system of elementary education respectability received a major reinforcement; 'habits of cleanliness and of order have been formed; a higher standard of dress and of decency have been attained', wrote Charles Booth, 'and this reacts upon the homes; and when children who have themselves been to school become parents, they accept and are ready to uphold the system, and support the authority of the teachers'.[65]

Twentieth-century affluence and welfare provision have eroded the culture of thrift, though faint echoes of the Victorians' world of scarcity are now again being heard. Thrift was essential near the breadline if the working man was to raise the credit needed to impress customers and equip himself with stock and tools. The savings bank (reinforced after 1862 by the Post Office) and the friendly society gathered in the respectable; skilled workers contributed by far the largest percentage of members to Edinburgh savings banks analysed for the 1860s and the 1890s.[66] Gambling seemed the antithesis of thrift; there was no reason to accentuate life's uncertainties, and Lovett and Burns denounced it in no uncertain terms.[67] Savings must be

[64] E. P. Thompson, *The Making of the English Working Class* (rev. ed., 1968), p. 691; J. F. C. Harrison, *Robert Owen and the Owenites in Britain and America. The Quest for the New Moral World* (1969), p. 230.

[65] Quot. in B. Webb, *My Apprenticeship*, p. 218.

[66] R. Q. Gray, *Labour Aristocracy*, pp. 122–3.

[67] [W. Lovett], in *Bee-Hive*, 5 Dec. 1868, p. 1; Lovett, *Life and Struggles*, p. 439; K. D. Brown, *John Burns* (1977), p. 113.

accumulated as a hedge against disaster, and a 'clean' rent-book became a symbol of respectability, whereas pawn-brokers, money-lenders, and tallymen were spurned (in theory, at least) as threats to integrity.[68]

At its most modest, thrift aimed simply to ward off the pauper's funeral, to which some York working people were still sacrificing their diet even in the 1930s;[69] but it was the friendly society, with its commitment to regular saving, which attracted the more strenuously respectable. Skilled workers outpace every other category as a proportion of both membership and trustees in the Early- and Mid-Victorian friendly societies of Kentish London, and their rule-books carefully enshrine respectable values;[70] but over a third of the adult occupied male population in the area joined at this time, and the high turnover in membership suggests that even more were at least temporarily exposed to the friendly society's ethos.[71] The anniversary meeting of the Foresters' friendly society seemed, to A. J. Munby in 1860, 'of all others the scene and the time to see the English working classes',[72] and by 1900 the membership of affiliated and ordinary friendly societies had risen as high as 5,400,000 (in a United Kingdom population over twenty of about twenty-four million).[73] The building-society movement did not begin its take-off till the twentieth century—with only £9 million advanced in mortgages in 1910[74]—but its earliest development, in the 1840s, owed much to the working man's involvement in the temperance and freehold-land movements.

Trade unionism was a relatively modest affair; as compared with the six million in affiliated and ordinary friendly societies in 1905, its membership was only two million, but

[68] See F. Place, *Autobiography*, p. 117.

[69] B. S. Rowntree, *Poverty and Progress*, pp. 201, 213.

[70] G. Crossick, *Artisan Élite*, pp. 183, 185-6, 193; G. Crossick, 'The Labour Aristocracy and its Values: A Study of Mid-Victorian Kentish London', *Victorian Studies*, Mar. 1976, p. 316.

[71] Crossick, *Artisan Élite*, pp. 182-3.

[72] D. Hudson, *Munby. Man of Two Worlds* (Boston, USA 1972), p. 71.

[73] Friendly society statistics, to which Paul Johnson kindly referred me, are in 15th Abstract of Labour Statistics, *Parl. Papers*, 1912-13 (Cd.6228), CVII, p. 254; B. R. Mitchell and P. Deane, *Abstract of British Historical Statistics* (Cambridge, 1962), pp. 12-14, population figures for 1901.

[74] A. H. Halsey (ed.), *Trends in British Society since 1900* (1972), p. 317.

rose to four million in 1915 and to eight million in 1920. Trade unionism was not yet clearly distinct from the friendly-society movement. In the seven years up to 1905, 100 leading trade unions spent 27s. 10d. annually per member—of which only 3s. 3d. went on dispute pay, and 6s. 3d. on unemployment benefit, whereas as much as 5s. 8d. went on sickness and accident benefit, 3s. 8d. on pensions, and 2s. 8d. on funeral benefit.[75] Mobilizing only a small segment of the working class, trade unions were often led by workers deeply influenced by the ideal of respectability, men whose resources and integrity enabled them to put up a stiff fight against threats to their living standards; but as Engels pointed out in 1892, their role was scarcely to promote conflict between employer and employee. He preferred to see them as 'useful means of spreading sound [i.e. non-Marxist] economical doctrines amongst the workers'.[76] Broadhurst's memoirs take pride in the fact that in the 1870s he had guided his own trade union towards preventing strikes by arbitrating between the members and their employers.[77]

The genuine working-class following for the culture of thrift enabled those in other classes who criticized indiscriminate charity and poor relief to pose plausibly as champions of the working man's 'independence'; the dignity of the poor must not be infringed, nor must the thriftless be seen to profit from their sins. As Herbert Spencer put it, 'protection of the vicious poor involves aggression on the virtuous poor'.[78] Contempt for charity as degrading and zest for economy in local government runs through the labour movement as a continuous theme, from Chartist local councillors of the 1840s through the Lib–Lab MPs of the 1890s and on into the Labour Party; all were keen to assault

[75] Phelps Brown, *Growth of British Industrial Relations*, pp. 222, 224; the figures cited in fn. 73, and see also the figures in *Parl. Papers*, 1890-1 (C.6475), XCII, p. 3, and in D. E. Butler and A. Sloman, *British Political Facts 1900–1975* (4th ed., 1975), p. 299.

[76] Engels, *Working Class*, p. 366.

[77] H. Broadhurst, *Story of his Life*, p. 44; cf. the argument in R. Price, *Masters, Unions and Men. Work Control in Building and the Rise of Labour 1830–1914* (Cambridge, 1980), pp. 118–19.

[78] H. Spencer, *The Man versus the State* (1940 ed.), p. 89; cf. B. Webb, *My Apprenticeship*, p. 173.

pauperism at both ends of the social scale. Octavia Hill, one of the keenest enthusiasts for working-class 'independence', noted that when attempts were made to prevent indiscriminate payment from the Mansion House Fund in 1886, 'the working-men on the Committees, especially those who represent the Oddfellows and Foresters, are the greatest help'.[79]

Social status is established as much by patterns of spending as of saving. Mid-Victorian respectability increasingly made two demands here: shopping for routine items at the co-op, and shunning the pub. The Rochdale Pioneers' prospectus of 1844 linked the two from the start, with its suggestion that the Society should open a temperance hotel as soon as convenient.[80] By the 1860s the co-op was mobilizing the respectable through offering them unadulterated goods without tempting them with offers of credit.[81] Co-op shopping was but one dimension of the respectable housewife's prudent housekeeping. The co-op's ancillary educational and thrift facilities reflected its initial aim of regenerating mankind, but here, as so often elsewhere, the values of respectability faced continuous threat. Although the co-op movement's official leadership right up to 1914 strongly condemned the extension of credit because it condoned thriftlessness in the customer and absorbed capital which could have been more usefully channelled into expanding the movement—the members forced the practice of the branch to diverge from the ideal. By 1886, 511 of the 946 registered industrial and provident societies in England admitted to giving credit, a proportion which by 1911 rose to 1,168 out of 1,426. In 1907 it was found that each co-op society member in England was on average a week behind in his payments. None the less the co-op movement never captured the entire working class. Skilled workers dominate the membership and officialdom of the Royal Arsenal Co-op Society in the 1870s, and at Oxford in 1912 the local co-op catered only for the better-off working people, with a membership 'chiefly of the artisan and shopkeeping class'.[82]

[79] C. E. Maurice (ed.), *Life of Octavia Hill* (1913), p. 468.
[80] F. Podmore, *Robert Owen. A Biography* (1906), ii, p. 584.
[81] Crossick, *Artisan Élite*, p. 169.
[82] C. V. Butler, *Social Conditions in Oxford*, p. 122; Crossick, *Artisan Élite*,

Only gradually during the nineteenth century did respectability become suspicious of the pub, which housed improving institutions of all types—reading-rooms, debating societies, museums, discussion groups, and meeting-places. The devil could not at first be convincingly portrayed as possessing all the best tunes, and the attack on the publican's respectability entailed a schism among the respectable. Long before teetotalism was launched in the 1830s, Francis Place and William Lovett were shunning pub company for rationalist and secular reasons, but they were wary at first of the new Preston-based teetotal movement. Its ethos never completely harmonized with the respectable ideal; it was too indiscriminate in its recruitment, too evangelical, and even patronizing in its tone. By the 1860s, however, an institution's decision to sell beer determined the type of working man it wished to attract; there was intense argument inside the Working Men's Club and Institute Union, and a series of ructions in the London Working Men's College.[83] Teetotallers had by then become the essential constituent of any demonstration mobilizing the respectable, and had established firm links with the friendly-society movement. Within the Rechabites, the leading temperance friendly society, the distinction between the two was dissolved; their membership rose from 23,109 in 1870 to 356,457 in 1910, not to mention several smaller temperance friendly societies. By 1900 the temperance movement numbered perhaps half a million activists and in some sense spoke for between three and six million abstainers.[84]

Here again the censoriousness of respectability faced two ways; prohibitionists relished a simultaneous attack on effete aristocrats and drunken paupers, and at one of the United Kingdom Alliance's meetings at Banbury in 1870,

pp. 167–8. Paul Johnson most kindly allowed me to use information on credit at the co-op from his 'Working-Class Economy and the Co-operative Movement 1870–1914' (unpublished paper), pp. 19–26.

[83] London Working Men's College, Crowndale Road, Scrapbook 1854–84, pp. 271–2, and file P.7; J. F. C. Harrison, *A History of the Working Men's College 1854–1954* (1954), pp. 81–2.

[84] A. E. Dingle, 'The Agitation for Prohibition in England. A Study of the Political Activity and Influence of the United Kingdom Alliance 1871–1895' (unpublished Ph.D. thesis, Monash, 1974), p. 604.

a prominent local Primitive Methodist teetotaler and white-smith R. Brazier expressed the wish that teetotalers could be required to support only their own poor; teetotalers rarely entered the workhouse, so that 'all the money dragged out of their pockets in the shape of poor rates went to pay for the evil and misery caused by the drinking system'.[85] Improvidence repelled both Late-Victorian teetotal working men in local government and Edwardian parents spurning free school meals for their children. Universality of benefit—whether in elementary-school fees or school meals—was adopted largely because it was difficult to distinguish between those who could and those who could not afford to pay. One must protect the sensitivities of the pauper child, but one must also avoid exploiting the good feelings of the respectable parent.

The institutions catering for working-class respectability should not be viewed in isolation; collectively their influence was greater than the sum of the parts. J. S. Mill, analysing the source of social power at the national level, detects three elements: numbers (or muscular strength), property, and intelligence. On the basis of 'plausible guesses', Hobsbawm estimates the size of the labour aristocracy at about 10 per cent of the Mid-Victorian male industrial work-force; others feel that this is an underestimate,[86] while Pelling questions whether the labour aristocracy even exists. For Pelling to argue that there is 'no aristocracy' in the factory and mining populations of the nineteenth century may be true if status gradations are viewed in purely occupational terms, but respectability's cultural influence in such areas was immense. No attempt will be made to reach numerical estimates here, partly because the ideal of respectability influenced many more than could ever be classified as belonging to a 'labour aristocracy', including many women with no formal occupation; and partly because respectability's ramifications can never be fully captured by figures for the membership of

---

[85] *Alliance News*, 30 July 1870, p. 246; cf. B. Harrison and B. Trinder, *Drink and Sobriety in an Early Victorian Country Town: Banbury 1830–1860* (*English Historical Review*, Supplement No. 4, 1969), pp. 44–6.

[86] E. J. Hobsbawm, *Labouring Men*, p. 279; cf. H. J. Dyos (ed.), *The Study of Urban History* (1968), pp. 146, 148.

specific institutions, let alone the varying intensity of its influence from one individual to another. Numbers are beside the point; it is influence that is relevant. 'We seek not a mere exhibition of numbers', declared the LWMA; the aim was rather 'to draw into one bond of UNITY the *intelligent* and *influential* portion of the working classes in town and country'.[87] The respectable working man also dominated his class in Mill's attribute of property, for his income and pattern of expenditure placed him in a relatively strong position. As for intelligence, his self-education and self-confidence guaranteed public attention for his views.

Mill went on to emphasize the importance of investigating how far his three attributes are organized; a social group can be inferior in all three to those it governs, he says, yet remain supreme because 'the advantage in organisation is necessarily with those who are in possession of the government'. The working man who could read, write, speak, publish, and organize—who was active in social, moral, and political movements—exercised an influence quite disproportionate to his numbers. He set standards, established precedents, and moulded the community conscience through the gossip that was exchanged in trade-union meetings, Sunday chapel, workshop discussions, friendly-society gatherings, and pub talk. Josephine Butler recognized this in 1871, when describing the type of working man who supported her campaign against state-regulated prostitution; her working-class sympathizers, she said, 'gather round them all the decent men in the place; when they start a movement they get all the rest to follow; and properly so, because they are men of character'.[88]

Public visibility enabled the respectable to make converts; they made the most of their numbers by advertising themselves and their life-style. It was partly a matter of clothing, to which they attached great symbolic importance. A working man must keep up a respectable public appearance, said

[87] H. Pelling, *Popular Politics and Society*, p. 61; LWMA *Address and Rules* (n.d.—in BL shelf mark 8138 a 55), pp. 2, 6.

[88] J. S. Mill, *Representative Government* (Everyman ed. 1960), p. 183; R. C. on the administration and operation of the Contagious Diseases Act, *Parl Papers*, 1871 (C.408), XIX, Q.12921 [henceforth cited as *C. D. Acts Commission*].

Place, because he 'will have resolution to struggle with, and frequently if not generally to overcome his adverse circumstances'.[89] Respectable clothing was not only the symbol of respectability attained, but the guarantee that respectability would persist. Temperance processions enabled teetotalers simultaneously to boost one another's confidence and influence a hostile environment. Nor was it simply a matter of clothing; Cassell's *Popular Educator* in 1852 (itself an important influence on working-class self-education) included a diagram showing how respectability could mould even facial appearance.[90] 'Sobriety will make you into new men', Joseph Livesey declared in his influential *Malt Lecture* of 1833 (the major theoretical basis for early teetotalism); 'it will remove from your faces those scars and blotches and pimples which you are obliged to exhibit to the public. It will put new shoes on your feet, and new clothes on your backs.'[91]

Processions and demonstrations often capitalized upon the working man's strong sense of occupational identity and corporate membership. The friendly societies of Mid-Victorian Kentish London gained social approval by extending honorary membership to community leaders, and invited them to their public functions.[92] Respectability's egalitarianism was primarily concerned with equality of opportunity. It sought to get respectable working men and their organizations entrenched among the recognized estates of the realm, and to propagate respectable values as widely as possible. This entailed a combination of exclusion and evangelism. To establish that co-ops, friendly societies, and other respectable organizations were influential, there is no need to argue that these were 'the exclusive preserve of the highly-skilled or even the highly-paid' (Pelling).[93] Mood is as important as membership criteria; the tone was set by those who formed and managed things, and struggling aspirants to the

---

[89] F. Place, *Autobiography*, p. 128.
[90] Reprinted in S. Nowell-Smith, *The House of Cassell. 1848-1958* (1958).
[91] J. Livesey, *The Malt Lecture* (Ipswich Temperance Tract. no. 133, n.d.), p. 30.
[92] G. Crossick, *Artisan Élite*, pp. 103, 196-7; R. Q. Gray, *Labour Aristocracy*, p. 92.
[93] H. Pelling, *Popular Politics and Society*, p. 55.

respectable life-style were content to follow. Indeed, it was one of the strengths of these institutions that working men frequently crossed and recrossed the divide between rough and respectable. In social institutions, at least, precise definition of membership is by no means a prerequisite for social influence. Respectability continuously recruited itself from below through aggressive propaganda, energetic example-setting, and even attempts at getting its values legislatively endorsed.

New recruits were not lightly admitted, for respectability's essence lay in the power (though not necessarily in the desire) to exclude, to impose tests of quality. But many Victorians held a view of society founded on the idea of an expanding middle rather than of social polarization; respectability seemed destined to make converts from both social extremes. In 1847 Marx claimed that the proletariat would recruit drop-outs from the employing class as skills became redundant and firms expanded in size, whereas the respectable knew that respectability was 'at once a select status and a universal motive. Like Roman citizenship, it could be indefinitely extended, and every extension fortified the State.'[94] Pre-eminent among the institutions aggregating the respectable have been all three political parties, but before their role is considered, due attention should be paid to two related institutions, the chapel (which here denotes Anglican and Catholic mission-stations as well as nonconformist communities), and the reforming movement.

'If any of the workers do possess some veneer of religion', Engels wrote in 1844, 'it is only a nominal attachment to some religious body, and does not indicate any spiritual conviction.' Though he excluded from his generalization the Irish, a few of the older workers, 'and those wage-earners who have one foot in the middle-class camp—overlookers, foremen and so on', he was deceiving himself.[95] Chapels and their ancillary week-night organizations—together with the secularist bodies which (despite their irreligion) shared so many of the chapel's essential features—made a major

[94] G. M. Young, *Victorian England. Portrait of an Age* (Oxford paperback ed. 1960), p. 25; see also K. Marx and F. Engels, *Selected Works* (Moscow, 1962), i, p. 41.   [95] F. Engels, *Working Class*, p. 141.

cultural (though not necessarily religious) impact on nineteenth-century working people. Halévy even attributes the absence of revolution in early nineteenth-century Britain to evangelical nonconformity's influence over working people.[96] This is an over-simplification, if only because respectability (and, for that matter, nonconformity) could in certain circumstances actually foment revolution, but religion and revolution were certainly sometimes rivals. Discussing the local obstacles to Chartism, Abram Duncan, Chartist missionary to Cornwall in 1839, points out that 'between the religious and teetotal agitation, a considerable amount of enterprise and talent is absorbed'.[97] Popular religion gained much from the harsh choices facing the working man: between drunkenness and sobriety, improvidence and thrift, ignorance and literacy, self-neglect and self-control—in short, between roughness and respectability. Given these polarities, the crude alternatives inherent in evangelical religion (as in political economy) bore some relationship to the realities of daily life.

Here the Methodist contribution was crucial. In its great growth period after the mid-eighteenth century it attracted extensive support from the artisans, who shared the anti-aristocratic mood and provincial assertiveness of the shopkeeping and manufacturing groups whom it also recruited at that time; in early nineteenth-century evangelical nonconformist communities, the percentage of labourers was lower than in the wider society, but the percentage of artisans and miners was much higher.[98] They fostered a moral self-scrutiny with their twin process of evangelical recruitment and austere selectiveness. The long-term outcome for many chapel-goers was perhaps social elevation, but Beatrice Potter at Bacup in 1883 could still see the local chapels as a leaven for the working class as a whole, and remark on 'what an excellent thing these dissenting

---

[96] E. Halévy, *England in 1815* (Tr. E. I. Watkin and D. A. Barker, Benn paperback ed., 1961), p. 425; E. Halévy, *Victorian Years 1841–1895* (Tr. E. I Watkin, Benn paperback ed., 1961), p. 395.

[97] *The True Scotsman*, 30 Mar. 1839, p. 1; cf. *Robert Lowery. Radical and Chartist*, p. 236.

[98] A. D. Gilbert, *Religion and Society in Industrial England. Church, Chapel and Social Change, 1740–1914* (1976), pp. 60–7.

organisations have been for educating this class for self-government'.[99]

Only the working man whose receipt and deployment of income emancipated him from a continuous and desperate battle against poverty could develop an intelligent interest in religion. Within the chapel, the newly respectable could not only shield himself from corrupting former acquaintances, but could also move in the right circles where custom and credit could be acquired. 'A steady young man commencing life in Liverpool', wrote B. G. Orchard in 1893, 'without capital or good friends, cannot do better for his own business future than by joining and becoming active, useful and respected in a large dissenting congregation.'[1] William Smith, converted in a Wellington revival of the 1830s, joined a friendly society, became a teetotaller and local preacher, married a young woman he met at a class-meeting, and took a better job all in a remarkably short space of time. To many working men, there seemed no middle way between the old life and the new; clean breaks had to be made, compromise was impossible. 'It has always been my aim in life to meet and associate with the best men and women I could find', wrote Smith in his autobiography. This is not snobbery, for it respects personal qualities rather than social rank, though the two could of course overlap. The chapel offered the respectable an association, largely defensive in nature, against a hostile environment. 'It is said you can always tell a man by the company that he keeps', is the concluding comment in Smith's memoirs; 'they that walk with the wise shall be wise'.[2]

Nineteenth-century chapels organized recreations of every kind as counter-attractions to the traditional and rather drunken election saturnalias, race-meetings, feasts, fairgrounds, and brutal sports. In this they resembled some radical organizations; Samuel Bamford, for example, described the public execution of the Cato Street conspirators as the very last occasion 'at which persons of our

[99] B. Webb, *My Apprenticeship*, p. 139; cf. J. Obelkevich, *Religion and Rural Society*, p. 246.

[1] Quot. in R. B. Walker, 'Religious Changes in Liverpool in the Nineteenth Century', *Journal of Ecclesiastical History*, Oct. 1968, p. 204.

[2] 'Memoir of William Smith, Wellington, 21 Oct. 1904', n.p., kindly loaned to me by Mr Barrie Trinder, of Shrewsbury.

description should be seen'.[3] Temperance societies safe-
guarded their members with excursions and picnics, just as
many modern African towns develop organizations designed
to set standards for personal conduct, guide careers, provide
a moral structure within an unfamiliar urban world, and
cultivate less traditional and more progressive attitudes.[4]
A purely introverted concern for self-insulation often pervaded nineteenth-century chapels and temperance societies.
They developed internal hierarchies whose gradations of
status and badges of office came to seem all-important, so
that a careerist mobility within the chapel, trade union,
friendly or temperance society seemed more important
than wider considerations, and political quietism was often
the outcome. The pioneer Socialist Ellen Wilkinson recalled
that 'to my father, who started to preach at the age of
fifteen as a "local preacher", chapel meant everything.
There he was taught to read, was lent books. It was his only
contact with education, its pulpit his only means of self-
expression.'[5] Yet if political quietism might be the immediate
outcome, the long-term and politically elevating impact of
planting such a group within the working-class community
was considerable, as testified, perhaps, by Ellen Wilkinson's
own career. Chapel life, with its rhetoric of popular
Christianity, its democracy of all believers, its sense of
community—could widen respectability's horizons and
cause it to elevate a class, as well as to elevate the individual
within his class. Education and public speaking were among
the chapel's major attractions; about a tenth of Lincolnshire's Primitive Methodist chapel membership between 1831
and 1874 were local preachers;[6] these were skills which
could readily be transferred elsewhere.

---

[3] S. Bamford, *Passages in the Life of a Radical* (1967 ed.), ii. p. 160.
[4] M. Banton, *West African City. A Study of Tribal Life in Freetown* (1957),
p. 180; W. B. Schwab, 'Oshogbo—an Urban Community?', in H. Kuper (ed.),
Urbanization and Migration in West Africa (University of California Press, 1965),
pp. 102–3; M. Banton, 'Social Alignment and Identity in a West African City',
in H. Kuper (ed.), ibid., pp. 143–4. I owe several of these references to Dr Alan
Macfarlane.
[5] Margot Asquith (ed.), *Myself When Young. By Famous Women of To-Day*
(1938), p. 401.
[6] J. Obelkevich, *Religion and Rural Society*, p. 244.

What is striking about chapel society is its capacity for reaching forward ambitiously (even absurdly, by twentieth-century standards) to broader preoccupations. Radiating out from chapels, and from secularist organizations (which combined intellectual with moral selectivity in their membership), came a sequence of moral and political reform movements, international in aim and assertive in tone. From anti-slavery to Roman Catholic emancipation to franchise reform and abolition of the Corn Laws, and on to Liberationism and the attack on drunkenness, on Bulgarian atrocities, on Governor Eyre, and on state-regulated prostitution—they were convinced that individual energy and idealism could make the world a better place. Respectability sharpened itself first on the immediate environment. Recalling her opponents at the Colchester by-election of 1870, Josephine Butler emphasized 'that these were not of the class of honest working people, but chiefly a number of hired roughs, and persons directly interested in the maintenance of the vilest of human institutions'.[7] But when such local villainy had been crushed, the victor could move forward to the national crusade.

W. T. Stead, for instance, confidently expected provincial working men to help him in purging London's corrupt Babylon in 1885; he spoke of 'the soundest part of the nation—the sober, hard-working, intelligent men who in North and Central England constitute the saving strength of our land'. Such provincial assertiveness frequently reappears, and is reinforced by a moralistic evangelism. Livesey's message, 'drunkards! We are your best friends . . . we pity your case, and are trying to save you', had first been trumpeted from Preston; the Anti-Corn-Law League had operated from Manchester, the Bulgarian atrocities agitation from Darlington.[8] When William Gregson the temperance advocate came down from Lancashire to campaign among Brighton working men, his biographer tells us how 'the amount of dissipation, trickery, deception, and wretched fawning that he came across . . . was, as he expresses it, something fearful'. Yet the point is that Gregson did go to

---

[7] J. Butler, *Personal Reminiscences of a Great Crusade* (1896), p. 44.
[8] *Pall Mall Gazette*, 11 July 1885, p. 1; J. Livesey, *Malt Lecture*, p. 27.

Brighton; he aimed at extending the ranks of the respectable. And when Britain had been won for respectability, attention could turn to elevating the world; or rather (since the relationship was more complex) Britain could be won for respectability partly through mobilizing an idealism that transcended the bounds of the nation state.[9]

Working-class respectability, when operating in the public arena, did not always show an attractive face. The struggle against poverty, the continuous pursuit of self-discipline, did not foster the mildly congenial and pliable temperament. 'The world owed very little to the men who had conformed to its institutions, and almost everything to those who had not conformed', said Henry Vincent, discussing Luther in a lecture at Bristol in 1850; he thereby anticipated a remark which appeared in J. S. Mill's *Representative Government* eleven years later.[10] Victorian nonconformity had important implications for character and conduct as well as for belief. Joseph Arch was by no means alone among his kind in being 'a Nonconformist by nature and by conviction'.[11] Felix Holt the radical watchmaker was determined not to get tangled 'in affairs where I must wink at dishonesty and pocket the proceeds, and justify that knavery as part of a system that I can't alter'.[12] This was the mood in which posts were obtrusively resigned on principle, toasts were conspicuously not drunk, honours were publicly refused, social conventions deliberately breached, ceremonial clothing contemptuously rejected, uncompromising standpoints provocatively taken up—actions which did much to uphold civil liberties and personal freedom in nineteenth-century Britain. But working-class respectability ramified much more widely than this; from the 1790s to the present day it has fertilized all three major British political parties.

---

[9] J. G. Shaw, *Life of William Gregson. Temperance Advocate* (Blackburn, 1891), pp. 41–2.

[10] *Bristol Examiner*, 9 Mar. 1850, supplement, p. 1; cf. J. S. Mill, *Representative Government*, p. 211.

[11] J. Arch, *Life*, p. 48.

[12] G. Eliot, *Felix Holt the Radical* (Blackwood ed., n.d.), p. 235; cf. J. F. C. Harrison, *Underground Education*, p. 7.

III

The 1840s launch Hobsbawm's labour aristocracy into its 'classical period'; before then, 'it is doubtful whether . . . we can speak of a labour aristocracy at all'.[13] Yet respectability had long been influential in the land as an ideal of conduct. Instead of hunting for the origins of a 'labour aristocracy', it seems more helpful to stress the continuous importance of respectable traditions among British working people, and to specify the economic and intellectual changes bringing that respectability into political prominence at different times, in different places, and in different ways.

When does working-class respectability first impinge on party politics? From the earliest period when politicians regarded working-class views as being of any account. Respectability was not at first seen as a matter for party policy; early nineteenth-century party politics were not much concerned with social policy, and working people first impinged on national politics through movements that were only tangential to party structure. If by 'labour aristocracy' we mean the existence of a self-selected grouping which aims to set standards of conduct for working people in general, we must go back at least to the London Corresponding Society of the 1790s which (says Place) 'induced men to read books, instead of wasting their time in public houses' and 'taught them to respect themselves, and to desire to educate their children'.[14] In 1822 Place objected to labelling a whole class by reference to its dissolute elements; among the working people, he wrote, 'I do not include (neither ought they ever to be included) that class of wretched beings who seldom or never labour, but live or linger on in existence by the habitual practice of vice, and the perpetration of crime.'[15]

By 1834 Place was convinced that 'a separation has taken place between those who are informed and those who remain in ignorance: they no longer associate in common, as they

---

[13] E. J. Hobsbawm, *Labouring Men*, p. 276.

[14] F. Place, *Autobiography*, pp. 132, 196, 198–9.

[15] F. Place, *Illustrations and Proofs of the Principle of Population* (1967 reprint), p. 156; cf. F. Place, *Autobiography*, pp. 216, 247.

formerly did';[16] his views were published in his *The Improvement of the Working People* of that year. He thought this change had occurred during his lifetime. Morals and manners among all classes had greatly improved since the late eighteenth century; there had been relatively few respectable London families then, whereas 'now, the difference between skilled workmen and common labourers is as strongly marked as was the difference between the workman and his employer; and in many cases the difference is nearly as great and as well defined between the skilful and unskilful workman in the same business'.[17] He told the same story to the select committee on drunkenness in 1834, claiming that 'the drunken part of the community has separated very much from the orderly part of the community, as the thieves have; they now form a separate class of the community'.[18] William Lovett echoed his views, and found improvement particularly noticeable among younger men. In 1840 J. S. Mill thought that 'a larger and larger body of manual labourers' were rising above the lowest class, 'and acquiring at once decent wages and decent habits of conduct'.[19]

It is difficult to get beyond personal impressions of this type, notoriously fallible, to more precise measures of social change, given that we are concerned with a cultural change affecting a minority. But Place's analysis gains credibility from the profound influence of the respectable ideal on the Chartist movement. The better-paid working men were prominent in the three movements feeding into Chartism: Owenite branches thirsting for enlightenment; critics of the new poor law who loathed its ill-informed, indiscriminate, and insensitive herding of working people into the workhouse; factory reformers shocked at the new factory system's disruption of respectable values. The LWMA manifesto of 1836 which gave Chartism its original leadership championed respectable values in their purest form. Although Chartism always owed its numbers and dynamic impetus to mass

[16] F. Place, *Improvement of the Working People. Drunkenness—Education* (1834), p. 10.

[17] Ibid., p. 6; see also F. Place, *Autobiography*, pp. 36–7. 73.

[18] S. C. H. C. on Drunkenness, *Parl. Papers*, 1834 (559), VIII, Q.2039.

[19] BL Add. MS 27827 (Place Papers), f.30: Lovett to Place, 17 Nov. 1834; [J. S. Mill], 'Democracy in America', *Edinburgh Review*, Oct. 1840, p. 13.

support from the manufacturing districts, a London-based respectability was integral to the outlook of its leaders, who strongly resented press denigration of their characters. Like J. S. Mill in 1839, they knew that the Chartist leaders were 'almost universally its most respectable and well-conducted men'.[20]

Chartist leaders felt threatened as craftsmen by the plight of the hand-loom weavers, which stirred them to eloquent comment whenever they saw it.[21] They felt insulted by the idea that inferiority in property should disqualify for the franchise; 'it is in the very nature of the intelligent and virtuous to feel self-respect', Robert Lowery recalled in 1856, 'and the claims of manhood as man'. They resented the view of the rich that inferiors in wealth were 'not capable of being equal in intelligence, integrity, and manhood'.[22] They were disgusted at being lumped together with common criminals in prison—William Lovett protesting vigorously at having his hair shorn by a common felon.[23] Not for the only time in their history, respectable working men in the 1830s were being forced to look beneath them for political allies, but not too far below.

Why then did Lovett and other Chartist pioneers secede during the early 1840s? Because they wanted to hold Chartism on its respectable course, whereas O'Connor's vulgar populism seemed to involve pandering to the lowest instincts. Lovett and Collins's *Chartism* (1840) envisages financing schools, mobile libraries, and places for mutual improvement out of the money saved from the pub; thereby the children of the respectable could escape the bad language and bad habits of the slum. ' "Unwashed faces, unshorn chins", and dirty habits', Lovett later declared, disgusted at O'Connor's rhetoric, 'will in nowise prepare you for political or social

---

[20] J. S. Mill, 'Reorganization of the Reform Party', in G. Himmelfarb (ed.) *Essays on Politics and Culture by John Stuart Mill* (Anchor Books, 1963), p. 291; cf. H. Mayhew, *London Labour and the London Poor*, iii (1851), p. 233; F. Engels, *Working Class*, p. 236.

[21] e.g. *Robert Lowery. Radical and Chartist*, pp. 102, 113–14.

[22] Ibid., p. 99.

[23] W. Lovett, *Life and Struggles*, p. 222; cf. P. Hollis, *The Pauper Press. A Study in Working-Class Radicalism of the 1830s* (1970), p. 184.

equality with the decent portion of your brethren.'[24] Henry
Vincent told the Complete Suffrage Union conference of
1842 that 'no man was fit to be a leader of the people unless
he would tell them of their own errors'. He often attacked
charity's degrading impact on the poor, and in 1871 urged
middle and working classes to unite against 'that brawny
pauperism, which allowed people to live in the labour of
others instead of their own'.[25]

Chartist respectability required far less deference to its
leaders, far more radicalism in policy, than O'Connorism.
Like the London Corresponding Society, it usually acknowledged the permanence of differentials in property; but it
fully recognized the need for political restructuring before
property differentials would reflect gradations in strength,
talent, and effort. An opportunity-society must be pursued
through undermining class and religious privilege, superstition, protection, chauvinism, ignorance, and brutality.
For this purpose an incorruptible élite must be thrown
up from within the working class to collaborate with progressive forces higher up. Only under Marx's influence
could Ernest Jones move forward to attack 'the fruitful
seminary of that worst of all aristocracies, the aristocracy
of labour', with its unjust and 'dictatorial trade-regulations
towards their poorer fellow-workmen'.[26] This was a late-
developing and minority Chartist theme; most Chartist
leaders in later life thought their respectability well catered
for by a democratizing Liberal Party.[27]

It is with Gladstonian Liberalism that respectable ideals
first move into influencing the structure and outlook of
a major political party; its educational and libertarian
idealism admirably suited all three types of social mobility—
mobility within the working class, mobility out of the
working class, and mobility of the class as a whole towards
a new acknowledgement of its national dignity. Add to this
the Party's encouragement of thrift, idealism, and broadened

[24] LWMA, *An Address to the Chartists of the United Kingdom* (1845), p. 7,
(shelved in BL at 8138 a 55).

[25] *British Statesman*, 16 Apr. 1842, p. 5; *Ashton Reporter*, 28 Oct. 1871, p. 3.

[26] J. Saville, *Ernest Jones, Chartist* (1952), p. 194.

[27] This theme is pursued in B. Harrison and P. Hollis, 'Chartism, Liberalism
and the Life of Robert Lowery', *English Historical Review*, July 1967.

political participation, and much of the Chartist programme is realized. 'What is Radicalism, but the claim of pre-eminence for personal qualities above conventional or accidental advantages?', J. S. Mill had asked in 1839; he was naturally led on into recommending direct working-class representation in parliament through men like Lovett and Vincent.[28]

By the 1880s their successors Broadhurst, Burt, Arch, and Howell claimed the Chartist inheritance. Trade unions could easily be accommodated within such a Party, so long as they concentrated on maintaining wage differentials and craft standards while negotiating freely with the employer. Co-ops were welcome, so long as thrift and high retail standards were their hallmark rather than an Owenite communitarianism or a socialist redistribution of wealth. Classical economists were confident about the expansive potential of respectable conduct and accumulative aspirations, and like many Gladstonians anticipated the Yellow Book's Liberal ideal of 1928 whereby 'everybody will be a capitalist, and everybody a worker, as everybody is a citizen'.[29] It might temporarily be necessary to reverse the device of Marx and Engels, and define its lower elements out of the working class as a disfranchised 'residuum', but in the long term, given the persisting individualism of the labourers and the legislative moral collectivism of middle- and working-class respectability, there might be hope even for them.

Such a philosophy hardly seems 'conservative' even now, and in the Late-Victorian period it seemed radical, even anarchic, in believing that landowners must justify their wealth through service to the state; that taxation policy should so foster morality and international peace as to enable governments to wither away; that equal moral standards and legal rights should extend to all classes and both sexes; that parliament and governmental posts should be open to all classes and denominations; and that self-government at home, in Ireland, and in the colonies should extend as far as was compatible with good order. Miners, textile workers, and urban and rural working men in those crafts, denominations,

[28] G. Himmelfarb (ed.), *Essays on Politics and Culture by John Stuart Mill*, pp. 280, 295; cf. J. S. Mill, *Representative Government*, p. 290.
[29] Liberal Industrial Inquiry, *Britain's Industrial Future* (1977 reprint), p. 261.

or open villages which fostered independence could rally round the Liberal standard which—in rural areas, at least— was still claiming new territory even in the early twentieth century. As one Edwardian Liberal electioneer wrote, if in a slum 'you find an oasis . . . a dwelling with white curtains, a bright door knocker and flowers in the window—you have found a Radical who has not lost hope and wants to get on'.[30] Respectability's policies only gradually made headway within the Party as a whole, but they advanced in a series of exciting crusades whose vigour and publicity alarmed monarchs, aristocrats, professional men, and even- tually even some progressive entrepreneurs, intellectuals, and working people.

Engels had little patience with all this. In 1889 he thought 'the division of society into a scale of innumerable degrees, each recognised without question, each with its own pride but also its native respect for its "betters" and "superiors" ' was 'so old and firmly established that the bourgeois still find it pretty easy to get their bait accepted'.[31] But this is to libel both leaders and led; Liberalism offered working men symbolic recognition—through enfranchisement and direct election to parliament, together with institutional incorporation into the Liberal Party machine. It also claimed to bring tangible benefits, in so far as their prosperity was thought to depend on reduced taxation, expanded oppor- tunity, moral progress, and the extension of peace through expanded trade. And if this 'bait' should prove insufficient, the mechanism had been created whereby further gains could be made.

Nor can we accept Marx's complaint of 1878 about 'venal trade-union leaders and professional agitators' mis- leading their class.[32] The attack on corruption was integral to success within mid-Victorian working-class organizations, and if men like Howell and Broadhurst were understandably concerned for their personal security, their careers (accom- panied by singularly little social or financial appetite)

---

[30] Quot. in P. Thompson, *The Edwardians*, p. 245.

[31] Engels to Sorge, 7 Dec. 1889, in Marx and Engels, *Correspondence 1846– 1895* (1934), p. 461.

[32] K. Marx and F. Engels, *Marx and Engels on Britain*, p. 509.

simultaneously developed the self-confidence of working people as a whole. Broadhurst's relations with the Liberal Party illustrate well the shared ideals and almost prickly independence that lay behind the Lib–Lab alliance. In 1876 Gladstone seemed 'a giant of unsurpassed strength wrestling with and conquering the powers of injustice and oppression' in his attack on Bulgarian atrocities, for he was carrying the respectable working man's assault on corruption and brutality to a higher and international plane. By March 1882 Gladstone was impressed with what he saw of Broadhurst in parliament, and told the Queen that he 'spoke as he always does with the utmost modesty and propriety, which might well teach a lesson to many, and with no small ability and clearness. Like Mr Burt, his fellow working-man, he does honour to his class.'[33] When offering him ministerial office in 1886, Gladstone reminded him of their collaboration ten years before. Yet neither here—nor when earlier turning down government offers of administrative posts, nor when refusing to wear a dress coat or court dress—did Broadhurst show any undue personal ambition; he saw a working man as being out of place in such a garb, and seriously doubted whether, in view of his lack of education, he was adequately equipped for office.[34] This was no false or servile humility, but a dignified recognition that working people had their acknowledged place in the social and political order, and should not risk looking ridiculous by trying to rise too high. Far from acquiescing in this self-respecting but static view of the working man's place, Gladstone overcame Broadhurst's protestation; he therefore became the first working man to hold ministerial office. He and Arch were among Gladstone's most enthusiastic followers on Home Rule in 1886, and for Arch the autobiographer Gladstone was 'a very great man indeed . . . one of the mighty men of the earth'.[35]

John Burns, whose portrait adorned Ernest Cassell's *A New Self-Help*, published early in the twentieth century, showed a similar loyalty to Asquith after 1908. As President

[33] H. Broadhurst, *Story of His Life*, p. 88; P. Guedalla (ed.), *The Queen and Mr Gladstone, II (1880–1898)* (1933), p. 181.
[34] H. Broadhurst, *Story of His Life*, pp. 149, 188, 206.
[35] J. Arch, *Life*, p. 380.

of the Local Government Board, Burns in 1912 had some
Home Office documents unearthed on the dock strike of
1889; 'my life seems like a romance when sitting here as
a minister', he wrote in his diary. The mere presence of
a working man in such a post, however unsuccessful, did
much for the over-all status of working men in British society
as a whole. Depressed at set-backs in his ministerial career
in January 1914, Burns none the less took justifiable pride in
the fact that he had been able to 'plant the banner of Labour
on the citadel of government'.[36] His practical achievement
has not impressed later generations, whose hindsight inter-
prets his later career as involving entry into a cul-de-sac, but
the Lib–Labs had been at least as radical and courageous in
the 1880s as the Labour Party's pioneers twenty years later,
their mood at least as directly in the line of Chartist continuity, and their practical achievements for working men at
least as substantial as anything Labour was later to supply.

For Marx, 'the more a ruling class is able to assimilate the
foremost minds of a ruled class, the more stable and dangerous becomes its rule'.[37] His dictum encapsulates an important
truth, but if it assumes that assimilation in Britain carried
no implications for government policy, it is mistaken; the
new recruits are indeed absorbed, but they exact their price.
Their absorption in itself constitutes enhanced recognition
for their class, but it has policy implications as well. The
'New Liberalism', whether of T. H. Green in the 1880s or of
Churchill and Lloyd George after 1905, involved advances
of substance on Liberalism of the individualist variety. Late-
Victorian Liberalism's universal and free elementary education, temperance legislation, and state arbitration between
Irish landlord and tenant infringed the night-watchman state
in such a way as to offer respectability the hope of new
recruits. Defending national elementary education against
libertarian objection in 1875, the Manchester Liberal William
McKerrow insisted that 'no man has a right to bring up his
family to be pests and nuisances and burdens to his fellow-
men . . . the industrious and respectable working-people of

[36] BL Add. MS 46334 (John Burns's Diary), entry for 9 Sept. 1912; Add MS
46336, entry for 31 Jan. 1914.
[37] K. Marx, *Capital*, iii, p. 601.

a neighbourhood have a right to defend themselves against unnecessary rates and against the offensive conduct of those by whom they are surrounded'.[38]

Edwardian 'New Liberalism' likewise indicates responsiveness to the demands of actual or potential working-class allies, and this too involved deferring to respectable values; state intervention was not designed to oust moral priorities from the Liberal programme, only to promote them the more effectively. Old-age pensions and national insurance aimed to remove from the pauper category those working men who patently could not be blamed for their own fate; if charity could be more efficiently organized, if the poor law could be broken up, and if national insurance could alleviate the poverty resulting from ill health, old age, structural and cyclical unemployment—labour colonies could grapple with that 'residuum' whose moral calibre could be faulted. The 'new Liberal' concept of an 'unemployable' class was destroyed only by the first world war, with its unprecedented demand for labour.[39]

John Burns at the Local Government Board did not of course epitomize the 'new Liberalism' in its more constructive aspect, but its moralistic dimensions found in him an eager exponent. 'New Liberals' were keen to work in harmony with trade unions and friendly societies, enthusiastic for economical administration.[40] John Burns delighted in blocking short-term relief schemes, which he saw as subsidizing malingerers; 'this man has debauched the poor' he wrote, after Lansbury had presented him with a particularly ill-informed set of proposals for a women's farm colony in 1909. He was apprehensive about the pauperizing tendencies of Lloyd George's national insurance scheme,[41] but like Place a century earlier he enjoyed observing the spontaneous

---

[38] J. M. McKerrow, *Memoir of William McKerrow, D.D.* (1881), p. 259.

[39] G. Stedman Jones, *Outcast London. A Study in the Relationship between Classes in Victorian Society* (Oxford, 1971), pp. 335-6.

[40] Cf. P. F. Clarke, 'The Progressive Movement in England', *Transactions of the Royal Historical Society*, 1974, pp. 173-4.

[41] BL Add. MS 46327 (John Burns's Diary), entry for 16 Jan. 1909; see also K. D. Brown, *John Burns* (1977), pp. 113, 142-3, 163, 197; J. Harris, *Unemployment and Politics. A Study in English Social Policy 1886-1914* (Oxford, 1972), pp. 182, 232.

elevation of his class, as demonstrated by their improved cleanliness and sobriety in public places.[42]

The advent of Socialism and the Labour Party at first sight seems to announce the political death of the respectable working man. Late-Victorian Socialists chose the muscular labourer as their symbol, not the skilled artisan,[43] who seems to disappear as a distinct political influence. Hobsbawm's labour aristocracy is shattered simultaneously from several directions—challenged by accelerated mechanization, larger firms, deeper cyclical fluctuations, declining major staple industries, and reduced differentials in pay, so as to merge politically and industrially with labouring groups. The new alignment is consolidated by the growth of a white-collar work-force, politically much more conservative, which intrudes itself between respectable working men and their one-time political allies, the employers.[44] Late-Victorian trade unions infiltrated by labourers and permeated by Socialism are familiar in the textbooks, together with the political unification of the working class through imprudent rejection of working-class Lib–Lab candidates by Liberal constituency parties. The Labour Party—operating in a society which lacks America's expanding frontier and assimi-lative political parties—mounts a distinct and ultimately successful challenge for leadership of the British left to a moribund Liberal Party tortured by class politics.

At the same time, respectability loses the battle of ideas. Bernard Shaw takes pot-shots at Samuel Smiles in *Fabian Essays* during 1889;[45] Chamberlain challenges free trade in 1903; Charles Booth after 1889 scales down the role of moral (as opposed to structural) factors in causing poverty, and his disciple Seebohm Rowntree virtually repudiates it in 1941 by jettisoning the concept of 'secondary' poverty. The dream of universal upward mobility succumbs before J. A. Hobson's objection of 1909 that there is insufficient

---

[42] BL Add. MS 46332 (John Burns's Diary), entry for 30 Dec. 1910; Add. MS 46333, entry for 11 June 1911; Add. MS 46334, entry for 10 Sept. 1912.

[43] E. J. Hobsbawm, 'Man and Woman in Socialist Iconography', *History Workshop Journal*, no. 6 (Autumn 1978), p. 136.

[44] E. J. Hobsbawm, *Labouring Men*, pp. 274–5, 297, 300–1; cf. R. Q. Gray, *Labour Aristocracy*, pp. 167–9, 174.

[45] B. Shaw *et al.*, *Fabian Essays* (1948 ed.), pp. 9, 22.

room at the top, so that this working man can rise only if that one does not.[46] Blatchford in 1902 can therefore see the ideal of self-help as inflicting 'a brutal insult upon the unsuccessful'.[47]

Cracks endanger the foundations of the respectable working man's institutions. Benefit societies 'flourish on the misfortune of their members', says Quelch, because the respectable are funded by members who default on their payments.[48] The co-op movement's real function, says William Clarke, is merely to raise 'certain persons out of the working into the middle class'.[49] The temperance society is dragged down by Quelch and others from tackling causes to tinkering with symptoms. Sobriety pays only because most working men drink; as soon as they abstain, employers will drive wages down because an abstainer can live on less than a drinker.[50] All this leaves the Lib–Lab MP high and dry. Broadhurst looks nostalgically and irrelevantly back to the harmonious industrial relations of his Norwich stonemason's workshop of the 1860s; Arch in his Gladstonian autobiography hopes against hope that 'present-day Socialism will die a natural death sooner or later'; and Howell finds himself in a predominantly middle-class Liberal backwater, cut off from new tendencies in the trade-union movement which he had done so much to develop.[51]

The portrait has a superficial plausibility, but it fails to bring out the vitality of respectability as a political influence; it also fails to recognize that the advent of the Labour Party constitutes collective self-help on a grand scale, under leaders profoundly influenced by the ideals of respectability. Engels comments on the respectability of Owenite working men as early as the 1840s,[52] and the careers of Hardie, Snowden, and Henderson illustrate how readily the career-ladder opened

---

[46] J. A. Hobson, *The Crisis of Liberalism* (1909), p. 204.
[47] R. Blatchford, *Britain for the British* (1902), p. 123.
[48] *Justice*, 2 July 1887, p. 2.
[49] *Fabian Essays*, p. 83.
[50] R. Blatchford, *Britain for the British*, p. 122; H. Quelch, *Literary Remains* (ed. E. B. Bax, 1914), p. 198; for further discussion, see my *Drink and the Victorians*, pp. 396–405.
[51] J. Arch, *Life*, p. 404; F. M. Leventhal, *Respectable Radical*, p. 210.
[52] F. Engels, *Working Class*, p. 270.

out from the chapel into the politics of labour. New movements in ideas seldom attract the poorest or least educated
groups in society; 'it is respectable, self-respecting men
and women who will make the great Social revolution',
wrote *Justice* in 1886, 'not the unfortunate starvelings and
paupers who have been crushed into misery by our brutal
civilisation'.[53] Middle-class opinion was so deeply affected
by events in 1889 only because they revealed the capacity
even of dockers for respectability.[54] Ramsay MacDonald
pointed out in 1908 that the early Labour Party prospered,
not in the poorest areas of London, but in constituencies
'with a large population of skilled artisans . . . An active
church and chapel organization with guilds, brotherhoods,
Sunday morning adult classes, is most advantageous to us.'[55]
Philip Snowden in the 1930s wistfully recalled the strongly
ethical flavour of the early ILP, and yearned for a modern
socialist movement that 'could recapture the spiritual exalta-
tion and religious faith of those early days'.[56]

The traffic between the new party and its respectable
recruits was by no means entirely one way. Like the Liberals
earlier, Labour was deeply influenced in its over-all outlook
by the mood of its new personnel. Whereas in France the
three functions of friendly society, industrial bargaining,
and working-class political representation came to be exercised by different organizations,[57] in Britain they were
combined in the Labour Party, the mood of whose branches
(and even the flavour of whose national policy) long reflected
a puritanism, a belief in self-education, and a suspicion of the
state which at this stage in the argument will not be unfamiliar. Even the early British Marxists combined secularist
zeal with an earnest desire for self-improvement; their

---

[53] *Justice*, 8 May 1886, p. 3; cf. H. Pelling, *Popular Politics and Society*, pp.
56, 58–9; J. Reynolds and K. Laybourn, 'The Emergence of the Independent
Labour Party in Bradford', *International Review of Social History*, 1975, p. 319.

[54] G. Stedman Jones, *Outcast London*, pp. 315–16.

[55] Quot. in J. W. Wolfenden, 'English Nonconformity and the Social Conscience, 1880–1906' (unpublished Ph.D. thesis, Yale, 1954), p. 152. See also
P. Thompson, *Socialists, Liberals and Labour. The Struggle for London 1885–
1914* (1967), p. 239.

[56] P. Snowden, *An Autobiographer* (1934), i, pp. 63–4, cf. pp. 71, 81.

[57] D. Thomson, *Democracy in France since 1870* (5th ed., 1969), p. 48.

laborious poring over their texts was spiced with a touch
of contempt for the mentality of the ordinary British worker.
In the absence of any substantial middle-class influx into Communism, this tradition survived into the 1920s until eroded
by Leninist variants of Marxism and by an improved system
of secondary education that channelled intelligent working
men elsewhere.[58] As for the Labour Party's pioneer leaders,
however vigorously they might attack the Liberal Party, or
even Liberalism, they remained Liberals in outlook and
conduct. Keir Hardie, Snowden, and Henderson were lifelong puritans, economical in their way of living, hostile to
notions of class war, idealistic exponents of free trade and
international peace.

There was a natural harmony of tastes, if not of argu-
mentation, between such men and the intellectuals who
entered the Labour Party via the Fabian Society and the
SDF. The intellectuals, too, were inspired by the distaste—
religious, medical, bureaucratic, feminist, humanitarian,
aesthetic—for a society which could produce 'the brutal
reckless faces and figures' glimpsed by Morris out of his
Hammersmith window in 1881. In its manifesto of 1885
the Socialist League deplored working-class degradation
and 'the terrible brutality so common among them'.[59] The
Labour Party was soon required to reproduce in a new guise
the Liberal Party's classless union of humanitarians.

Labour's affinity with the Liberals on respectability is
well illustrated by Labour's attitude to Liberal temperance
measures. Keir Hardie had once been a temperance orator,
and the personal abstinence of a Lansbury and a Morrison
owed much to the memory of a father who drank. It is
hardly surprising that Labour MPs heartily welcomed the
Liberals' Licensing Bill of 1908. Henderson said that during
his time in parliament he had never heard a scheme un-
folded 'which gave me such general satisfaction'; Snowden
gave the bill his strong support; Hardie did not think the

[58] S. Yeo, 'A New Life: The Religion of Socialism in Britain, 1883–1896',
History Workshop Journal, no. 4 (Autumn 1977), p. 15; S. Macintyre, *A Proletarian Science. Marxism in Britain 1917–1933* (Cambridge, 1980), pp. 70–2,
94–5, 98–9, 108.

[59] E. P. Thompson, *William Morris. Romantic to Revolutionary* (2nd ed.,
1977), pp. 247, 734.

bill went far enough.[60] Marxian restiveness at Labour's temperance alignment hardly surfaced in the debates; here, as so often elsewhere, Labour's political leadership shared the social outlook of the Liberal government. In the following year Snowden noted that the ILP 'contains among its membership a larger proportion of abstainers than any other political organisation in the country'. In good respectable tradition, Snowden was neither then nor later reluctant to inform his fellow working men of their weaknesses; his pamphlet of 1936 entitled *End This Colossal Waste* respectfully refers to the abstaining working classes as 'the backbone of the democratic political movement in this country'.[61]

Labour struck an equally respectable note in response to the Liberal welfare programme. On old-age pensions in 1908 Snowden's main complaint was that to omit those with an income of more than 10s. a week 'excluded from the pension a very large and most deserving section of the community'.[62] Labour leaders shared the Liberal distrust of state hand-outs as a threat to moral effort.[63] In a socialist society, said Blatchford, there would be work for all, so 'the answer to the able-bodied beggar would be "If you are hungry go and work". If the man refused to work he must starve.'[64] Labour was as divided as the Liberals on whether women should receive the vote via a restricted property franchise. Henderson, Snowden, and Hardie supported women's suffrage in any form; 'the strength of Toryism, of every vested interest, is in the working-class vote', wrote Snowden, advocating a property qualification for women in 1909, '. . . Let us disabuse our minds of the cant and humbug that all virtue resides in the wage-earning class . . .

---

[60] *H. C. Deb.*, 27 Feb. 1908, c.118; 28 Apr. 1908, cc.1180 ff; 20 Oct. 1908, cc.988 ff. See also P. Snowden, *An Autobiography*, i, p. 187; K. O. Morgan, *Keir Hardie. Radical and Socialist*, p. 9.

[61] P. Snowden, *Socialism and Teetotalism* (1909), p. 2; Viscount Snowden, *End This Colossal Waste. A Neglected Palliative for Unemployment* (1936), p. 16; cf. *The Common Cause*, 6 Oct. 1910, p. 410.

[62] P. Snowden, *An Autobiography*, i, pp. 190-1.

[63] H. V. Emy, *Liberals, Radicals and Social Politics 1892-1914* (Cambridge, 1973), p. 158.

[64] R. Blatchford, *Merrie England* (1894), p. 187.

The simple truth is that Socialism owes nearly all it has become to middle-class men and women.' Many labour activists, however, favoured women's emancipation only through adult-suffrage.[65]

On national insurance in 1911, Ramsay MacDonald felt that without the contributory principle 'the whole scheme would degenerate into a national charity of the most vicious kind, which would adversely affect wages and would not help the Socialist spirit'.[66] Of Labour's MPs, C. F. G. Masterman said that 'in their excellences as in their defects they stand sharply distinct from the excellences and defects of the average English artisan. They care for things he cares nothing for; he cares for things which seem to them trivial and childish.'[67] Like their Lib–Lab predecessors, the early Labour MPs saw working-class traditionalism and conservatism as the enemy, and sought to gain full recognition of working-class dignity through incorporation within the political system. Before the first world war, it seemed likely that this would occur through Labour's incorporation into a broadened Liberal movement, but in the transformed situation of 1917 the same destination had to be approached by a different route.

Ramsay MacDonald was ideally equipped to preside over this process, whatever his subsequent failures. As the illegitimate son of a Scottish servant-girl who became a pupil-teacher and learned his public speaking in a mutual improvement society, he seemed destined for respectable Lib–Labbery. And though in the 1880s he was influenced by Socialism, this is probably what would have happened but for the first world war's transformation of Labour's potential. Even in the 1890s, MacDonald was ready to work in alliance with Liberals, whom he saw in 1892 as but one of the 'two separate wings' necessary to build up 'a great progressive party'. His attacks on the Liberal Party before 1914 fell into a well-established tradition whereby its leadership was pushed

---

[65] *Christian Commonwealth*, 31 Mar. 1909, p. 458; cf. B. Harrison, *Separate Spheres*, p. 42.

[66] D. Marquand, *Ramsay MacDonald* (1977), pp. 138–41.

[67] Quot. in S. Yeo, *Religion and Voluntary Organisations in Crisis* (1976), p. 271.

leftwards by dissident sympathizers whose trenchant oratory was designed to conceal the fact that their bark was worse than their bite. In 1913–14 he would himself have favoured a new electoral pact with the Liberals, and when the Liberals offered cabinet office in 1912 and 1914, his refusals probably stemmed from tactical considerations rather than from personal inclination.[68]

In the transformed political situation of the 1920s, MacDonald's attacks on the Liberal Party became more destructive in intent, for Labour now had the hope, as it had not had before 1914, of actually supplanting the Liberals as the major party of the left. Its 1918 programme deliberately threw the Liberals on to the defensive with its collectivist rhetoric. But this was misleading as a guide to what the Labour Party would eventually do in office, as well as to what Liberal governments could not have done. Lloyd George predicted some such outcome in a conversation of December 1917; whereas Buckmaster envisaged labour dictating the policy of the next government and insisting 'that wealth shall pay', Lloyd George pointed out that ' "Labour" means skilled Labour and there is quite as great a gulf between skilled and unskilled Labour as between the propertied class and Labour generally.'[69] Labour's assault on the Liberals in the 1920s did not involve an attack on Liberalism. On the contrary, it sought to attract Liberals by itself espousing Liberal policies—free trade, extended political participation, international peace, moderate political and social reform, and the defence of the individual against the state. On public-works schemes in 1924 MacDonald viewed his attack on extemporized palliatives and his refusal to draw off large sums 'from the normal channels of trade' as 'the old, sound socialist doctrine'; his Gladstonian outlook here recalls John Burns's scorn for Lansbury before 1914. Burns's zeal for economical management at the Local Government Board also reappears in MacDonald's Chancellor of the Exchequer; in 1929, for example, Snowden branded family allowances as 'nothing but a proposal for pauperising

[68] D. Marquand, *Ramsay MacDonald* (1977), pp. 33, 41, 151, 160, 162; R. McKibbin, *The Evolution of the Labour Party 1910–1924* (1974), pp. 77, 79.
[69] BL Add. MS 50904 (C. P. Scott Diary), f. 223 (28 Dec. 1917).

outdoor relief'.[70] For MacDonald in 1929 'the State as Lady Bountiful' was not the beginning of Socialism but 'a fatal extension of Toryism'.[71]

1931 carries to its culmination the respectable working man's enthusiasm for political incorporation and economical administration. Dignifying his class in 1924 by assuming the role of prime minister, MacDonald in 1931 grasped the ultimate symbol of incorporation involved in becoming saviour of the nation. Nor did this require him to repudiate respectable attitudes, for it involved a frontal assault on what he described in August as the 'Poor Law frame of mind' that led Socialists to assume that handing out 'largesse to the community' would solve all problems.[72] He and Snowden fully agreed in opposing state doles for the unemployed as demoralizing,[73] and after forming the National Government MacDonald condemned a Labour Party 'whose ideal of Socialism is not much more than public subsidies'.[74] It is impossible to say how far MacDonald's standpoint in 1931 enabled him to carry Labour's rank-and-file respectables along with him. The government's scare about Post Office savings deposits at the election no doubt helped in this, and MacDonald was able to win even a mining constituency like Seaham with a majority of 5,951 over Labour. Nor had he lost the respectable working man's fear of the degradation threatening him from below. When contesting Seaham in 1935 he likened his female opponents to *tricoteuses*, their faces 'lined with destitution; their eyes flamed and gleamed with hate and passion; their hair . . . dishevelled; their language filthy with oaths and some obscenity' filling him 'with loathing and fear just like French Revolution studies. Night after night their misery was upon me.'[75]

Yet respectability can be found on both sides in Labour's schism of 1931—in Snowden and MacDonald, perhaps, but also in Lansbury, Morrison, Henderson, and Margaret Bondfield. The Party's internal history since 1931 has largely centred upon a debate about how to recapture the electoral

[70] P. Snowden, *An Autobiography*, ii, p. 628; City of London Polytechnic: Fawcett Library Autograph Collection, Snowden to Mrs Fawcett, 23 Apr. 1929.
[71] D. Marquand, *Ramsay MacDonald*, p. 525.
[72] Ibid., p. 609.
[73] Ibid., pp. 586-7.
[74] Ibid., p. 674, cf. p. 675.
[75] Ibid., p. 781.

dynamic which a relatively classless reformism had lent the
pre-war Liberal Party—all the more necessary for it, given
the diminishing number of electors who could be defined,
objectively or subjectively, as members of the working class.
The same Late-Victorian industrial changes that had caused
some respectable working men to cultivate the labourers
as political allies ensured that white-collar workers became
one of the trade unions' major twentieth-century growth
areas; their numbers increased by 147 per cent between
1911 and 1961, and their proportion of the labour force
during the same period rose from 19 per cent to 36 per
cent.[76] Educational and technological change were blurring
the clarity of the old divide between middle and working
class, and if Labour failed to adapt accordingly, other parties
might pre-empt its ground; indeed, the political conservatism
of white-collar workers is mentioned in passing by historians
of the labour aristocracy. Herbert Morrison for one was not
prepared to acquiesce in such an alignment; as a key figure
within the Labour Party's machine between the wars, he
went out to recruit women, intellectuals, 'middle opinion',
white-collar occupations, and meritocrats from the suburbs.

Morrison's practice receives retrospective theoretical
justification in Evan Durbin's *Politics of Democratic Socialism*
(1940), which outlines the arguments that were to become
familiar among Labour's revisionists in the 1950s: 'the
society in which we live', he announced, 'is an increasingly
bourgeois society'. Classes intermediate between bourgeoisie
and proletariat were growing instead of following the
patterns of contraction that Marx—in some, though not all,
his writings—had predicted. Durbin argued that in this non-
revolutionary situation, with a dwindling proletariat which
now had so much more to lose than its chains, the Labour
Party should work out a practicable, moderate, detailed
programme for a forthcoming Labour government in the hope
of implementing it through the existing political structure.[77]

---

[76] G. S. Bain, *Trade Union Growth and Recognition with Special Reference
to White-Collar Unions in Private Industry* (Royal Commission on Trade Unions
and Employers' Associations, Research Paper No. 6), p. 3.

[77] E. F. M. Durbin, *The Politics of Democratic Socialism. An Essay on Social
Policy* (1954 ed.), p. 112; see also pp. 109, 117, 144.

Revisionists' efforts to repudiate Labour's class-sectarianism since the 1930s stem from the belief that amid the affluence which economic growth now made possible, new political options were opening up for working-class respectability. Hugh Gaitskell found Durbin's message as relevant to the politics of the 1950s as to those of the late 1930s, and Crosland followed broadly similar lines in his *The Future of Socialism* (1956).[78] Given the dramatic rise in real living standards since 1945, the advent of television, and the mass ownership of cars and other consumer durables, revisionists felt that the Labour Party must make terms with a working-class home-centredness, the scale of which would have gratified the respectability of a Place, a Lovett, and a Broadhurst.

Yet Labour's revisionists were by no means always in harmony with respectable aspirations. Like others in the Party, their egalitarian and statist attitudes offended against that nurturing of pay differentials, that faith in free collective bargaining, which have long been hallmarks of respectability. In vain since 1945 have Socialists pressed upon their Party's trade-union rank and file the need to moderate inequalities of income, to repudiate 'the free-for-all society',[79] and to cease apologizing for the high taxes needed to finance welfare benefits.[80] 'Respectable' attitudes to poverty show a surprising twentieth-century persistence; poverty surveys of the late 1960s show the poor (however defined) as reluctant to admit dissatisfaction at their situation, and people who call themselves 'working class' as locating themselves above an inferior and workless under-class.[81] A poll of 1976 found the British much less sympathetic to the poor than the members of any other country in the EEC; for them, poverty stemmed largely from laziness and drink, whereas other countries

[78] Gaitskell's preface to Durbin, op. cit., p. 8; see also C. A. R. Crosland, *The Future of Socialism* (1956), p. 172.

[79] Barbara Castle, quot. in *The Times*, 21 July 1977, p. 8; cf. Ray Gunter, *Observer*, 18 Sept. 1966, p. 1; P. Jenkins, *The Battle of Downing Street* (1970), pp. 42–3.

[80] James Callaghan, in *Guardian*, 14 Mar. 1978, p. 6; cf. Mrs Castle in *Sunday Times*, 2 Mar. 1975, p. 6.

[81] P. Townsend, *Poverty in the United Kingdom* (Penguin ed., 1979), pp. 410, 431.

gave higher priority to lack of education or a deprived childhood. A fifth of the British respondents thought the government did too much to help the poor—by far the highest percentage in any of the countries surveyed.[82]

Labour's revisionists simultaneously offended respectable values with some of their policy standpoints—most notably through their 'permissive' outlook on immigration and personal conduct. They were eager to combat working-class hostility to immigration—a hostility which (as will be argued below) is deeply permeated with the values of respectability. At the same time Crosland's *Future of Socialism* challenged Labour's identification with austerity, and favoured relaxing the laws on abortion, licensing, drink, and censorship; Hugh Gaitskell was equally impatient with puritanical attempts at regulating popular pleasures. Later in his career Crosland, ever alert to his Party's electoral interests, sought to distance himself from Labour's preoccupation with middle-class moral and cultural issues, and urged his Party to seek a wider appeal. 'I have long been locked in conflict', he wrote, 'with a middle-class element on the left which seems to me to show an élitist and even condescending attitude to the wants and aspirations of ordinary people.'[83]

Conservatives were thus presented with many opportunities for encroachment. 'Conservatism is more than successful administration', said the Party's manifesto of 1959: 'it is a way of life. It stands for integrity as well as for efficiency, for moral values as well as for material advancement, for service and not merely self-seeking.'[84] Traditions of respectability cannot in fact be seen as operating exclusively on the British left. Mid-Victorian respectable radicals might see the Tory working man as a contradiction in terms, a freak, or a deception, and 'Tory Democracy' a fraud. Nor can it be denied that nineteenth-century popular Conservatism contained elements of what the radical saw as a rustic and

---

[82] European Commission poll, *The Times*, 21 July 1977, p. 5.

[83] Crosland in *Sunday Times*, 4 Apr. 1971, p. 16; see also his *The Future of Socialism* (1956), pp. 288, 290, 293, 521-4, and cf. P. M. Williams, *Hugh Gaitskell. A Political Biography* (1979), pp. 390-2.

[84] D. E. Butler and R. Rose, *The British General Election of 1959* (1960), p. 257.

benighted Anglicanism, a depraved loyalty to the publican, an unthinking taste for the racecourse and the boxing-ring, a traditionalist acquiescence in a landed hierarchy, a childish delight in warlike ceremonial, and a contented acquiescence in drink bribes and degrading doles: respectability's valuation of 'independence' could hardly be detected here. Indeed, it became part of the respectable working man's heroic story that he was sometimes required to stand up for his views against drunken jingo mobs—with John Burns on Mafeking night warding off the mob in the hallway of his house with a cricket bat.[85]

Yet Conservatives have always sought to cater for working-class ideals of respectability, not through political incorporation or through integrating working-class organizations into the political system, but in different areas of life and in a different way. They know that their Party's strength rests on attachment to the magic of the individual (whether locally or nationally known) and on direct calls to the nation as a whole rather than through sectional appeals. Once again the temperance question can act as a touchstone of party attitudes here. A Conservative Party with its paternalist, philanthropic, and humanitarian traditions might well have responded to temperance demands, but for their stridency, class-divisiveness, and sectarianism of tone. Yet only in the exceptional situation created by alliance with the Liberal Unionists in 1886 did the Party feel much temperance pressure. By 1908 the Liberal Unionists had either departed or had been digested, so that when Milner urged Conservatives not to alienate the temperance enthusiasms of the Party's increasing support 'especially in the middle and better working-class' by defeating the Liberals' Licensing Bill, his plea went unheard.[86] Yet when respectability took more overtly patriotic directions it could win enthusiastic Conservative backing.

The nineteenth-century volunteer movement drew on extensive Conservative working-class support from the start, and became increasingly Conservative in tone as the century

[85] K. D. Brown, *John Burns*, p. 94.

[86] A. M. Gollin, *Proconsul in Politics. A Study of Lord Milner in Opposition and in Power* (1964), p. 155.

wore on. And when patriotism took an anti-Irish direction, it could mobilize the respectable working man as vigorously in the 1880s against the outsider as against the Jews in the 1930s, or against Commonwealth immigrants in the 1960s. A Conservative leaflet of 1894 complained that the Liberals did so much for evicted Irish tenants, yet 'the industrious and honest poor of England have nothing done for them'. Conservative propaganda complained in 1904 of immigrants suffering 'from loathsome diseases' who filled the streets 'with profligacy and disorder', and stressed the Party's reluctance 'to see the honest Britisher turned out by these scourings of European slums'.[87] Alien cultures apparently threatened the respectability of the working-class community, which feared the drunkenness of the Irish Saturday night, the squalid poverty and alleged disease of the East European immigrant, the foreign customs and clothing of the Pakistani or the West Indian, not to mention competition from all three groups in the labour market. The Conservative Party could also appeal here to the respectable working man preoccupied with the education of his children, for in the area of immigration policy the concern was as much to prevent downward mobility (of individuals within the host nation) as to promote mobility upward. Joseph Chamberlain's firm declaration against Home Rule in 1885–6 (in the long run a major boost for the Conservative Party) owed much to his belief that 'the anti-Irish feeling is very strong with our best friends—the respectable artisans and the non-Conformists'. Again during the 1960s Conservatism in the Midlands was nourished by the more prosperous working man's fear of the immigrant as a threat to property values, educational standards, and social status.[88]

The Liberal and Labour parties have repeatedly tried to play down such sentiments as irrational, even Fascist. Hence the need felt by C. A. R. Crosland to brand such explanations as 'libellous and impertinent', and to emphasize that

[87] R. T. McKenzie and A. Silver, *Angels in Marble. Working Class Conservatives in Urban England* (1968), pp. 55, 60; see also H. Cunningham, *The Volunteer Force. A Social and Political History 1859–1908* (1975), pp. 108, 123.

[88] A. L. Thorold, *The Life of Henry Labouchere* (1913), p. 278, cf. p. 250 and J. L. Garvin, *Chamberlain*, ii, p. 120; N. Deakin (ed.), *Colour and the British Electorate, 1964* (1965), p. 166; I owe this last reference to Dr McKibbin.

working-class hostility to immigrants reflects 'a genuine sense of insecurity, and anxiety for a traditional way of life'; or by George Orwell to point out that 'the first step towards serious study of antisemitism is to stop regarding it as a crime'.[89] Conservatives are less embarrassed by the issue, and recognize that many of the problems thrown up by first-generation immigrants within the working-class community are real, and are rationally perceived by those who complain about them. Their standpoint here also accords well with their readiness, at least since the 1870s, to make populist assaults on the 'cosmopolitanism' of parties of the left. Nor does this exhaust the categories of respectable working man likely to be tempted into Conservative voting. Mid-Victorian Conservative working-class voters included groups labelled by Hobsbawm as 'on the whole . . . exceptional'—Anglican in allegiance, aristocratic in dependence, or (as champions of factory legislation) keen to preserve the working man's independence *vis-à-vis* his Liberal employer. The life cycle of the respectable working man discussed earlier led naturally into Liberal rather than Conservative politics during the nineteenth century. Yet the Blackburn poll-books of 1868 show the Conservative working-class voter as being not so very exceptional; allegiance to the employer's party (whether Liberal or Conservative) comes from every level of employee, and by no means only from a working-class élite.[90] In a society where personal service was so widespread an ideal and practice, working-class respectability could readily take a non-radical direction. In the twentieth century the growth of white-collar employment, with its close proximity to the employer, greatly extended the scope for respectability through emulation.[91]

[89] Crosland, *Observer*, 21 Jan. 1973, p. 8; G. Orwell, *Collected Essays, Journalism and Letters*, iv, p. 513, writing in 1948.

[90] E. J. Hobsbawm, *Labouring Men*, p. 274; P. Joyce, *Work, Society and Politics*, pp. 205, 210–11, 345 and ff. See also J. R. Vincent, *Pollbooks*, p. 16; H. Pelling, *Social Geography of British Elections 1885–1910* (1967), p. 58; R. Harrison, *Before the Socialists. Studies in Labour and Politics. 1861-1881* (1964), p. 161.

[91] On this issue see H. Pelling, *Social Geography*, p. 425; R. T. McKenzie and A. Silver, *Angels in Marble*, pp. 93–4, 97.

In twentieth-century conditions, however, the Conservatives could not content themselves with attracting only the deferential variant of working-class respectability; they had to capitalize upon the Labour Party's collectivism, and attract the working people who, for whatever reason, favoured those twin objectives once so vigorously canvassed on the British left—personal social mobility and a property-owning democracy. Even nineteenth-century Conservatives had felt able to accommodate social mobility through the advancement of talent and enterprise, provided that this was not accompanied by aggressive class attitudes. The prominent early Conservative practitioners of social mobility—Peel, Disraeli, F. E. Smith, Sir Edward Clarke—were moving up from the middle class towards the aristocracy. But during the twentieth century the Party has increasingly concerned itself with promoting social mobility lower down. The ideal of 'setting the people free', championing working-class enterprise and individual ambition, was espoused by Conservative leaders from Baldwin onwards, and there is some evidence that it has struck home. Survey material from the 1960s showed that working people who rose into the middle class were drawn to a disproportionate extent from children of working-class Conservatives.[92] Furthermore, far from being an ignorant lumpenproletariat, Conservative working-class voters were by then somewhat better informed than Labour working-class voters and more confident of being able to influence government policy.[93] It was noted even in the 1950s that manual workers who rated themselves as middle class were much more likely than any other social grouping to describe the working class in derogatory moral, rather than occupational, terms.[94]

By 1970 the Conservative Party's election manifesto was holding out promises that could have been drawn verbatim from a radical speech of a century before: 'we want people to achieve the security and independence of personal ownership, greater freedom of opportunity, greater freedom of

[92] D. E. Butler and D. Stokes, *Political Change in Britain. Forces Shaping Electoral Choice* (1969), p. 99.

[93] R. T. McKenzie and A. Silver, *Angels in Marble*, pp. 121-4.

[94] D. V. Glass (ed.), *Social Mobility in Britain* (1954), p. 61.

choice, greater freedom from government regulation and interference'.[95] In recruiting leaders who had risen from the lower middle class, the Party in the 1970s even came to display something of that censoriousness adopted by the socially mobile towards those who have been left behind.[96] The explicit advocacy of self-help as 'the only real lasting help we can give to the poor'[97] was once more heard in the land, and from unexpected quarters came praise for the 'artisan of Victorian days, who read serious literature, supported radical causes, was sober and self-improving'.[98] Like Liberals before them, Conservatives who argued in this way ignored the unreality of such an ideal for large sections of the population, yet this aspect of the Conservative appeal is likely to attract an extensive respectable working-class following in the future, and perhaps especially from within the more entrepreneurial sections of the immigrant community.

Since the late eighteenth century, therefore, all three major political parties have catered in their different ways for traditions of working-class respectability. To revert to the sevenfold classification of the working man's choices outlined earlier, the discussion of the respectable working man's life cycle, and of the institutions which catered for it, reveals that there has long been a close affinity between positions three and six, but that at times—in the 1830s, for example, or among Late-Victorian Socialists—position seven rises tentatively into view. Chartism and its antecedents showed a particular interest in positions two, three, and six, with elements of position seven in so far as their ultimate aim was to supersede aristocratic government; but much confusion was caused among contemporaries and since by their failure to distinguish between their four favoured positions. Gladstonian Liberalism was able to attract so many old Chartists because it also offered positions two, three, and six, but its appeal was always broader than that because it catered also

[95] *Guardian*, 27 May 1970, p. 8; cf. Mrs Thatcher, *The Times*, 12 June 1978, p. 2.
[96] Cf. Brian Walden, in *The Times*, 17 Apr. 1971, p. 22.
[97] e.g. for Sir Keith Joseph at Birmingham, *Observer*, 20 Oct. 1974, p. 2.
[98] *Guardian*, 16 Jan. 1975, p. 30 (Sir Keith Joseph).

for positions four and five. It is because the last two of these positions are sometimes confused with the first three that the Party's working-class appeal is sometimes underestimated.

Given its Whig component and the wily leadership it received from Gladstone, the Liberal Party could begin to cater for position seven only in the early twentieth century; but for Liberals throughout their history, position seven did not extend to anything more than the attack on aristocracy. Nor, despite its rhetoric, was the Labour Party very different; it simply carried into a new generation, and with a new energy, the Liberal preoccupation with positions two, three, and six, but without the Liberals' capacity to cater for positions four and five. Labour's successes in its chosen area were considerable, but its neglect of positions four and five left new territory for the twentieth-century Conservative Party to colonize—together with position one, for which Conservatives have always been happy to cater, and moderate variants of positions two and three. An important and continuing aspect of early twentieth-century British political history has therefore been the vigorous competition between Labour and Conservative for respectability's dimension of the Liberal legacy. Conservatives have lost much support here by their lack of interest in position six, but have recouped some of it by their firm repudiation of position seven, and since 1945 they have made special efforts with positions two, three, four, and five. Respectability therefore shows no sign of retreating from prominence as a theme in British political life.

V

Philanthropy and the Victorians[1]

'Among the social changes in my lifetime, in the London that I have known', wrote Beatrice Webb, 'none is more striking than the passing "out of the picture" of personal alms-giving.'[2] Victorian Britain cannot be fully understood without attempting to comprehend this vanished world in which the Victorians took such pride. 'In no other kingdom, we believe, under the sun', wrote the *Nonconformist* in 1842 on the May Meetings, 'is there such a periodical gathering of benevolence and piety.' After attending a crowded ragged-schools meeting in 1846, Shaftesbury noted in a diary normally prone to gloom that 'these things are now becoming "fashionable". Humanity will soon be considered "elegant", "genteel", &c. &c.'[3]

Of 640 London charities alive in 1860, no less than 279 were founded between 1800 and 1850, and 144 between 1850 and 1860; by the 1860s they were raising annually about as much as the total annual expenditure of the poor-law system in the whole of England and Wales—not to mention the voluntary labour involved and the numerous private and unrecorded acts of charity.[4] The process began at an early age, with children contributing £13,195 to the London Missionary Society in 1841–5 and £6,300 to the Wesleyan Missionary Society's juvenile Christmas appeal of 1855. 'They offered most willingly, nay joyfully', wrote Shaftesbury somewhat innocently of his children's contributions towards financing the bishopric of Jerusalem in

---

[1] This essay incorporates all I wish to preserve from the article with the same title which was published in *Victorian Studies*, June 1966; it adds a great deal of new material and has been completely rewritten.

[2] B. Webb, *My Apprenticeship* (2nd ed., n.d.), p. 167, n. 1.

[3] *Nonconformist*, 27 Apr. 1842, p. 265; E. Hodder, *Shaftesbury*, ii, p. 151. See also *Quarterly Review*, lxx (1842), p. 389.

[4] E. Lascelles, 'Charity', in G. M. Young (ed.), *Early Victorian England 1830–1865* (1934), ii, p. 320; McCord, in D. Fraser (ed.), *The New Poor Law in the Nineteenth Century* (1976), p. 97.

1841, 'and, wonderful to say, the little ones did it without a word on my part; I had spoken to the elder boys, who cheerfully acquiesced; the little ones, hearing from them, burned to do likewise.'[5]

It was a sign of Gladstone's political courage as Chancellor of the Exchequer in 1863 that he dared to contest some of philanthropy's privileges.[6] National celebrations and anniversaries illustrate how central philanthropy was within British society; coronations and jubilees inspired fund-raising for good causes and witnessed mass distributions of food and drink to children and the poor. 'Hospital Sunday' was an important annual social event in many Late-Victorian communities, and charitable meetings provided one of many nineteenth-century opportunities for royalty and aristocracy to display itself. The RSPCA's chairman, the Earl of Harrowby, explained the poor attendance at the Society's annual meeting of 1877 by referring to the unexpected absence of Princess Christian; 'humanity is a very popular thing, but Princesses are popular also, and still more attractive'.[7]

Through large-scale benefactions, knighthoods could be won.[8] The sale of honours was commonplace within the philanthropic world; a United Kingdom Alliance vice-presidency was at the disposal of anyone giving £1,000 or more to its guarantee fund. At the local level, too, prestige could be won in this way; this is the source of Mrs Henley's social distinction at Charlotte Yonge's fashionable summer resort of St. Mildred's.[9] Among nineteenth-century American millionaires, philanthropy was more likely to attract the self-made;[10] can the same be said of Britain? Before an answer to this and similar questions can even be sought, questions of definition must first be faced.

[5] E. Hodder, *Shaftesbury*, i, p. 381; F. K. Prochaska, 'Charity Bazaars in Nineteenth-Century England', *Journal of British Studies*, Spring 1977, p. 75.

[6] F. W. Hirst, *Gladstone as Financier and Economist* (1931), p. 286.

[7] RSPCA *53rd A.R., 1877*, p. 22.

[8] See e.g. Sir E. Hamilton, *Diary* (ed. Bahlman), ii, p. 653, and the help given by the RSPCA to Sir George Measom, in RSPCA *Minutes No. 16*, p. 141 (7 Feb. 1888); p. 322 (5 Jan. 1891).

[9] C. Yonge, *The Heir of Redclyffe* (Collins ed., n.d.), p. 205.

[10] M. Curti *et al.*, 'Anatomy of Giving: Millionaires in the Late Nineteenth Century', in S. M. Lipset and R. Hofstadter (eds.), *Sociology and History: Methods* (New York paperback ed., 1968), pp. 282–5.

I

Changes in the amount and direction of organized philanthropy can be charted from the abundant (if scattered)
annual reports, which usually contain subscription lists. In
the case of particular charities, it should also be possible to
estimate the proportion of the total contributed by donors
of specific amounts, and even the proportions given by
different regions and sections of the community. But it is
difficult to see how voluntary nineteenth-century transfer-
payments can ever be precisely measured, still less their
changing proportion of the national income. Charity was
often very informal; the cash which flowed between the two
streams of humanity whom Dr Phelps observed descending
on Edwardian Oxford at the beginning of term—the undergraduates and the 'perfect army of beggars and tramps'—
probably never entered a subscription list.[11] Much charity
was secret on principle. Dr Barnardo, for instance, did not
publish more than the initials of his donors; John Bright in
the 1840s made his donations anonymously through a Rochdale missionary; and Joseph Chamberlain's charity was often
deliberately channelled through Jesse Collings.[12] The Late-
Victorian writing of begging letters became almost an
industry; referring in a speech of 1886 to Rosebery's 'enor-
mous and unlimited wealth', Lord Randolph Churchill
evoked from Rosebery the complaint that as a result
'thousands of mendicant pens are being sharpened'.[13]

Victorian philanthropy will remain unmeasurable also
because it includes payments so varied in nature. The voluntary distribution of wealth from motives of benevolence
amply qualifies for inclusion, but this evades the questions
of how the wealth is distributed, to whom, with what motive,
and in what form. How could one measure the non-monetary
elements—the intellectual and physical voluntary labour, the
time and emotion expended? Or even the professional

[11] [L. R. Phelps], *Giving No Charity!*, n.p. (shelved in Bodleian Library,
Oxford, at G.A. Oxon 4° 165).
[12] Mrs Barnardo and J. Marchant, *Memoirs of the Late Dr. Barnardo* (1907),
p. 54; for Bright, see W. Logan, *The Great Social Evil: Its Causes, Extent, Results,
and Remedies* (1871), pp. 34–5; J. L. Garvin, *Chamberlain*, ii, p. 218.
[13] R. R. James, *Lord Randolph Churchill* (1959), p. 248.

person's adjustment of his fees in accordance with the client's capacity to pay? Philanthropy extends through a wide range of social behaviour—from the informal expression of kindness to a dependent at one end to legislative campaigning for social justice at the other.

The Oxford English Dictionary defines philanthropy as 'love to mankind; practical benevolence towards men in general; the disposition or active effort. to promote the happiness and well-being of one's fellow-men'. At the informal end of the philanthropic spectrum, this might be thought to include the distribution of wealth within the family, an institution with broad ramifications and firm loyalties before the days of public welfare. To ignore charity within the family would be to blind oneself to many major changes in social life, and even to the existence of forgotten institutions like the 'marriage settlement', which ensured that women within the family were 'provided for'. The family included a host of co-opted members with legitimate claims—employees, servants, and hangers-on, not to mention obligations to employees in the family firm and within the local community. Altruism here was never undiluted, if only because such institutions flourished on continuing relationships involving mutual obligation. Looking back from the early 1920s, Willoughby de Broke admitted that the employees on his family's Warwickshire estate received small wages, 'but they had security. And above all, there was a mutual bond of affection that had existed for many generations between their families and the family of their employer, a bond that cannot be valued in terms of money.'[14]

Employment with an aristocratic family or a large industrial firm did not necessarily inspire resentment at the employer's affluence, which seemed a source of security. Many northern textile manufacturers, for example, supported local schools, religious bodies, and self-help institutions, and saw themselves as being in the same protective relationship towards dependents as a feudal lord. If the Cadburys and Rowntrees had been more widely imitated, public welfare in Britain—instead of being financed through compulsory

[14] Lord Willoughby de Broke, *The Passing Years* (1924), p. 48.

taxation—might have been voluntarily conceded, and channelled by the employer through the wage-packet, with all the consequences for industrial relations flowing from that. For these serious-minded Quakers, philanthropy merged into good business management; their factory-based welfare measures merely extended and systematized that good neighbourliness which any nineteenth-century community expected from its leading figures. Working-class neighbourhoods were communities too. Without the mutual exchange of favours slum life would have been intolerable; social observers from Engels to Rowntree commented on the mutual generosity to be observed there.[15] Official philanthropy did not always approve of the form the gift would take; recalling the Harp public house at Uxbridge in the 1840s, the radical J. B. Leno noted that 'whips round were of frequent occurrence, and I have seen as much as twenty pounds speedily collected to set a hard-up frequenter of the "Harp" on his legs again'.[16] Amidst the great uncertainties of life near the poverty line, the poor were in a position to know what kind of help would be most appropriate, if only because they had probably themselves received similar help at an earlier stage.

The exchange of mutual favours at Victorian elections is pejoratively labelled bribery, yet was widespread because a gentleman was then expected to show hospitality and good-neighbourliness. This seemed anyway a small price for him to pay for being returned to a parliament which was then thought incapable of doing much to benefit the population, but which—for social and other reasons—the candidate wished to enter. Treating was a form of charity that did nothing for wife and child, and perhaps in the long term little for husband and father. But until quite recently, the MP's generosity also extended to local charities; first attacked by the Liberals, the practice eventually became discredited even among Conservatives. But it was not until the 1920s that Conservative headquarters encouraged constituency parties to supplement the candidate's donations with the fund-raising drives and small subscriptions which are now familiar, and

---

[15] F. Engels, *Working Class*, pp. 102, 140; B. S. Rowntree, *Poverty*, p. 70.
[16] J. B. Leno, *The Aftermath* (1892), p. 75.

not until 1949 that the practice was consolidated by the Maxwell-Fyfe reforms.[17]

Merging on one side with the traditional mutual exchange of favours, philanthropy merges on the other with progressive campaigns for legislative reform. We conventionally distinguish between the philanthropist who distributes his own money and the social reformer who promotes what may even be the same cause by legislating to distribute the money of others. But this distinction dissolves before the philanthropist's critic who urges him to promote his cause more efficiently and comprehensively through invoking legislative aid, and even before the philanthropist himself when his ambitions draw him ineluctably into the legislative sphere. 'The philanthropist who was endeavouring to alleviate human misery', the Chartist Robert Lowery declared in 1838, 'would find that bad laws would be able to create more misery than he would ever be able to remove.' The Anti-Corn-Law League aimed at relieving poverty in an up-to-date and 'scientific' way; provident and respectable working men, once freed from the Corn Laws, would stand on their own feet. Jowett regarded political economy as 'in this imperfect world to be Humanity on a large scale'; its free trade and other reforms had done more for the labouring classes 'than all the Philanthropists put together'.[18]

We cannot even make a distinction between the philanthropist who makes personal sacrifices and the social reformer who does not. Social reformers were not of course required to do more than articulate the cause in parliament, and many advanced their own political standing thereby—but dedication of a personal kind did not come amiss. Richard Cobden and his wife often pined for a life shielded from public and political demands, and getting the Corn Laws repealed severely damaged Cobden's personal finances. Wilfrid Lawson gave thousands of pounds to his prohibitionist movement, and Josephine Butler expended a personal dedication on

[17] N. Gash, *Politics in the Age of Peel* (1953), p. 173; J. Ramsden, *The Age of Balfour and Baldwin*, pp. 245, 248.

[18] *Robert Lowery. Radical and Chartist*, p. 222; F. P. Cobbe, *Life*, i, pp. 352, 317–18.

repealing the Contagious Diseases Acts which involved far more than her slender finances.

The temperance movement illustrates well the philanthropic purposes which social reform could attain, for it aimed at eliminating poverty through encouraging the poor to reassign their expenditure so as to escape dependence on hand-outs by the rich. As the National Temperance League put it in 1893, 'no investment in benevolent work yields a better return than that which aims at the removal and prevention of our national intemperance'. Benjamin Whitworth in 1872 said that enacting local option would be equivalent to raising working-class wages by 25 per cent; his fellow Lancashire manufacturer William Hoyle predicted that employers who subscribed to the United Kingdom Alliance would get more than their money back in ten years.[19] The situation of the NSPCC was rather similar; at first the public sometimes failed to see that its role was to remove cruelty through legislation, inspection, and encouragement of parental responsibility—not to hand out direct relief to the children concerned.[20]

Individual philanthropists naturally gravitated into social reform on seeing that personal altruism was not enough. The National Education League—campaigning for legislation to make elementary education compulsory, unsectarian, and free—launched itself only after Birmingham's energetic voluntary efforts had failed to produce the desired result. Likewise, it was partly disappointment at the slow progress of voluntary rescue work that led Josephine Butler to campaign against state-regulated prostitution after 1869. The legal distinction between charities and political bodies, which still applies, is in many respects arbitrary, and charities often get restive when brought up against its restrictiveness.[21]

The distinctions so far drawn between the different types of benevolence—from the exchange of mutual favours,

[19] National Temperance League, *A.R. 1892-3*, p. 24; Whitworth, in *Alliance News*, 7 Sept. 1872, p. 648; Hoyle, ibid., 21 Oct. 1871, p. 666, and cf. Hoyle in ibid., 28 Oct. 1876, p. 690.

[20] R. Waugh, *The Life of Benjamin Waugh* (1913), pp. 286, 288, 290-1; NSPCC, *A.R. 1895-6*, p. 52.

[21] e.g. Oxfam, discussed in *Guardian*, 24 Jan. 1970, p. 11; *The Times*, 6 Oct. 1972, p. 14; *The Times*, 12 Feb. 1974, p. 14.

through altruistic philanthropy to the pursuit of legislative reform—do not rule out any one individual from participating in all; in nineteenth-century circumstances these distinctions might not even have been perceived. Wilberforce's anti-slavery campaigning, for example, did not cause him to neglect personal charity; Gladstone's energy and idealism enabled him to operate with some effect in all three types of benevolence. A single essay cannot hope to bring out the full richness of the subject, especially as systematic research has hardly yet begun. Discussion will therefore concentrate on two topics that seem well calculated to bring out the major contrasts between nineteenth-century and present-day attitudes: first, philanthropic motive; and secondly, the critique that eventually removed philanthropy from her high Victorian pedestal.

II

The analysis of philanthropic motive is beguiling, if only because altruism implicitly reproaches the bystander, who is at once disappointed and reassured to discover a touch of self-interest here, a hint of human weakness there. The Victorian philanthropist's personal sacrifices were often considerable, and the personal contact with the beneficiary involved in nineteenth-century welfare machinery ensured that these were far more than merely financial; they included sufferings both psychological and physiological. 'I ·hated standing knocking on a door, waiting till some one opened, uncertain of the reception I might get,' wrote Mrs Louise Creighton, of visiting the Cambridge poor in the 1880s. This seems a small worry, of course, in the modern context of relatively egalitarian manners and equality between the sexes, nor is it easy now to share the young Edmund Gosse's distaste for visiting the cottages of the poor: 'I dreaded and loathed the smells of their cottages. One had to run over the whole gamut of odours.'[22] Many years later Mrs Rackham recalled the smell pervading her clothing for days afterwards

---

[22] Louise Creighton, MS Autobiography, n.p., in the care of Mr T. Creighton, and kindly loaned to me by Professor B. Heeney, of Trent University, Peterborough, Canada; E. Gosse, *Father and Son*, p. 106.

as a Notting Hill child in the 1880s after visiting a charitable play-centre in Fetter Lane; when a class of young servants met in the family dining-room, 'there always had to be an interval before we sat down to tea for all the windows to be opened and the room thoroughly aired'.[23] In the tide of reaction against Victorianism which has only recently begun to ebb, it is tempting to see altruism as a mask for self-interest, particularly when Victorian diary-keeping and self-scrutiny provide the critic with such ample ammunition.

But if the analysis of motive is tempting, it is an extremely complex business, and perhaps requires skills—psychological, even medical—which the historian does not possess. Indeed, for a rich evocation of the philanthropist's mixture of motives, each interpenetrating at different levels, one turns not to the historian but to novelists like George Eliot or George Meredith, who can bestow on a Bulstrode and a Mrs Crambourne Wathin a rich characterization which the historian can prise out of his raw material only rarely, and which he is professionally barred from imaginatively re-creating. A further hindrance is the deliberate concealment of motive rife in the philanthropist's publicity-conscious world—as witness the remarkable efforts made by Dr Barnardo and his wife to polish up his life story for public consumption.[24] Altruism rarely appears in unadulterated form at any time, and certainly not in this period. Were Lancashire manu-facturers altruistic, for example, when they opposed the Corn Laws in the belief that their own interests coincided with those of humanity? Did not self-interest mingle with the altruism even of the pioneer Socialist distressed at the very sight of poverty? He resented poverty's degradation and injustice, but he also felt an anguished desire to abolish the poor.[25]

Difficult as the topic is, the preoccupation with philan-thropic motive will particularly attract the historian, for here

[23] Mrs Clara Rackham, MS Notebook, 'Recollections of Childhood 1875–1891', which her niece (Miss Tabor of Stevenage) kindly allowed me to consult and to quote, n.p.
[24] This matter is ably discussed in G. Wagner, *Barnardo* (1979).
[25] Cf. R. Michels, *Political Parties* (New York paperback ed., 1959), pp. 263–4; Viscount Knutsford, *In Black and White* (1926), p. 133; E. P. Thompson, *Working Class* (2nd ed.), p. 864.

he will discover forgotten values, personalities, and institutions. Many of these are religious in essence, or at least in phraseology and mood; they are easily neglected or depreciated by the secularized twentieth-century mind, which is often also surprised to find them frequently yoked to entrepreneurial values. Some philanthropists did of course yearn for the organic harmony of pre-industrial society and bitterly criticize the factory's ugliness; they are allowed to remain on their pedestals because they are seen as pioneers of collectivism. Yet in their day they jostled for attention with the much-admired but now almost completely forgotten Octavia Hill, whose faith lay in cultivating individual character rather than in setting up public institutions. For this reason, and because she hated publicity, she has been swept into the backwaters of history.

It is best to begin with motives that can be labelled as in some sense 'religious' and then move outwards. Religious motive has its own internal complexities. It may occasionally be expressed as an appeal to store up treasures in heaven, or as a claim that what is donated will bring a blessing on what is retained. Yet although so crude a motive may be held out to others, it can hardly satisfy oneself; more relevant were the incentives provided by the churches in their social role. Prosperous Victorians made an impressive effort individually and at a personal level to grapple with problems we would now label as structural or governmental. Their deference relationships were never purely one-sided; a nineteenth-century aristocrat lived in the glare of publicity, his social position carried with it important obligations, and his conduct was closely scrutinized to see whether he carried them out. Sober men became teetotalers to help rescue their drunken neighbours; humanitarians abandoned sugar to emancipate the slaves; Lord Shaftesbury met the Irish potato famine in 1846 with an order that no more potatoes should be bought in his house. 'We must not, by competing in the market, raise the cost on the poor man', he wrote; 'he has nothing after this to fall back upon.'[26] It was perhaps a wrong-headed (though oft-repeated) response, but it illustrates

[26] E. Hodder, *Shaftesbury*, ii. p. 183; cf. the Balfour family's response to the cotton famine, in B. E. C. Dugdale, *Arthur James Balfour* (n.d.), i, p. 21.

the strong and widely held Victorian sense of personal responsibility for solving social problems, reinforced by a preparedness to make personal sacrifices of a more than merely financial kind.

Religious influences helped to ensure that it was philanthropy rather than some other object (sport, for example) that claimed surplus wealth. Shaftesbury, mixing freely in middle-class company, described as the 'dangerous classes' in 1848 not the masses but 'the lazy ecclesiastics of whom there are thousands, and the rich who do no good with their money'.[27] Aristocratic philanthropy for him, as for Gladstone, provided justification for rank and wealth. Like Florence Nightingale and the Barnetts, Shaftesbury felt uncomfortable at fashionable London functions, whose accoutrements contrasted so completely with the poverty so uppermost in his mind.[28] Two middle-class instances of the same sense of personal responsibility can be cited—Gladstone, whose 'engagement' with fifteen other men in 1845 led him to tackle the problem of prostitution through personal attempts at reclamation; and Josephine Butler, who felt that venereal disease could and should be tackled through the voluntary reclamation she had herself practised, and not through state action. 'It only requires more voluntary agency, and a fuller measure of the true spirit of charity and justice', she told the royal commission of 1871, 'and the thing is done.'[29]

Religious commitment made philanthropy a natural way of escaping from family tragedy. Distraught at the death of her daughter Eva in the 1860s, Josephine Butler's sole wish was, according to her own later account, 'to plunge into the heart of some human misery, and to say . . . to afflicted people, "I understand. I, too, have suffered" '.[30] Death was

[27] Broadlands Papers, Romsey: Lord Shaftesbury's Diary, 19 June 1848; this diary is quoted by permission of the trustees of the Broadlands archives; cf. Reginald, Twelfth Earl of Meath, *Memories of the Nineteenth Century* (1923), p. 245.

[28] E. Hodder, *Shaftesbury*, ii, p. 166; Sir E. Cook, *The Life of Florence Nightingale* (1914), i. p. 83; Mrs S. A. Barnett, *Canon Barnett. His Life, Work, and Friends* (1918), i, p. 216.

[29] C. D. Acts Commission, *Parl. Papers*, 1871 (C.408), XIX, Q.13052; see also H. C. G. Matthew, introduction to W. E. Gladstone, *The Gladstone Diaries*, vol. 3 (ed. H. C..G. Matthew, Oxford, 1974), p. 436, n. 1.

[30] J. E. Butler, *Recollections of George Butler* (2nd ed., Bristol, n.d.), p. 183; cf. O. C. Malvery, *A Year and a Day* (1912), p. 8.

a direct and indirect ally of many nineteenth-century charities; it delivered the legacy, but it also inspired commemorative gifts and effort by those who lived on. Bereaved parents commemorated lost children with gifts to Dr Barnardo, who was himself inspired to greater effort by the death of his nine-year-old son Herbert in 1884.[31] In personal affairs, philanthropy could provide solace of a surprisingly direct sort—for Mary Carpenter, for instance, in her quest for affection; for the tensions seething inside Mr Gladstone; and for the 'agonising suffering' of Beatrice Potter, whose unhappy courtship of Joseph Chamberlain gave her 'an almost passionate desire that not a drop of my bitter suffering shall be wasted'. Keble told Hurrell Froude in 1826 that 'when you find yourself . . . over-powered as it were by melancholy, the best way is to go out, and do something kind to somebody or other'.[32] Given rather different cultural pressures, the Barnardos and the Butlers might have responded differently to personal tragedy—by writing a novel, as did Mrs Gaskell when her only son died, or by plunging more deeply into politics, as did Althorp in 1818, John Bright in 1841, or Bonar Law in 1909 when depressed at the death of a wife.

Religion provided not only a major impulse to philanthropy, but also abundant opportunity for it. The churches offered parish visitation, mission outposts, ragged schools, and week-night functions, as well as the direct encounter and even friendship between rich and poor that many regarded as the antidote to Chartism and Socialism. The relief of suffering was not necessarily expected to be rapid; many Victorians felt that it could be effectively tackled only through the time-consuming business of cultivating character, or 'independence' as it was often called. For them, suffering seemed less avoidable and less uniformly harmful than it is for us; given their situation of scarcity, this was perhaps making a virtue of necessity.

Furthermore philanthropy was seldom single-minded. Even

[31] G. Wagner, *Barnardo*, pp. 81, 202.

[32] London School of Economics, Beatrice Webb's typescript diary, 26 Apr. 1890; P. Fraser, *Joseph Chamberlain. Radicalism and Empire 1868–1914* (1966), pp. 121, 126; Sir J. T. Coleridge, *A Memoir of the Rev. John Keble, M.A.* (Oxford, 4th ed., 1874), p. 142. See also J. E. Carpenter, *Life and Work of Mary Carpenter* (1879), p. 138; P. Magnus, *Gladstone. A Biography* (1954), p. 107.

when poverty was the prime target, moral growth was thought desirable in both donor and recipient. Burke disliked the idea of public welfare provision because it would dispense with the voluntary donations that foster virtue.[33] The personal nature of Mr and Mrs Gladstone's philanthropy reflects a very unfamiliar preoccupation with individual sin in both donor and recipient. Personal philanthropy also seemed necessary to enable benefactor and beneficiary to enlighten one another. Florence Nightingale when nursing was of course concerned about preventing disease, but for her this entailed educating the patient. Overcrowded housing was of course Octavia Hill's concern, but she wanted to train the tenant in the qualities that would enable him to solve the housing problem for himself.

The philanthropist's desire for moral growth ensured that religious and secular motives imperceptibly merged. His overriding concern for the dignity of the individual often involved repudiating the aristocratic institutions which seemed to foster a medieval servility—misappropriated or misconceived ancient charities, for example, or extravagant City guilds. Though seldom direct in its attack, and frequently using individual aristocrats for its own purposes, Victorian philanthropy none the less aimed to erode aristocratic values by assisting the social and political integration of three hitherto politically excluded and partly interlinked groups: the middle classes (broadly defined so as to include the upper reaches of the working class), religious groupings outside the Establishment, and educated women. Philanthropy's integrating role in these three dimensions can now be discussed in detail.

The gulf between aristocracy and middle class is central to the philanthropic story. The link between Victorian entrepreneurship, humanitarianism, and philanthropy was close; a relationship that now seems somewhat incongruous and even self-contradictory then seemed natural. Philanthropists, like entrepreneurs, were seen as undertaking society's risk-taking free of charge—as pioneering philanthropic inventions with the ingenuity and energy which also inspired their

---

[33] E. Burke, *French Revolution*, p. 203.

commercial innovations. The point should not be overdone, because in practice the causes backed by philanthropists were relatively conventional in nature. Yet J. S. Mill defended philanthropy on precisely this ground, and Samuel Morley— an enthusiast for what he saw as 'businesslike' philanthropy —was one of many Victorians who straddled both worlds.[34] Commerce was expected to banish superstition, ignorance, war, and brutality; and by introducing a contractual relationship between employer and employee, it could supersede slavery. The spread of international trade would eliminate the need for war, with all the justifications for aristocratic dominance which that provided. The educated and sober population required by modern industry would gradually eliminate brutality. Inventions would directly supersede the cruelty to climbing-boys and animals, for example; 'as the introduction of mechanical power proceeds and becomes diffused over the country', Henry Aggs told the RSPCA in 1834, 'the temptation to cruelty will of course be decreased'.[35] Commercial ventures were launched specifically to eliminate brutality; trading companies in Africa, mechanical chimney-sweeping firms, inventions of non-intoxicating drinks, and so on. Indeed, as soon as a philanthropic cause had been successfully pioneered, commerce often took it over; the early temperance movement, for example, had been a matter of self-denial and self-sacrifice, yet by 1859 one temperance reformer could complain that 'it is now a thing made up of sordid interests'—with temperance building societies, insurance schemes, land societies, excursions, and so on.[36]

The tension between aristocracy and middle class often pervaded the philanthropic organization. Aristocrats might feature as figure-heads, but middle-class secretaries and treasurers took a pride in doing the work. Association with aristocrats might constitute one of philanthropy's attractions for middle-class people, but middle-class philanthropists

[34] D. Owen, *English Philanthropy 1660–1960* (Harvard, 1965), pp. 326, 474–5, 557; E. Hodder, *Life of Samuel Morley* (1888 ed.), p. 219. See also Lady Reading, *Voluntary Service* (privately printed, n.d.), p. 15.

[35] RSPCA *8th A.R., 1834*, p. 38.

[36] *Temperance Spectator*, June 1859, p. 85.

took pleasure in discovering their own superiority in efficiency and energy. Octavia Hill repeatedly depreciates 'ladies'
in her correspondence, and at a Girls' Friendly Society conference of 1883, the Hon. Mrs Oldfield, making the same
point from the opposite direction, could not speak too
highly of the middle-class women. 'Their efforts do indeed
put ours to shame. We think we require rest and change of
air and scene for three months in the year, or even more,
and seldom refuse a pleasant invitation into the country
for our work's sake, while they toil on unremittingly from
week to week, seldom if ever missing being present at the
Mothers' Meeting on Monday or Tuesday, refusing all invita-
tions for that afternoon or evening, going away from home
for perhaps one fortnight only on the long, hot summer;
doing all this so cheerfully, quite as a matter of course.'[37]

Through philanthropy, middle-class values percolated
lower down as well as higher up. Middle-class attitudes to
the poor that now seem harsh, even callous, stem from the
conviction—most notably within the Charity Organisation
Society [COS]—that aristocratic open-handedness corrupted the poor into servility, whereas the refusal of indiscriminate charity would train the poor in self-help. Eglantyne
Jebb pointed out that such refusal was not necessarily the
easy option: 'we can soothe our feelings by quieting the
whining voice or causing the distressing object of the beggar
to pass quickly again out of our sight, and this luxury costs
only a few pennies. Such self-indulgence is, however, positively cruel in its effects upon others.' She saw the temptation as 'often almost irresistible to do something which is
really unkind in order to escape the odium of *appearing*
unkind'.[38]

Middle-class needs were also involved in the second department of philanthropy's integrating role, whereby religious
groupings outside the Established Church were assimilated
into the British social and political system. Political exclusion

[37] Girls' Friendly Society, *Associates' Journal and Advertiser*, Aug. 1883, p.
103. See also C. E. Maurice (ed.), *Octavia Hill*, p. 92; E. M. Bell *Octavia Hill.
A Biography* (1942), p. 41; cf. N. Annan, 'The Intellectual Aristocracy', in J. H.
Plumb (ed.), *Studies in Social History* (1955), p. 245.

[38] E. Jebb, *Cambridge. A Brief Study in Social Questions* (Cambridge, 1906),
pp. 188, 190.

produced in the dissenter a gnawing but helpless sense of
responsibility for the evils around him without opportunity
for outlet, and without experience of the compromises
necessary in government. Even a Cambridge-educated Anglican like Thomas Clarkson could burn up with frustration at
being unable to grapple directly with the evil of slavery
that he now so vividly perceived. Walking alone with his
thoughts in the woods during 1785, he tells us, 'I . . . began
to envy those who had seats in parliament, and who had
great riches, and widely extended connexions, which would
enable them to take up this cause.'[39] Philanthropy enabled
denominational superiority to be displayed and complicity
shed—a holy rivalry which, like the competition in social
reform between aristocracy and middle class, helped to
ensure that the ground was more completely covered.

While Anglicans might seek to consolidate their position
through their local educational monopolies, university
settlements, and slum parishes subsidized from elsewhere—
Catholics and nonconformists tried to raise themselves by
their own bootstraps through sponsoring from purely local
resources a completely separate range of charities and reforming movements. Some of these directly reproached the laxity
of the Establishment; 'numbers of people used to go to the
rectory for soup', wrote Joseph Arch, 'but not a drop of it
did we touch. I have stood at our door with my mother, and
I have seen her face look sad as she watched the little children
toddle past, carrying the tin cans, and their toes coming
out of their boots. "Ah, my boy", she once said, "you shall
never, never do that . . ." '.[40] Nonconformists and Catholics
were unlikely to channel their funds towards Oxford and
Cambridge till the end of the century, but put immense
energy into subsidizing elementary education and temperance.[41] These larger denominational contests left ample
scope for smaller-scale personal rivalry; many people were
active and admired in the world of the chapel who could gain

[39] T. Clarkson, *History of the Rise, Progress, and Accomplishment of the
Abolition of the African Slave Trade by the British Parliament* (1839 ed.), p. 139.
[40] J. Arch, *Life*, p. 15.
[41] For Oxford and Cambridge, see D. Owen, *English Philanthropy*, p. 346 and
ff. For Catholics, see A. E. Dingle and B. Harrison, 'Cardinal Manning as Temperance Reformer', *Historical Journal*, 1969, pp. 500–4.

respect nowhere else. 'It was a principle with Mr Bulstrode', wrote George Eliot, 'to gain as much power as possible, that he might use it for the glory of God.'[42]

A third middle-class subgroup launched by philanthropy on to a wider social and political stage was the educated woman. Women's relative sensitivity in personal relationships was invaluable here.[43] From the Social Science Association's first meeting in 1857 onwards, women were prominent in its proceedings and gained considerably from its feminist offshoots. Through voluntary work a woman could attain considerable status at local and even national level; Charlotte Yonge's *Daisy Chain* ably demonstrates how the Cocksmoor project enlists the political skills of leisured women in Stoneborough; 'it all interests me like a game', says Vida Levering, organizing a charity concert in Elizabeth Robins's *The Convert.*[44]

The rising number of female charitable societies (whether feminist or not) in the early nineteenth century, and the rising proportion of total donations drawn from women in charities as a whole, were important for pioneering women's emancipation in Britain.[45] Philanthropy could liberate women in the most trivial ways—by encouraging Mrs Wightman, the Shrewsbury temperance reformer, to overcome her fear of going out alone at night, for example: 'I never could be happy again to sit down in a drawing-room', she remarked later, 'subject to the conventional rules of society.'[46] Relative longevity perhaps explains why the 150 women whose wills are listed by the *Daily Telegraph* in the 1890s gave a far higher percentage (25 per cent) of their estates to charity than the 316 men (11 per cent); but it does not explain why women volunteers were so prominent in distributing the charity organized by a fashionable parish like the Revd

[42] G. Eliot, *Middlemarch* (Penguin, ed. W. J. Harvey, 1970), p. 184, cf. p. 15.

[43] J. Hall, 'Female Intuition Measured at Last?', *New Society*, 9 June 1977, p. 502.

[44] E. Robins, *The Convert* (1907), p. 50.

[45] F. Prochaska, 'Women in English Philanthropy 1790-1830', *International Review of Social History*, 1974, pp. 428, 442. See also his excellent *Women and Philanthropy in Nineteenth-Century England* (Oxford, 1980).

[46] Mrs C. Wightman, *Haste to the Rescue; or, Work While it is Day* (1862), p. 116.

G. H. Wilkinson's St. Peter's Eaton Square in the 1870s, or why in the COS by 1911 'in a town with a population of anything up to 50,000 the secretary, whether honorary or paid, will almost certainly be a woman'.[47]

Philanthropy took all three excluded groups—middle class, nonconformists, and educated women—further than they had originally intended. Middle-class voluntarists did not at first recognize the scale of the injustices they would be required to tackle; still less did they recognize the implications of this for their attitude to the state. They were drawn ineluctably forward by a twofold dynamic—in both range of concern and elaboration of remedy. Anti-slavery acknowledges the human qualities of enslaved peoples and extends the boundaries of citizenship, thus setting a precedent for prostitutes (via Josephine Butler), children (via the NSPCC), and even animals (via the RSPCA). Drunkards, lunatics, orphans, tramps, and climbing-boys are all brought into the sphere of public concern. The exposure of one injustice uncovers others, and with these the individual or even the voluntary society eventually cannot cope. A campaign for state intervention may then ensue, which often creates the inspectors who can initiate that dynamic of accelerating state involvement so ably portrayed by Professor MacDonagh. Enthusiastically voluntarist at first in outlook, and often anti-bureaucratic in mechanism when driven into interventionism, the early philanthropists often seem in retrospect more like harbingers of public welfare, pioneering recognition of new areas of concern but ultimately making it clear that voluntarism is not enough.[48]

The philanthropist thus eventually uncovers the full ramifications of social inequality. At first J. S. Mill wanted the poor-law system to provide minimum provision and leave charity to discriminate between the deserving and

---

[47] L. V. Shairp (Organizing Secretary, Leeds COS and Travelling Secretary in the North of England for the London COS), in *Charity Organisation Review*, xxx (1911), p. 69. For wills, see D. Owen, *English Philanthropy*, p. 471; and see A. J. Mason, *Memoir of George Howard Wilkinson. Bishop of St. Andrews* ... (1909), i, pp. 272-3.

[48] See O. MacDonagh, 'The Nineteenth Century Revolution in Government: A reappraisal', *Historical Journal*, 1958. See also p. 421.

the undeserving.[49] The COS then set about systematically encouraging independence and organizing the voluntary redistribution of wealth, only to convince its critics of the need to move on towards public welfare. Beatrice Webb highlights the 'tragic dilemma of charitable relief' in 1889, whereby 'if we help a man to exist without work, we demoralize the individual and encourage the growth of a parasitic or pauper class'; but if the man is raised out of demoralization through being brought into competition with others, 'we save him at the cost of all those who compete with him'.[50] Moving on from voluntary provision, the philanthropist aimed to channel central-government money or local-government assistance towards bodies that had once been purely voluntary in origin and intent. It is not surprising that state intervention appears relatively early in the areas of education and drink, for if ignorance and drunkenness could be removed, the free-acting, atomistic society might still be made to work. With the formation of the United Kingdom Alliance in 1853 the voluntarist temperance movement embarked on its prohibitionist phase; by the 1870s, in the form of 'local option', it was penetrating the Liberal Party machine. Likewise in 1870 the educational world, hitherto largely voluntarist in nature, moved forward into ever extending state management; 1871 therefore saw a reversal of the earlier rising trend in the number of teachers employed by ragged schools.[51] The long-term outcome was the subordination of voluntarily financed schools within a nation-wide state system.

A similar sequence can often be detected elsewhere. In the 1880s philanthropists provide school meals for the needy, only to be superseded later by public provision. Octavia Hill rouses opinion on the housing question in the 1870s, only to demonstrate in the 1880s that respectability and the counter-cyclical deployment of savings within the family cannot cope with a problem now seen to be much more formidable than

---

[49] J. S. Mill, *Principles of Political Economy*, pp. 967, 969.

[50] B. Potter [later Webb], in C. Booth, *Life and Labour of the People in London. First Series, Poverty* (1904), iii, p. 176, cf. B. Webb, *My Apprenticeship*, pp. 215–17.

[51] C. J. Montague, *Sixty Years in Waifdom* (1904), p. 191.

even she had imagined. Voluntary schemes for labour exchanges, first pioneered by the Egham exchange of 1885, soon make way for state-run schemes more comprehensive in scope. On old-age pensions Joseph Chamberlain speculated in 1891 that 'perhaps, as in the case of education, when the voluntary system has been exhausted, then public opinion will agree to a compulsory measure';[52] in 1908, it did. The philanthropist does not supersede the state, whatever his initial intentions; he skirmishes on its frontiers and prepares the way for its further advance. Theorists (Fabians, constructive Liberals, Socialists) then intellectually justify what has already been done and urge the process further forward, sometimes transcending the narrower perspectives of the movements that initially inspire their concern. The gulf between the Late-Victorian philanthropist and Socialist was therefore not as great as it often seemed at the time. They sometimes quarrelled fiercely, but both believed it would be possible to transform society in the near future; both tried to uphold human dignity; and both, through championing the ideal of 'independence', repudiated deference to aristocracy—though perhaps occasionally replacing it by deference to the social worker.

Eventually even the initial intention of some philanthropists was for the state to take over the voluntary bodies they created. This applies to many Edwardian schemes for child welfare and to many inter-war schemes for birth-control, nutrition reform, and improved health care; 'the traditional philanthropic drive to perform good works was allied', writes Paul Addison, 'to the modernizing, technocratic motive'.[53] William Beveridge epitomizes the compatibility within one individual of the impulses to private philanthropy and public welfare; nearly half his income between the wars went on donations to good causes and on gifts and loans to family and friends. He always regarded the philanthropic organization, rather than the trade union, as the ideal type of voluntary association, and disliked the phrase 'welfare state', with which the public identified his later

[52] J. L. Garvin, *Chamberlain*, ii, p. 522.

[53] P. Addison, *The Road to 1945. British Politics and the Second World War* (1975), p. 183.

career, because of its Santa Claus connotations. Philanthropy's resort to the state culminated in the 1970s, a decade when personal donations were in relative decline, but when one of charity's growth areas had become transfers of revenue from central government; these totalled £186,000,000 in 1975.[54]

A rather similar falsification of expectations occurs with the non-Anglican groupings who embark on philanthropy; in the process they lose much of the denominational distinctness and even some of the religious motivation which initially inspired them. Though Barnardo followed church congresses around searching for funds to the end of his career, his initially evangelical rather than philanthropic motive faded into the background.[55] Both political quietism and denominational exclusiveness became impossible for the philanthropist who was in earnest. Philanthropic platforms witnessed an unprecedented ecumenicalism in practice which could only retrospectively be justified in theory; the evils being tackled seemed so formidable, the reformer's resources so feeble by comparison, and still feebler when internally fragmented. Philanthropy united a Shaftesbury not merely to a Congregationalist like Samuel Morley, but even to Catholics, utilitarians, Unitarians, and humanitarian agnostics.

A further casualty of philanthropic work was the continued predominance of other-worldly concerns; T. H. Green's high-minded altruism involved continuity with earlier generations in seriousness, but an increasingly secularized quest for salvation. Poverty gradually came to seem worth eliminating for its own sake, and the biblical ideal of an open-handed and indiscriminate charity came to seem inappropriate in modern conditions, unlikely to produce either prevention or cure; if poverty was to disappear, charity must endure the higher criticism and become scientific. Symbolic of the tendency was Lord John Russell's response to the Chartist demonstrations of 10 April 1848; rejecting the Court's plea for prosecutions and Archbishop Sumner's

[54] J. Harris, *William Beveridge. A Biography* (Oxford, 1977), pp. 275, 448, 459, 473; P. Falush, 'Trends in the Finance of British Charities', *National Westminster Bank Quarterly Review*, May 1977, p. 37.

[55] Mrs Barnardo and J. Marchant, *Barnardo*, p. 248; G. Wagner, *Barnardo*, pp. 15, 19.

proposal for a day of thanksgiving. Russell got up a subscription for a free hospital.[56] Philanthropists increasingly
focused on medical matters, and by the 1900s medical
charities were absorbing eight shillings in every philanthropic
pound contributed.[57]

This secularization process was by no means obvious to
those who experienced it, if only because the churches were
so eager to embrace the change. Consciousness of sin there
might be among thinking people in the 1880s, but as Beatrice
Webb pointed out, it was less an affair of the individual
conscience than a matter of collective class guilt. 'We have
sinned against you grievously', wrote Arnold Toynbee to the
working classes, '. . . but if you will forgive us . . . we will
devote our lives to your service.' By alerting society to the
problem of poverty, the philanthropist eventually secured
a more vigorous political response than perhaps he had
originally intended, for the sentiment he conjured up led
the politicians to move on in their remedies from voluntary
to compulsory redistribution of wealth between the classes.
By 1912 Lord Hugh Cecil felt the need to emphasize that
the compulsory transfer of wealth from rich to poor does
nothing to develop the ideal of Christian self-sacrifice. Compulsory acts of self-denial 'lose the only thing that gives
them their Christian character if they are done by compulsion'; unselfishness must be voluntary, whereas 'compulsory unselfishness is an absurdity, a contradiction in
terms'. Yet here he was mounting one of those numerous
hobby-horses which in later life drew him away from practical
politics altogether.[58]

Philanthropy also led the pioneer women philanthropists
in unexpected directions, towards a political participation
more open and complete than they had at first envisaged.
MPs cited their achievements as evidence for women's
suffrage; even the anti-suffragist Octavia Hill's career was
adduced in support of the cause.[59] Woman philanthropists

[56] J. Prest, *Lord John Russell*, p. 285.

[57] D. Owen, *English Philanthropy*, pp. 479, 489.

[58] M. Richter, *The Politics of Conscience. T. H. Green and his Age* (1964),
p. 322; K. Rose, *The Later Cecils* (1975), p. 275.

[59] Woodall, *H.C. Deb.*, 10 June 1884, c. 1948.

felt hampered by male control, male perspectives, at the same time as they realized that voluntarism was not enough; the vote seemed the obvious remedy. So suffragism came to divide the philanthropic world. The more conservative in temperament saw philanthropy as woman's natural sphere, where she could complement the male's involvement in politics, commerce, and war. Several women deeply involved in philanthropy—Mrs T. H. Green, Mrs Humphry Ward, Beatrice Potter, Mrs Arnold Toynbee—signed the anti-suffrage protest of 1889, with its conviction that citizenship 'is not dependent upon or identical with the possession of the suffrage', but 'lies in the participation of each individual in effort for the good of the community'; political involvement might pollute women's impartiality and lower their ideals.[60] So firmly did Octavia Hill hold this view that she could not even bring herself to campaign against getting the vote; she had to screw herself up even to writing a trenchant letter to *The Times*.[61] In her *Diana Mallory* (1908), Mrs Humphry Ward juxtaposed the good works of the ailing Miss Vincent and the worldliness of the suffragette Miss Fotheringham, and in *Delia Blanchflower* (1915) she expressed her profound concern at the wastefulness involved in diverting women's creative energies into militant suffragism. Even a suffragist like Florence Nightingale (though hardly a militant one) accepted Jowett's advice in 1865 that 'it would seriously injure your influence if you were known to have influence'.[62]

On the other hand, the suffragist rejoinder to the anti-suffrage protest included a special section for signatories headed 'social and philanthropic', together with thirty women doctors, thirty-two women poor-law guardians, and philanthropic names as distinguished as Emma Cons, Josephine Butler, Margaret Llewelyn Davies, and Lady Knightley of Fawsley. Such women repudiated unobtrusive-

[60] 'An Appeal against Female Suffrage', *Nineteenth Century*, June 1889, p. 783; cf. the anti-suffrage petition in *The Times*, 20 Feb. 1907, p. 11, and my *Separate Spheres*, p. 84.

[61] C. E. Maurice (ed.), *Octavia Hill*, p. 263; E. M. Bell, *Octavia Hill*, p. 240; *The Times*, 15 July 1910, p. 9. See also archives of Messrs Baring, *Cromer Autograph Collection*, f. 51: Octavia Hill to Cromer, 16 July 1910.

[62] Sir E. Cook, *Florence Nightingale*, ii. p. 97.

ness in good works.[63] In these ways, then, the philanthropist's largely religious and non-political motives became interventionist, secularized, and politicized, while simultaneously assisting the threefold social and political integration of middle-class people, non-Anglicans, and educated women. Given these powerful incentives to charity, this complex interpenetration between philanthropy and prevailing social values —the nineteenth-century philanthropist could present a bold front to his enemies. For enemies there were, and they now deserve more attention.

III

The critics often shared the philanthropist's over-all aims; they often simply aimed to make him more effective— arguing that his efforts were, broadly speaking, inefficient, ignorant, insufficient, and even insulting. Each of these four accusations will be discussed in turn. They were not all voiced by the same social groups, but cumulatively they cast down the philanthropist from his seat.

Efficiency was no more the prime consideration in the philanthropic world than in J. S. Mill's view of government; philanthropists, if obliged to choose, would have preferred participation to efficiency. Like local authorities, voluntary bodies—from this point of view the more of them the merrier—usefully broadened out the citizen's experience of public affairs. The same subscribers and beneficiaries were pursued by a host of organizations, each clinging sect-like to whatever distinctive quality it might possess. In 1833 there were four London organizations catering for animal welfare; in 1840, four temperance organizations claiming national status; in the 1870s, five national bodies campaigning to reduce Sunday gloom. There was also a certain intellectual, as well as institutional, fragmentation involved in the notion of raising money for individual 'causes'—a tendency to ignore the interconnection between social ills. In philanthropy as in business, pressure for rationalization

---

[63] 'Women's Suffrage: A Reply', *Fortnightly Review*, July 1889, p. 132 and ff.

eventually resulted; the formation of the COS in 1869 was the philanthropist's equivalent of the cartel—the move towards public welfare his equivalent of nationalization. Both breathed a passion for efficiency and a distaste for waste.

A charity's heavy dependence on volunteers intensified the pressures for yet another threat to efficiency: an internal participatory structure. The authoritarianism of a Barnardo, or even of an Octavia Hill, might at that time suit the master's relationship with his servant, the factory owner's management of his work-force, but it could hardly be implemented here without offending against the participatory values the middle classes were cultivating in national and local politics. The volunteer, whether as donor or activist, was inspired not by financial gain but by 'the cause'; he had contributed time, energy, and enthusiasm, and wanted a democracy of volunteers—free to criticize, free to withdraw. An unpaid volunteer could hardly be ordered to neglect his family or other personal obligations; he might also lack experience of businesslike methods and structures. Problems of reliability and continuity among philanthropic staff inevitably resulted.

The authoritarian direction which was often forthcoming, and which in other circumstances might have been welcome, therefore risked actually accentuating problems of management. 'I am essentially what may be called a strong man', said Barnardo, '*i.e.*, I rule'; Josephine Butler spoke of 'the awful abundance of compassion which makes me fierce'. The philanthropic pioneer's occupational hazard is an almost obsessive and humourless, though selfless, dedication to a cause; an overriding preoccupation with the evil in question can be transmuted into a ruthlessness which results in scandals, splits, and disputes. His own generalized love of humanity makes his subordinates' tiresomely petty jealousies and disputes seem incongruous. Because in day-to-day matters he has so little concern for himself, he is surprised and impatient at the scarcity of such intense dedication in others. Yet to the outsider the philanthropist's abrasive, even harsh personality consorts ill with the elevated nature of his objectives. 'Tact, sir, I despise it,' retorted the NSPCC's Benjamin

Waugh, when criticized for being aggressive in defending children.[64]

Qualities of efficient management are not necessarily present in those whose vision and commitment initiate a new crusade. Yet unless the founder is sometimes prepared to conciliate subordinates, forsake exclusive concern with beneficiaries, and focus on the efficiency of the philanthropic machine, trouble results. It is hardly surprising that Mayhew in the 1840s was able to mount vigorous criticism of ragged schools and sailors' charity finances in London. In the 1870s the surprising informality of Barnardo's accounting methods won him the lifelong hostility of the COS; Barnardo was rescued by an unpublicized change of status whereby trustees assumed managerial responsibility for his homes.[65] Division of labour like this, reproduced after 1874 in the crusade against the CD Acts through the separated spheres of Josephine Butler and James Stansfeld, was one way out of the problem, but such solutions were by no means always found.

Ignorance was the critic's second accusation. He could emphasize four discouragements to serious thought within the philanthropic body: its permanent mood of interruption and haste, its non-political and non-legislative outlook, its preoccupation with the distractions of fund-raising, and its over-all tendency to anti-intellectualism. All four tended to frighten off specialist skill and knowledge. The twentieth-century administrative state makes the nineteenth-century philanthropist look depressingly amateur.

Haste and urgency were built into his situation from the outset; the evil seemed obvious and pressing, and there was no time to ponder whether, when, or how to intervene. Wilberforce became so obsessed with his reform that he dreamt of slaves at night. When founding the temperance movement in Scotland, John Dunlop said he 'got no sleep except dozing all night, and dreamed of drunken women

---

[64] Mrs Barnardo and J. Marchant, *Barnardo*, p. 300; G. Petrie. *A Singular Iniquity. The Campaigns of Josphine Butler* (1971), p. 97; R. Waugh, *Benjamin Waugh*, pp. 167–9.

[65] *Morning Chronicle*, 2 May 1850, p. 6; 6 May 1850, p. 6; 9 May 1850, p. 5; 16 May 1850, p. 2. G. Wagner, *Barnardo*, pp. 87, 93, 118–19, 158, 170, 269.

and boys, till I overheard myself groaning, so that I was afraid I might disturb those that slept in the next room'.[66] It was not easy to resist the temptation to plunge into the heart of the evil, acting only on impulse. Hence the superficiality of diagnosis, the poverty of legislative expedient. Given the urgency of action, argument and criticism seemed almost a betrayal of the victims who were being championed. 'Hurried beyond all precedent; never a moment to myself', wrote Shaftesbury in 1843, '. . . I have lost all power of consecutive meditation.'[67]

The one respite from what Josephine Butler called 'the deadening effect on the soul of the enforced whirl of active engagements'[68] was, for her and many other nineteenth-century reformers, prayer; but this was hardly likely to encourage constructive thought on the more worldly dimensions of the reforming process—legislative expediency and empirical research, for example. Florence Nightingale and Edwin Chadwick, for whom statistics revealed elements of the divine plan to mankind, were decidedly unusual among reformers here. Social problems were usually viewed in terms of individual sinfulness, whether in government or in society at large. The philanthropist's hope of sudden social transformation through mass conversion therefore supplants concentration on gradual and long-term structural and legislative change.

Then there was the need to combine the befriending of the beneficiary with a hopeful pursuit of the benefactor. Voluntarist expertise can mean skill at fund-raising or thorough understanding of the relevant subject-area, but the two do not necessarily go together. The professionalization of philanthropy in the first sense risks amateurism in the second. Furthermore, neither quality is necessarily combined with the initial perception that an evil exists. Instead of focusing exclusively on the reasons for Late-Victorian child neglect,

[66] J. Dunlop, in *Weekly Record of the Temperance Movement*, 22 Mar. 1862, p. 98; cf. E. Hodder, *Shaftesbury*, ii, p. 112; R. I. and S. Wilberforce, *Life of William Wilberforce* (1838), iii, pp. 213, 215.

[67] E. Hodder, *Shaftesbury*, i, p. 496, cf. pp. 466, 514; ii, p. 67; Broadlands Archives, Lord Shaftesbury's Diary, entries for 9 Apr. 1848, 8 July 1848.

[68] J. E. Butler, *The Life of Jean Frederic Oberlin, Pastor of the Ban de la Roche* (n.d.), p. 62.

a Barnardo therefore spends much of his time writing stories for religious magazines, founding children's periodicals, and organizing huge annual birthday fêtes for his Young Helpers' League at the Albert Hall. A continuous sense of insecurity about finance—which some charities sought to tackle by launching 'guarantee funds' lasting for a time-span longer than the year—obstructed long-term planning.

Victorian charities also needed to impress potential sub-scribers; one critic saw the lavish structure of a Late-Victorian penitentiary as being designed less for the welfare of the inmates, more for 'the gratification and convenience of the ladies in charge'.[69] A modern visitor to the London head-quarters of the British and Foreign Bible Society, for instance, finds himself amid positively Medicean architectural splen-dour. The numerous charity balls, philanthropic dinners, and conversaziones, the pretentious central offices, the pages of print devoted to listing subscriptions, the elegant member-ship cards—the very organization of the philanthropic world itself (not to speak of the causes on which its resources were spent)—all ensured that such nineteenth-century redistribution of the national income as did take place gave pleasure to, and even financially profited, many of the not-so-poor before it finally filtered down to those in real need. The structure of Victorian philanthropy therefore supports those critics who say that sufficient capital was in theory available for industrialization without depressing popular living standards, but that this did not occur because 'much of what was available was not in fact pressed into the most useful investment'.[70] Public welfare therefore came to seem preferable to philanthropy because it facilitated specializa-tion and expertise in two dimensions: by relieving the experts of their perennial worry about funds, and by producing economies of scale. The minority report on the poor laws of 1909, with its zeal for specialization, epitomized the new mood.

Ignorance also stemmed simply from the anti-intellectual atmosphere in which the philanthropist moved. Philanthropy

---

[69] Anon., *Penitentiaries and Reformatories* (Edinburgh, 1865), p. 6.

[70] E. J. Hobsbawm, 'The British Standard of Living. 1790–1850', *Economic History Review*, 1957, p. 47.

was often only a part-time activity, and although it attracted highly educated and intelligent people, their perspectives were severely practical. Typical was Octavia Hill's instruction to fellow-workers of 1879 to 'beware of well-meant failures. Have your drainage, and your clean stairs, your distempering and your accounts all as perfect as possible.' Training for her consisted not in the economist's and sociologist's grasp of the housing question's social complexities or legal technicalities, but in comprehending practical household management and the personality of the tenant. 'It is not often', she wrote, 'that I turn away from the very engrossing detail of work here, to think much about general questions.'[71] If the worlds of the housing manager and the sociologist came together at all, they did so in the area of 'social administration', not in that of social science. J. A. Hobson thought the COS too myopic in its conception of what constitutes a 'fact'—too preoccupied with individual casework, insufficiently concerned with the over-all social framework.[72] Charles Booth, by contrast, was beginning to shift discussion away from the poor and towards poverty.

Anti-intellectualism intrudes at other levels. Preoccupation with fund-raising ensures that 'failures must be hushed up, and successes advertised from the house-tops'.[73] At annual meetings, charity officials praised each other's self-sacrifice and dedication, and the platform rallied round the chairman to rebut the occasional irreverent critic from the floor. All this made life easier for the new category of criminal noted by *The Times* in 1860: the official who gained the confidence of the benevolent and then ran off with the funds.[74] By the 1880s, Labouchere's *Truth* was making a speciality of exposing financial and charity swindles. The charitable

---

[71] Quotations from E. S. Ouvry (ed.), *Extracts from Octavia Hill's 'Letters to Fellow-Workers' from 1864 to 1911* (1933), p. 21; C. E. Maurice (ed.), *Octavia Hill*, p. 228. See also E. M. Bell, *Octavia Hill*, pp. 65, 278; A. S. Wohl, 'Octavia Hill and the Homes of the London Poor', *Journal of British Studies*, May 1971, pp. 126-9.

[72] J. A. Hobson, *The Crisis of Liberalism*, p. 205; cf. S. Ball, in S. Webb *et al.*, 'Socialism and Individualism', *Fabian Tract No. 3* (1908 ed.), pp. 82-3.

[73] T. S. Simey, *Principles of Social Administration* (1937), p. 136.

[74] *The Times*, 2 Jan. 1860, p. 8; for examples of charity frauds, see E. Hodder, *Samuel Morley*, p. 295; C. L. Mowat, *The Charity Organisation Society 1869–1913. Its Ideas and Work* (1961), p. 48.

body's eulogistic official history avoids offending valued co-workers and seeks the continued prosperity of the cause; it therefore hurries over disputes and failures as irrelevant to the ongoing story. Philanthropists were often more energetic in denouncing alternative remedies for their problem than in developing a coherent policy of their own. It was easier to brand a friendly critic as a renegade than look sympathetically on his ideas. Mayhew's criticisms of the ragged schools, for instance, were rebutted as assaults from an enemy, and philanthropic periodicals prefer righteous indignation and comfortable words to constructive debates, case-studies, social investigation, or comparative analysis. Beatrice Webb found it 'a curiously demoralising life' moving amid 'the subservient and foolish admiration of followers' during her brief essay in pressure-group management after 1909, and began to wonder 'whether the expenditure of money and energy on mere passing propaganda is as socially useful as research'.[75]

Philanthropy had already become a pejorative term for some Mid-Victorians, a synonym almost for soft-headedness. By the 1860s the Social Science Association was often being attacked for its sentimental views of social problems. J. S. Mill made female sentimentality one of his major reasons for enfranchising women; political experience might render their philanthropy more discriminating. Already in 1875 we find the term being used to denote more government rather than less; Gladstone told Granville in December that if W. E. Forster became party leader he would be tempted towards over-government, and 'in . . . the propagandism of a vague philanthropy, he might go constantly astray'. In June 1877 G. J. Goschen complained in the House of Commons that political economy had been dethroned there, 'and Philanthropy had been allowed to take its place. Political Economy was the bugbear of the working classes, and philanthropy, he was sorry to say, was their idol.'[76]

[75] B. Webb, *Our Partnership* (ed. B. Drake and M. I. Cole, 1948), pp. 432, 453.

[76] Lord E. Fitzmaurice, *The Life of . . . Earl Granville K.G. 1815–1891* (2nd ed., 1905), ii. p. 148; Hon. A. D. Elliot, *The Life of George Joachim Goschen 1831–1907* (1911), i, p. 163; cf. Salisbury on Gladstone's 'vague philanthropic phraseology' in Lord Newton, *Lord Lansdowne. A Biography* (1929), p. 74.

The early twentieth century brought a certain professionalism to voluntary organizations; they recruited more paid
workers, and with academic and governmental encouragement developed more expertise. Their voluntary status now
stemmed more from their origins and structure than from the
situation of their employees. None the less, within the
increasingly self-confident labour movement, charities—
with their air of upper- and middle-class patronage, their
inefficiency, their suspicions of the state, and their links
with the sour sectarianism of the later COS—came to seem
not only old-fashioned and morally bankrupt, but also
intellectually outmoded. For G. D. H. Cole, that major
early nineteenth-century philanthropist Joseph Sturge had
'in effect, the essential qualities of the great philanthropist,
but lacked those requisite for the successful political
reformer'. In the Workers' Educational Association in the
1930s, R. H. S. Crossman recalled, 'all disliked the do-good
volunteer and wanted to see him replaced by professionals
and trained administrators in the socialist welfare state of
which we all dreamed'. Philanthropy, he went on, 'to us was
an odious expression of social oligarchy and churchy bourgeois attitudes'.[77] Even the Conservative Lady Astor was
apologetic by 1933 about the old charity, and claimed that
an open-air nursery school was 'a particularly good effort,
because it is not charity. I don't believe in charity in the
sense in which we usually speak of it, because I don't think
it does people very much good unless there is some effort
on their own part.' She went on to repudiate the old self-
regarding element of charity: 'it always gives the man who
gives charity the feeling that he is so much better than his
neighbour and encourages self-righteousness'.[78]

Philanthropy was also accused of being insufficient; 'the
givers are few, and those few are over-tasked', Shaftesbury
complained, and the level of philanthropic donations had
not paralleled the growth in national income. 'If you take
fifteen societies', he wrote in 1848, 'I will undertake to say

[77] G. D. H. Cole, *Chartist Portraits* (1941), p. 186, cf. F. Place, *Autobiography*, p. 282; R. H. S. Crossman, *The Role of the Volunteer in the Modern
Social Service* (1973), p. 9.

[78] *Louth Standard*, 25 Feb. 1933, p. 15.

the names of the same persons will be found in ten of them.'[79] His point is borne out at the local level by the Revd A. Hume, whose researches showed that only 1,243 people subscribed to Liverpool charities in the early 1850s, and that no less than 85 per cent of subscriptions came from people who supported more than one charity; half the total subscribed to Liverpool charities came from a mere 689 persons.[80] The point could be corroborated from the biographical direction; Emily Kinnaird claimed that her brother the Eleventh Baron was president or treasurer of twenty-eight different societies and on the committees of as many more.[81] Such dispersed philanthropic concern both reflected philanthropy's fragmented approach to social problems and illustrated the failure of the greatest moral and political pressure to create a sufficiently large donating public.

Furthermore there was no necessary relationship between the urgency of a social problem—as measured by the quantity of human suffering involved—and philanthropists' willingness to give. A colliery disaster-fund, for instance, could attract funds only if the colliery was adjacent to a local community, or if the disaster attracted publicity, or if there were no distracting news stories about at the time. Late-Victorian colliery disaster-funds could cater for the families of only one-eighth of the men killed in the coal-mining industry, and for only four-fifths of the families of those killed in serious accidents which claimed more than four lives.[82] Furthermore charities, like local authorities later, often found that funds were not forthcoming for use in the areas that most needed them; a philanthropist often wanted to see his donations benefit his immediate locality rather than the slum areas where aid was most needed, but which he might well be too fastidious or frightened to visit.[83]

[79] E. Hodder, *Shaftesbury*, iii, p. 177; ii, p. 251; cf. Broadlands Archives, Lord Shaftesbury's Notebook, 1864 and 1880-1, n.p.; D. Owen, *English Philanthropy*, p. 408.

[80] The Revd A. Hume, 'Analysis of the Subscribers to the various Liverpool Charities', *Transactions of the Historic Society of Lancashire and Cheshire*, vii (1854-5), pp. 22-5.   [81] G. Wagner, *Barnardo*, p. 41.

[82] J. Benson, 'Colliery Disaster Funds, 1860-1897', *International Review of Social History*, 1974, pp. 75-6, 84.

[83] H. Solly, *'These Eighty Years'*, or, *The Story of an Unfinished Life* (1893), ii, p. 237; cf. Broadlands Archives, Lord Shaftesbury's Diary, 3 May 1857.

Philanthropy's risk-taking, entrepreneurial aspects involved the risk of quirkiness and even eccentricity in range of concern. There was a large element of vanity in charitable bequests, together with a penchant for widows, sailors, children, and animals.[84] The Early-Victorian philanthropic preoccupation with the moral state of the donor helps to explain the popularity of animals; as William Ewart told the RSPCA's annual meeting of 1845, 'benevolence assumes its purest form when its author is not only unrequited, but unknown'.[85] The philanthropist's beneficiaries sometimes seemed the more attractive for being far off and abstruse; George Eliot cited the wag's definition of a philanthropist as 'a man whose charity increases directly as the square of the distance'.[86] Early-Victorian radicals complained that factory children at home were subordinated to those of black overseas; Joseph Rowntree found it easier in 1904 to get Indian famines relieved or soup-kitchens established than to finance an inquiry into the causes of poverty; Ray Strachey complained in 1938 that philanthropists' focused on present misery instead of helping (through her Women's Employment Federation) to prevent misery in the future.[87] In the same year George Orwell ridiculed the later Galsworthy as 'the perfect Dumb Friends' Leaguer, seeing virtually nothing wrong in contemporary society except over-population and cruelty to animals'.[88]

There was even a danger that, where a charity had been formed in an area which patently required it, its formation would in itself be deemed sufficient; the conscience would thereby be satisfied, and the problem would mistakenly be regarded as dealt with. This was particularly likely in view of the philanthropist's tendency to seek further donations by stressing the successes so far achieved. As Mayhew complained, the annual reports of the ragged schools in the 1840s

[84] D. Owen, *English Philanthropy*, pp. 325, 538.
[85] RSPCA *19th A.R., 1845*, p. 19; cf. *23rd A.R., 1849*, p. 18.
[86] G. Eliot, *Middlemarch*, p. 418.
[87] A. Briggs, *Social Thought and Social Action. A Study of the Work of Seebohm Rowntree. 1871–1954* (1961), p. 93; Ray Strachey Papers: Ray Strachey to her mother, 17 Nov. 1938; cf. Ray Strachey to her son Christopher, 21 June 1935.
[88] G. Orwell, *Collected Essays, Journalism and Letters*, i. p. 342.

were all too reluctant to measure their achievement against the scale of the problem they tackled.[89] The existence of ample untapped wealth became apparent at times of social and economic crisis. The forcing of donations through violent intimidation was not unknown in Victorian Britain, and in 1848 and 1886 even the threat of violence was sufficient to produce a sudden access of philanthropic zeal. 'Aye, truly, this is the way to stifle Chartism', wrote Shaftesbury in his diary when Prince Albert responded to his suggestion in 1848 and appeared in person at a meeting of the Labourers' Friend Society.[90] Shaftesbury and Barnardo quite publicly harped upon fears of the 'dangerous classes' in their fund-raising, and in February 1886 Lord Salisbury was worried about the deductions the poor might draw from the large charitable donations evoked by the Trafalgar Square riots.[91]

For the most virulent of philanthropy's critics, the labour movement, charity seemed actually insulting—simultaneously undemocratic in mood and hypocritical in motive. The large donor wielded immense power within the philanthropic organization when (if dissatisfied) he threatened to withdraw his support, and when (if satisfied) he 'challenged' other donors to match his own increased contribution. The average donation given to Barnardo in the thirteen years from 1894 to 1906 was £1. 16s. 7d., and 67.7 per cent of the donations given at that time were under £1. But this was probably unusual among charities, because Barnardo emphasized the need for subscriptions of any size; the United Kingdom Alliance in its great days was far less democratic in its pattern of donations.[92] Nor should one assume that a small donation necessarily comes from a small person, particularly when rich

---

[89] *Morning Chronicle*, 29 Mar. 1850, p. 5.

[90] E. Hodder, *Shaftesbury*, ii, p. 249; cf. Broadlands Archives, Lord Shaftesbury's Diary, entries for 12 May 1848, 19 June 1848; RSPCA *22nd A.R., 1848*, pp. 29-30.

[91] *H. L. Deb.*, 18 Feb. 1886, c.573; cf. J. Harris, *Unemployment and Politics*, p. 111; G. Stedman Jones, *Outcast London*, p. 300.

[92] Calculated from figures in Mrs Barnardo and J. Marchant, *Barnardo*, p. 385. See also my *Drink and the Victorians*, p. 220, and my article, 'The British Prohibitionists, 1853-72. A Biographical Analysis', *International Review of Social History*, 1970, pp. 383-4.

men tended to disperse their donations very widely. Cobden was well aware of subscribers' control over policy; he told the enthusiastic C. D. Collet of the newspaper-tax agitation that before committing himself to vigorous rhetoric he should cast his eye 'over the subscription list . . . and you will see how exclusively, almost, we comprise steady, sober, middle class reformers. Free Trade, temperance, education, peace advocates who will stand by you from year to year, and gather about them a constantly increasing moral power, provided you handle them judiciously.'[93]

No working man had enough leisure or social status to get elected on to an Early-Victorian philanthropic committee. At its anniversary meeting in 1838, a man named Wightman attempted from the floor to substitute some working men for respectable nominees to the New British and Foreign Temperance Society's committee, but was told by the chairman Earl Stanhope that appointees 'should be those who by their leisure, and other qualifications, were enabled fully to attend to its duties'.[94] Philanthropy sometimes even seemed designed to advertise the charity of the rich and thereby throw into the shade the less formal, less co-ordinated mutual helpfulness of the poor. John Collins the Chartist said that if any middle-class person 'gave a few pounds for a charitable purpose, every body was sure to hear of it; but nobody heard of the kindly sympathies of the working man, for his unfortunate brother, when he sat whole nights by his sick bed, or when he clothed his ragged children, and shared his hard crust with his family'.[95] Again, nineteenth-century philanthropists (like some twentieth-century sociologists) allowed the informal nature of so many working-class organizations to blind them to their philanthropic functions; the pub facilitates the exchange of benefits quite as effectively as the voluntary associations whose membership is sometimes seen as an indicator of relatively high social status.[96]

[93] BL Add. MS 43677 (Cobden Papers), f. 42: Cobden to Collett, 5 Dec. 1853.
[94] *The New British and Foreign Temperance Intelligencer*, 26 May 1838, p. 171.   [95] *Northern Star*, 22 Aug. 1840, p. 8.
[96] Cf. T. Bottomore, 'Social Stratification in Voluntary Organisations', in D. V. Glass (ed.), *Social Mobility*, p. 372.

Philanthropists sometimes seemed even to be reinforcing their own status by harping upon the defects of the poor. 'Notions of contempt', wrote Francis Place, 'freely and frequently expressed, of the grades below that in which any one has entered and been accepted are necessary not only to his advancement towards a higher grade, but even to a continuance in his own grade.' Temperance reformers enlarged on the drunkenness of the poor while claiming to be curing it; humanitarians argued that if the poor became kinder to animals, they might then 'behave with greater kindness and good feeling towards those who fill a superior station in life to themselves'.[97] At times charity required actual subservience—in the humiliating scramble for prizes at traditional aristocratic sports, for example, and in the abject supplications addressed to subscribers of 'voting charities'. 'Observe the pauper fawning with abject vileness upon his rich benefactor', wrote William Godwin, 'speechless with sensations of gratitude for having received that which he ought to have claimed . . . with the spirit of a man discussing with a man, and resting his cause only on the justice of his claim.' It became the mark of respectable working people to refuse charity; M. K. Ashby describes how one countrywoman accepted some red flannel from the local charity in Tysoe, but washed it thoroughly and hung it on the line. Asked by passers-by why she was washing the new flannel, she replied, 'why, I bin washin' the charity out on it'.[98]

Hypocrisy seemed another of philanthropy's defects. For the radicals of the 1790s, through Cobbett and the Chartists and on to Marx and the early Labour Party—charity merely involved returning a small portion of the wealth unjustly seized from the people, and added insult to injury by claiming credit for the activity. In 1842 the *Northern Star* alleged that some employers' philanthropy was financed by deliberately underpaying their employees.[99] By the 1890s, Keir Hardie was exposing the long hours and low pay at the

[97] BL Add. MS 27790 (Place Papers), f. 115, cf. Add. MS 27823 (Place Papers), f. 60; RSPCA *19th A.R., 1845*, p. 40.

[98] W. Godwin, *Enquiry concerning Political Justice and its Influence on Morals and Happiness* (2nd ed., 1796), ii, p. 447; M. K. Ashby, *Joseph Ashby of Tysoe. 1859–1919. A Study of Village Life* (Cambridge, 1961), p. 46.

[99] *Northern Star*, 16 July 1842, p. 5; cf. A. R. Schoyen, *The Chartist*

Shawfield chemical works of the philanthropic Scots Presbyterian Lord Overtoun, and the Reading branch of the SDF was attacking those local heroes of philanthropy, Huntley and Palmer, for sacking politically uncongenial workmen and building up a fortune 'by sweating the workers of Reading'. A late variant of this approach can be found in Tom Driberg's description of Lord Nuffield's benefactions to Oxford as 'a welcome but inadequate instalment of conscience-money'.[1] Philanthropists seemed to invert the truth by claiming credit for the huge sums they distributed; for Mayhew and Ernest Jones, these figures merely indicated the scale of Britain's maldistribution of wealth. 'What thoughtful rich people call the problem of poverty', wrote Tawney, 'thoughtful poor people call the problem of riches.'[2]

Philanthropists seemed to make matters worse by their intrusiveness. The *Guardian*, discussing the role of the Anglican clergy in 1856, considered it 'no small security for the peace of this nation that 17,000 men scattered throughout the country, in positions which give them access to the poor at all times when they are most open to influence, are connected in habits and prospects, by blood and acquaintance and prepossessions with . . . the upper 10,000'. Instead of being seen as bids for friendship, visits from the rich to the homes of the poor were seen as intrusions, and their leading advocate Octavia Hill by the SDF as 'inquisitrix-general into the homes of the poor'.[3] Such visitors were for working men what domestic servants were for some wealthy Parisians in 1848—spies within a potentially enemy camp.[4] Matters were made worse when the visitor displayed, in cultivated but patronizing tones, a complete ignorance of

Challenge. A Portrait of George Julian Harney (1958), p. 8; K. Marx, *Capital*, i, pp. 234, 242, 288, 730; T. Burt, *Autobiography*, p. 250.

[1] S. Yeo, 'Religion in Society. A Study from the Standpoint of Reading, Croydon and Hornsey, 1890–1914' (unpublished D.Phil. thesis, 1971), p. 334; *The Times*, 3 Dec. 1970, p. 11; see also K. O. Morgan, *Keir Hardie*, p. 96.

[2] Quot. in P. Mathias, *Living with the Neighbours. The Role of Economic History* (Oxford, 1971), p. 13.

[3] Quotations from S. H. Mayor, 'The Relations between Organised Religion and English Working-Class Movements 1850–1914' (unpublished Ph.D. thesis, Manchester, 1960), p. 22; Wohl, 'Octavia Hill', *Journal of British Studies*, May 1971, p. 119.

[4] A. de Tocqueville, *Recollections* (Tr. A. T. de Mattos, New York, 1959), pp. 157–8.

working-class domestic economy. In 1909 J. A. Hobson thought the cultivated COS enthusiast would never discover the truth about poverty: 'the "case" does not truly reveal itself because it feels it is regarded as a "case" '.[5]

Socialists felt the need to expose as bogus the philanthropist's claim that he could effectively tackle social problems; they felt as much threatened by philanthropy's stabilizing image of upper-class social concern as by the reality of the social benefits it produced. Here, as so often elsewhere, they were merely continuing nineteenth-century radical traditions. Lord Cochrane led radicals in breaking up the meeting held in 1816 to reorganize the Association for the Relief of the Manufacturing and Labouring Poor.[6] Chartists interrupted a sabbatarian meeting at Carlisle in 1839, anti-slavery meetings at Norwich and Cumnock in 1840, and the annual meeting of the Society for Improving the Condition of the Labouring Classes in 1850;[7] and teetotallers of the 1830s broke up the meetings held by the more moderate anti-spirits movement.[8]

Such confrontations became the more bitter because the aims of the two sides were so similar. Both were discontented with present evils, and Socialists even practised personal philanthropy within their tight, almost hermetic, local branch communities. Samuel Smith was the type of philanthropist whose approach involved him in frequent controversy with Socialists, and he published pamphlets in reply to their arguments.[9] When the future Lord Swaythling told the young Lansbury in 1889 that he gave away a tenth of his income to the poor, Lansbury replied that 'we socialists want to prevent you getting the nine-tenths'. The future Earl of Meath faced interruption and insult when, as a prominent philanthropist, he tried to address socialist audiences in London during the 1880s.[10] At the level of

---

[5] J. A. Hobson, *The Crisis of Liberalism*, p. 212.

[6] E. Halévy, *The Liberal Awakening*, p. 12.

[7] *Carlisle Journal*, 21 Dec. 1839, p. 3; *Northern Star*, 28 Nov. 1840, p. 6; *Scottish Patriot*, 28 Mar. 1840, p. 203; *The Times*, 7 June 1850, p. 8.

[8] B. Harrison, *Drink and the Victorians*, p. 146.

[9] S. Smith, *My Life-Work* (1903 ed.), pp. 144–5.

[10] R. Postgate, *Life of George Lansbury* (1951), p. 38; Meath, *Memories*, pp. 232, 234; Meath, *Social Aims* (1893), pp. 84–5.

public argument, philanthropists were now rapidly being
thrown on to the defensive.

Progressive-minded people even began undermining the
psychology of philanthropy at the levels of both benefactor
and beneficiary. The beneficiary's moral defects were transformed into mere outcrops of a corrupt environment,
peripheral among the causes of poverty. As for the philanthropist's benevolence, that had never gone uncriticized.
'It is better sometimes *not* to follow great reformers beyond
the threshold of their homes', wrote George Eliot, sympathetically describing the rather lax parson Mr Irwine.
A generalized benevolence does occasionally, if incongruously,
accompany lack of consideration for immediate dependents;
so total was Barnardo's dedication that he even used his
wedding as a fund-raising device. Virginia Woolf closely
scrutinized Mrs Besant's performance at a public meeting
in 1919 and speculated about the 'many discreditable desires'
harboured by social reformers and philanthropists 'under the
disguise of loving their kind'.[11]

Suspicions of the philanthropist were nourished by the
Late-Victorian fashion for individual spontaneity, and by
the prestige of a new psychology which repudiated repression
and espoused fulfilment. Edward Carpenter in 1907 professed to regard the altruist as usually 'painfully dull and
uninteresting' by comparison with the egotist, and in
Daughters of the Vicar D. H. Lawrence in 1914 memorably
recorded the psychological deprivation which could accompany a woman's 'charity and high-minded living'.[12] By 1925
he could portray Yvette, the vicar's daughter in *The Virgin
and the Gipsy*, as a rebel against Victorianism, and as a
young woman who 'struck absolutely against Sunday School,
the Band of Hope, the Girls' Friendlies—indeed against all
those functions that were conducted by determined old
maids and obstinate, stupid, elderly men'.[13]

---

[11] G. Eliot, *Adam Bede* (New York paperback ed., 1966), p. 60; V. Woolf,
Diary, I (ed. A. O. Bell, Penguin ed., Harmondsworth, 1979), p. 293, cf. p. 256. See
also G. Wagner, *Barnardo*, pp. 76-9, 201; A Boyle, *Only the Wind will Listen.
Reith of the B.B.C.* (1972), p. 36.

[12] E. Carpenter, 'Morality under Socialism', *Albany Review*, Sept. 1907,
p. 628; D. H. Lawrence, *The Prussian Officer* (Penguin ed., 1969), p. 68.

[13] In D. H. Lawrence, *The Short Novels*, ii (1968 ed.), p. 9.

IV

By the end of the nineteenth century, therefore, philanthropy was losing its plausibility as an over-all national
solution to social problems. Sir Robert Peel's father had
been among the rich men who made voluntary tax contributions in 1797, but the permanence of the income tax
reintroduced by his son in 1842, together with Harcourt's
major extension of death duties in 1894, made volunteering
of this kind seem antique. Lloyd George made things worse
in 1909; anti-suffragists trying to raise money from wealthy
individuals in 1910 encountered resistance from critics of
what one of them called 'that d——d little Welsh attorney'.
By contrast, Maud Selborne in the same year viewed the
supersession of private philanthropy by public welfare with
some relish; she told her brother she was not frightened of
Socialism much, because she knew it would not work, and
one advantage of 'having the State spend your charity money
for you . . . is that several old screws who never will subscribe to anything will have to stump up'. By the 1960s so
central had government funding become to social welfare
that Richard Crossman was 'astonished by the strength of
the resistance among my civil servants' when (as Secretary
of State for the Social Services) he suggested encouraging
private donations to the National Health Service.[14]

The vigour of the entrepreneurial ideal, reinforced by the
frontier mentality and a federal political structure, ensures
the continued vitality of philanthropy in the United States,
and in recent years American historians have crossed the
Atlantic to analyse the very different situation in Britain.
By 1977, income from investments, public-sector grants,
and donations from business firms accounted for a rising
proportion of British voluntary organizations' over-all receipts,
whereas personal donations accounted for a dwindling
proportion. Personal donations to charity were also falling
as a percentage of consumer expenditure—from 0.6 per cent
in 1934 in England and Wales to 0.3 per cent in 1975 in the

---

[14] India Office Library, Curzon Papers, MS Eur. F. 112/32: Hanbury to
Curzon, 27 July 1910; Hatfield House MSS, CHE 56/71: Maud Selborne to Lord
Robert Cecil, 18 Nov. [1910]; R. H. S. Crossman, *Role of the Volunteer*, p. 29.

United Kingdom.[15] At the same time, increased size of firm was eroding commitment to local charities.[16]

Yet philanthropic decline in Britain should not be ante-dated or exaggerated. A. J. P. Taylor describes voluntary workers between the wars as still 'the active people of England' who 'provided the ground swell of her history'.[17] And the remarkable post-war rise in the number of blood-donors (from 1.4 per cent of the eligible population in 1947 to 6.0 per cent in 1968) illustrates how individual altruism can effectively collaborate with public welfare. Crossman in the late 1960s was surprised at the abundance of volunteers still active in the social services.[18] British charities such as Oxfam, Shelter, and Child Poverty Action Group have recently shown considerable resourcefulness in fund-raising technique. Furthermore in the 1970s one of the major political parties showed renewed enthusiasm for the philan-thropic ideal. Viewed through his own eyes, 1926 was the finest hour of the volunteer, when the Supply and Transport Committee managed to enrol 300,000 and perhaps half a million people in helping to break the General Strike,[19] and Conservatives came to see voluntary welfare work as a way of obtaining social welfare without state intervention or higher taxation, of securing participation without bureau-cracy or trade-union domination over policy. Conservatives had never been convinced by the Socialists' critique of nineteenth-century philanthropy. For them it embodied a welcome recognition that government cannot solve all prob-lems, a welcome proliferation of choices—at least for some. They saw the volunteer as equivalent in the welfare sphere to the entrepreneur in the sphere of production; both were far more efficient than any other agency at discovering and meeting local needs.[20]

---

[15] P. Falush, 'Trends in the Finance of British Charities', loc. cit., p. 42.

[16] *The Times*, 3 Sept. 1968, p. 2.

[17] A. J. P. Taylor, *English History 1914–1945* (1965), p. 175.

[18] R. M. Titmuss, *The Gift Relationship. From Human Blood to Social Policy* (1970), pp. 42–4; *The Times*, 8 Aug. 1973, p. 14.

[19] G. A. Phillips, *The General Strike. The Politics of Industrial Conflict* (1976), p. 153.

[20] See e.g. Mrs Thatcher, *Financial Times*, 28 May 1980, p. 8; 20 Jan. 1981, p. 5. See also *The Times*, 8 Aug. 1973, p. 14.

Nor were Conservative politicians alone in thinking that the early twentieth-century reaction against philanthropy had gone too far. Public provision has not monopolized initiative in social welfare; numerous commercial and philanthropic bodies have sprung up on the frontier of state organizations to cater for new needs or desires: Securicor, BUPA, the Samitarians, play-groups, consumer groups, Help the Aged, Denticare, not to mention the recent resurgence in private education, privately-run railways, and women's self-help organizations. Nor are these bodies merely pioneering the advance of the state like so many of their predecessors. Many of them illustrate the fact, frequently embarrassing to the Labour Party, that there is little enthusiasm for paying compulsory rates and taxes, however excellent the institutions and functions they finance,[21] and that state-run social-security arrangements, however professionalized, leave insufficient scope for initiative and altruism,[22] and are insufficiently sensitive in their handling of their beneficiaries. The twentieth-century growth of public welfare has been associated (not, perhaps, inevitably) with the rise of huge institutions—hospitals, old people's homes, asylums, welfare centres, and the rest—highly capitalized and specialized in their facilities, but somewhat impersonal in character.

Nineteenth-century philanthropists often emphasized this; they disliked state action partly because they disliked interference from London and favoured a personal bond between the deprived and the privileged. In 1869 Josephine Butler distinguished between the 'feminine' method of individual ministration and the 'masculine' method of legislating to create large relief organizations and systems, and pleaded for a compromise between the two; 'the large and magnificently-ordered Institution', she wrote, 'is in danger of becoming as fatally a pauperizing influence as the Lady Bountiful'. She wanted an infusion of 'home elements' into large institutions, believing that 'the wholesale system tends to turn human beings into machines instead of training them to be self-

[21] See Barbara Castle's complaint at Scarborough, *Sunday Times*, 2 Mar. 1975, p. 6.
[22] R. H. S. Crossman, *The Role of the Volunteer*, p. 24; see also p. 21.

depending responsible beings'.[23] It is perhaps no accident that those three pioneers of public welfare—Edwin Chadwick, Beatrice Webb, and William Beveridge—felt little personal identification with the victims of social distress: 'to me "a million sick" have always seemed actually more worthy of self-sacrificing devotion', Beatrice wrote, 'than the "child sick in a fever", preferred by Mrs Browning's *Aurora Leigh*'.[24]

The reaction against institutionalization and against the increasing size of institutions has now been in progress for some time, and credit now tends to be given to the COS for pioneering systematic social casework. The COS also recognized how difficult it is to tackle poverty without a rounded appreciation of the individual's over-all situation. The specialist services so efficiently developed by the welfare state are now co-ordinated on to the individual through an individual casework which C. S. Loch would not have found unfamiliar. 'The truth is that the ascertainment of the actual need of the individuals cannot be done by government officials taking time off from the desk', wrote Crossman.[25] We are now increasingly aware of the scale of the error and the degree of insensitivity that both administrator and planner can commit. Late-Victorian criticisms of philanthropy had force and effectiveness, but they did not destroy the case for a balance in any democratic society between centralized welfare and decentralized self-help. Now that the Victorian age is securely behind us, we can perhaps acknowledge the substantial and continuing contribution made by volunteers and philanthropists to our history.

[23] J. E. Butler, introduction to J. E. Butler (ed.), *Woman's Work and Woman's Culture* (1869), p. xxxviii.

[24] S. E. Finer, *Edwin Chadwick*, p. 3; B. Webb, *My Apprenticeship*, p. 221, cf. pp. 104, 222, 228; J. Harris, *William Beveridge*, p. 60.

[25] R. H. S. Crossman, *The Role of the Volunteer*, p. 20.

VI

Finding out how the Other Half Live:
Social Research and British Government since 1780 [1]

Commenting in 1914 on the mood of the *Daily Herald*, H. G. Wells said he enjoyed reading the paper, but disliked its uncritical enthusiasm for revolt and its limited political outlook. The paper's editorial columns and Will Dyson's cartoons made a simplistic juxtaposition between on the one hand the fat cigar-smoking capitalist and on the other hand 'the lean, large-limbed, small-headed, pathetic *Worker*'. In neither personage did Wells see much hope for the future, and he went on to ask: 'isn't there, indeed, between these two, something as yet inadequate in which the hope of man resides, something that is neither pride and greed on the one hand nor blind anger and revolt on the other—Intelligence and Will?' In his view, the future lay with science and education, for these would put an end both to serfs and to fat men; 'in schools and laboratories to-day', he went on, 'there are heroes at work'.[2] Wells's optimism about the directness of the relationship between science and social progress would not now go uncontested, but he rightly drew the paper's attention to the continuous and, in the long term, revolutionary impact made by intellectual inquiry. Nowhere has such inquiry been so relevant to improving social conditions than in the growth of social investigation; such a theme is central to the story of how social and political stability has been secured in modern Britain.

In the histories of British sociology, the Booths and the Rowntrees receive ample but somewhat disproportionate attention. Sociological textbooks in their historical sections tend to concern themselves with founding fathers, and label

---

[1] This chapter originated as a radio programme for the Open University, made in 1970. It has been substantially amplified and recast for publication here.

[2] *Daily Herald*, 15 Apr. 1914, p. 10.

Booth as 'the father of scientific social surveys' whose off-spring—Rowntree, Bowley, and others—refine the techniques he pioneers.[3] Yet the history of social investigation cannot be seen simply in terms of a relay-race whereby one founding-father hands on his methodological baton to the next. First, the main-line direction of the social survey has never been free of criticism; from Henry Mayhew onwards, critics have emphasized the price investigators pay for their technical advances, together with hints of alternative approaches; some of this criticism will be briefly considered at the end of this chapter. But secondly, in so far as social investigation has advanced, it has done so not in a linear way, but through a syncopation or dialogue. The wits of Britain's pioneer freelance sociologists were sharpened on the official inquiry, a form of investigation which has received much less attention; their exchanges constituted a sort of workshop which forged improved technique on both sides.

The dialogue was well under way by the 1820s, for Cobbett's *Rural Rides* originated in his desire to rebut the evidence for a duty on imported corn which the select committee on agriculture had collected in 1821. *Rural Rides* eventually transcended its original purpose, but its mood of finding fault with parliamentary inquiries persisted, and Cobbett later assailed a committee of 1818 on church accommodation and an emigration committee of 1824.[4] Mayhew carried this mood forward into the 1840s; official inquiries were very much in his mind throughout *London Labour and the London Poor*, which he described as 'the first "blue book" ever published in twopenny numbers'. Its whole procedure implicitly and explicitly reproached the official inquiry, and Mayhew took a delight in exposing inconsistencies between different sets of government statistics.[5] He also complained of the defective statistical categories adopted by officials ignorant of working-class life, and contrasted

---

[3] C. A. Moser and G. Kalton, *Survey Methods in Social Investigation* (2nd ed., 1971), p. 6; cf. R. and D. Glass, in *Chambers Encyclopaedia* (1966 ed.), xii, p. 665.

[4] W. Cobbett, *Rural Rides* (1930 ed.), i, p. xix; ii, pp. 377, 415–16.

[5] H. Mayhew, *London Labour and the London Poor*, i, p. iii; see also iii, p. 234.

official information with what working men told him.[6] Charles Booth enjoyed more influence than Mayhew over the compilation of government statistics, yet he too was critical of them. In his case, the interaction was fruitful, and he was largely responsible for securing a select committee on sweated labour in 1888, and for accumulating valuable information on housing through the census of 1891—not to mention the help he gave Beatrice Webb in enabling the poor law commission of 1905 to gain full control over its agenda.[7]

With Beatrice Webb, the exchanges between official and freelance social investigators virtually becomes a dialogue between the government machine and the London School of Economics; its location, traditions, and distinction in the field of social science made it the twentieth-century continuator of a nineteenth-century critique which, in the absence of any firmly based home for social science in Britain, had hitherto been merely intermittent and unintegrated. Beatrice Webb and other freelance sociologists, convinced that 'reforming society is not a light matter, and must be taken by experts specially trained for the purpose'— condemned the amateurism of the official investigation, and its concentration on collecting opinions, as distinct from engaging in social research.[8] They did not of course object to surveys of opinion as such, but to their undue prominence in investigations of this kind, and to their unsystematic procedure. A related criticism was their distaste for the impressionism of the official inquiry. Charles Booth had resolved 'to make use of no fact to which I cannot give a quantitative value', and under his supervision Beatrice 'became aware that every conclusion derived from observation or experiment had to be qualified as well as verified by the relevant statistics'.[9] Like Booth, but unlike so many of her predecessors on official inquiries, she operated within the increasingly professional world of sociology, and like him she could draw upon the expertise of many informed people.

[6] Ibid., i, p. 5; ii, pp. 1, 5, 162, 166, 189, 196, 288; iii, p. 234; iv, pp. 6–7, 28, 30.   [7] T. S. and M. B. Simey, *Charles Booth*, pp. 67, 107, 122, 174.

[8] M. Cole, *The Story of Fabian Socialism* (paperback ed., 1963), p. 70.

[9] Booth quot. in C. A. Moser and G. Kalton, *Survey Methods*, p. 7; T. S. and M. B. Simey, *Charles Booth*, p. 102.

In view of the major contribution made to the history of British social investigation by this dialogue—not to mention the immense scale of official investigation by comparison with the work done by freelance sociologists, and its major importance as a historical source in its own right—surprisingly little has so far been written about the official inquiry, perhaps partly because the subject superficially lacks dramatic appeal. The census has received most attention, yet even there the focus has rested on its potential as a historical source rather than as an important historical event in its own right. There are no historical studies of nineteenth-century select and departmental committees as political instruments, though some individual select committees have now been studied. The nineteenth-century royal commission has fared rather better; there is Clokie and Robinson's valuable general survey of 1937; but their interests were severely limited, and the gap has not been entirely filled by the more detailed subsequent studies of individual royal commissions, nor have these aimed at painting a dynamic picture, or at relating the changes they discuss to wider social, political, and intellectual developments.

A comprehensive discussion of these inquiries would be impossible here. The aim will simply be the fourfold one of narrating the over-all expansion and diversification of the official inquiry since the late eighteenth century, outlining the obstacles overcome in the process, and explaining the criticisms it encountered from the professional sociologist and the scepticism it received from critics whose ideal of social investigation assigned a larger role to the layman. From this discussion it should become clear how far the roles of official inquiry and freelance social survey are distinct, interact, or overlap.

I

The select committee was the first type of offical inquiry to grapple with the host of social problems thrown up by industrialization. Parliament simply appointed a committee from its own members to question witnesses, and a parliamentary debate on their report would often result. After

1780, the House of Commons began printing some of its papers for sale or circulation, and the reports of some committees were independently published by the booksellers.[10] The growth in the quantity of parliamentary papers published annually was striking—7 volumes in 1801, 24 in 1824, and an annual average of between 60 and 70 after 1850; only after 1890 did the rate of production begin to fall.[11]

The increasing government control over the appointment of select committees, and the limited number of MPs and peers available for such purposes soon increased the attractions of a second form of public inquiry, the royal commission, an old institution revived in the 1830s as a more flexible instrument of government investigation. It had less power to compel the giving of evidence, but was broader in recruitment, more versatile in location and method of inquiry, and better able to remedy both parliament's lack of expertise and Whitehall's lack of authority and personnel. Formally responsible only to the Crown, it was free to develop its own procedures *de novo* according to need, and its prestige soon won it more public co-operation than any number of formal powers would have bestowed. After 1801 the number of royal commissions appointed annually rose fast, culminating in eight per year between 1851 and 1860; thereafter the number annually appointed went into decline, though between 1881 and 1890 the annual average was still as high as four.[12] Overseas observers in the 1930s were impressed at the social prestige still attaching to service on a royal commission, and noted that volunteers were not hard to obtain.[13]

Perhaps most impressive of all was the third instrument for inquiry, the census, the eighteenth of which was held in 1981. The early nineteenth century saw a continuous improvement in its range and accuracy. In 1841 in England and Wales the parish overseers were replaced in conducting it by the registrars acting under the registrar-general. Ever more

[10] J. Ehrman, *The Younger Pitt. The Years of Acclaim* (1969), p. 605; see also C. S. Emden, *The People and the Constitution* (2nd ed., 1956), p. 65.

[11] H. McD. Clokie and J. W. Robinson, *Royal Commissions of Inquiry. The Significance of Investigations in British Politics* (Stanford, 1937), p. 67.

[12] Ibid., pp. 73–5, 79.

[13] Ibid., p. 157; H. F. Gosnell, 'British Royal Commissions of Inquiry', *Political Science Quarterly*, 1934, p. 118.

information was accumulated at each census. 1851 saw the first census of educational provision, and of religious facilities and observance; 1861 saw (for Scotland) the first survey of housing accommodation. 1881 saw the first language census (of Scottish Gaelic-speakers), extended to Welsh-speakers in 1891.[14] The census of housing accommodation was first extended to England and Wales in 1891, and in 1908 a census of production was first taken. Organized by the Board of Trade and the Board of Agriculture and Fisheries, it issued specified employers with a questionnaire—part compulsory, part voluntary—which requested information on output, materials and fuel used, numbers employed, days worked, and plant used during 1907. It collected a wealth of information on factories, agriculture, mines, and certain specified workshops. 1911 saw the first fertility census, and the process of elaboration went into reverse only in 1921— 'the first time in the modern history of census-taking in this country', according to the general report of that year, 'that any enquiry once introduced into the schedule has been omitted therefrom on a subsequent occasion'.[15] A passion for planning eventually succeeded inter-war governmental economies, so that the scope of the census was further broadened in 1951 and 1961.

Except for the census, these official inquiries were irregular in timing, and were usually launched in response to concern about distress of some kind. The early official inquiries were like explorers entering an unmapped jungle from different directions; they had hardly begun to move towards mutual reinforcement. When engaged in Irish administration, the young Peel did not even possess the trade statistics necessary to provide adequately against famine; and when devising governmental policy at the national level in 1841, he complained (in a cabinet memorandum on the corn duty) that 'we must legislate on speculation and conjecture, and on assumptions which rest on no satisfactory data'.[16] The mining

[14] See the useful table in R. Lawton (ed.), *The Census and Social Structure. An Interpretative Guide to Nineteenth Century Censuses for England and Wales* (1978), pp. 292-3.

[15] Census of England and Wales 1921, *General Report* (HMSO, 1927), p. 2.

[16] Sir R. Peel, *Memoirs* (1856), ii, p. 349; see also N. Gash, *Mr Secretary Peel*, p. 221.

commission of 1842 found it extremely difficult to investigate an area never hitherto surveyed, and much of Mayhew's lack of system stemmed from the fact that he was exploring unknown territory.[17] Victorian franchise reform was often implemented amid remarkable ignorance of the classes destined for enfranchisement, and as late as 1900 pension policy was hindered by a serious lack of accurate statistics on old age.[18] At the end of the first world war, after almost a decade of labour exchanges, policy on unemployment insurance had to be formulated without adequate information on the incidence of unemployment in Britain or on the prospects of particular British industries.[19] There was a circular problem: statistics could be improved only after legislation, but effective legislation could be devised only with the aid of adequate statistics.

The pioneer official inquiries were also inevitably forced into operating at an early stage in the formulation of their problem, and aimed for the moment simply to collect useful information. Legislation was, as yet, somewhat far off, and the immediate aim was simply to fertilize public debate with relevant facts. Such inquiries produced a miniature encyclopaedia rather than a set of conclusions arranged with elegantly scientific precision; praising the 'practical utility' of the evidence given to Sadler's inquiry into the factory question in 1832, Samuel Kydd saw it as 'a cyclopaedia of physiological, social, and moral knowledge, by the most eminent professional men of their age in the departments of anatomy and medicine'.[20] Mayhew's subtitle reveals that this was also one purpose of his *London Labour and the London Poor*.

Long-term and structural trends could be clarified and problems precisely formulated only if inquiry became a continuous and integrated process, conducted as a matter of

[17] R. C. . . . Children in Mines and Manufactories, First Report, *Parl. Papers*, 1842 (380), XV, pp. 2, 4; H. Mayhew, *London Labour and the London Poor*, iii, pp. 301, 312.
[18] R. Harrison, *Before the Socialists*, p. 115; D. Collins, 'The Introduction of Old Age Pensions in Great Britain', *Historical Journal*, 1965, p. 248.
[19] B. B. Gilbert, *British Social Policy 1914–1939* (1970), p. 74.
[20] [S. Kydd], *The History of the Factory Movement* (1857), i, p. 312, cf. pp. 275–310.

routine by government departments. A fourth instrument, the departmental inquiry, eventually emerged to meet this need. An outstanding early example of it is Chadwick's sanitary report of 1842, which Chadwick afterwards always saw as a model. The poor law commission's machinery was used for issuing questionnaires to poor-law medical officers, assistant commissioners, and other officials. Chadwick's firsthand observations were then injected, together with the results of his reading in the British and overseas literature. The information could then all be worked up into an argument that was much more lucid and concise than was customary in other official inquiries at the time. Experts were invited to comment on the draft, and proof copies were sent to distinguished men of letters. The whole enterprise drew on governmental resources and expert knowledge in an unprecedented way.

As the government machine grew in size and competence, its inspectors and departments produced a stream of annual reports, and the departmental inquiry began to seem an obvious way of conducting inquiries that did not require publicity; its calibre emerges clearly from contrasting Beveridge's social insurance committee of 1942 with the poor law commission of 1905-9. Its use varied markedly between departments, and was particularly popular with the Home Office and the Scottish Office.[21] Already by 1900-9 as many as 209 departmental committees were being appointed per decade as compared with forty-four royal commissions. The Liberal Party's Yellow Book in 1928 felt that the work done by royal commissions and departmental inquiries could now be speeded up and co-ordinated by the Economic General Staff which it wished to see appointed. In 1960-9 departmental committees kept their total up to 206, whereas the number of royal commissions had fallen to ten.[22] Continuous research became incorporated into regular departmental activity in other ways. By 1923 the

[21] T. J. Cartwright, *Royal Commissions and Departmental Committees in Britain. A Case-Study in Institutional Adaptiveness and Public Participation in Government* (1975), p. 60; J. Harris, *William Beveridge*, pp. 383-4.

[22] T. J. Cartwright, *Royal Commissions*, p. 36; Liberal Industrial Inquiry, *Britain's Industrial Future* (1977 ed.), p. 119.

Ministry of Labour, for instance, was taking sample surveys of the unemployed.[23] Between the wars, governmental inquiries were supplemented by social surveys sponsored in universities, which were themselves in some respects becoming outcrops of government. The interests of academic empirical sociologists overlapped with the needs identified by civil servants, for British empirical sociology has never been remote from government, whether local or national.

The various types of social investigation—official and freelance—were now moving towards mutual reinforcement and clearer definition of their problem. Numerous private consumer surveys were set up after the 1920s for product planning,[24] and when Rowntree and Lavers investigated English life and leisure in the late 1940s they were able to draw on numerous private surveys. They could also make extensive use of Research Services Ltd.—so that at times they merely aggregate and analyse data collected by others. With this explosion in information came an increasing commitment to 'planning'. By 1945, the pieces of the jigsaw seemed to be coming together at last, and Herbert Morrison was keen to complete the picture. Claiming in 1946 to be 'well launched on a campaign for statistical flood-lighting', he pointed out that 'in the past, government has made the worst of both worlds by demanding a mass of information which was only useful for limited purposes and did not fit together. The need now is for facts and figures to give all concerned—not only government—a clear up-to-date picture of what is happening with the minimum of effort.'[25]

Under governments of both parties, the process of 'statistical flood-lighting' has continued ever since. The periodical *Economic Trends* was launched in 1953, the family expenditure survey in 1957, the Central Statistical Office's *Abstract of Regional Statistics* in 1965, *Trends in Education* in 1966, and *Social Trends* in 1970. The Wilson governments of the 1960s accelerated the collection of official data, and in 1967 the sample size for the family expenditure survey

[23] D. C. Jones, *Social Surveys* (n.d.), pp. 79-82.
[24] On these see M. Abrams, *Social Surveys and Social Action* (1951), pp. 54, 61.
[25] H. Morrison, *The Peaceful Revolution. Speeches* (1949), pp. 14-15.

was increased from 5,000 to over 10,000.[26] The amalgamation of the General Register Office for England and Wales with the government social survey in 1970 aimed at improving both the quality and the quantity of government data so that, in C. A. Moser's words, 'the census, instead of being an isolated event, can become part of a coherent programme of population enquiries'.[27] In 1973 the general household survey aimed to carry still further the integration of social investigation with the needs of government departments. They themselves helped design the survey, which aimed to collect in a co-ordinated way the information they separately required on topics such as health, education, housing, employment, and population. It saw itself 'as a kind of co-operative government research activity in which the information collected was related as closely as possible to needs of the departments, as they saw them'. In this way the gaps between decennial censuses could be bridged, and 'a government research instrument' could be created to 'examine the way in which different policy areas interacted'.[28]

The government machine has now become so large that official inquiries cannot always be co-ordinated. Nor do related problems necessarily force themselves to the political forefront simultaneously. Even when this does occur, co-ordinated research does not necessarily result; it has been argued, for instance, that there was insufficient collaboration between the Annan committee on broadcasting and the concurrent royal commission on the press.[29] And for two reasons, official research will continue to encounter the difficulties involved in exploring the unknown. First, government is continually involving itself in new areas of conduct. Twentieth-century concern about the economic structure of the press, for instance, caused the appointment of the first (Ross) royal commission on the subject in 1947, which mapped out the territory for its successors, the Shawcross

[26] C. A. Moser, 'Some General Developments in Social Statistics', *Social Trends*, no. 1 (1970), p. 9.

[27] Ibid., p. 8.

[28] Office of Population Censuses and Surveys, Social Survey Division, The General Household Survey, *Introductory Report* (HMSO, 1973), p. 1.

[29] J. Tunstall, in M. Bulmer (ed.), *Social Research and Royal Commissions* (1980), p. 126.

(1961) and Finer/McGregor (1974) commissions. In seeking
to grapple with their subject, each looked to its predecessor
for guidance; as one participant in the Finer/McGregor
commission put it, 'the earlier reports were benchmarks . . .
in the sense of a standard to be surpassed: "We must at least
do better on this than Shawcross." '[30] Secondly, in a changing society, government does not even enjoy the option of
staying in the same place; changes in social behaviour and
technology compel existing procedures and relations to be
thought out afresh—road transport, the media, drug abuse,
and the location of airports all provide recent examples.
Official inquiries could perhaps be ranged on a scale—
moving from the preliminary foray into the subject at one
end, through the detailed fact-gathering type of inquiry,
and on towards the type of investigation at the other end
which aims simply to mobilize opinion behind a legislative
change already favoured by government.

Will this process of official factual accumulation ever
cease? There have been set-backs to it in recent years; and in
retrospect the Wilson government's 'national plan' of 1965
within which 'each industry will know both what is expected
of it and what help it can expect—in terms of exports,
investment, production and employment', looks like the
denouement of the inter-war all-party enthusiasm for
planning.[31] Since the 1960s, for reasons of politico-economic
doctrine, economy, and disillusionment with the results of
planning—there has been a certain retreat. The national
plan was abandoned, the proposed mid-term census of 1976
was withdrawn for reasons of economy, the Diamond commission on the distribution of wealth was discontinued in
1979, and by then there was widespread disillusionment
with the high-rise housing, the demand management of the
economy, the improved motorways, the industrial mergers,
the impersonal and highly technical medical treatment, and
the large bureaucratic structures that seemed to grow out
of planning at national and local level. Yet it is difficult to
see this mood as anything other than temporary. Not only

[30] J. Tunstall, ibid., p. 124.
[31] F. W. S. Craig (ed.), *British General Election Manifestos 1918–1966*
(Chichester, 1970), p. 233.

does the Labour Party retain its faith in planning; it is not at all clear how any continuing retreat from planning could be compatible with tackling the social problems thrown up by the greater population density, faster industrial change, rising expectations of life, dwindling natural resources, and an increasingly complex technology. The improbable alternatives to planning are the abandonment of all attempts at rational control over man's environment and/or a drastic reduction in public expectations of life. The recent retreat of the state from social investigation will surely prove as temporary as the set-back initiated by the Geddes Axe in 1922.

The twentieth-century growth of the departmental committee has been accompanied by the decline of the royal commission and the select committee. Twentieth-century government requires advisory bodies more permanent than the royal commission, or bodies that respond more flexibly and quickly to governmental need. The 24 royal commissions held between 1945 and 1969 met on average 89 times, received information from an average of 200 witnesses, and issued a report averaging at 330 pages. By contrast, the 358 departmental committees that met during the same period were much less cumbersome; they met on average only 33 times, received information from an average of 100 witnesses, and issued reports averaging at only 110 pages.[32] The royal commission now tends to be used primarily to resolve wide-ranging questions that do not require rapid settlement, and that straddle government departments.[33] When the royal commission falls naturally into the sphere of a single government department, it can virtually become part of it. The Diamond commission for instance embarked from the outset on systematic research, and aimed to provide the factual foundation for government policy. It took oral evidence only with the aim of guiding its research, not as the raw material for its conclusions. With a statistical support unit of its own, it worked closely with government statisticians who provided much of its data; it was less like a royal commission than a small statistical department of

[32] T. J. Cartwright, *Royal Commissions*, pp. 116, 131, 195.
[33] Cf. A. Beattie, 'Commissions, Committees and Competence', *New Society*, 29 July 1965, pp. 10–11.

government.[34] The parliamentary select committee has also gone into decline. Whereas between 1867 and 1900 there were thirty-three select committees per session, by 1945–61 there were only fifteen a year, involving fewer MPs and on topics less likely to arouse major public interest.[35] But too much should not be made of the distinction between the select committee, the royal commission, and the departmental committee; the public often fails to distinguish between them because in practice they often turn out to do much the same kind of thing.[36]

This vast accumulation of information has a double interest for the historian. It provides him with a wealth of raw material, but it is also an event in its own right. By the 1840s, politicians were attaching great importance to official inquiries. In September 1849 Disraeli was found immersed at Hughenden in the blue books of the previous session; he had classified them by subject, and attributed Peel's 'great power and effect in the House to having always had Blue Books by heart, and having thereby the appearance of a fund of general knowledge greater than he really possessed'. Towards the end of his life, he saw these reports as 'pregnant with prudent and sagacious suggestions for the improvement of the administration of affairs'.[37] Pressure groups also valued them highly. The anti-slave-trade movement in the late 1780s took great trouble to drum up witnesses for a parliamentary investigation into the evil,[38] and Cobden in the 1840s wanted a select committee to cross-examine the protectionist leaders; as he told parliament in March 1844, 'there is no tribunal so fair as a Select Committee'.[39] Chadwick saw the royal commission as a major help in mobilizing

---

[34] M. Bulmer, in M. Bulmer (ed.), *Social Research and Royal Commissions*, pp. 164–5, 167, 174.

[35] H. McD. Clokie and J. W. Robinson, *Royal Commissions*, p. 192; B. Crick, *The Reform of Parliament* (2nd ed., 1968), p. 100.

[36] R. A. Chapman (ed.), *The Role of Commissions in Policy-Making* (1973), p. 175; cf. T. J. Cartwright, *Royal Commissions*, pp. 23–31.

[37] W. F. Monypenny and G. E. Buckle, *The Life of Benjamin Disraeli* (two-vol. ed., 1929), i, p. 1035; *H. L. Deb.*, 19 July 1877, c.1478.

[38] E. C. Toye, 'Abolitionist Societies. 1787–1838. A Half-Century of Abolition' (unpublished MA thesis, London, 1936), p. 48.

[39] *H. C. Deb.*, 12 Mar. 1844, c.890.

public opinion,[40] and pressure groups occasionally reprinted parliamentary papers for their own purposes; temperance reformers plundered the report of the select committee on drunkenness of 1834 for ammunition for decades.[41] The Tariff Reform League in 1903 even appointed a commission of its own to frame a scientific tariff, composed of experts and representatives from the empire and from every major industry.

British official inquiries were not praised only by the Establishment. In 1845 Engels thought German Socialism suffered from its ignorance of the real world, because 'only in England is adequate material available for an exhaustive enquiry into the condition of the proletariat'.[42] Engels depends heavily on official inquiries throughout his book, while simultaneously assaulting the inhumanity and indifference of the society that produced them; for him, the offence is merely compounded when social evils are so elaborately investigated, yet left without remedy.[43] Marx too recognized Britain's superiority here; 'the social statistics of Germany and the rest of Continental Western Europe are, in comparison with those of England, wretchedly compiled', he wrote in 1867. Germany's bad social conditions would be exposed, he says, if she could draw upon 'men as competent, as free from partisanship and respect of persons' as Britain's government inspectors and parliamentary investigators.[44]

II

This investigative achievement seems all the greater in the light of the obstacles that had to be overcome. In some respects, government inquiries faced difficulties even greater than the freelance investigators. For both groups, transport

[40] S. E. Finer, *The Life and Times of Sir Edwin Chadwick* (1952), p. 480.
[41] See my 'Two Road to Social Reform', *Historical Journal*, 1968, p. 292; cf. G. L. Phillips, *England's Climbing-Boys. A History of the Long Struggle to Abolish Child Labour in Chimney-Sweeping* (Harvard, 1949), p. 21.
[42] F. Engels, *Working Class*, p. 3 (preface to 1st German ed., 1845); see also p. 4 and Chaloner and Henderson's introduction, p. xxviii.
[43] e.g. ibid., pp. 109, 123.
[44] K. Marx, *Capital* (Tr. S. Moore and E. Aveling, New York paperback ed., 1967), i, p. 9.

difficulties were formidable. As late as April 1802, two remote Scottish counties had still not made their returns for the census taken in the previous November.[45] Engels often stressed how difficult it was for a stranger to find his way around the Manchester slums in the 1840s.[46] Houses were often not precisely numbered, if only because tenements were not divided into distinct homes. Street-numbering systems did not become formalized in most British towns till the 1850s at the earliest, and in 1871 the compilers of the census found their work especially difficult where this had still not been done.[47] Difficulties were compounded by the fact that many slum children lacked even a name; Chadwick's sanitary report records Captain Miller, a police superintendent, as saying that 'within this range of buildings I have no doubt I should be able to find a thousand children who have no names whatever, or only nicknames, like dogs'.[48] Probably a majority of adults surveyed by the census of 1891 did not know their exact age.[49]

A circular problem beset pioneer social investigators of every type. Accurate information could be obtained only from a literate and even numerate population which could both provide and process the information desired; yet only with the aid of accurate information could the economic and educational systems effectively cultivate universal literacy and numeracy. Even the use of graphs was a technique only painfully acquired and laboriously rendered familiar from the late eighteenth century onwards.[50] Only since the 1950s have people become accustomed to the regular use of statistics in public debate; every general election campaign since then has been at some stage affected by the routine publication of statistics—inflation rates, trade figures, and the rest[51]— but this is something new in British public life.

[45] E. A. Wrigley (ed.), *Nineteenth-Century Society* (Cambridge, 1972), p. 24.
[46] F. Engels, *Working Class*, pp. 61-3.
[47] R. Lawton (ed.), *The Census and Social Structure*, pp. 128-9.
[48] M. W. Flinn (ed.), *Report on the Sanitary Condition of the Labouring Population of Great Britain* (by Edwin Chadwick, Edinburgh, 1965), p. 199.
[49] E. A. Wrigley (ed.), *Nineteenth-Century Society*, p. 21, cf. pp. 75, 88.
[50] M. J. Cullen, *The Statistical Movement in Early Victorian Britain. The Foundations of Empirical Social Research* (Hassocks, 1975), pp. 11-12.
[51] D. Butler and D. Kavanagh, *The British General Election of October 1974* (1975), p. 110.

Nor do trained social investigators spring out of the ground when required. Objectivity and reliability had to be sought out and trained; investigators who could gain the trust of both informant and investigator had to be located. Once obtained, the information had to be processed. The sheer scope and scale of governmental inquiry posed special problems. By modern standards the early census was prodigal in its demand for routine arithmetical and secretarial operations. Only in 1890 did a departmental committee on the census discuss using Hollerith punched cards; the census of 1901 was the last to copy householders' schedules into enumerators' books before tabulating the results of the census by hand; Hollerith punched cards were first used in the census of 1911.[52] Intellectual statistical breakthroughs were also required if the cost of processing was to be kept down. Of these the most important was perhaps the sample survey; this major source of economy gained general acceptance only after 1936, when Seebohm Rowntree checked the findings of a complete survey against what a sample survey would have revealed.[53] Not till 1961 was the sample survey introduced into the national census for certain purposes. Furthermore increased information is not necessarily to be had for the asking. There is a tension between seeking more information and securing completeness and accuracy of return; the inverse relationship between the two can be countered only by expensive follow-up inquiries. Quantity of information also has the disadvantage of taking longer to process, and becomes that much the less useful for planning purposes; as late as 1975 it was being objected of the 1971 census that 'the main tabulations required for policy work are only just coming out'.[54] Twentieth-century office technology, though, may well accelerate fast enough to overcome this problem.

The difficulties were by no means all purely intellectual in nature. When it came to detailed investigation of slum conditions by educated observers, there were health hazards. Historians rightly express concern for those who spent their

[52] R. Lawton (ed.), *The Census and Social Structure*, p. 20.
[53] B. S. Rowntree, *Poverty and Progress*, p. ix.
[54] *The Times*, 7 Jan. 1975, p. 13; cf. *The Times*, 10 Jan. 1975, p. 15.

daily lives in such conditions, but the social investigator
who voluntarily incurred such dangers also deserves respect.
The fleas so readily picked up by slum visitors were the least
of it. We are told that nearly all the mining commissioners
in 1842 'incurred serious indisposition' in the course of their
work, 'such was the severity of the season'. On the health of
towns commission in 1843, as Chadwick told Major Graham,
'Dr Playfair has been knocked up by it and has been seriously
ill. Mr Smith has had a little dysentery. Sir Henry De La
Beche was obliged at Bristol to stand up at the end of alleys
and vomit while Dr Playfair was investigating overflowing
privies. Sir Henry was obliged to give it up.'[55] Then there
was the ugliness of slum life, all the more vivid to outside
observers unaccustomed to it. 'Where is the wish for better
things in these myriads of beings hurrying along the streets
night and day?', Beatrice Webb asked herself when investigating East End conditions for Booth in 1886: 'even their
careless, sensual laugh, coarse jokes, and unloving words
depress one as one presses through the crowd, and almost
shudders to touch them'.[56]

While governmental influence and resources lent the
official inquiry many advantages in getting public co-
operation, the official investigator was in some ways at
a disadvantage by comparison with the freelance sociologist,
for nineteenth-century society deeply distrusted state interference. Nineteenth-century French and German bureau-
cracies enjoyed ready access to information directly acquired
by reliable officials on the spot,[57] but in Britain a relatively
corrupt, inefficient, and weak central-government machine
was hampered at every point by autonomous self-governing
local communities and corporations, jealous of London's
pretensions. Opposition to inquiry might stem from the
belief—of Robert Lowe in 1869, for instance—that governments should have the courage to act without waiting for

---

[55] R. C. . . . Employment and Condition of Children in Mines and Manufactories, First Report, *Parl. Papers*, 1842 (380), XV, p. 2; S. E. Finer, *Edwin
Chadwick*, p. 234.

[56] B. Webb, *My Apprenticeship*, p. 237.

[57] A. Oberschall, *Empirical Social Research in Germany 1848–1914* (The
Hague, 1965), p. 17.

inquiry,[58] but it more commonly sprang from the fear that if information is collected interference and perhaps also taxation will follow.

In the late eighteenth century the very idea of preparing a national census had been opposed on libertarian grounds, and the early nineteenth century saw many vigorous protests against royal commissions as intrusions on the Englishman's traditional liberties.[59] Parliament so loathed the income tax that when it was discontinued in 1816 orders were given for all its records to be destroyed. When Brougham tried in 1834 to get a complete survey prepared of all landed property in the country he was defeated by the argument that this would be a dangerous instrument to place in government hands.[60] From the objectors' viewpoint, such opposition was often justified. The history of the ordnance survey illustrates the intimate relation between government research and government interference; the survey provided the data essential for implementing many types of legislation, and when government later short-sightedly cut back on map-making investment, its own legislative needs subsequently forced it to rectify its earlier cut-backs.[61] The twentieth-century social investigator has in fact carried forward the nineteenth-century philanthropist's role as skirmisher on the frontiers of the welfare state, as publicist of its inadequacies. Even the market survey and opinion poll, often nowadays criticized for reinforcing conservative attitudes, were seen as aids to progressive politics as recently as the 1940s.[62]

Suspicions of government inquiry affected all sections of the population—nineteenth-century pressure groups, for example. On the slavery question in the late 1780s it was the slave-owners who were obstructive, and their critics

[58] R. Lambert, *Sir John Simon 1816–1904 and English Social Administration* (1963), p. 448.

[59] E. A. Wrigley (ed.), *Nineteenth-Century Society*, p. 20; [S. Kydd], *The Factory Movement*, ii, pp. 50–1.

[60] P. Deane and W. A. Cole, *British Economic Growth*, p. 323; E. Halévy, *The Triumph of Reform*, p. 103.

[61] See e.g. W. A. Seymour (ed.), *A History of the Ordnance Survey* (Folkestone, 1980), pp. 230, 235, 250, 257–8.

[62] G. Orwell, *Collected Essays, Journalism and Letters*, iv (Penguin ed., Harmondsworth, 1968), p. 356; see also *The Times Literary Supplement*, 2 Oct. 1937, p. 709.

found it difficult to get evidence against the trade from places like Bristol where intimidation was rife. Clarkson describes how retired sea captains 'whenever they met me in the street, they shunned me as if I had been a mad dog', for fear of giving evidence. By the early 1830s it was the opponents of slavery who were unhelpful, in the belief that they had already amply demonstrated their case. A similar position was taken up in 1833 by the ten-hours movement, which ridiculed the idea of a royal commission on 'whether our children shall be worked more than ten hours a day'.[63] For some reforming leaders, a principle was involved which no inquiry could affect. Opposing state-regulated prostitution in 1871, Josephine Butler felt that her principles 'must be vindicated as axioms, not debated as doubtful questions'; empirical inquiry in such cases was inappropriate.[64] She gave evidence on this occasion but was not in a co-operative frame of mind, and did not help her case by casting doubts on the morality of the commissioners.[65] Nor could antivivisectionists have gained much by the extraordinary wrangles over procedure conducted by George Jesse and Sir George Duckett in 1876, which caused the exasperated chairman to remark at one point that 'there are some limits to all things'.[66] A similar mood sometimes inspired refusal to collaborate with the census; the suffragettes in 1911, for instance, refused to complete census forms, though by doing so they risked mistaking notoriety for publicity.

More obstruction came from the poor who, in retrospect, perhaps had most to gain from inquiry. Chadwick often complained of the almost oriental traditionalism nourished in working people by slum life; the recurrent set-backs and emergencies there became tolerable only if the slum-dweller habituated himself to expecting the worst. Yet there was more than mere obscurantism here; if the legislative machine

[63] T. Clarkson, *History of . . . the Abolition of the African Slave Trade*, p. 199, cf. Buxton, in *Anti-Slavery Reporter*, May 1832, p. 144; B. L. Hutchins and A. Harrison, *Factory Legislation*, pp. 54–5.

[64] J. E. Butler, *Reminiscences*, p. 33; cf. Association for Promoting the Extension of the CD Acts, *4th A.R. 1872*, p. 8. See also pp. 392–7.

[65] G. Petrie, *Singular Iniquity*, p. 116.

[66] R. C. Vivisection, *Parl. Papers*, 1876 (C.1397), XLI, Q.5561, cf. QQ. 6473–9 and appx. 2.

was (as it seemed) in the hands of the enemy, or at least in the hands of people lacking sympathy or understanding, inspectors and administrators had to be kept at a distance; information was therefore refused, lies were told, obstacles were set up. Even Mayhew encountered suspicion from his informants: 'they *will* suspect an ulterior object', he complained.[67] One census enumerator in 1871, suspected of being connected with the poor-law authorities, aroused great suspicion, because 'all these people . . . high and low, had one feeling in common—an insurmountable dread of going into "the house", and "breaking up their home" '.[68] In Ireland a wary population was reluctant even to supply demographic information in 1841, and Irish doubts reappeared in 1971 when the IRA claimed that the security forces would use census information to build up detailed dossiers on the riot areas within Belfast.[69]

The elusiveness and strong sense of privacy among working people were almost as serious a problem as suspicion of government intentions. An enumerator in 1871 was struck with the ignorance of one another displayed by people in a North London slum: 'families that had occupied different rooms in the same little house for months were ignorant of each other's names and occupation . . . and they referred me from one to another, or tapped at each other's doors to attract the attention of the inmates, without intruding on one another, and with an evident delicacy that would have well become a higher station'.[70] Particularly reticent were those who felt they had something to hide. Like most social investigators, Seebohm Rowntree found it difficult to get information on the spending habits of the unrespectable poor. His twentieth-century surveys of working-class diet were incomplete because drinking families could not be relied upon to keep accurate family accounts. Elementary education and special efforts with the relevant population eventually helped overcome these problems. In 1911, for

[67] H. Mayhew, quot. in A. Hookham, 'Literary Career of Henry Mayhew' (unpublished MA thesis, Birmingham, 1962), p. 175.

[68] *Morning Advertiser*, 11 Apr. 1871, p. 4.

[69] N. Mansergh, *The Irish Question 1840–1921* (1965 ed.), p. 29; *The Times*, 19 Apr. 1971, p. 1.

[70] *Morning Advertiser*, 11 Apr. 1871, p. 4.

example, lessons on the census were given in the state
schools, and an enlarged copy of the census schedule was
supplied for demonstration purposes. The TUC parliamentary
committee helped to explain the census to trade unions,
who also assisted with the occupational inquiry; shortly before
census day the press received a wider appeal by circular letter
describing the aims of the census.[71] By 1931 the BBC was
instructing the public on why the census was being compiled
and on how to complete its schedules.[72]

Ethnic minorities caused special difficulties. At the census
of 1901, great efforts were made to ensure a complete return
of Jewish immigrants, and circulars were sent round in
Yiddish and English prepared by the Chief Rabbi and issued
in the name of the Jewish Board of Guardians.[73] By 1971
the chairman of the Community Relations Commission felt
the need to assure a new generation of immigrants that
'rumour is the enemy we must vanquish', and that this could
be done only through collecting accurate statistics.[74] Pilot
surveys designed to prepare the way for questions on ethnic
origins in the 1981 census were so unsuccessful that the
questions were abandoned.[75] But the difficulty should not
be exaggerated; of the 18,000,000 people required to complete census forms in 1971, only 3,000 refused to do so.[76]

Underlying many of these difficulties lay the class divide
—not simply between employer and employee, but between
aristocracy and middle class. Working people to some extent
gained from the second of these polarities because political
capital could be accumulated from being seen to treat working people better than the other side; aristocracy and middle
class used the official inquiry to scour the country for
ammunition that could be marshalled against one another.
But when aristocracy and middle class encountered some
groups of working people, even their shared humanity was
called into question; working people laboured at different

[71] 1911 Census, General Report, *Parl. Papers*, 1917–18 (Cd.8491), XXXV,
p. 11.
[72] *The Woman's Leader and Common Cause*, 24 Apr. 1931, p. 91.
[73] R. C. Alien Immigration, *Parl. Papers*, 1903 (Cd.1741), IX, p. 13.
[74] *The Times*, 15 Apr. 1971, p. 1.
[75] *Daily Telegraph*, 3 Sept. 1979, p. 2; cf. *Guardian*, 21 Mar. 1980, p. 1.
[76] *Guardian*, 7 Dec. 1971, p. 13.

times of day, wore different clothes, spoke differently. Public officials could hardly have been expected immediately to grasp the intricacies, for example, of working-class occupational categories or of wage structures. The advent of the term 'interview', first mentioned in its modern sense in 1869, indicates recognition that the retreat of the face-to-face society had left problems behind in several areas, and not solely in respect of class relations.

It was in throwing bridges across the class divide, however, that social investigation could make its major contribution. Oastler had been living near Bradford's factory area for ten years before John Wood told him of the terrible conditions prevailing there, and so launched him on the crusade to limit factory hours. Edwin Chadwick says that when he and Dr Arnott were investigating Scottish slum housing during the early 1840s, 'we were regarded with astonishment; and it was frequently declared by the inmates, that they had never for many years witnessed the approach or the presence of persons of that condition near them'. Wealthy neighbours found his discoveries 'as strange as if they related to foreigners or the natives of an unknown country'.[77] The theme of discovery and exploration among alien peoples often recurs among nineteenth-century social investigators—from Mayhew to G. R. Sims, from Disraeli to Dickens. 'In these pages I propose to record the results of a journey with pen and pencil into a region which lies at our own doors', wrote Sims in 1883, '—into a dark continent that is within easy walking distance of the General Post Office.'[78]

III

Given the seriousness of this social problem, the official inquiry's efforts to grapple with it were inevitably controversial, and nowhere more so than with the freelance investigators also operating in the field. Their criticisms of the official inquiry, their contributions to the syncopated evolution of British social investigation, now deserve more detailed consideration. Engels's repudiation of piecemeal reform was

[77] *Sanitary Report* (ed. Flinn), p. 397.
[78] F. Engels, *Working Class*, p. 54; G. R. Sims, *How the Poor Live* (1883), p. 5.

too uncompromising to be helpful to government; in the 1840s he welcomed 'any circumstances which bring the disease to its climax',[79] in the belief that things must get worse before they could get better. Among those aiming to frustrate such predictions were members of several professional groups later prominent in social investigation—the medical and religious missionary, the high-minded business man, the humanitarian and/or prurient journalist, and, from the early 1870s, the School Board Officer. Here is an important dimension of the unwritten history of the British middle class, for paradoxically the entrepreneurial qualities that created the need for social investigation were also relevant in its development. Charles Booth ran his inquiry into London life and labour like a business enterprise, and Seebohm Rowntree, when introducing his second poverty survey of York in 1941, made the entrepreneurial analogy explicit: 'in every well-conducted business', he wrote, 'a balance sheet based on a physical stock-taking is prepared periodically'.[80]

Behind this mood of self-dedication lie the nonconformist conscience and its secularized successors; these required a simultaneous commitment to social welfare and to humane ways of attaining it. Rowntree dismissed the idea 'that everything must be destroyed before a worthy social structure can be raised'—every one of poverty's causes can be remedied, he insisted in 1941, 'without dislocating industry or our national finances. They can be removed just as the slums, once thought to be inevitable, are being removed to-day.'[81] Booth's route to social investigation lay through the anguish felt by a pious Unitarian in the 1870s who knew that his faith was slipping away. Respectful, even half-envious of working-class ways of life, he three times took up lodgings incognito with a working-class family for several weeks at a stretch. By eating a piece of fruit for lunch while standing at his high desk in the office, he conserved time for his major contribution to British empirical sociology that was building

[79] F. Engels, *Working Class*, p. 139.

[80] B. S. Rowntree, *Poverty and Progress*, p. v; see also T. S. and M. B. Simey, *Charles Booth*, pp. 22, 26–7, 101.

[81] B. S. Rowntree, op. cit., pp. x, 476.

up during his evenings and week-ends.[82] Seebohm Rowntree's sympathy with working people dates from his twenty years' teaching in a York adult school, which enabled him to visit his scholars in their homes. Behind the spare-time achievement of both men lies a deep sense of the employer's responsibility not simply to his work-force, but to society as a whole —a conscientious stewardship of time and resources for purposes that seemed more important than getting and spending.

To freelance social investigators who gave up so much for their studies, and who were usually only on the fringes of the political élite—official inquiries seemed defective in composition, procedure, and over-all approach. Chadwick was shocked at how casually even the members of royal commissions were appointed. In 1844 he mentioned a doctor appointed to the factory commission who 'himself avowed his utter want of preparation for such a task. "Then how came you to enter upon it?" was my question. "Why, I know Lord Althorp, from having attended some of his family at Leamington. I was passing down the street accidentally the other day, when who should accost me but Lord Althorp, with 'Hallo, Loudon', would you like to be on a Commission?" Thinking it might lead to something good, I said "Yes", and his Lordship put me on.' Edward Thring was shocked in 1869 at the endowed schools commission's presumption in dispatching outsiders to Uppingham to pronounce on 'an intricate professional question' like running a school.[83]

Official inquiries were usually composed of upper-class English gentlemen. The select committee, confined in its membership to MPs, was still further limited in composition, and was not even able to recruit leading politicians because their time was usually already committed; its composition also needed to reflect the balance of parties in the House as a whole. As the Webbs knew, an inquiry's composition influences its conclusions. Discussing with Lloyd George in 1919 the composition of the royal commission on the

[82] T. S. and M. B. Simey, *Charles Booth*, pp. 98–9.
[83] S. E. Finer, *Edwin Chadwick*, pp. 52–3; G. R. Parkin, *Edward Thring. Headmaster of Uppingham School* (1898), i, pp. 169, 178, 187.

miners' claims, Beatrice asked 'who wants the Commission and what is the conclusion you want it to come out at?', and was followed up by Sidney with 'the membership must depend on the report you wish it to make'.[84] The Welsh were furious in 1846 when the three members of the royal commission on Welsh education (English gentlemen and lawyers all) assaulted the morality, religion, and language of the Welsh people.[85] By the Edwardian period, male dominance of the official inquiry was beginning to cause trouble; Edward VII opposed female membership of the royal commission on divorce because 'the nature of the subject is one which cannot be discussed openly, and in all its aspects, with any delicacy, or even decency, before ladies'.[86] Like other anti-suffragists of his day the king was fighting a losing battle, and the desire to make parliamentary committees more representative was one of Herbert Samuel's arguments in 1918 for admitting women to parliament; if this occurred, it would be less necessary, he said, to use departmental committees.[87]

Part of the problem for the Webbs lay in the official inquiry's concept of the impartial layman who judiciously weighs the evidence laid before him. 'Seven or eight members sat round a table in a lofty room open to the public', questioning expert witnesses, wrote Hippolyte Taine of a Mid-Victorian investigation into the British Museum: 'notes were taken. The general tone was even, moderate; there were occasional smiles, it was all rather like an informative private conversation. And that, in fact, is what it was.' He praised the detail and precision of such inquiries as 'the way to be well informed'.[88] Informality was perhaps well suited to the discussion among social equals required on such a topic, but there was less to be said for inviting Austen Chamberlain to

[84] B. Webb, *Diaries 1912–1924* (ed. M. Cole, 1952), p. 148. See also BL Add. MS 49880 (Balfour Papers), ff. 181–2: Balfour to Cardinal Bourne, 10 Mar. 1896 (copy).
[85] R. Coupland, *Welsh and Scottish Nationalism. A Study* (1954), pp. 186–94.
[86] BL Add. MS 45985 (Viscount Gladstone Papers), f. 105: A. Davidson to Herbert Gladstone, 10 Sept. 1909; cf. J. A. Spender and C. Asquith, *Life of Herbert Henry Asquith, Lord Oxford and Asquith* (1932), i. p. 243.
[87] *H. C. Deb.*, 23 Oct. 1918, c.816.
[88] H. Taine, *Notes on England*, pp. 184–5.

chair the royal commission on the currency in 1913. He
confessed privately that he did not know 'the elements of
the subject', but supposed 'that I shall be able to feel my way
as I go along. At any rate, I shall begin by simply eliciting
what the witnesses themselves wish to say and leaving cross-
examination to others.'[89] There were of course instances
of open-mindedness in the face of the evidence. Witnesses
before the royal commission of 1871 on the Contagious
Diseases Acts seem to have inclined Charles Buxton and
F. D. Maurice against state-regulated prostitution, and the
conversion of Sir Ernest Gowers away from capital punishment on the royal commission of 1953 was very influential,
particularly with Herbert Morrison.[90] But to Beatrice Webb,
at least, such instances were not sufficiently frequent, nor
were they worth purchasing at the price of expertise.

The official inquiry did display professionalism of a sort,
but it was a legal professionalism, involving skill at cross-
examination rather than expertise in social investigation or
in the subject under discussion. As a witness who had herself
once been tripped up when giving evidence to an official
inquiry, Beatrice had reason for feeling strongly on the
matter, and thought that witnesses should when necessary be
allowed to correct their evidence.[91] Josephine Butler objected
when the royal commission on the CD Acts of 1871 asked
her, without prior warning, to prove several of her public
assertions; random spot questions were, she thought,
unfair.[92] Convinced that the official inquiry aimed at trap-
ping her, she reveals (in a letter to her husband written at
the time) how distant from the official inquiry even the
wife of a cultivated headmaster could be: 'I felt rather like
Paul before Nero, very weak and lonely. But there was One
who stood by me. I almost felt as if I heard Christ's voice
bidding me not to fear.' When giving evidence before the

---

[89] Sir A. Chamberlain, *Politics from Inside. An Epistolary Chronicle 1906–
1914* (1936), p. 542; see also B. Wootton, *In a World I never made. Autobiographical Reflections* (1967), p. 257.
[90] J. B. Christoph, *Capital Punishment*, p. 132; B. Donoughue and G. W.
Jones, *Herbert Morrison. Portrait of a Politician* (1973), p. 545.
[91] B. Webb, *My Apprenticeship*, p. 277.
[92] *C. D. Acts Commission, Parl. Papers*, 1871 (C.408), XIX, QQ.13065,
13075; J. E. Butler, *Personal Reminiscences of a Great Crusade* (1896), p. 242.

select committee of 1882 she took care to learn off her answers by heart.[93]

Critics of the official inquiry also disliked the prominence given to the self-confident and the articulate among witnesses. If water supply was the topic, for instance, the water companies were fully able to publicize their case, but rare indeed was the water-drinking working man who could organize the counter-case.[94] Also rare was the working-class witness able to testify from personal experience. The working men's committee of twelve interviewed informally by mines inspector H. S. Tremenheere at Newcastle during a strike in 1845 'were greatly pleased' at being questioned so carefully, and asked, 'Why don't gentlemen such as you come among us and listen to what we have got to say? There wouldn't be half so much trouble if they did.'[95] There were too few working men represented on the official inquiry. Joseph Arch grumbled at the absurdity of a royal commission on the agricultural depression with no agricultural labourer among its members.[96] Octavia Hill, on the royal commission on the aged poor, argued that it would be as foolish to listen to the very poor on poor relief as to consult patients on the treatment of disease, but George Lansbury was able to produce a pauper, T. H. Walker, and a shaft of light was at once shed on the callous treatment of aged paupers in workhouses. Walker was encouraged to talk quite freely to the commissioners, and at one point in his evidence produced a specimen of oakum, saying that 'picking that for eight hours a-day, sir, is enough to drive you mad'.[97]

Employers sometimes discouraged their employees from giving evidence. Sadler's inquiry into factory conditions faced opposition of this type in 1832, and in 1892 several railway

[93] J. E. Butler, *Recollections of George Butler* (2nd ed., Bristol, n.d.), p. 234; City of London Polytechnic, Josephine Butler Papers, Box 1, Envelope 1: Josephine Butler to George Butler, n.d., letters relating to the 1871 commission and the 1882 committee.
[94] R. A. Lewis, *Edwin Chadwick and the Public Health Movement. 1832–1854* (1952), p. 135, cf. p. 12.
[95] R. K. Webb, 'A Whig Inspector', *Journal of Modern History*, 1955, p. 359.
[96] J. Arch, *Life*, p. 308.
[97] R. C. Aged Poor, *Parl. Papers*, 1895 (C.7684–II), XV, Q.15563; F. B. Smith, *The People's Health. 1830–1910* (1979), p. 400.

employees were dismissed for giving evidence to a select committee.[98] Joseph Arch, when giving evidence in 1873 to the select committee on the game laws, was perhaps wise to resist pressure for information about working-class attitudes to legislation on matters other than game: 'I should refuse to give any definite reply', he told his questioner Mr Winterbotham, 'I will keep to the game laws.' Later Mr Cameron hoped to probe more deeply into the social depths; 'may I ask, without offence', he enquired, 'were you ever convicted of poaching?' 'No, I was not', said Arch, 'but I know those that have been.' Arch recalled these exchanges many years later: 'a man with the weight of many masters on him', he wrote, 'learns how to be dumb, and deaf, and blind, at a very early hour in the morning'.[99]

Underrepresentation of working men was but one aspect of the official inquiry's reluctance to consult what it saw as the enemy. Alone among the CD Acts commissioners in 1871, Robert Applegarth visited the Devonport area and interviewed women confined by the Acts in the Royal Albert Hospital.[1] The royal commission of 1889 on the Welsh Sunday Closing Act was typical among nineteenth-century inquiries into the drink question in failing to consult the drinkers, nor did the royal commission on divorce (1951–5) make much effort to consult the divorced or those aiming at divorce. The Pilkington committee's failure to seek out the typical viewer and listener produced a document inevitably filled with official opinions rather than with factual information; Hugh Gaitskell thought its tone 'priggish, arrogant, puritanical'.[2]

Formality of procedure made things worse. At first sight, statements from the knowledgeable supplemented by cross-examination from the clear-headed seems a sensible way of

[98] [S. Kydd], *Factory Movement*, i, pp. 317, 319; R. C. K. Ensor, *England 1870–1914* (1936), p. 301; G. Blaxland, *J. H. Thomas. A Life for Unity* (1964), p. 29.

[99] SCHC Game Laws, *Parl. Papers*, 1873 (285), XIII, QQ.8064, 8618; J. Arch, *Life*, p. 147.

[1] J. R. Walkowitz, *Prostitution and Victorian Society. Women, Class, and the State* (Cambridge, 1980), p. 103.

[2] P. M. Williams, *Gaitskell*, p. 391; cf. B. Wootton, *In a World I never made*, p. 257; O. R. McGregor, *Divorce in England. A Centenary Study* (1957), pp. 176, 199.

proceeding, particularly to politicians who feel at home
in the world of the lawcourt. In practice, however, such
a method runs into a host of difficulties. The best-informed
and most competent witnesses are not necessarily the most
willing to come forward, nor are they likely to speak freely
in a formal situation, nor does defeat in cross-examination
necessarily render their ideas uninteresting, unimportant, or
invalid. The 96,333 questions and answers of the royal
commission on labour of 1894 consisted, said Beatrice Webb,
'for the most part, not of statements of fact, but of the
answers to abstract conundrums put in cross-examination
by the commissioners . . . The greatest triumph was, by
skilful questions, to lead the witnesses, especially the working-
men witnesses, into some logical inconsistency.'[3]

Thorough inquiry was easier for royal commissioners, free
as they were to roam about the country and interview
informants in less formal situations, but their visits were
often fleeting, their questions inevitably ignorant, their
informants nervous. 'I am sure nobody has told me what to
say', May Holmes, who had worked eight years in the pit,
told a commissioner in 1842; he was suspicious at her failure
to complain about her working conditions.[4] An official
inquiry could never produce the wealth of information
collected by investigators who 'dropped out' and engaged
in participant observation—Charles Booth, Beatrice Webb,
Jack London, George Orwell. The mining commission of
1842 had the best of non-partisan intentions; complaining
that the employers who were so ready to supply information
'seldom or never descend into the pits', its commissioners
took the trouble to enter the pits themselves.[5] But here, as
with the children's employment commission in the following
year, the employers were well placed to challenge much of
the evidence. As Engels pointed out, the conducted tour
of the factory led by the employer himself was hardly likely
to elicit the whole truth. Yet when working people were
able to break through the barrier in an organized way—as

[3] S. and B. Webb, *Methods of Social Study* (1932), p. 143.

[4] R. C. . . . Employment and Condition of Children in Mines and Manufactories, First Report of the Commissioners (Mines), *Parl. Papers*, 1842 (380),
XV, p. 77.   [5] Ibid., p. 13.

with the Women's Co-op Guild evidence to the royal commission on divorce-law reform of 1909—a considerable
impact was made.[6]

In fairness to the official inquiry it should be said that the
unprepared spontaneous answer is not completely without
value. It was probably right that Emanuel Klein, for example,
was not allowed to correct the rather discreditable evidence
he gave the vivisection commission of 1876.[7] Furthermore
in her evidence to the inquiry on the Jameson Raid, Flora
Shaw demonstrated that victory did not always lie with the
questioners.[8] The question-and-answer method could also
usefully instruct a politician like Peel, who educated himself
by playing devil's advocate before the parliamentary committee of 1819 on cash payments. It could usefully expose
the shallow knowledge of a public figure—as with Parson
Bull before the select committee on the poor laws appointed
in 1837 and with Winston Churchill before the joint committee on Indian constitutional reform in 1933.[9] The process
of preparing to answer questions, or the experience of failing
to answer them, could also achieve the important function
of educating the witness.

But for Beatrice Webb and others the official inquiry
added to its offences by attempting to mould its evidence.
This process began early—when terms of reference were
framed, the chairman appointed, the secretary chosen, and
the members selected. Thereafter the inquiry's conclusions
could be manipulated through summoning the right witnesses,
guiding them in their statements, and then choosing selec-
tively within the evidence when writing the report. Inquiries
were often consciously and overtly partisan. Even Engels
admitted that Sadler's select committee on the factory
system was 'a very partisan document . . . drawn up entirely

[6] F. Engels, *Working Class*, p. 210 and ff.; L. Middleton (ed.), *Women in the Labour Movement. The British Experience* (1977), pp. 133–4.

[7] R. D. French, 'Medical Science and Victorian Society: The Anti-Vivisection Movement' (unpublished D.Phil. thesis, Oxford, 1972), p. 96.

[8] J. Wilson, *CB. A Life of Sir Henry Campbell-Bannerman* (1973), pp. 268–9.

[9] N. Gash, *Mr Secretary Peel. The Life of Sir Robert Peel to 1830* (1961), p. 241; D. Roberts, *Victorian Origins of the British Welfare State* (New Haven, 1960), p. 255; R. R. James, *Churchill. A Study in Failure 1900–1939* (1970), pp. 208–9.

by enemies of the factory system for purely political purposes';[10] utilitarian skills elicited from the factory commission evidence of a very different kind in the following
year. Free traders and utilitarians of the 1830s, especially
Chadwick, skilfully chose congenial witnesses and groomed
them to say the right things.[11] 'Professional witnesses' made
their appearance in the 1830s, sometimes giving evidence
before more than one committee. Nearly all the witnesses
before the select committee on import duties in 1840 had
connections with the Anti-Corn-Law League or the Board of
Trade.[12] For the health of towns commission of 1843, Chadwick wrote the questions, prepared the report, and gave all
the direction required. Florence Nightingale powerfully
affected the composition of the royal commission on the
health of the army in 1856, and influenced both the composition and the report of the royal commission on the
Indian army in 1859-63.[13]

The spontaneous opinion of the witness was not necessarily what was wanted. Urging Place to get a working man
to testify before the committee on postal reform in 1838,
Cobden told him 'you will not shrink from the trouble of
finding and properly *priming* such a person. Were he of the
rank of a day labourer or artisan it would be most desirable.'
Gravener Henson was later fed with questions which enabled
him admirably to bring out the moral and other benefits
a cheaper postal system would bring to the working people
he knew so well, and his remarks were much cited in the subsequent report.[14] The London moderates' manipulation of
the inquiry into trade unions in 1866 is well known, but
similar arts seem to have been applied to the royal commission on the agricultural depression of 1879, which greatly

[10] F. Engels, *Working Class*, p. 192.

[11] S. E. Finer, in G. Sutherland (ed.), *Studies in the Growth of Nineteenth-
Century Government* (1972), pp. 19, 22.

[12] D. Bythell, 'The Hand-Loom Weavers in the English Cotton Industry during
the Industrial Revolution: Some Problems', *Economic History Review*, Dec.
1964, p. 351; L. Brown, *The Board of Trade and the Free-Trade Movement 1830–
42* (Oxford, 1958), p. 73.

[13] S. E. Finer, *Edwin Chadwick*, p. 234; Sir E. Cook, *Florence Nightingale*, i,
p. 330; ii, pp. 19, 21-2.

[14] BL Add. MS 37949 (Place Papers), f. 386: Cobden to Place, 11 May 1838;
SCHC on Postage, *Parl. Papers*, 1837-8 (658), XX Pt. 2, QQ.9074 ff.

overrepresented the arable farmers and unjustifiably assumed that the depression equally affected all types of farming.[15] The Webbs successfully frustrated the Local Government Board's attempt to rig the poor law commission of 1905, but they did so partly by rigging it in reverse—carefully timing the presentation of Beveridge's evidence on labour exchanges and grooming him meticulously on what he should say and on how his ideas could be publicized.[16] Likewise the feminist Ray Strachey in 1934 described her role as 'busily stage managing the evidence to be given' to a Foreign Office inquiry on the appointment of women to civil-service posts.[17]

Stage management continued during the hearings. Robert Owen endured what he saw as a vindictive cross-examination on his religious views from a committee on factory legislation in 1816, and was excluded from testifying before a poor-law committee in exchanges that were not published.[18] In nineteenth-century conditions, an argument could be effectively neutralized as much by casting doubt on the respectability of the speaker as by refuting the argument directly. By the 1780s anti-slavery witnesses were already being brow-beaten in this way,[19] and Marx refers to the 'impudent, unexpected, equivocal and involved questions, put without connexion' addressed by the select committee on mines in 1866 to its miner witnesses, 'to intimidate, surprise, and confound'.[20] Beatrice Webb, on the labour commission of 1894, noticed that the cross-examination of working men— a 'game of cat and mouse'—gave enjoyment to the questioners, but 'aroused the deepest resentment among the

[15] G. D. H. Cole, 'British Trade Unions in the Third Quarter of the Nineteenth Century', in E. Carus Wilson (ed.), *Essays in Economic History*, iii (1962), p. 215, cf. T. Burt, *Autobiography*, p. 165; T. W. Fletcher, 'The Great Depression in English Agriculture: 1873–96', *Economic History Review*, 1960–1, p. 426.

[16] A. M. McBriar, *Fabian Socialism and English Politics 1884–1918* (Cambridge, 1962), p. 265; J. Harris, *William Beveridge*, p. 134.

[17] Ray Strachey Papers: Ray Strachey to her mother, 8 Feb. 1934; cf. Ray to her mother, 16 Mar. 1934.

[18] F. Podmore, *Robert Owen. A Biography* (1906), i, p. 197; R. Owen, *The Life of Robert Owen* (1857), i, p. 133.

[19] T. Clarkson, *History of the Rise, Progress, and Accomplishment of the Abolition of the African Slave Trade . . .* (1839 ed.), p. 422.

[20] K. Marx, *Capital*, i, p. 495; cf. SCHC on Bleaching and Dyeing of 1857, discussed in B. L. Hutchins and A. Harrison, *Factory Legislation*, p. 137.

working-class witnesses'.[21] She noted 'the evident irritation shown by intelligent working men' at the official inquiry's ignorance about the realities of working-class life.[22] Mayhew also emphasized such mistakes, and some twentieth-century historians have echoed their complaints.[23] The trade unions were so suspicious of the lawyers on the royal commission on trade unions of 1903 that they refused to give evidence altogether.

There were problems even at the basic level of language. Thomas Burt was once asked by a reporter to give his evidence slowly and distinctly so that it could all be written down, and an interpreter was required on at least one occasion to render Tyneside miners intelligible to a committee.[24] There was distortion in the process of reporting, which eliminated much of the informality and immediacy of working-class speech—leaving only a palimpsest of the vigorous statements Mayhew had been able to capture verbatim. Claiming that his *London Labour and the London Poor* is the first survey to describe working-class conditions in their own language,[25] he includes a superb series of self-portraits with none of the official inquiry's attempts at précis or translation; indeed, so interested is he in their modes of speech that he includes small specialist dictionaries at three points in his inquiry.[26] Once the evidence had been collected, there was yet another opportunity for manipulation—during the selection of evidence to be used in making up the report. This was all the easier because the inquiry's internal discussions were private and because the evidence at its disposal was so abundant. A preconceived case could easily be made out and decorated with some of the new information that had been collected.

[21] B. Webb, 'The Failure of the Labour Commission', *Nineteenth Century*, July 1894, p. 17.

[22] B. Webb, *My Apprenticeship*, pp. 359–60.

[23] e.g. R. Samuel (ed.), *Village Life and Labour* (1975), pp. 3, 5; cf. the criticism of crude quantification on pp. 206, 219; R. Samuel (ed.), *Miners, Quarrymen and Saltworkers* (1977), p. 4.

[24] T. Burt, *Autobiography*, pp. 165–6.

[25] H. Mayhew, *London Labour and the London Poor*, i, p. iii.

[26] For dictionaries, see ibid., i, pp. 23, 207, 217; for colloquial speech, see ibid., i, pp. 22, 69, 158, 224.

Beatrice Webb's remedy for the defects in the official inquiry lay in expertise at two levels: in its composition, and in the type of evidence it acquired. She wanted investigators whose expertise lay both in the relevant subject area and in methods of social investigation. The trouble with the formal hearing was that it accumulated opinions rather than facts. The Webbs in their historical work felt impatient with 'interminable question and answers', which merely accumulated hearsay evidence.[27] Like Chadwick Beatrice believed that investigators should survey their problem personally, if possible penetrating below the topmost administrative layers. 'It is . . . almost axiomatic with the experienced investigator', she wrote, 'that the mind of the subordinate in any organisation will yield richer deposits of fact than the mind of the principal'; the subordinate would be less on his guard, less conventional in outlook, in closer touch with the realities.[28] Others had preceded her here. Engels in the 1840s talked informally to Manchester working men; Mayhew in London visited them in their homes and, when inquiring into London's lodging-houses, stressed the importance of conversing with some of their inmates. Interviewing was for Mayhew simply a way of getting information which he could follow up in other ways—through personal observation, reading, and statistical analysis. Beatrice Webb merely applied these insights within the framework of a better-formulated and more systematic scheme of inquiry.

'The less formal the conditions of the interview the better', she declared, and emphasized that although a careful plan of inquiry should be made beforehand, this should not be flourished before the informant, nor should notes be taken during the discussion. She sought in the interviewer 'a spirit of adventure, a delight in watching human beings quite apart from what you can get out of their minds, an enjoyment of the play of your own personality with that of another'. Here was that ideal combination of artistic and scientific opportunity that would bring out her talents to the full. The informant should neither be interrupted nor argued

[27] S. and B. Webb, *Methods of Social Study*, p. 142; cf. O. R. McGregor, *Divorce in England*, p. 176.
[28] B. Webb, *My Apprenticeship*, p. 362.

with; on the contrary, he 'must be permitted to pour out his fictitious tales, to develop his preposterous theories, to use the silliest arguments', in the hope that eventually something useful would emerge.[29]

A freelance social investigator could afford to do this because he needed to write down only information useful to his inquiry. In 1910 a departmental committee on the procedure of royal commissions pointed out that oral evidence cost £50 a day (allowing for travelling expenses, transcription, and printing), and recommended each royal commission 'to carefully consider the relative cost and relative productiveness of the different methods of investigation which might be employed'. The committee wanted witnesses to make an initial submission in writing; commissioners could then reduce costs by deciding whether to interview the witness, and if so what questions to ask.[30]

Beatrice saw the interview as no more than a route to the documents that contained the facts[31]—for informal research, rather than formal cross-examination, was her method. She felt that the royal commission on labour began to produce worthwhile information only when it sponsored research into social conditions. The combination of her two criticisms led her to urge a far more professional and co-ordinated approach to social investigation. 'All efficient public careers consist in the proper direction of secretaries', Altiora Bailey pronounced in H. G. Wells's *The New Machiavelli*.[32] Equipped with pilot survey, statistical precision, and expert assistance, and fully briefed by preliminary reading, she felt herself far better qualified to probe social problems than any royal commission. She felt that most of the poor-law commissioners' cross-examination was not worth attending, and most of her efforts went into private research when the commission was not in session. On the coal industry commission of 1926, William Beveridge tried

[29] B. Webb, *My Apprenticeship*, pp. 362-3; S. and B. Webb, *Methods of Social Study*, p. 140.

[30] *Parl. Papers*, 1910 (Cd.5235), LVIII, pp. 9-10; see also pp. 11, 15.

[31] B. Webb, 'Methods of Investigation', in *Sociological Papers*, iii (1907), p. 348.

[32] H. G. Wells, *The New Machiavelli* (Penguin ed., Harmondsworth, 1966), p. 161.

unsuccessfully to get reporters excluded from the hearings
so as to encourage candour; oral evidence formally collected
seemed useless to him, and he sat through it making calculations. He later took pleasure in the fact that his famous
national insurance committee took no notes in the course of
its investigations.[33]

The freelance sociologists' critique of the official inquiry
was formidable, but it did not go unheard. The official
inquiry has always been a flexible instrument—especially
the royal commission, whose constitutional status neither
subordinates it to any other body nor constricts its procedure. The factory commission of 1833, for instance,
divided up the country into four districts and sent commissioners to each under the direction of a central board
based in London; the royal commission on children's employment (1842-3) organized itself rather similarly. To illustrate
the emancipation from hearsay evidence which this made
possible, one need only cite the incident in 1842 when the
mining commissioner S. S. Scriven was able to test the assertions of one boy witness about his ill-treatment as a hurrier
by getting him to reveal the scars which had resulted.[34]

During the twentieth century, the official inquiry diversified
in composition and technique. The eagerness of pressure
groups to gain representation upon it helped considerably
to broaden out its membership, but other influences worked
in the same direction. Of the 1,843 royal commissions
appointed between 1900 and 1965, nearly half have been
described as 'impartial', 39 per cent as 'expert', and the rest
'representative'.[35] The modern official inquiry aims in its
composition rather at a balance between interested experts;
even if he were still wanted, the leisured and gentlemanly
amateur is, after all, in diminishing supply. Like parliament
and government as a whole, official inquiries fall short of
complete representativeness. Seven per cent of their members
between 1900 and 1965 were women, though Mary Stocks

[33] W. Beveridge, *Power and Influence* (1953), pp. 217-18, 300.

[34] R. C. . . . Employment and Condition of Children in Mines and Manufactories, First Report, *Parl. Papers*, 1842 (380), XV, p. 43.

[35] C. J. Hanser, *Guide to Decision. The Royal Commission* (Totowa, New
Jersey, 1965), pp. 42-3.

claimed that many of these between the wars were 'a kind of stage army appearing on one government assignment after another'. Twenty-three per cent have been drawn from local or central government in this period, 15 per cent from business, 15 per cent from law, 13 per cent from social science, 7 per cent from natural science, and 6 per cent from labour. Still, the composition of royal commissions has become in several respects broader than parliament, the cabinet, or the higher civil service.[36]

As for improvements in research technique, the twentieth century has seen further moves towards direct observation. In 1903 the royal commission on alien immigration visited Stepney to hear witnesses unable to provide it during the day, and sent Major Evans-Gordon to Poland and Russia for relevant information. The coal industry commission of 1926 insisted on visiting collieries in all the main coal-producing areas, and embarrassed the managers by personally investigating the coal-face.[37] There were improvements in other directions too, for Beatrice Webb in the 1890s was to some extent pushing at an open door. The royal commission on the depression of trade and industry in 1886 did not confine itself to question-and-answer sessions with witnesses in London; it began by addressing questions to Chambers of Commerce and other relevant bodies, both on their impressions of what was occurring and on certain areas of fact which the commissioners thought relevant. Comparative information on other countries was provided through the diplomatic service on this as on many other occasions, and civil servants provided digests of the relevant official statistics. In the event of disagreement there was always the option of preparing a minority report; on the poor law commission of 1905–9 Beatrice Webb amply demonstrated what this could achieve. The Haldane committee on the machinery of government supplied all the opportunity for informal discussion that Beatrice had long been advocating, and the Webbs later described how 'in the

---

[36] M. Stocks, *My Commonplace Book* (1970), p. 165; cf. E. Rathbone, *The Disinherited Family. A Plea for the Endowment of the Family* (1924), p. 171. Figures from C. J. Hanser, *Guide to Decision*, pp. 182, 258.

[37] J. Harris, *William Beveridge*, p. 335.

ease and comfort of a private house, sanctified by the portraits of philosophers and jurists, exhilarated by tea and soothed by tobacco, all sorts of interesting sidelights emerged from this friendly clash of official minds'.[38]

During the twentieth century, the oral evidence she so strongly condemned has slipped markedly from its nineteenth-century prominence; rather more than half the major departmental committees and royal commissions between 1945 and 1969 chose to rely on written evidence alone. Of the 24 major royal commissions operating between 1945 and 1969, 15 engaged in visits of inspection, 13 issued questionnaires and surveys, and 14 appointed research subcommittees; only four used none of these methods.[39] On the delicate matter of homosexuality and prostitution, the Wolfenden committee felt entirely free, as a departmental committee, to take its oral evidence in private; 'only in genuinely private session', it wrote, 'could our witnesses, giving evidence on these delicate and controversial matters, speak to us with the full frankness which the subjects of our enquiry demanded'.[40]

The royal commission on population of 1949 marks a further stage in technical sophistication. In a Royal Statistical Society discussion of 1937, A. M. Carr-Saunders and D. V. Glass argued that in demographic matters, at least, royal commissions could contribute little until some basic research had been done, and Glass suggested that a thorough revision of the registration system would be helpful 'so as to provide researchers with adequate vital statistics'.[41] After the war, Glass was able to bring the worlds of academic demography and official inquiry closer together, for here we have an investigation that operated through three specialist subcommittees—statistical, economic, and biological/medical—each chaired by a member of the main body, with all four bodies serviced by a common secretariat. As part of its work, it inspired an official family census in 1946 and an inquiry into fertility by the Royal College of Obstetricians and

---

[38] S. and B. Webb, *Methods of Social Study*, p. 150.

[39] T. J. Cartwright, *Royal Commissions*, pp. 133, 147.

[40] *Parl. Papers*, 1956-7 (Cmnd. 247), XIV, p. 7.

[41] Discussion of 20 Apr. 1937 in *Journal of the Royal Statistical Society*, vol. 100 (1937), pp. 403, 411.

Gynaecologists. This inquiry also illustrates how royal commissions often create permanent or semi-permanent institutions in their area; David Glass's Population Investigation Committee long outlived its parent inquiry.

In the Robbins report on higher education of 1963 the worlds of professional sociology and official social investigation virtually merge. The opportunity was taken to conduct research of major academic importance, and £45,000 of the £128,770 over-all costs was assigned to sample surveys. In this case as in others, the real cost of preparing the report was probably much higher, because much of the research sponsored by official inquiries is done free, or at less than cost, by civil servants on secondment or by the Government Social Survey.[42] The Redcliffe-Maud commission on local government reached a new plateau for official inquiries in the elaborateness of its research. With its twelve research committees it was able to commission ten research studies by outsiders, and took evidence from 2,156 witnesses, whose published evidence alone took up 6,745 pages.[43]

The official inquiry has therefore shown a remarkable adaptiveness during the twentieth century—in institutional structure, composition, and methods. Yet it could never meet all the freelance sociologists' criticisms, for it has never been purely an instrument for sociological research. As the Webbs themselves later acknowledged, official inquiries are 'primarily political organs, with political objects . . . frequently set up as a safety valve, or as a channel for current agitations and counter agitations', which enable governments to sound out public opinion;[44] in such a situation, the opinions of significant witnesses are themselves facts. Like other ways of moulding public opinion—the petition, for example—official inquiries were attacked when their information was uncongenial, eulogized when it was welcome.

Official inquiries are not so much agencies impinging on government from without as themselves part of the

[42] J. S. Maclure (ed.), *Educational Documents. England and Wales. 1816 to the Present Day* (2nd ed., 1974), p. 289; R. A. Chapman (ed.), *The Role of Commissions in Policy-Making*, p. 182.

[43] J. Stanyer, in R. A. Chapman (ed.), op. cit., pp. 114-15.

[44] S. and B. Webb, *Methods of Social Study*, p. 157.

governmental process, part of government's machinery for
'mobilising consent' behind its policies.[45] Governments quite
often unobtrusively point an inquiry in the right direction;
indeed, the government may itself help to initiate the inquiry
and provide much of its evidence. In June 1908, for example,
Leonard Courtney wrote to Asquith volunteering to mount
a public agitation for the inquiry into electoral reform that
he wanted Asquith to appoint. In 1933 the feminist Ray
Strachey told her mother about giving evidence to the joint
committee on the Indian constitution for women's suffrage;
'we got the tip to be rather violent. So I was'; Lord Lothian,
the chairman, told her afterwards 'that bombs were what
they needed, and that I had thrown them'.[46] It was partly
because Winston Churchill recognized the political role of
this committee that he accentuated its biased composition
by refusing to serve on it. As he told Hoare, 'I see no advantage . . . in my joining your Committee merely to be voted
down by an overwhelming majority of the eminent persons
you have selected.'[47]

Once the official inquiry's political function is recognized,
many of its defects as an instrument of research become
virtues. The purpose of oral evidence, in an inquiry that aims
simply to assist government by preparing the ground for
legislation, is to lend the inquiry a good public image, or to
publicize the known views of significant people—not to find
out anything new. Again, if the inquiry aims to influence the
political system and/or public opinion, a membership composed largely of politicians (experts in both) is not inappropriate. Given the official inquiry's political function, it is
hardly surprising that its academic members are somewhat
suspect to those whose presence on the inquiry stems from
expertise of a more practical kind and who know that there
is little point in making recommendations which government
will not accept.[48] The academic researcher, who often aims to
move ahead of public opinion, will in such situations be

[45] Cf. G. Rhodes, *Committees of Inquiry* (1975), p. 208.
[46] Ray Strachey Papers: Ray Strachey to her mother, 28 July 1933. See also
Bodleian Library, MS Asquith 11, ff. 141, 143: Courtney to Asquith, 5 June
1908.   [47] M. Gilbert, *Winston S. Churchill*, v (1976), p. 476.
[48] L. J. Sharpe, in M. Bulmer (ed.), *Social Research and Royal Commissions*,
p. 25; cf. A. R. Prest, ibid., p. 181.

almost professionally bound to make himself a nuisance with his continual tendency to rock the political boat.[49] He will certainly feel uncomfortable amid such unfamiliar pressures. When campaigning to break up the poor law in 1909, Sidney Webb himself experienced such conflicts, and longed 'to get back to the state of a pure seeker after truth, which *cannot* be maintained while campaigning'.[50]

The official inquiry's perspective has always been primarily administrative and governmental, with legislation as the aim. Even now, its female and working-class members tend to be drawn from the organizing classes. Housing conditions are therefore seen through the eyes of the sanitary reformer, education through the eyes of the teacher, and so on; the perspective of the slum-dweller and the child all too easily gets left out.[51] The very selection of the topic for inquiry will be determined largely by governmental need. Cobbett's mouth watered at the thought of the many embarrassing inquiries he would launch if he had his way, but in vain; and when Josephine Butler told the royal commission on the CD Acts of 1871 that upper-class immorality should be investigated, she was not encouraged in the idea.[52]

If all this is so, the official inquiry can never entirely satisfy the social investigator's wishes because its time-scale can never by governed solely by the requirements of research. It will be designed either to accelerate or to slow down legislative action according to circumstances. If its role is to accelerate, the facts are often collected in a hurry to enthuse rather than to instruct a lay readership. Where government wishes to act, there is neither the time nor the need for academic research; the inquiry's purpose is to prepare public opinion for legislative change which the government knows

[49] L. J. Sharpe, 'The Social Scientist and Policy-Making: Some Cautionary Thoughts and Transatlantic Reflections', *Policy and Politics*, iv, no. 2 (Dec. 1975), p. 24.

[50] As reported by Ernest Simon, quot. in M. Stocks, *Ernest Simon of Manchester* (Manchester, 1963), p. 25; see also BL Add. MS 49880 (Balfour Papers), f. 181: Balfour to Cardinal Bourne, 10 Mar. 1896 (copy).

[51] R. Samuel (ed.), *Village Life and Labour*, p. xiii; see also B. Wootton, *In a World I never made*, p. 256.

[52] W. Cobbett, *Rural Rides*, i, pp. 131–2; E. M. Bell, *Josephine Butler. Flame of Fire* (1962), p. 88.

is needed. Such situations were no doubt in Keynes's mind when he pointed out that 'there is nothing a government hates more than to be well-informed; for it makes the process of arriving at decisions much more complicated and difficult'.[53] Like the early statistical surveys the official inquiry is often not an inquiry at all, but an instrument employed by those who already know.

The official inquiry which aims to accelerate legislation, such as the royal commission on the press of 1974-7, may well be forced into pronouncing quickly despite operating in relatively uncharted territory; it may recognize many of the relevant questions only at the point of writing its report. This conflict between political requirements and systematic research was perhaps at its most severe with the select committee, which was always liable to be disrupted by political events—by the fall of a government, for example, or even by parliamentary vacations.[54] 'The academic's time scale is relative posterity', writes L. J. Sharpe; 'the policy-maker's can seldom be longer than next week to next year.'[55] Suggestions have sometimes been made on how to overcome this intractable problem. The departmental committee of 1910 on royal commission procedure rejected the idea of a permanent secretary of royal commissions with a nucleus staff that could be expanded to meet the needs of all royal commissions simultaneously at work; but it favoured the idea of a permanent staff for such purposes, including shorthand reporters, indexers, typists, a statistician, and a bibliographer. A more recent and less practicable suggestion has been that government departments should systematically collect information on subjects that they think may in the future become subjects for official inquiry.[56]

On the other hand, when a government is distracted by other problems, divided on the question, or embarrassed by it—the inquiry aims at delay. This is frustrating for the

---

[53] Quot. in R. M. Titmuss, *Poverty and Population* (1938), pp. 5-6.

[54] O. R. McGregor, in M. Bulmer (ed.), *Social Research and Royal Commissions*, pp. 154-5.

[55] L. J. Sharpe, art. cit., p. 21; cf. W. E. S. Thomas, *The Philosophic Radicals: Nine Studies in Theory and Practice, 1817-1841* (1979), p. 267.

[56] *Parl. Papers*, 1910 (Cd.5235), LVIII, p. 14; G. Rhodes, in M. Bulmer (ed.), *Social Research and Royal Commissions*, p. 120.

social investigator, and still more for the social reformer. In 1842 Shaftesbury branded the inquiry on the employment of women and children in agriculture as a government trick to 'oppose my efforts' for factory reform. Joseph Arch thought parliamentary inquiries a very slow way of getting things done, and complained that 'there is too much sitting and talking, and not enough pushing and acting'.[57] Similar accusations have been made retrospectively by labour historians—by E. P. Thompson, for example, who sees the hand-loom weavers and framework-knitters as being 'duly enquired into as they starved', and who notes Irish poverty as receiving 'an average of five parliamentary enquiries per year' without result.[58] Whether designed to accelerate action or to postpone it, official inquiries therefore only partially overlap—in mood and objective—with those of the professional social investigator.

Given the glare of publicity that surrounds official inquiries, and the public argument that so often envelopes the topics they study, their internal mood can hardly be one of patient study. A distinction perhaps needs to be made between investigation, which systematically seeks factual information not hitherto accessible, and inquiry, which seeks truth through free debate between those who hold opposed opinions.[59] The two could be yoked in harness, but in a pluralist political situation they could never be identical. During the early twentieth century, when it became common to appoint large 'representative' official inquiries, the inquiry's internal structure more closely resembled a mini-parliament than a research team. When each member's role is largely to speak up for his own interest, an agreed report can hardly emerge, and by the 1930s the role played by this type of royal commission had been transferred to the representative conference.[60] Beatrice Webb's criticisms of the official inquiry perhaps rest partly on a belief that argument over values can conveniently be removed from discussion on public policy, as reflected in her enthusiasm of the 1930s

[57] E. Hodder, *Shaftesbury*, i, p. 441; J. Arch, *Life*, p. 171.
[58] E. P. Thompson, *Working Class* (2nd ed.), p. 375.
[59] Cf. T. J. Cartwright, *Royal Commissions*, p. 226.
[60] H. McD. Clokie and J. W. Robinson, *Royal Commissions*, p. 314.

for Soviet Russia's 'scientific' administration and efficiency. A similar trait can be detected in Beveridge, whose confidence in the impartial expert's capacity to resolve hotly contested social problems resulted in abrasive questioning of both mine-owners and miners on the coal industry commission of 1926; yet the well-documented and accurate report took all too little account of the political factors bedevilling the whole area.[61]

Any notion that an uncontroversial official inquiry is possible on a subject when the political parties disagree involves wishful thinking. Political parties reflect real sources of divergence within the community; if they did not exist it would, given human propensity to disagree, be necessary to invent them. Each naturally uses the instrument lying most conveniently to hand. When refused an official inquiry, an opposition party may even think it worth appointing an inquiry of its own. Early in 1920 the Labour Party sent its own delegation to investigate the situation in Ireland, and the government later in the year refused Henderson's request for an inquiry into Irish reprisals. The Labour Party then sent its own commission to investigate, chaired by Henderson himself. It took evidence, visited the scenes of reprisals, and a national Labour Party campaign for peace in Ireland followed.[62]

There is even a political situation within the official inquiry itself; its report does not emerge from conclusions spontaneously reached by individual members through hearing and reading the evidence, but is often the product of energetic effort by some of the members to convert the rest. Internal political conflicts are still more likely to arise when the inquiry appoints its own special researchers. Tension between them and the inquiry's members easily results over such matters as the shape and duration of the investigation. The researchers can even 'capture' an inquiry for a particular political position; critics of the Donovan commission on the trade unions, for instance, point to the dominance upon it of the Oxford approach to trade-union

[61] J. Harris, *William Beveridge*, pp. 336, 339.
[62] D. G. Boyce, *Englishmen and Irish Troubles. British Public Opinion and the Making of Irish Policy 1918–22* (1972), p. 62.

studies, with its commitment to voluntarism, to the labour movement, and to an incomes policy.[63] For all these reasons, what Beatrice Webb enthusiastically described as 'this slow stepping towards truth' through 'the careful measurement of facts' cannot govern the official inquiry's proceedings,[64] whose analogy with academic research procedures can never be complete.

IV

The official inquiry could not therefore fully respond to criticism from the professional sociologist; and in so far as it did respond, it became even more vulnerable to that under-current of criticism which the dominant trends in social investigation have long had to face. Two of these criticisms can briefly be discussed in conclusion: the danger of separating social research from social reform, and of distancing investigator from investigated.

On the first of these points, the professional social investigator cannot of course confine himself to seeking information congenial to any particular political grouping; yet he is no more able to denude his inquiry of political implications than any other student of human behaviour. His personal outlook will affect his choice of topic, the relevant facts he selects within that topic, and the shape of the argument he builds out of them. During the nineteenth century, the distinction between publicly campaigning for reform and systematically collecting information relevant to it was not strongly argued for. The social investigator usually wanted to catch the public attention, and this required an arresting literary style and even—in the case of the Midland mining commission—memorable illustrations. Social investigation and literary skill were prised apart only through the increased influence of mathematical precision—salutary in itself, but damaging to an inquiry's public impact and misleading in so far as it promised some sort of scientific objectivity; for the quantitative technique itself had implications for policy,

---

[63] T. J. Cartwright, *Royal Commissions*, p. 161; R. Kilroy-Silk, in R. A. Chapman (ed.), *The Role of Commissions in Policy-Making* (1973), p. 58.
[64] B. Webb, *My Apprenticeship*, p. 338.

in that its practitioners were less likely to possess either the desire or the capacity for directly educating the public about social conditions.

When training herself as a social investigator, Beatrice Webb felt a need actually to suppress her (very marked) literary talents. Dismissing her doubts about doing so in 1889, she thought of the many novels she had read and wondered what they had 'accomplished for the advancement of society on the one and only basis that can bring with it virtue and happiness—the scientific method?'[65] Booth played down the importance of literary merit partly because (unlike Mayhew) he was not obliged to sell his copy; on the contrary, he subsidized his survey from the profits of his Liverpool shipping firm. Its descriptive material therefore appears in the purely subordinate role of giving 'life to statistics'. Individual case histories and descriptive passages interpenetrate the statistics and render them less abstract, but it is the statistics that are seen as important. 'From the individual workmen we wish if we can to get as vivid pictures as possible of their working life', he wrote, 'as these alone will make the book readable.'[66] Booth still felt the need to attract readers, but the audience he wanted was smaller and more select than Mayhew's, and he was prepared to make few concessions to them. Given such an outlook, Booth could not hope for the directness of Mayhew's impact on public opinion. In this situation the professional investigator may rely on others to publicize his findings, or journalists and amateur sociologists may offer themselves for the purpose; in either case intermediaries are intruded between the investigator and his public.

In this situation it becomes all too easy actually to distance the investigator from the investigated. There is a danger that with the investigator's increasingly administrative preoccupation, a certain psychological as well as technical change will be introduced whereby the social survey—whose initial purpose is to bring investigator and investigated together—gradually and unconsciously shifts its purpose into holding

[65] Ibid., p. 340.
[66] T. S. and M. B. Simey, *Charles Booth*, pp. 78, 124; see also pp. 105, 107, 129, 163.

them apart. In contrast to the approach adopted by personal charity, the administrative perspective associated with legislative reform risks viewing the administered as an undifferentiated mass,[67] and social investigation moves away from comprehending the administered in their own terms. Mary Booth urged her husband to purge 'the excessive colloquialism of some of the quotations' he proposed to include in his survey. 'After all', she remarked, 'what passed the lips of your interviewed people is not a sacred text, verbally inspired.'[68] The difference between Mayhew and Booth here is significant. Mayhew sought to comprehend what he regarded as an almost alien culture, to absorb from his informants new ideas and perceptions almost for their own sake. For Booth, the language and imagery used by his working-class informants were much less important. His purpose was much more firmly administrative, much more confidently corrective. Likewise Rowntree, who might have written of Booth's and Beatrice Webb's work as of his own that 'no fact has been stated which has not a direct bearing on the steps which should be taken if the evil of poverty is to be remedied'.[69] There is a double sacrifice involved: the role of experience in the whole investigation has been devalued, and in so far as it is discussed at all, it is filtered through a middle-class vocabulary and perception. Even when administrative preoccupations were not in view—as with the social investigators mobilized by Mass Observation in the late 1930s to explore popular culture—it was difficult at first to prevent middle-class observers from doctoring their reports of demotic speech.[70]

For some social investigators, the pursuit of precision even became an end in itself. Carlyle's objection to statistical tables as 'abstractions . . . difficult to read the essence of',[71] like Dickens's merciless portrayal of Gradgrind's zeal for fact,

[67] Cf. B. Webb, *My Apprenticeship*, p. 221, and cf. pp. 104, 222, 228.

[68] B. Norman-Butler, *Victorian Aspirations. The Life and Labour of Charles and Mary Booth* (1972), p. 132.

[69] B. S. Rowntree, *Poverty and Progress*, p. 40.

[70] Mass-Observation, *May the Twelfth* (ed. H. Jennings and C. Madge, 1937), p. 146.

[71] T. Carlyle, 'Chartism', in *Miscellaneous Essays*, iii (Ashburton ed., 1888), p. 260.

overdoes the point; but Mayhew showed in his practice the fruitfulness of a method described by commentators as 'anti-statistical'.[72] Correcting generalities by constant reference to the particular, Mayhew pays the price of a certain shapelessness and inconclusiveness that renders his inquiry of small assistance to the administrator and politician. Yet in other ways the gain is immense: a vivid resurrection of a significant section among London's working people that invigorates the reader generations later. Social investigation in the 1840s had not become so sophisticated in technique nor (partly in consequence) so insulated from contact with the observed, as it became later. The investigator needs always to maintain a balance between three objectives: precise investigation, where statistical precision is appropriate, but also sensitivity to the outlook of those whom he investigates, and preservation of contact with the general public. For it is the general public which directly or indirectly finances his investigation, and whose welfare provides its ultimate justification.

Mass Observation responded to this tension between the social investigator's objectives by organizing the participant-observer on a mass scale. It described its observers in 1937 as 'trying to act as recording systems'.[73] Imagination and receptiveness, informed by insights from social anthropology, were to return to the social inquiry, but with the safeguard provided by expanding the number of investigators and welding together their spontaneous comments. It recognized the importance of educating the observer—of heightening 'his power of seeing what is around him' and giving him 'new interest in and understanding of it'.[74] Mass Observation soon merged with the more impersonal opinion survey and market research, and no major impact on social investigation was then made. But in 1970 Tom Harrisson felt that Mass Observation's original techniques were 'still relevant'; the opinion polls which had now become dominant could reveal but a thin segment of a community's life,

[72] E. P. Thompson, 'The Political Education of Henry Mayhew', *Victorian Studies*, Sept. 1967, p. 58.
[73] Mass-Observation, *May the Twelfth*, p. 337.
[74] Ibid., p. x.

because 'many of the things which count most cannot be said to a stranger. Many of them, indeed, are not said to the wife in bed.'[75]

Nobody would now advocate jettisoning the remarkable advances in precise social investigation made since Mayhew; their administrative and legislative value can be considerable. But the historian, at least, will also hope for the continued perpetuation of the more impressionistic type of survey that thinks it important to record the perception of experience in an open-ended way. Historians have been rightly warned to consult official inquiries only if prepared to work 'against the grain of the material', and if continuously aware of how categories and opinions are distorted by the investigative procedure.[76] Mayhew may have been overtaken by investigators statistically more proficient than himself, but their machine-readable categories and multiple-choice questions risk merely confirming the investigator's preconceptions; they create an unnecessary separation—which H. G. Wells, for one, never envisaged—between literature, social science, and social reform. Necessary for us, perhaps, though never for Mayhew, is the warning uttered by that perceptive Edwardian social observer Miss Loane: 'if we would solve even the simplest of problems, we must be willing to learn from the working classes, as well as to teach'.[77]

[75] *The Times*, 20 Jan. 1971, p. 14.
[76] R. Samuel (ed.), *Village Life and Labour*, p. xvi.
[77] M. Loane, *Neighbours and Friends* (1910), p. 57.

VII

The Centrist Theme
in Modern British Politics

I

To all appearances, there is no centrist theme in modern British politics, if only because the two-party system closes the two most obvious and overt routes to government by the centre. Halifax's Trimmer took the first of these routes; in a boat of men, says Halifax, when one group wants it weighted down on one side, and another to the same extent on the other, 'it happeneth there is a third opinion of those, who conceive it would do as well, if the boat went even, without endangering the passengers'. Halifax himself tried to stabilize the political system by shifting his position against the tendencies of the time—always infusing the party he joined with principles from the party he had just left, always more severe on the extremists among his new friends than on the moderates among his old.[1]

Yet even in the seventeenth century this was hardly the way to win friends; Halifax's career did not prosper, and the verb 'to trim' acquired pejorative overtones from the start—denoting the sort of self-interested caution that plays safe. In Burke's *Reflections* the art of trimming can still be seen in effective operation a century later,[2] but the nineteenth century's entrenchment of the two-party system discredited trimming in the sense of groups or individuals shifting between political factions or parties. Since then it has been possible for an individual to trim once (Hartington, Haldane) between the parties without loss of reputation, or precariously twice (Winston Churchill), but not more often (Oswald Mosley), let alone continuously; henceforth the Trimmer was free to operate only with circumspection, and could find

---

[1] George Savile, Marquess of Halifax, *Complete Works* (ed. J. P. Kenyon, Penguin Books, 1969), p. 50; see also T. B. Macaulay, *Works* (Edinburgh ed., 1896), i, pp. 192-3.

[2] E. Burke, *French Revolution*, p. 377.

no trimming group among politicians to shield him. Hence William Hamilton's attack on Reginald Prentice in 1978: 'the most contemptible and pathetic figure is the guy who crosses the floor'.[3]

The second of the direct routes to government by the centre—the distinct centrist political grouping—has persisted for longer than Halifax's strategy. The dream of government without party alternation is integral to the argument of J. S. Mill's *Liberty* (1859), for example, which regrets the fact that progress seems to involve the old being supplanted by, rather than harmonized with, the new. It is also the aim of his *Representative Government* (1861), which seeks a political system that can simultaneously attain the twin objectives of order and progress through a legislature undistracted by party antagonism. Politicians, too, have dreamed of an institutionalized centre, and several have even promoted it, but in the end they have all stumbled against the two-party system. As Roy Jenkins pointed out in 1956, 'centre parties have never had a happy or successful existence in England . . . their lives have been difficult and depressing'.[4] *The Oxford English Dictionary*'s first citation (in 1893) of the term 'centrist' dates only from 1872, and refers to the French legislature; the term is defined as 'a member of the Centre Party (in France)'. The term 'centrism' enters the *Dictionary* in its own right only in its 1972 supplement, shorn at last of its Continental overtones as '(the policy of adopting) a middle position'. But in the English context, the term remains somewhat exotic; although 96 per cent of those questioned in a survey of the 1960s admitted to some degree of party commitment, only 21 per cent of the respondents thought of the political parties in terms of right and left, and only 25 per cent saw themselves as belonging to right, left, or centre.[5]

A long sequence of ephemeral centrist groupings lies behind this situation. Formed only with difficulty, their

[3] *The Times*, 11 Mar. 1978, p. 3.
[4] R. Jenkins, 'A Genius for Compromise? A Debate on the British Party System', *Encounter*, Mar. 1956, p. 11; I owe this reference to Mr Anthony Teasdale, formerly of Nuffield College, Oxford.
[5] D. E. Butler and D. Stokes, *Political Change*, p. 206.

leaders rapidly succumb to offers of office, their rank and file are squeezed out by the constituency machines, and their popularity is destroyed through quick-thinking strategic moves by party leaders on right and left. Given nineteenth-century changes in the relationship between legislature and executive, in the role of parties, and in the role of the opposition, the discussion of centrist impermanence can conveniently begin with the Grenvillite 'third party' set up in 1818. It has been seen as the first of the centre parties, but it was absorbed into the Liverpool government in 1821. Canning's centre combination of 1827 against Grey and Wellington hardly outlived its creator, and in 1830 Canning's leading followers gravitated into the Whig government. When the followers of Stanley and Graham seceded from that government in 1834 and formed the 'Derby Dilly', their centrist appeal was undermined from the start (like the abortive scheme for a Lyndhurst/Whig coalition) when Peel advertised the moderation of his Toryism during his government of 1834-5, and when the Whigs allied with radicals and Irish in the Lichfield House Compact of 1835. The Dilly soon began travelling light, and in 1841 its two creators joined Peel's new Conservative government. As for the Peelite secession from the Conservatives in 1846, although 119 Conservative MPs had originally voted with Peel, Peelite numbers fell to between forty and fifty after the general election of 1852. When Gladstone joined Palmerston's government in 1859, they disappeared.[6]

Adullamite rebels against a Liberal franchise reform in 1866-7 foundered as a distinct centrist grouping on their greed for posts in a hypothetical coalition with the Conservatives; Disraeli was thereby enabled to take office and to pose with Derby as a moderate and safe reformer. And the Liberal Unionists, despite their successes of 1886, immediately found themselves (in Joseph Chamberlain's words) 'without efficient organization, isolated, and uneasy' in their constituencies, loathed by old friends and distrusted

---

[6] A. D. Harvey, 'The Third Party in British Politics 1818-21', *Bulletin of the Institute of Historical Research*, vol. 51 (1978); J. B. Conacher, *The Peelites and the Party System 1845-52* (Newton Abbot, 1972), pp. 30, 110, 118.

by new.[7] Their subsequent parliamentary representation registers a long-term undulating decline, concluding with a Conservative merger in 1912; but their freedom of manœuvre had ceased long before then. Still more ephemeral as centrist groupings were the Liberal Imperialists and the Conservative free traders. Rosebery's Liberal Imperialism aimed at recovering reasonable men of the centre for the Liberal Party, and never formally broke with it. But Liberal Imperialism lacked support from the constituency parties, and Rosebery lacked sympathy with Liberal Party traditions; it was killed in 1903 by the unifying impact on the Party of tariff reform's challenge to central features of the Liberal creed. Tariff reform, after much speculation about more centrist groupings, dispatched some Conservative free traders (including Winston Churchill) into the Liberal camp, and provided the dwindling number who remained behind with a decade of worried and precarious existence until their Party's overriding fear of Socialism and Home Rule healed its internal wounds.

The first-world-war coalitions involved a retreat from party infighting between 1916 and 1922, but their Labour members departed early, and Conservative back-benchers later forced their leaders into making a similar choice. The new-found vigour of the Labour Party and of back-bench Conservatism frustrated Lord Robert Cecil's dreams of a centre party led by Sir Edward Grey in 1921, and Baldwin completed his task of restoring the two-party system by offering posts to several Conservative coalitionists in his government of 1924. Modern scholarship now makes it clear that the National Government of 1931—like its predecessor of 1918-22—does not, at least in its early months, deserve the reactionary image it later gained; initially, at least, it occupied the centre ground. The National Labour grouping might be small in the number of its own candidates, but it was large in the number of votes it could marshal behind National Government candidates of any type, and the coalition provided a vehicle for collectivists who found the Labour Party distasteful. The outcome, if not the intention, was therefore that Baldwin received an

---

[7] J. Chamberlain, *A Political Memoir 1880-92* (ed. C. H. D. Howard, 1953), p. 276.

excellent excuse for resisting his own right wing. His Party could then resume its steady devouring and peaceful digesting of votes which would earlier have been cast for the Liberal Party and eventually capture the National Government in all but name.[8] The National Labour Party wound up in 1945 and the Liberal National Party amalgamated with the Conservative Party in the 1960s.

The suspension of party conflict during the second world war gave centrist ideas (Beveridge) their memorable moment. But events between 1940 and 1951 so liberalized both parties that the demand for centrist structures did not become vociferous again till the 1960s. Yet nothing came of Dick Taverne's Democratic Socialist Party, based on Lincoln in 1972-4, or of the many predictions[9] that a new centrist party would emerge in 1974-5 from the campaign to maintain British membership of the European Economic Community—nothing, that is, beyond the continuous secession of disaffected individuals from an allegedly *Marxisant* Labour Party: from Desmond Donnelly (1969) to Ray Gunter (1972) to Christopher Mayhew (1974) to Lord Chalfont (1974) to George Brown (1976) to Reginald Prentice (1977) to Richard Marsh (1978).

Centrist groupings vanish so quickly largely because of the great power of the party machine in a simple-majority single-ballot electoral system; but there is also a lack of centrist conviction among the centrists themselves—not on the merits of a centrist policy, but on whether an institutionalized centre is the best way to get it. Centrists secede from right or left more out of disillusion at and defeat within their own party than from enthusiasm for centrist structures as such. Espousing an overt centrist standpoint has the effect of easing the transition from right to left—or, more commonly, from left to right—in a two-party system, and is usually only the preliminary to a further move or merger. This was certainly true for the Canningites, the Derby Dilly, the Peelites, the Liberal Unionists, and the Labour and

[8] R. Bassett, *Nineteen Thirty-One. Political Crisis* (1958), pp. 332-3; J. Ramsden, *The Age of Balfour and Baldwin*, pp. 325-6; A. Marwick, 'Middle Opinion in the Thirties. Planning, Progress and Political "Agreement" ', *English Historical Review*, Apr. 1964, pp. 289-90.

[9] e.g. *The Times*, 2 June 1975, p. 2.

Liberal members of the National Government of 1931.

The point can again be briefly demonstrated in detail. The idea of 1835 for a Whig/Lyndhurst coalition, energetically promoted by the young Disraeli, was not centrist in inspiration; it was a mere device for dishing the Whigs. The Peelite rank and file after 1846 found itself under leaders—Peel and later Aberdeen—who refused to mobilize their followers as an effective centre grouping. Offers of office from the other parties, internal Peelite disputes about strategy, and hostility from the constituencies complete the picture. Even Gladstone, quick to criticize Peel for his lack of centrist leadership, seems not to have believed in a distinct centrist party; throughout the 1850s he inclined towards joining the Conservatives until distaste for Disraeli and enthusiasm for Italy, among other things, caused him to plump for the Liberals in 1859. Hartington in 1886 was equally unenthusiastic for a permanent centre grouping; he retained the Liberal prefix because this seemed the best way of getting a wider following for his overriding purpose—to defeat Home Rule—and because (like so many centrists before and since) he wanted to disguise even from himself the enormity of his personal leap in the dark. Joseph Chamberlain, aware of the Peelites' fate a generation earlier, at first sought devices for staving off absorption into the Conservative Party: championing Liberal policies apart from Home Rule, negotiating for Liberal reunion, and/or (briefly) flirting with the idea of a 'national' or centre party which would unite his own forces with moderate Conservatives and Gladstonians. But the familiar story of centrist fragmentation soon ensued—G. O. Trevelyan and W. S. Caine rejoining the Gladstonians, Goschen entering the Carlton Club, and Chamberlain eventually becoming the Conservative Party's Edwardian rejoinder to Socialism.

The Liberal Imperialist and Conservative free-trade groupings possessed ample talent but displayed little centrist drive, and Liberal coalitionists within Lloyd George's government were centrists less from conviction than from inability to make up their minds.[10] Baldwin's progressive Conservatism

[10] K. O. Morgan, in A. J. P. Taylor (ed.), *Lloyd George. Twelve Essays* (1970), pp. 238, 247.

and MacDonald's cautious Socialism jointly purloined the electorate on which Lloyd George's hopes of creating a progressive centre party after 1922 were founded. A centre party that merely compromised between policies developed elsewhere would never have suited his temperament, yet a Liberal Party that made bids for the leadership of the left risked dispatching moderates to the other two parties.[11] The ambiguity of Lloyd George's politics at this time may owe much to temperament, but it also owes much to situation. As for the National Government of 1931, its Labour leaders did not at first envisage it as being more than a temporary expedient, and were inspired less by centrist zeal than by distaste for tendencies within their own Party, and by the urgency of warding off a pressing financial crisis.

Liberal leaders since 1945 have hesitated between seeking realignment on the left, retaining the centre ground, or going it alone as the one party of radicalism; their followers divided fairly equally between centrists, radicals, and anti-system protesters.[12] As for the seceders from the Labour Party since 1967, far from opting vigorously for centrism a few have validated by their conduct Anthony Crosland's dictum that a social democrat is 'somebody about to join the Tory Party', and of the rest those who have stayed in politics were probably described accurately by the *Daily News* in 1871, when it portrayed an earlier group of deserters from the left. They 'are off with the old love and not on with the new', stragglers from the party of the left 'who will hang for a time between the two armies, and then gravitate to the Conservative ranks'.[13] In a two-party system, the centrist who leaves one party but cannot nerve himself to join the other, must usually retire from politics altogether, as did many Liberals between the wars.

From the mid-1960s, however, a rather different situation began to develop: whereas in several earlier periods there had

---

[11] Cf. J. Campbell, *Lloyd George. The Goat in the Wilderness 1922–1931* (1977), pp. 88, 251.

[12] On this see M. Steed, 'The Liberal Party', in H. Drucker (ed.), *Multi-Party Britain* (1979), p. 89.

[13] Crosland quot. in *Guardian*, 21 Feb. 1977, p. 11; *Daily News*, 2 Dec. 1871, p. 4.

been centre groupings without centrist enthusiasm, there now developed centrist enthusiasm without centre groupings —partly because the parties of right and left began drawing more widely apart, each condemning any consensus policy that sought compromise between the extremes. Sir Keith Joseph in 1975 therefore repudiated any Conservative pursuit of the political 'middle ground' as allowing the direction and even the pace of British politics to be determined by the extreme left, just as his Labour counterparts embraced Bentham's view that *'done gradually* means *left undone*, left undone for ever if possible'.[14] Whereas in the past critics of the two-party system complained that it failed to present the electorate with policies sufficiently distinct, and that there was too much bipartisan collusion between the two front benches—in the 1970s it became modish to complain about the width of the gulf between the two major parties.

'Where conflict does not exist', wrote Nevil Johnson in 1975, 'adversary politics manufactures it; where genuine conflict is present, adversary politics exacerbates it, and yet may frustrate its resolution; and where the clash of opinions and interests is many-sided and complex, adversary politics offers little hope of creating that basis of consensus which is indispensable if there is to be effective political authority'. The two-party system was now accused of imposing a crude, class-bound polarity of policy choice; 'it is absurd to talk of only two alternatives', writes Johnson again; 'instead we face multiple possibilities and can secure consent to a course of action only by combining in some way several of them'.[15] Electoral reform thus becomes the gateway to a new-born political liberation. 'I have believed for a long time', writes David Steel, 'that Britain is both a more diverse and, at root, a more united country than our political system allows us to express', and his Party's manifesto of 1979 attacked a political system which 'rewards parties based on class

---

[14] Sir K. Joseph, *Stranded on the Middle Ground? Reflections on Circumstances and Policies* (1976), p. 25, cf. pp. 19–21; Bentham quot. in S. E. Finer, *Edwin Chadwick*, p. 14.
[15] In S. E. Finer (ed.), *Adversary Politics and Electoral Reform* (1975), p. 76.

distinctions and reinforces class divisions'.[16] Whereas pro-
portional representation attracted J. S. Mill as a way of
protecting the minority against an overwhelming majority,
it had now become a way of protecting the majority against
two excessively powerful minorities.

It will now be argued that the two-party system since the
1820s has offered a third route to government from the
centre that is far more powerful for centrism than any
distinct centre grouping. Its swings in policy are less violent
and its operation is more subtle than its critics sometimes
perceive, because centrists are well entrenched within the
parties of right and left, and enjoy unrivalled opportunities
there both for influencing policy and for extending the
political range of their influence. Social anthropologists
could perhaps usefully export to other disciplines the idea
that a society can be united by its conflicts—by a precarious balance between opposed loyalties. Only in this way
can we resolve the paradox of a centrist community surviving
in the absence of centrist institutions, for in the British two-
party system, as Bagehot pointed out in 1874, 'though a
middle party is impossible, a middle government—a government which represents the extreme of neither party, but the
common element between the two parties—is inevitable'.[17]

II

Who, then, are the British centrists? We are concerned with
a combination of personality, strategy, and situation. The
centrists under discussion operate within a two-party system,
but favour compromise and moderation, and seek to stabilize
the political structure as a whole. Their beliefs make them
tolerant of, and even accessible to, ideas, attitudes, and
policies widespread outside their own party. They resist the
extreme within their own party partly because they fear it
will nourish the extreme in the other party as well. They
also know how governmental authority in a pluralist society
can suffer as a result of legislative attempts to coerce those

[16] D. Steel, *A House Divided. The Lib–Lab Pact and the Future of British
Politics* (1980), p. 163; *Financial Times*, 11 Apr. 1979, p. 13.
[17] W. Bagehot, *Works* (ed. N. St. J. Stevas), vii (1974), p. 198.

sectors of public opinion which the legislation in question most deeply affects. They are modern variants of Halifax's Trimmer, best denoted here by the term 'centrist' because this is less of a hurrah-word than 'moderate', and because it consorts more comfortably with the term 'fundamentalist', which seems preferable to the pejorative 'extremist'.

So much for personality and strategy; but what of situation? The fact that, at an outside estimate, only a fifth of British citizens over eighteen were members of the two major parties during the 1970s left ample territory for centrist politicians to colonize. Centrists in the community at large seldom organized themselves formally, but they lent new hope to the Liberal Party by contributing towards its 6,059,519 votes at the general election of February 1974; they also helped to produce a large majority for staying within the European Economic Community during the referendum of 1975. They regularly informed opinion pollsters and newspaper editors of their enthusiasm for 'Governments of National Unity', of their distaste for the party bickering they heard in radio broadcasts of parliament (particularly at question time), and of their preparedness to vote for a centre party that had any hope of power. A *Times* leader of September 1972 thus felt able to speak of 'twelve million Jenkinsites', and a rash of opinion polls in 1981 announced substantial—even landslide—support for an electoral alliance between Liberals and social-democratic dissidents from the Labour Party.[18] These are the millions allegedly unrepresented by the adversary system.

Centrists operate at several levels—as voters, writers, journalists, civil servants, politicians, cabinet ministers, and statesmen. This discussion focuses only on the last three, and especially on the last two—though the first four will feature in so far as the last three are influenced in their conduct by the knowledge that they exist. We are concerned, then, with politicians who occupy high position towards the left of the Conservative Party and towards the right of the Labour or pre-1914 Liberal parties, but also with a few who shift from one party to the other. Centrist politicians are by

[18] *The Times*, 30 Sept. 1972, p. 15; for opinion polls, see *The Times*, 19 Jan. 1981, p. 2; 28 Jan. 1981, p. 2; 9 Feb. 1981, p. 4; *Observer*, 1 Feb. 1981, p. 1.

no means moderates in all dimensions of life; here the focus rests only on the political dimension. Even there, the centrist's moderation does not necessarily permeate the full range of policy, though it will apply to whichever segment of policy at any one time determines a politician's location along a political spectrum running from right to left. In the Mid-Victorian period the crucial area might concern religious or fiscal policy; in the 1880s, Irish policy; in the Edwardian period, tariffs, social and imperial policy; between the wars, foreign policy; since 1945, industrial relations, state intervention, economic policy, and membership of the Common Market. The centrist politician is by no means necessarily centrist for a lifetime; the focus here rests only on the portion of a career which seems genuinely to have assumed centrist objectives.

The centrist category cannot include confirmed fundamentalists such as the Ultras in the 1820s; Durham, Cobden, Bright, Dilke, and Labouchere; the protectionists after 1846; the Diehards of 1911; Keir Hardie and the Clydesiders; the third, fourth, and fifth Marquesses of Salisbury; Lansbury, Sir Charles Trevelyan, Sir Frederick Banbury, Bevan, the later Enoch Powell, the earlier Michael Foot, Mrs Thatcher and her closer associates, and the later Benn. Nor can it include those who temporarily pass through the centre as a sort of transit camp, but whose temperament causes them rapidly to move on; it is a testimony to the power of the centrist theme in modern Britain that several politicians feel it worth laying claim to a centrist label which they do not really deserve. Here Joseph Chamberlain takes his departure; as St. Loe Strachey told Rosebery in 1910, 'the truth is that so English an Englishman from many points of view, he is in other ways utterly unEnglish. Almost every Englishman has a touch of the essential Whig in him and a liking for moderation and the via media. Joe has none. Once a Jacobin always a Jacobin.'[19] For rather similar reasons Joseph Cowen, Lloyd George, Winston Churchill, Milner, Mosley, and L. S. Amery are excluded; they all also display a touch of the radical

[19] House of Lords Record Office, St. Loe Strachey Papers, S/12/7/21: St. Loe Strachey to Rosebery, 26 Apr. 1910 (carbon copy). Mr Vernon Bogdanor, of Brasenose College, very kindly provided me with this reference.

imperialism that simulates centrism only in combining ideas prevalent in more than one party, but diverges from it because those ideas are located at the two extremes. 'I have long believed that most of our countrymen are Radical and Imperialist', wrote Austen Chamberlain in April 1913, 'and that the irony of our political history consists in the fact that at most great crises the Parliamentary Radicals have been on the one side and the Parliamentary Imperialists on the other.'[20] The two-party system forces some within this group to leap from left to right in abrupt transition, or even (Lloyd George) to attempt both simultaneously. Despite Mosley's claim always to have been politically 'a man not of the parties but of the centre', his capacity for relating apparently disconnected ideas and his yearning (incongruously reminiscent of J. S. Mill) for a combination of order and progress—he was eventually forced to remove himself from practical politics altogether.[21]

In failing to make full use of such formidable talents, the two-party system can fairly be criticized, and Nevil Johnson hopes that the decline in adversary politics will compel politicians 'to recognise more fully the complexity and difficulty of many of the issues they deal with'. The right/ centre/left political categorization is certainly crude; Sam Brittan in 1968 even thought it more misleading than helpful, and—together with Eysenck and others—tried to supplement it with distinctions between the 'tough' and the 'tender-minded', between egalitarians and élitists radicals and orthodox, liberals and authoritarians.[22] Still, by no means all political misfits can be blamed on the two-party system; some of them blame the system for defects in themselves. Nor has any political system infallibly succeeded in producing ministries of all the talents; nor would such concentrations of talent in government necessarily produce the best outcome.

A very diverse grouping remains, including several who are

[20] BL Add. MS 46392 (Spender Papers), f. 92: Austen Chamberlain to J. A. Spender, 2 Apr. 1913.
[21] O. Mosley, *My Life*, p. 100; see also R. Skidelsky, *Oswald Mosley* (1975), pp. 80-1, 151.
[22] N. Johnson in S. E. Finer (ed.), *Adversary Politics*, p. 89; see also S. Brittan, *Left or Right. The Bogus Dilemma* (1968).

driven by age (like Goschen) from left to right, or less frequently (like Gladstone and the fifteenth Earl of Derby) from right to left; several (possibly the same group as the Goschen category) who, like Hartington after 1886 or several social-democratic seceders from Labour after 1967, think they stay in the same place while the world moves on; several who were born or projected too young into a party which they later discover is unsuited to their mature ideals (middle-period Rosebery, vintage Viscount Cecil), or which they realize (as did Lord James of Hereford after 1902, J. E. Gorst in later life, or Desmond Donnelly in the late 1960s) does not appreciate their talents; and some who are centrists from principle (some nineteenth-century Whigs, for example, or Eleanor Rathbone and some Liberals since 1918), shifting from one party to the other as circumstances or prudence seem to dictate, or even advocating a centrist grouping.

These centrists are not necessarily enthusiastic for inter-party coalition; their attitude towards it is pragmatic, as illustrated by Baldwin's disruption of one but crucial importance in another. For centrists know that although England does not love formal coalitions, she has never ceased to love them when they take the form of ranging a wide spectrum of opinion within each of her two major political parties. There may be few politicians who 'cross the floor' from one party to the other, but those few reflect the fact that in the two-party system most politicians experience a continuously fermenting intra-party debate; this accustoms them to the need for conciliation and compromise well before they become ministers. Centrists know that inside the parties of right and left they enjoy sources of influence far greater than if segregated into a formal centrist grouping.

There would be no point in systematically listing centrists and tabulating their personal qualities, if only because the centrist category gains so much strength from being blurred at its edges, and because individual centrists can vary markedly in the political weight they carry; even a single centrist politician can profoundly influence the whole political tone of his generation. The following list, by no means exhaustive, suggests itself without difficulty: Althorp, Huskisson,

Canning, Macaulay, Sir James Graham, Melbourne, Palmerston, Aberdeen, Sidney Herbert, Clarendon, the fifteenth Earl of Derby, Granville, Goschen, Northcote, R. A. Cross, Sir Henry James, Hartington, Rosebery, Bryce, Campbell-Bannerman, Asquith, Sir Edward Grey, Haldane, H. A. L. Fisher, Baldwin, Lady Astor, Dalton, Lothian, Eleanor Rathbone, Halifax, Hoare, Sir John Anderson, Attlee, Macmillan, Monckton, Gaitskell, R. A. Butler, Maudling, Macleod, Michael Stewart, Boyle, Heath, Crosland, Callaghan, Healey, Rippon, Prior, and the founders in 1981 of the Social Democratic Party.

Others qualify for at least part of their career—Gladstone, at least between 1841 and 1865, and probably later; the fourteenth Earl of Derby in his earlier career; Charles second Earl Grey, Peel, Lord John Russell, W. E. Forster, Curzon, Balfour, Austen Chamberlain, Bonar Law, McKenna, MacDonald, Lord Robert Cecil, Clifford Allen, Morrison, J. H. Thomas, Sir John Simon, Fred Pethick-Lawrence, Cripps, and Michael Foot in their later careers; Henderson, at least till 1931; Eden, at least until Suez; Harold Wilson at least after 1963, and perhaps throughout his career. There are some doubtfuls; Lord Randolph Churchill, W. V. Harcourt, Neville Chamberlain, the later Bevin, George Brown, and Reginald Prentice, for instance, qualify in some respects on strategy and situation but not on personality.

The centrist politician's fullest influence comes into the open only when the political situation seems to demand an appeal that transcends political party. Bagehot says that Palmerston was not loved by party zealots but enjoyed great influence 'over the common, sensible, uncommitted mass of the nation who nowadays do not strictly or rigidly adhere to any party'—over those 'fair, calm, sensible persons, who have something to lose, who have no intention of losing it, who hate change, who love improvement'. He goes on to claim that 'these are the men who really rule in all localities, in all undertakings, in all combinations; and it was over these that Lord Palmerston possessed unequalled and marvellous influence'.[23] Their successors were to follow

[23] W. Bagehot, *Works*, vii, p. 160.

Hartington in 1886 and Baldwin between the wars, to support the National Government in 1931, Beveridge in 1942, and the Conservatives between 1951 and the early 1960s.

Centrist politicians are difficult to analyse as a category, for they come from all political parties by several routes. Furthermore the argument here is not that they constitute a coherent grouping, but that their influence is all the greater for being bifurcated so as to penetrate opinion simultaneously to right and to left. Perhaps this is why they tend to be studied only as individuals. Biography is procedurally the easiest of the historian's activities; group-biography is more difficult, though still feasible; but the collective biography of politicians who operate independently of one another, engage in formal combat, and include many who dislike one another (Aberdeen versus Palmerston, Gaitskell versus Macmillan, Heath versus Wilson) would be difficult to write and aesthetically unpleasing. Nor do conflicts between centrists occur only when they are moving apart; preoccupation with political consistency can produce friction as they move closer together—between Liberal Unionists and moderate Conservatives in the 1880s, for example, or between Liberals and the social democrats who seceded from the Labour Party after 1967. Internally fragmented, formally split by interparty conflict, and without an institutional base —how can centrists perpetuate themselves? National temperament cannot be invoked, if only because centrism was relatively weak in seventeenth-century Britain and may well become so again. British centrism is cultivated through a number of political institutions, of which the most powerful is the two-party system. This will be discussed first, then the other institutions which reinforce its centrist tendency.

Centrist pressures in Britain date from long before the emergence of the two-party system; they owe much to memories of seventeenth-century civil strife. Those memories were reinforced (with Burke's aid) by events in France after 1789, and (with Macaulay's aid) by the reform debates of 1831–2; they entered the traditions of the Whig Party. It developed a set of political responses which eventually became almost instinctive, and not expressly related to the events that had originally inspired it. Such traditions were consolidated by identifiable pressures within the nineteenth-century parties. For both parties the earliest of these pressures was inevitably family, whose traditions frequently determined political allegiance. Especially important here is the Whig family tradition. 'Perhaps as long as there has been a political history in this country', wrote Bagehot, discussing the Whigs in 1855, 'there have been certain men of a cool, moderate, resolute firmness, not gifted with high imagination, little prone to enthusiastic sentiment' but with 'a steady belief that the present world can, and should be, quietly improved'.[24] Careful sponsorship encouraged young Whigs like Hartington to assume their historic role. His family had been prominent in resisting the Stuarts, and the second Duke of Devonshire had married a daughter of William, Lord Russell, beheaded in 1683. Hartington's relaxed, rather sceptical, political style reflected his family's well-developed political tradition. Palmerston promoted him early, and Hartington looked back respectfully to him when Liberal fundamentalists seemed to be threatening the union with Ireland in 1885: 'he was beyond everything an Englishman . . . I believe that he never on any occasion allowed party sympathies to blind him in the discharge of what he thought to be his duty in the interest of England'.[25] Palmerston's sponsorship, later reinforced by Gladstone's appeals to his family sense of duty, helped overcome Hartington's indolence and so ensured that in 1885–6 his political conduct became of crucial national significance.

The Whigs were particularly preoccupied with governmental methods, as distinct from substantive policy. Their seventeenth-century legacy made them wary of coercive reactions to extra-parliamentary agitation; in their view, this could be most effectively restrained through at least appearing to respond to it. Rather than endanger political continuity, the Whigs risked broadening out the political system by enfranchising new groups, by maintaining contact with potentially dangerous extra-parliamentary leaders, and even by admitting them to government's innermost councils where they could be watched and perhaps even converted. Whig

---

[24] W. Bagehot, *Works*, i, p. 318.   [25] *The Times*, 9 Oct. 1885, p. 7.

conduct in 1831-2 supplied Liberal ministers with a model for decades afterwards. Conservatives were somewhat embarrassed by their own Party's equally dramatic responsiveness to extra-parliamentary movements in 1829 and 1867, but such embarrassment was gradually muted by their continuous ingestion of Whig traditions and personnel; in this way, Whig traditions were perpetuated long after the Whig grouping formally disappeared in 1886.

The Conservative Party has contained no grouping equivalent in role and coherence to the Whigs' function within the Liberal combination. But this is partly because the Conservative Party's capacity to win recruits from the other party, reinforced by the strategy of its leaders, renders any such grouping unnecessary. Under Peel's leadership, and even under Disraeli's leadership in the Commons during 1866-7, Conservative conduct seemed diminishingly distinct from Whig traditions. Furthermore those traditions were strengthened within the Conservative Party by the continuous accession of Whig, Liberal, and even Labour refugees from the left—from Canning to Graham and Stanley, forward to Lansdowne, the Duke of Argyll, and the Liberal Unionists in the 1880s, and on to coalitionist Liberals after 1922 and non-Conservative members of the National Government in 1931. It was a bid for Liberal votes that inspired Baldwin's centrist variant of Conservatism after 1923. After making his name by helping to break up Lloyd George's anti-Socialist coalition, Baldwin devoted the rest of his career to re-creating it in a new and far more effective form. Laski once told him that he detected 'something in you of the temper of George Savile, Lord Halifax, which tinges all principles that claim finality with a recognition that novelty is inescapable'.[26] But trimming now had to be unobtrusive; with the Liberal Party crumbling, Baldwin thought 'the next step must be the elimination of the Communists by Labour. Then we shall have two parties, the Party of the Right and the Party of the Left.'[27]

Interviews conducted in the 1960s suggest that the Conservatives won more of these inter-war Liberal voters than

[26] G. M. Young, *Stanley Baldwin* (1952), p. 54.
[27] Quot. in J. Ramsden, *Age of Balfour and Baldwin*, p. 265.

Labour.[28] Liberals may have been conservatized, but Conservatives were certainly liberalized through Neville Chamberlain's domestic policy and through the Party's conciliatory imperial and foreign policy culminating in appeasement. 'What an infernal world!' exclaimed the Liberal Ernest Simon in January 1937: 'I find the really cheering thing to be the liberalism and decency of the bulk of the Conservative party in England, who might be going Fascist but are conservative enough to stick to the decent things that we have built up here.'[29] Nor does Whiggish Conservatism cease with Baldwin; with strong Whig family connections of his own, Harold Macmillan includes a chapter on 'The Whig Tradition' in his *The Past Masters* (1975). There he outlines their 'strange but not inglorious story', but preserves a Whiggish reticence about their influence on his own career. His espousal of interparty coalition in 1976—hinted at in 1975 as a possible 'desperate remedy'—would, if acted upon, have provided Conservatives with yet another opportunity for attracting recruits from the left.[30]

Whig traditions have also been carried forward into the British left. In his social attitudes, his friendships, his privately stated intentions and his over-all strategy, Gladstone carried forward Whig traditions within the Liberal Party even after the Whig secessions of 1886. Gladstonian Liberalism pursued the decidedly Whiggish aims of stabilizing the political system through fully incorporating Catholics, Irish, Jews, nonconformists, and working men into it, and through retaining contact with their leaders even when they seemed (as with Parnell in 1882) at their most dangerous. But Gladstone is never easy to categorize, and some felt that his centrist purposes were frustrated by the radical methods he used to promote them; the mass meetings and the timely surrenders, for instance, alarmed the Queen. His successors' relatively assured control over the party machine enabled them to dispense with country-wide crusades and adopt an

---

[28] Butler and Stokes, *Political Change*, p. 252.

[29] Manchester City Library, Simon of Wythenshawe Papers, M/11/14: Simon to Mrs Swanwick, 4 Jan. 1937 (copy).

[30] H. Macmillan, *The Past Masters. Politics and Politicians 1906–1939* (1975), p. 197, cf. pp. 190, 232; *The Times*, 22 Oct. 1976, p. 2.

approach that was in some ways more Whiggish than his own. Confronted by organized labour before 1914, Liberals had at least as good a chance of consolidating a new connection—in view of the weakness of Labour's challenge to Liberal values—as the Whigs had earlier achieved with the radicals and the Irish. As late as 1922 Lloyd George saw Sir Edward Grey as 'a real Whig seeking to reap the fruits of Radical achievement. It was in the family', his great grandfather having done just the same in 1832.[31]

By 1918 events had excluded this outcome, but Labour could now carry forward the Whig/Liberal strategy of annexation, incorporation, and stabilization with renewed effect. Haldane, whose move from Liberals to Labour in the early 1920s personally testifies to the continuity, sounded a decidedly Whiggish note when justifying adult suffrage in the House of Lords franchise debates of January 1918. And when arguing in December 1923 for Labour to be given its chance of power, his reference to the Whig tradition was direct (if somewhat anachronistic in its specific reference): 'three quarters of a century since', he wrote in the *Sunday Times*, 'the old Whigs, wise in their limited way, refused to meet the Chartist movement merely with a blank refusal. Thereby they earned our gratitude.'[32] By taking office in the minority Labour government, Haldane added one more coping-stone to the Liberals' nineteenth-century assimilative achievement. But the need for psychological assimilation is continuous in any democratic polity, and at that role the twentieth-century Labour Party has so far been adept.

In November 1929 Ramsay MacDonald saw it as 'our immediate duty' to 'place every obstacle we can in the way of the survival of the three party system'.[33] His combination of romantic exterior, humble birth, and vague but inspiring oratory enabled his Party to attract disaffected Liberals, nonconformists, and middle-class progressives; with him as with Gladstone, a bewitching ambiguity gave hope to all

[31] BL Add. MS 50906 (C. P. Scott Diary), f. 161 (1 Mar. 1922).
[32] Quot. in K. Martin, *The Crown and the Establishment* (1962), p. 88; see also R. B. Haldane, *An Autobiography* (1929), p. 330, cf. p. 321 and *H. L. Deb.*, 9 Jan. 1918, c.428.
[33] D. Marquand, *MacDonald*, p. 483.

sections of the Party. But the new Party required distinctive credentials and so could not advertise Labour's immense debt to the Liberals—organizationally, intellectually, and in personnel; it must confine itself to bidding for dissident Liberal votes by stressing its liberalism in policy. In October 1974 Roy Jenkins was still emphasizing that Labour's internationalism, humanitarianism, conscience, and approach to reform 'embraces the best part of the liberal tradition'. Far from being in decline between the wars, Liberalism was rapidly making converts; as Lord Lothian pointed out in 1933, 'thanks to their own work in the past, two-thirds of the Conservative Party and two-thirds of the Labour Party are in fundamentals still Liberally minded'.[34]

Supplementing centrist Whig traditions were relationships, structures, writings, and attitudes internal to the Conservative and Labour parties; these deserve brief consideration. Close friendships were inevitable within a political élite educated together and associating in the same clubs, salons, and country houses; this still lends the Conservative Party as a whole the advantage of relative cohesion. There were first the great 'vertical' centrist discipleships between generations and the 'horizontal' linkages between centrist politicians of the same generation, usually acting inside each party separately. The Conservatives boasted the line from Pitt to Canning and Aberdeen, and from Peel to the Peelites and out (via Gladstone) to fertilize the party of the left after 1859; in the 1880s Gladstone repeatedly claimed that Peel would have backed his position on many issues. Old impinged on young less through doctrinal influence than through sponsorship and apprenticeship in political technique. Gladstone told Tollemache admiringly about Peel's overmastering sense of public duty and 'exact sense of the proportion between one Bill, and the general policy of the Government; also of the proportion between the different parts of the same Bill'. Discipleship readily merged into friendship— between Peel and the Peelites, for example—but in more diluted form it could jump the political generations and enable a youthful R. A. Butler to find, when studying the

---

[34] Jenkins, *The Times*, 4 Oct. 1974, p. 6; P. Kerr, *Liberalism in the Modern World* (1933), quot. in J. R. M. Butler, *Lord Lothian* (1960), p. 170.

crisis of 1846, that his sympathies 'were for Peel against Disraeli', and to see in Peel his 'mentor among historical figures'.[35]

The trauma of 1845–6 masks the continuity in Party strategy and even the importance of Peel's personal influence on Disraeli. In his later career Disraeli, by personally sponsoring statesmen with a middle-class following—Stanley, Cross, Northcote, W. H. Smith—ensured that his Party's over-all strategy virtually reverted to Peel's. But centrist Conservatism takes different forms in different political situations. In the divided and demoralized state of the Liberals after 1886, the main centrist pressure on Lord Salisbury came from his Liberal Unionist allies rather than from the need to outbid the Liberals in progressive reforms. Again between 1917 and 1922, centrist pressures came from Liberal allies within an anti-Socialist coalition, but back-benchers' rejection of this strategy in 1922 enabled Baldwin to rebuild a broad-ranging Conservative Party reminiscent of Peel's, and capable of governing on its own. Devolution in India, a conciliatory approach towards Labour, and the origins of appeasement were centrist Conservative policies resting on the close horizontal linkage between Baldwin and Neville Chamberlain, with Halifax strategically placed as Viceroy in India or later at the Foreign Office. ' "Then there's Edward" was really the key to Baldwin's India policy', writes Butler; 'he was devoted to Irwin.'[36] Sir Samuel Hoare, with his formidable industry and devotion to Baldwin and Chamberlain, brought up the rear.

Baldwin and his allies produced a vertical centrist linkage by training a younger generation of Conservatives through their one disciple who survived the Party's trauma over appeasement in reasonably good order: R. A. Butler. 'He was my patron in politics', wrote Butler of Hoare in 1935, 'and I owe him a great deal.'[37] It was from Hoare that Butler obtained his first junior office, and the debt was acknowledged

[35] Hon. L. A. Tollemache, *Talks with Mr Gladstone* (2nd ed., 1901), p. 116; R. A. Butler, *The Art of the Possible* (1971), pp. 17, 29; see also C. W. R. Cooke, *Four Years in Parliament with Hard Labour* (2nd ed., 1890), pp. 58–9.

[36] Ibid., p. 39.

[37] J. A. Cross, *Sir Samuel Hoare. A Political Biography* (1977), p. 261, cf. p. 152.

in Butler's foreword to Cross's biography of Hoare in 1977. Of the seven prime ministers he served, Butler saw Baldwin as his mentor,[38] and it was in Baldwin's tradition—whether acknowledged or not—that Butler rejuvenated the Party after 1945 with new centrist horizontal and vertical linkages. Macleod is a key figure here, with Maudling as a close friend and with Neville Chamberlain as a newly discovered exemplar. As Minister of Health, Macleod found himself frequently continuing Chamberlain's earlier work—another example of the centrist discipleship that jumps the generations. The affinity later led Macleod to write Chamberlain's biography. But centrist friendships spring not only from affinity or shared apprenticeship, but from collaboration at dangerous political junctures—between Peelites braving protectionist wrath in 1846; between the Conservative advocates of devolution in India, nerving themselves to resist die-hard back-benchers in the 1930s; or among R. A. Butler's team between 1945 and 1951, struggling to guide their Party towards challenging an apparently triumphant Labour in the most effective way.

In the party of the left, Hartington's vertical bond with Palmerston was replicated at many levels among Whig politicians, and supplemented by the horizontal association between leading Liberal imperialists under Rosebery. Likewise with the Labour Party. It was Ramsay MacDonald's assault on syndicalist and revolutionary tendencies that tempted Herbert Morrison, for one, away from fundamentalist politics towards his subsequent centrist role; his decision not to follow MacDonald in 1931 was allegedly far less easy than it became convenient later to avow. Horizontal connections among non-Marxist Labour activists between the wars owed much to the capacity of Herbert Morrison and Hugh Dalton separately to attract and enthuse a band of experts and friends.[39] Tawney inspired personal admiration as well as intellectual respect among the circles in which Gaitskell, Dalton, and Durbin moved in the 1930s. Hugh Gaitskell's gift for friendship in the 1950s lent his following a cliquish image which was resented in some

---

[38] R. A. Butler, *Art of the Possible*, p. 29.
[39] B. Donoughue and G. W. Jones, *Herbert Morrison*, pp. 19, 177.

quarters; 'he cared desperately about his friends', writes Roy Jenkins of Gaitskell, 'and the small change of social inter- course assumed an unusual importance in his life'.[40]

Centrist linkages were consolidated not only by the club-like atmosphere of the House of Commons but, at least till the 1880s, by London's great political clubs. The Whigs clustered in those *bêtes noires* of the Victorian provincial radical— Brooks's and the Reform. The radical back-bencher Labou- chere told Chamberlain in 1883 that the radicals were 'a miserable lot, and seem ashamed of their opinions. The Whigs, on the contrary, out of office act solidly together.' Three years later he urged Chamberlain not to underestimate them: 'they hang together: they have . . . the machine: they dominate in Clubs and in the formation of Cabinets'.[41] With the decline in club-life, centrist groupings in both parties gradually became more formal and specific. The Fabian Society, combining the personal approach to the influential with sociability among the membership, marks a transition point here. Thereafter political life gradually became more segregated from social life, and centrists organized themselves within their parties in formal groupings such as the Tory Reform Group, the One Nation Group, the Campaign for Democratic Socialism, the Campaign for Labour Victory, the Manifesto Group, and Labour Solidarity.

Books and theories were less important as consolidating influences; centrist Conservatives even make a virtue of having no theoretical commitment. The directness of the impact made by economic theory on the Conservative government after 1979 was unusual in the Party's history, and encountered considerable suspicion within Conser- vative ranks. Governments, said Geoffrey Rippon, 'should not go nap on one statistic or one economic expert'; politics and policies, he said, 'are about people. That is why they must be sensitive and flexible.'[42] Likewise on the left. Whigs refused to push rival objectives—freedom and order, for

---

[40] W. Rodgers (ed.), *Hugh Gaitskell* (1964), pp. 115-16; see also pp. 120, 150; P. M. Williams, *Gaitskell*, p. 475.

[41] A. L. Thorold, *Labouchere*, pp. 206, 278.

[42] Rippon, *H. C. Deb.*, 21 Nov. 1980, c.241; cf. Alport, *H. L. Deb.*, 2 Apr. 1980, c.1423.

example—to their logical extremes in the belief that if combined in moderation they could be reconciled. Whiggism,
said Bagehot, 'is not a creed, it is a character', espoused by
men indifferent to large general theories, but 'with a clear
view of the next step, and a wise intention to take it'.[43]
C. W. R. Cooke's 'class of prigs, professors, philosophers,
and pedants' in 1890 were likely to be found on the left of
the Liberal Party, and were unlikely to cluster with centrists
in the House of Commons smoking-room—an institution
integral to the House's club-like role which Mosley later
claimed would 'very quickly rob a people's champion of his
vitality and fighting power'.[44]

Books (as distinct from theory) were more important for
strengthening centrism within the Labour Party, if only
because the left could now no longer deploy the tactical
resources of inherited family tradition. Drawing heavily upon
British rather than European socialist traditions, the social-
democratic writers from Tawney to Dalton to Durbin to
Crosland were firmly empirical in outlook at two levels:
in their attempt to relate their programme to observed
tendencies within British society, and in their detailed
knowledge of its political institutions, through which they
hoped to work. Their preoccupation with detail indicates
a concern for political effectiveness, not an absence of
commitment. Dalton's *Practical Socialism for Britain* (1935)
is anti-utopian, undoctrinaire, and down-to-earth in mood,
proud of Britain's traditions and respectful towards her
political institutions, with a full knowledge of their detailed
working. Evan Durbin praised its preoccupation with the
details of legislative and administrative change,[45] and showed
similar qualities in his own *The Politics of Democratic
Socialism* (1940). Durbin insists that the social-democratic
tradition is 'in no sense inferior' to the Marxist when it comes
to its historical and intellectual foundations; indeed, that its
position 'is more firmly grounded in the evidence of history,

[43] W. Bagehot, *Works*, i (ed. St. J. Stevas, 1965), p. 318.
[44] C. W. R. Cooke, *Four Years in Parliament*, p. 54; O. Mosley, *Tomorrow We
Live*, quot. in R. Skidelsky, *Mosley*, p. 311.
[45] *Political Quarterly*, 1935, p. 384; I owe this reference to David Bryan,
Nuffield College, Oxford.

psychology and economics'. Whig influences once again surface when Durbin adduces a detailed analysis of events in 1831-2 to illustrate how it is entirely possible in Britain for one class peacefully to prevail over another; all four franchise Acts, he says, transformed 'the economic, cultural and political status of the working class' without any resort to force.[46]

In 1953 Hugh Gaitskell, one of the book's dedicatees, found Durbin's book 'just as relevant to our current problems as it was to those of the thirties', and throughout the 1950s Labour's revisionists drew heavily on Tawney, whose views were promoted in *Socialist Commentary*, and whose non-Marxist outlook informs the Campaign for Democratic Socialism manifesto of 1960.[47] Social-democratic ideals were now so well rooted that the next major revisionist text, Crosland's *The Future of Socialism* (1956), was able to take libertarian political institutions for granted and abandon exhortation for a largely administrative and technical argument. But Crosland knew the importance of books, and towards the end of his life often told friends of the need to reinvigorate democratic Socialism by applying its principles to a new situation.[48]

More important for fostering centrism than internal party traditions and relationships is the search by both parties in a two-party system for an electoral majority, and for ministerial talent once this has been won. If the right to trim is a luxury now denied to politicians, political leaders know that centrist voters retain it to the full, and assume that the profile of British public opinion is strongly concentrated towards the centre and that therefore the richest electoral prizes are to be won by capturing it.[49] Hence the ambiguity of their response to party activists marshalled in the party conference. Political parties unceasingly scour the country for new sources of support and respond rapidly to shifts in opinion. If at any time the centrists in one party lose ground,

[46] E. Durbin, *Politics of Democratic Socialism*, pp. 320, 199; see also pp. 192, 195-6.

[47] Ibid., p. 8 (foreword); see also S. Haseler, *Gaitskellites*, pp. 74, 212.

[48] *Listener*, 18 Oct. 1973, p. 523.

[49] Cf. A. Downs, *An Economic Theory of Democracy* (New York, 1957), pp. 118-19.

centrists in the other party can in most circumstances adroitly guide its almost instinctive move to occupy the vacated territory. The separate existence of small centre groupings offers a salutary reminder of the need to respond in this way, and the ever present possibility that a party's centrists will depart reinforces that reminder.

Conservative centrists gain much from a period in government (1841-6, 1924-9, 1951-64, 1970-4), for this normally makes the Party's right wing captive to its centre (Ultras after 1828, Protestant Tories on Maynooth in 1845, opponents of Disraeli's Reform Bill in 1867, imperialists in the 1930s and 1950s, Powellite nationalists after 1970) unless unskilful handling of back-benchers (as in 1845-6) provokes it into impossibilism. In 1907 Lord Hugh Cecil, urging Balfour to conciliate Conservative free traders, reminded him of 'one of the great canons of political tactics'—that 'a secession from a party is much more formidable on the side nearest its opponents than on the more remote side . . . because the near side can easily join the opponents, but the far side have nowhere to go'.[50] Rare indeed is the situation of 1886 whereby fundamentalists are among those in one party who join the other. Furthermore, in the absence of formal dividing-lines between the various gradations of opinion within the parties of right and left, centrists can exert a continuous pull on fundamentalists. Particularly important here is the influence of the party leader, whose situation compels him to foster centrist tendencies within his party, however unobtrusively. It is no accident that of the twenty-eight prime ministers since 1830, twenty feature in the list of centrist politicians printed above. It is through this route, among others, that Conservative ingestion of Whig attitudes and Labour ingestion of Liberal attitudes takes place. 'A national Party like ours', wrote Macmillan in 1958, '. . . must by its very character and tradition avoid sectional or extremist policies. It must, therefore, by definition, occupy the middle ground.'[51]

The situation of the party leaders to right and left is similar

[50] Cecil quot. in A. Sykes, *Tariff Reform in British Politics 1903–1913* (Oxford, 1979), p. 147.

[51] H. Macmillan, *The Middle Way* (1966 ed.), pp. xx–xxi.

but not identical. Both parties embrace a broad spectrum of opinion; 'what is my party?', Baldwin once asked: 'Diamond Jubilee die-hards and Tory Democrats pulling me two ways at once.'[52] In both parties their governmental capacity makes centrists inevitable ministerial material. But the parties differ in their leaders' relationship to the fundamentalists. The process of edging the Conservative Party towards the centre can be fast or slow, according to circumstances, and at times (as in the era of Lord Salisbury, and perhaps after 1979) division and demoralization on the left enable Conservative leaders to remain stationary or even apparently to go into reverse. But the long-term tendency in the political system as a whole is leftwards, and the process eventually resumes. The Conservative leader's prime problem is therefore usually to move the Party discreetly towards the centre without splitting it. Not only is this usually necessary for effective government; it is also necessary if the Party is to attract and assimilate the new recruits, often with ministerial experience, that it receives from the left. Given the social recruitment of Conservative politicians, and their Party's traditional deference to its leaders when in office, governmental necessity can frequently be pleaded with some effect in justifying this move towards the centre—though never without strain, as witness events in 1829, 1846, 1867, 1929, and 1975.

Party leaders on the left, by contrast, preserve party unity less by encouraging a move from the left towards the centre than by slowing down the drift towards the left. This contrast becomes clear from comparing the mechanism for mobilizing ministerial talent on right and left. Centrists' major assets lie in their talent for government, and in the pull towards centrism exerted on politicians by governmental experience. While Conservative leaders do of course seek out ministerial talent among their fundamentalists (Knatchbull in 1834, Buckingham in 1841, Salisbury in 1874), they do not need to be as energetic in this as party leaders on the left, partly because their back-benchers are usually less restive, and partly because the over-all leftward drift of the political system causes ministerial talent to shift towards the party of

[52] G. M. Young, *Baldwin*, p. 55.

the right. 'The army of so-called reform, in every stage of its advance, necessarily converts a detachment of its force into opponents', said Lord Salisbury in 1869, and the more vigorous its reforms the more substantial the desertions from the party of the left, so that equilibrium between the parties is more rapidly reached.[53] Conservative governments rarely send the mechanism into reverse by embracing reforms that can be avoided. Conservative leaders can often therefore recruit centrist defectors from the left who possess ministerial experience or calibre (Stanley and Graham in 1841, Goschen in 1887, Chamberlain, Hartington, and James in 1895, Churchill in 1924, and, in a sense, MacDonald and Sir John Simon in 1931); likewise at lower levels of promotion.

In parties of the left, the need for ministerial talent requires the leader to live more dangerously. The left does of course occasionally attract distinguished ministerial recruits from the right—Peelite leaders in 1859, the fifteenth Earl of Derby in 1880, Winston Churchill after 1903, for example. In 1923 Lloyd George even hoped to filch Austen Chamberlain, F. E. Smith, Balfour, and other former coalitionists from the Conservative Party for some more progressive combination. 'The Tory party from time to time absorbed Liberals . . .', he told C. P. Scott: 'why sh[oul]d not the Liberal party absorb Tories?'[54] But he failed, and secession from right to left is in general less frequent, so that leaders of the left are more frequently required to draw upon fundamentalists whose attitude to office-holding is often equivocal. Left fundamentalists know that accepting the loaves and the fishes will shake the extra-parliamentary following and restrain the tongue; so concerned about this was Richard Cobden that he could never bring himself to accept the offer, and John Bright accepted only reluctantly, and with small success, in later life. The left fundamentalist also wonders whether his skill at criticizing authority can be reconciled with the arts of administration, and fears being surrounded in office by centrists who will expose his inadequacies and drain him of national influence.

[53] P. Smith (ed.), *Lord Salisbury on Politics. A Selection from his Articles in the Quarterly Review, 1860–1883* (Cambridge, 1972), p. 36.
[54] BL Add. MS 50907 (C. P. Scott Diary), f. 31 (26 July 1923).

Fortunately for leaders of the left, the distinction between fundamentalists and centrists is never clear-cut; it has been made here only for analytic purposes, but in reality there is an infinite gradation between the two within a party at any one time, and individuals continuously meet opportunities for altering the shade of their political colouring as time passes. The party constitutes a continuously moving escalator whereby individuals can unobtrusively and painlessly shift their positions towards the centre. This process would be greatly obstructed by that institutionalizing and crystallizing of the divergence between centre-left and left, centre-right and right which is desired by some advocates of electoral reform. 'The whole idea is wrong', said Shirley Williams of the centre-party idea in November 1980, 'because it means the only alternatives to the Centre are the extremes.'[55] Fundamentalist governmental capacity is cultivated by the numerous opportunities for internal compromise and bargaining presented within any party in a two-party system. Furthermore each party has its own source of professional conciliators; Conservative and Liberal lawyers and diplomats, like Labour trade unionists, pursue conciliation as their stock-in-trade. Some one-time fundamentalists—MacDonald, Clifford Allen, Morrison—eventually transfer to the national or even international stage powers of conciliation initially developed inside their own party. The leader of the left must make ministerial recruits among his fundamentalists not just to maintain party unity, but to protect himself against being left high and dry as leader of a centrist rump which the over-all leftward shift of opinion drives towards the Conservatives, as was MacDonald in 1931.

Some might regard this process as uninspiring, or even as entailing cynicism and deception. Yet this would be to ignore the training in mutual conciliation that the system provides and the extensive political participation it facilitates —participation for a wide spectrum of opinion not just in practical politics, but also in periodic access to governmental experience. Centrists must grapple with fundamentalist ideas, energy, and idealism, while fundamentalists are exposed to centrist experience, judgement, and governmental skill. Fundamentalists thereby enhance their understanding of governmental processes and get their chance of influencing policy at the same time as centrists extend their contacts more deeply into the fundamentalist camp. As Joseph Chamberlain pointed out, 'the legislative work of a Liberal administration is always decided by the maximum which the moderate section is ready to concede, and the minimum which the advanced party will consent to accept'. J. S. Mill as Liberal MP in the 1860s recognized this, and therefore pressed for reforms which he knew could not be conceded in their entirety; he later pointed out that 'it is the character of the British people, or at least of the higher and middle classes who pass muster for the British people, that to induce them to approve of any change it is necessary that they should look upon it as a middle course'.[56] The alternation in power of two parties (each with its complement of fundamentalists) is a centrist educational process far more comprehensive for a society than the proliferation of irresponsible fundamentalist groupings confronted by a governmental centre.

If this process of centrist consolidation invites suspicion from the fundamentalist left it also worries the fundamentalist right, who see unending opportunities here for trimming in the pejorative sense. The two-party system facilitates unobtrusive shifts of position at several points: from the centre to the extremes, from one party to another, and from the extremes to the centre. At any one time the distinction between the principled type of trimming which aims at political stability and the trimming which merely makes for a quiet life is by no means always clear. The Liberal Unionist shift towards the Conservatives in 1886 involved trimming in the first of these two senses, and *The Oxford English Dictionary*'s first entry on trimming when used in the intransitive sense is a citation from the *Daily Telegraph* for 6 November 1885: 'Lord Hartington is not the sort of statesman to trim his opinions according to the expediency of conciliating or not conciliating.' On the other hand the

[56] J. Chamberlain, *Political Memoir*, p. 116; J. S. Mill, *Autobiography* (ed. J. Stillinger, 1971), p. 174.

leader of Liberals or Labour who finds himself positioned
somewhere between his party's right and left may well be
forced to trim towards a party-centre which may be (because
of fundamentalist pressures within his party) far removed
from the centre in parliament as a whole, and perhaps even
further removed from the centre in the nation as a whole;
he may then find himself among colleagues whose views
differ markedly from his own.[57] Trimming in the second
sense is the more likely for the fact that centrists, as men of
government, are familiar with the need for compromise in
practical affairs, suspicious of the rigidities involved in
adherence to principle, and accustomed to getting through
short-term emergencies without too much thought about
long-term consequences; they do not therefore always
recognize the point at which a practical willingness to seek
accommodation degenerates into a sacrifice of essentials.
For L. S. Amery in 1914, Asquith seemed a statesman
'holding a season-ticket on the line of least resistance',
going 'wherever the train of events has carried him, lucidly
justifying his position at whatever point he has happened
to find himself'. For Reginald Prentice in April 1979, Wilson
and Callaghan had degenerated into trimmers in the second
sense, and had 'just trimmed and trimmed again'.[58]

Yet such objections ignore the fact that fundamentalists
within the party of the left can also trim towards the centre;
once the new fundamentalist recruit has accepted office—
Bright in 1868, Dilke and Chamberlain in 1880, Lloyd
George in 1905, Wheatley and Sir Charles Trevelyan in
1924, George Lansbury in 1929, Bevan and Cripps in 1945,
Frank Cousins and Barbara Castle in 1964, and Michael Foot
in 1974—he is subjected to centrist pressure and is rarely
presented with convenient moments for effective resignation
over a question of principle; perhaps he ceases even to seek
them. He will know that his party has not normally won
support from more than half the electorate during the
preceding election, and that in a pluralist political structure,
governments inevitably respond to non-party or other-party

[57] S. E. Finer (ed.), *Adversary Politics*, p. 12.
[58] L. S. Amery, *My Political Life*, i (1953), p. 459; Prentice, *Daily Telegraph*,
11 Apr. 1979, p. 11; cf. *The Times*, 21 Dec. 1979, p. 2.

pressures; these weaken the fundamentalist minister's standing. 'It's easy to pass laws', Prior told the Conservative Party conference in October 1980, 'but nothing is more damaging for parliamentary democracy than to pass laws you can't enforce.'[59] Democracy has always involved something more than mere majority rule; it also entails a certain deference to the views of the minorities most likely to be affected by legislation, provided that such deference does not unduly damage the interests of the majority. There are also local authorities with their powers of resistance, judicial restraints on governmental freedom of action, and the pragmatic pressures exerted by the civil service.

The last of these is for many fundamentalists the villain of the piece. They load the civil servant with responsibility for all their frustrations, self-doubts, betrayals, and disappointments when in office; by contrast, centrists find administrators congenial, whether at the national or local level. This is hardly surprising, because the attempt to enable a pluralist democracy to run smoothly while effectively tackling day-to-day practical problems ensures that (as Lord Armstrong told an interviewer in 1976) most senior civil servants are Butskellites: 'after all those years you tend to be within a narrow line either side of the centre. Most of them would like a government with Heath as prime minister and Jenkins as chancellor.'[60] It is not a Machiavellian desire to frustrate democratic processes that causes Fabians to urge pioneer Socialists into town-hall committee-rooms, or social democrats when in opposition to emphasize the importance of adequate preparation for power; it is a recognition, readily comprehended by civil servants, that a grasp of detail is central to practical achievement. 'It is necessary to mix a ton of detail with every ounce of general principle', wrote Durbin, urging Labour in 1940 to prepare a practicable programme for its next government, 'before the result is administratively edible. We need, as democratic socialists, a clarion call, a religious conversion to, and a rising passion for, detail.'[61] Centrists—the Whigs, the Peelites, Northcote, Hoare,

[59] *Guardian*, 9 Oct. 1980, p. 6.
[60] *The Times*, 15 July 1980, p. 14.
[61] E. F. M. Durbin, *Politics of Democratic Socialism*, p. 319.

Morrison, Macmillan, Butler, Gaitskell (though not Palmerston)—get on well with their civil servants not because they have been steam-rollered, but because they have spontaneously arrived at the same destination. Beveridge, Anderson, and later Armstrong—as outstanding administrators in difficult times—even found themselves being drawn into politics by the centrists of their day, though all three felt embarrassed by the partisan attachment which inevitably resulted.

The House of Commons also works in a centrist direction. The two sides of the debating chamber, reinforced by two lobbies which force MPs to divide themselves between 'ayes' and 'noes', offer the appearance of confrontation and help to explain the unfamiliarity in Britain of the left/right/centre terminology. The terms 'right' and 'left' originated in the French Revolution and were rarely used in Britain till the 1920s.[62] They have never been welcomed as labels by either party, and Edwardian volumes of *The Oxford English Dictionary* use the terms in a Continental context—though the 1976 supplement defines 'left' as a term 'now usually applied to a political grouping holding radical or socialist views'. Yet it is not at all clear that semicircular legislatures moderate extremism; in reality, the adversary seating plan helps to restrain fundamentalists in several ways.

First, a vigorous 'adversary' style of debating helps to channel potentially violent dissidence into parliament, and is often designed primarily to restrain the party's back-benchers and rank and file in the country; through the politics of theatre, recruits for the centre are unobtrusively won. The House of Commons is, after all, divided on two planes, not merely in one; if the leadership of one party became too conciliatory towards the leadership of the other, back-benchers on both sides, and still more those they represent, would seek other outlets. The parties' presentation of policy therefore exaggerates the extent of their divergence, but helps to mute the even cruder polarity between government and anti-government which is so often seen elsewhere, while simultaneously ensuring that government actions are always fully exposed to public criticism. This mechanism is

[62] S. Brittan, *Left or Right. The Bogus Dilemma*, p. 29; cf. D. Thomson, *England in the Twentieth Century (1914–1963)* (1965), p. 116.

perhaps more readily understood by the participants than by the spectators, but its function is conciliatory none the less. As Anthony Eden once said of Ernest Bevin's foreign policy, 'I would publicly have agreed with him more, if I had not been anxious to embarrass him less.' Political speeches, whether in or out of parliament, need to be decoded if their true significance is to be grasped. Winston Churchill admitted as much privately to Austen Chamberlain at a time of intense party conflict over Ulster in 1913: 'both sides had to make speeches full of party claptrap and no surrender, and then insert a few sentences at the end for the wise and discerning on the other side to see and ponder'.[63]

This is but one aspect of the important educational function performed by the House of Commons—that of forcing opponents to hear one another's arguments and of projecting them into a shared situation which involves collaborating in many non-party activities; in this way, the House erodes that insulation from disagreement which nourishes sectarian opinions. Much House of Commons business takes place in a non-party mood outside the debating chamber—in the small cross-party committees that focus on specific practical problems, regional interests, or matters that concern all MPs. It was in this world that a centrist Conservative like Hoare—in his own phrase 'a liberal amongst conservatives and a conservative amongst liberals'—felt most comfortable; it was day-to-day administration that really interested him, not the partisan confrontations at elections and on the floor of the House. Lord Robert Cecil in 1864 referred to the House's aversion 'for anything approaching to abstract reasoning'— to its 'indifference to any considerations which do not promise a distinct practical advantage'.[64] During the past two centuries, parliament has helped to tame the middle-class radical, the provincial nonconformist, the Irish and Welsh nationalist, and the early Socialist, few of whom held to their initial aim of insulating themselves socially from their political opponents.

---

[63] Eden, quot. in R. Miliband, *Parliamentary Socialism. A Study in the Politics of Labour* (1964, paperback ed.), p. 303; R. S. Churchill, *Winston S. Churchill*, ii, pp. 481-2; cf. A. Chamberlain, *Politics from Inside*, p. 574.

[64] J. A. Cross, *Sir Samuel Hoare*, p. 354; *Saturday Review*, 17 Sept. 1864, p. 358. See also pp. 433-41.

This moderating function has been fostered by parliament's location well away from the major areas of early industrialization. To Bagehot, Palmerston seemed to represent 'above all things, *London*,—that easy worldly Belgravian crowd, which we can none of us describe or define, but which we all know so well'.[65] Politics there seemed less a matter of principle and doctrine, more a question of expediency and personal loyalty. Furthermore, parliament's influence extended well beyond Westminster. Enshrined in its magnificent new complex of buildings, parliamentary procedure in the Victorian period acquired a prestige that enabled it to penetrate widely into numerous mini-parliaments throughout Britain—from public-house debating societies to trade unions to religious assemblies. When Baldwin portrayed himself as defending the British constitution (during the General Strike) against external threat, he played a winning card.

These moderating influences ensure that there is far more collaboration between the parties at Westminster than meets the eye. Among the centrist's strengths is the fact that when pressed by his own fundamentalists he can often rely on support from the other party. Only in unusual situations can fundamentalists on the two sides conceive of collaborating; but informal collaboration between one party and the centrists in the other is common. Peel helped the Whigs to outwit the radicals after 1832 just as the Whigs enabled Peel to outmanœuvre his own fundamentalists on the Maynooth question in 1845 and on the Corn Laws in 1846; and from then until his death, Peel reciprocated by lending his support and expertise to the Whig government at crucial moments. Gladstone could often rely on Conservative support against radical sectarians: temperance zealots, disestablishmentarians, Home Rulers (till 1886), and rebels on imperial and foreign policy. It was a strategy which the Home Rule crisis, by integrating both parties more tightly within themselves, rendered more difficult but also less frequently necessary.[66]

---

[65] W. Bagehot, *Works*, iii (1968), p. 280; cf. R. Cobden, *Speeches*, ii, p. 68.

[66] H. Berrington, 'Partisanship and Dissidence in the Nineteenth-Century House of Commons', *Parliamentary Affairs*, xxi (1967-8), pp. 371-2—an important and curiously neglected article.

But even this did not prevent more subtle forms of collaboration between the parties. Late-Victorian centrist Liberal MPs could temporarily embrace fundamentalist policies in the secure knowledge that Conservatives would defeat such policies in the House of Lords. The best-known instance of this occurred with Home Rule in 1893, and after the general election of 1906 Balfour aimed to use the House of Lords in such a way as to frustrate this convenient Liberal unifying device. The centrist's reliance on the other party could extend even further; when outmanœuvred by his fundamentalists he could confidently but covertly rely on the electoral swing of the pendulum against his own party. 'I am not in the least afraid of a Radical Government', the Whig Granville told Mrs Grote in 1858, 'firstly because I am rather Radical myself; and, secondly, because if other Radicals went further than I wished, I am sure that there would be a strong Conservative opposition in Parliament, and a Conservative reaction in the country.'[67]

Parliament moderates confrontation in another way, too: its adversary seating plan entails contiguity within each of the two sides. Followers are encouraged in the confrontation to cohere behind a leader who struggles to present his grouping as a rival governmental team. In the two-party system, centrist tendencies are fostered not only by governmental experience, but also by the hope of it. As Roy Jenkins argued in 1973, the entrenched centre favoured by some electoral reformers may drive Labour's left out of the mainstream of British politics, and so 'remove from a large and significant section of the nation both the discipline and the benefits of participation in a governing party'. The reform would not cause fundamentalists on right and left to vanish; it would merely reduce the strength of the centrist pull upon their loyalties. George Orwell's question 'in such and such circumstances, what would you *do*?' was a question that Hugh Gaitskell perhaps asked himself too frequently, but which a multi-party system would require fundamentalists to answer all too rarely.[68]

[67] Lord E. Fitzmaurice, *Granville*, i, p. 320.
[68] Jenkins, *The Times*, 10 Mar. 1973, p. 4; G. Orwell, *Collected Essays, Journalism and Letters*, ii, p. 228; cf. P. M. Williams, *Gaitskell*, pp. 296, 474, 773.

The gulf between the party's leaders and its rank and file will normally be at its widest at the end of a period of government, and at its narrowest at the point of access to power. Periods of opposition enable the centrist to restore links with his extra-parliamentary and parliamentary fundamentalists; the men of government resume their dialogue, after the compromises inevitable in office, with the men of ideas—evolving new priorities, seeking new recruits for the centre, and engaging in the rest, recuperation, and reflection that are necessary after a testing period of governmental power. But if centrists lack influence in opposition, and are unable to get their party to prepare adequately for power, one of four undesirable outcomes may result: the party will lose the next general election; or if it wins, it risks being unable to carry out commitments undertaken while in opposition, with all the consequent disillusion for rank and file; or if it succeeds in carrying them out, it may later have to reverse them, thus risking accusations of betrayal; or if the changes have failed to win all-party acquiescence, they may be reversed by the incoming government when the second general election is lost.

Critics of the two-party system often link their attack on Britain's so-called 'adversary', or (in David Steel's phrase) 'yah-boo politics',[69] to Britain's disappointing economic performance. Alternation between governments dominated by their fundamentalists would certainly damage an economy so much more heavily dependent than it once was on government policy. But such alternation can hardly be assigned any large role in producing an economic performance that has proved relatively disappointing since as long ago as the 1870s—for the disappointment has persisted under coalition and single-party government, under periods of frequent and infrequent party alternation, under class and non-class politics. Furthermore party alternations also occurred during much of Britain's industrial growth-period. The nationalist and early Labour parties were usually incorporated into the Liberal alliance and were thus yoked into the two-party alternation; the brief period of governmental instability

---

[69] Steel, *Guardian*, 18 Apr. 1979, p. 4 (speech at Louth).

between 1846 and 1859 was far from typical of nineteenth-century politics, and its effects were widely deplored at the time. The economy may well gain more by the political stability the two-party system ensures than it loses by the economic inefficiencies thereby entailed. Its wastefulness and confrontation are already fully apparent; the disruption it prevents will not become manifest until the system is removed. Besides, when contrasts in presentation are allowed for, the fluctuations in policy that have occurred in modern times—while sometimes embarrassing or inconvenient (1880, 1905, 1951, 1974, 1979)—have usually preceded eventual agreement. The need of one party for governmental success and of the other for electoral victory keeps such fluctuations to a minimum.

Some of the inefficiencies associated with two-party confrontation may well turn out to be civil liberty under another name. Centrist coalitions fragment the opposition into two halves, with all the threat to the integrated defence of citizen against executive which that entails. The two-party system's relative openness of government and responsiveness to opinion made it easier for colonial nationalities to gain their freedom and set a term to Balfour's resolute government in Ireland; it is hardly surprising that the critics of the adversary system have included more than one imperial proconsul. As Peel told Gregory in January 1828, repudiating the Ultras' approach to Irish policy, 'this country ought not, and cannot, be governed upon any other principles than those of firmness no doubt, but of firmness combined with moderation'.[70] 'Without a generation of resolute government', said Hoare in 1917, 'the Union is impossible and I am convinced that in the quick changes of English politics there is never going to be any resolute government of Ireland for any considerable time.'[71] Maximum political efficiency is by no means the only criterion for evaluating a political system; indeed, there may be something rather sinister about a political system that places a very high valuation upon it.

The cohesion of two 'sides' encouraged by House of

---

[70] Quot. in R. Peel, *Memoirs*, i, p. 16.
[71] D. G. Boyce, *Englishmen and Irish Troubles*, p. 37, cf. Austen Chamberlain on p. 36.

Commons adversary politics reinforces the centrist pull on the political community not only by drawing fundamentalists and centrists together into a potential party of government, but also by integrating into the two larger parties potentially schismatic and irresponsible groupings. Hence politicians' preoccupation with seating arrangements—during the confused party situation created by Canning's premiership in 1827, for example; after 1832, when the Tories had to decide whether they or the radicals should occupy the opposition benches; after 1846, when the protectionists caused a stir with their initial decision to remain on the government benches, and when the Peelites wondered which location accurately reflected their view; after 1886 when, after some discussion, the Liberal Unionists and Gladstonians sat together on the opposition side of the House, neighbours as uncomfortably sited as the Peelites and protectionists had been after 1847; and after the general election of January 1910, when Labour MPs had to move to the government benches so as to leave room for the increased number of Conservative MPs opposite. After each general election or political crisis, schismatic groupings are forced to take seats on one side or the other.

'Adversary politics' promotes centrism in one further way; by institutionalizing the polarities of the past, it hinders new polarities from breaking into the system. This reinforces in the policy sphere that bias against new political groupings which the simple-majority single-ballot system operates in the electoral sphere. It cannot prevent the emergence of a new polarity, but it slows down its advent. The newcomer is forced to organize support and formulate proposals, but is not obstructed so far as to deter him altogether from setting his sights on parliament. Both middle-class radicalism and working-class consciousness were held (admittedly sometimes precariously) on parliamentary course, nor did either ultimately disrupt the two-party system. Late-Victorian aristocrats before 1886 recognized the advantages of the contest between Liberals and Conservatives (both led by aristocrats) for an aristocracy threatened by an aggressively radical middle class. Edwardian Marxists saw in the same polarity (between parties now both deeply penetrated by the middle

class) a serious obstacle to the national advent of working-
class politics. The polarity between Conservatives and Labour
now tends to be criticized for perpetuating old class antagonisms—yet the eventual departure of the Whigs from the
Liberal Party in 1886 and the Liberal Party's adaptation by
1910 to cater for working-class politics illustrate how the
old mould can eventually be broken without disrupting
the two-party system; parties are in the end too thirsty for
support for such disruption to be necessary.

Centrism in the British two-party system profits from
a circular relationship between attitudes and institutions;
the notion of compromise and arbitration lends new functions to, or actually creates, institutions which in their turn
consolidate such attitudes. When faced by conflict, human
beings do not normally sit back while it gets worse. The idea
that reconciliation is feasible even in the most difficult
disputes—political, industrial, religious—permeates modern
British society, and is epitomized by the constitutional role
of the Speaker. His impartiality between the parties was
established by Shaw Lefevre between 1839 and 1857, and
was maintained by all his successors; only once during the
nineteenth century, in 1835, did the parties divide on who
should be elected to this post. From the Mid-Victorian
period onwards, the Speaker's conference emerged as an
unexpected but effective remedy for disputes between the
parties over the franchise, just as the conference between
party leaders evolved pragmatically as a way of solving
serious constitutional disputes.[72]

Surveys in the late 1950s showed that among working-class
Conservative and Labour voters the notion of 'balance' was
widespread—each seeing their party as necessary to secure
fairness by moderating the policies of the other, and neither
expecting dramatic change from the electoral success of their
own party.[73] It is from these widespread notions of 'fair play'
and balance that opportunities for compromise—'the usual
channels', institutional opposition, bipartisan policy, moderating moods, attitudes, and institutions—derive their force.

---

[72] J. D. Fair, *British Interparty Conferences. A Study of the Procedure of Conciliation in British Politics, 1867–1921* (1980), pp. 3, 270.

[73] R. T. McKenzie and A. Silver, *Angels in Marble*, p. 245.

Balfour told Blanche Dugdale in 1925 that the essence of British parliamentary government lay in 'the intention to make the thing Work', such an outlook being 'so deep in us that we have lost sight of it'. His much-quoted remark of 1927 described a political machinery which 'presupposes a people so fundamentally at one that they can safely afford to bicker; and so sure of their own moderation that they are not dangerously disturbed by the never-ending din of political conflict'.[74]

Belief in the feasibility of arbitration lies at the heart of the British judiciary, which reproduces the notion of an umpire between two competing teams that is familiar from the world of sport; it contrasts here with the inquisitorial role expected of the judge in (for example) France or Russia. It is perhaps no accident that the centrists specified earlier include several lawyers—James, Asquith, Simon, Monckton —members of a profession which has become less contro-versial between the parties since the nineteenth century. Whereas 54 per cent of United Kingdom judges could be described as in some sense political in 1820-75, and 52 per cent in 1876-1920, only 30 per cent could be so repre-sented in 1921-50 and only 11 per cent in 1951-68.[75] Allegations against the judiciary of class bias have of course long constituted a staple of Labour rhetoric, but this formal public standpoint does not necessarily reflect the private conduct of individual working men, or even of working-class institutions with specific grievances. A preparedness to prosecute for theft extends well below the middle class even in the Early-Victorian period. Chartist argument, firmly directed towards parliament, assumed a traditional radical constitutionalism, and Chartists were fully prepared to exploit opportunities the lawcourts presented. By the 1860s the trade unions in Kentish London were using the lawcourts to achieve aims which they might have been expected to seek through industrial action.[76]

[74] B. E. C. Dugdale, *Balfour*, ii, p. 267; R. T. McKenzie and A. Silver, *Angels in Marble*, p. 48.

[75] J. Morgan, 'The Judiciary of the Superior Courts 1820-1968: A Sociological Study' (unpublished London M.Phil. thesis, 1974), p. 151, defining 'political' as a former MP or parliamentary candidate; I owe this reference to Lord McGregor.

[76] D. Phillips, 'Crime and Authority in the Black Country 1835-60. A Study

Centrists also profited by the gradual nineteenth-century retreat from party politics of the Church of England and the monarchy. The Established Church always held within itself the potential for acting as the exponent of compromise in society as a whole, and its concessionary response to Catholic and dissenting claims freed it to occupy a conciliatory role in conflicts between the classes, especially when these involved conflicts between Lords and Commons. Itself originating in a compromise between Rome and Geneva, the Church of England embraced a breadth of opinion which threw up many leaders (Blomfield, Samuel Wilber-force, Tait, Temple, Randall Davidson) whose conciliatory role broadened naturally out from the religious into the secular sphere. Bishops gave timely help to progressive forces in the House of Lords—in getting the Navigation Acts repealed in 1849, for example, and in getting franchise reform enacted in 1884, when Gladstone wrote a persuasive individual letter to each of them. On the second reading of the 1909 budget most of the bishops abstained, including Randall Davidson, and three bishops joined the Archbishop of York in supporting the Liberal government. In 1911 it was a combination of 'the bishops and the rats' who frustrated the die-hard opponents of House of Lords reform. The Queen gave ample encouragement; in discussing church appointments with Randall Davidson in 1882, she pointed out that 'both extremes of High and Low church are to be avoided'. She had much to do with advancing those two Anglican conciliators, each profoundly influenced by the other—Tait and Randall Davidson.[77] Moving with calmness, tolerance, patience, and common sense amid a host of clerics who seemed at times to have lost all sense of propor-tion, these two archbishops held quietly but firmly and single-mindedly to their policy of maintaining Anglican unity while simultaneously conciliating nonconformists and Catholics through judicious concession.

of Prosecuted Offences and Law-Enforcement in an Industrialising Area' (un-published Oxford D.Phil. thesis, 1973), pp. 217–18, 220, 483–4; G. Crossick, *Artisan Élite*, p. 160; cf. F. Engels, *Working Class*, pp. 317–18.

[77] G. K. A. Bell, *Randall Davidson. Archbishop of Canterbury* (1935), i, p. 61, cf. p. 143; P. Guedalla (ed.), *The Queen and Mr Gladstone*, ii, p. 273.

Under Prince Albert's influence, the Queen had herself begun to lift monarchy above party, and thus to assume mediating functions, particularly when party warfare inflamed relations between Lords and Commons. Her personal views were of course strongly partisan; by the 1880s even her enthusiasm for a coalition of 'moderates' had much to do with her desire to wreck Gladstone's Irish policy. None the less, in the crises of 1869 and 1884–5 she helped facilitate consultation between party leaders—a process greatly assisted in 1884 by her private secretary Ponsonby, that subdepartment of monarchy's conciliating role whose 'tact[,] discernment and constancy' Gladstone generously acknowledged.[78] Under George V, the monarchy moved more publicly into a role of conciliation. On Ulster he tried to enhance the arbitrating role of the conference between party leaders, finding it inconceivable (as he told Asquith in September 1913) that 'British commonsense will not ultimately find a solution to this terrible prospect of rebellion and bloodshed'.[79] Like his predecessors, but unlike many centrists, he often saw interparty coalition as the best way of resolving national problems, and his crucial role in creating the National Government of 1931 is well known. But in disliking party conflict he was probably, like his grandmother, more in harmony with public opinion than the party politicians; certainly the electorate endorsed the monarchy's standpoints at the general elections of 1886 and 1931.

Two more general features of centrist opinion deserve brief mention at this point: its middle-class connections and its patriotic image. Positioned midway between aristocracy and labour, the middle class features recurrently in the centrist story—from Canning's popularity with merchants and financiers to Macaulay's eulogies of the middle class during the reform debates, and on to Peel's Tamworth Manifesto of 1834. There is the middle-class popularity of Palmerston and the fifteenth Earl of Derby, and the middle-class affinity of Liberal Unionists and Liberal Imperialists, of Baldwinite

[78] Quot. in P. Guedalla (ed.), *The Queen and Mr Gladstone*, ii, p. 319, cf. pp. 302, 306, 315; Sir E. Hamilton, *Diary* (ed. Bahlman), ii. pp. 650, 738.
[79] Quot. in H. Nicolson, *King George the Fifth. His Life and Reign* (1952), p. 228, cf. pp. 121, 157.

Conservatism and Labour's social democrats between the wars. The centrist's governmental situation enables him also to display the caution, self-restraint, and industriousness associated with the middle-class self-image—qualities they seek to propagate in other classes. It took many years before Disraeli could overcome the suspicions of this class, whose personal situation between the 1820s and the 1950s inclined it to perform a trimming function by shifting periodically in long cycles between right and left. An Aristotelian notion of the expanding middle moulds the class outlook of many centrists—Whigs, progressive Conservatives, and social democrats. From Durbin through Crosland to the Jenkinsites of the early 1970s, social democrats stressed the need for the Labour Party to respond adventurously in the face of manual labour's reduced proportion of Britain's electorate.

Integrating and invigorating British centrism as a whole is the recurrent conviction that this is an essentially English political standpoint. For G. M. Trevelyan, the events of 1832 were 'a characteristically English business from beginning to end'. For *The Times*'s obituarist of Lord John Russell, Westminster Abbey might contain memorials to more brilliant names, but 'there is the record of no more thoroughly English career'.[80] Baldwin contributed as much as anyone to this classic emphasis on the English talent for compromise, reinforcing it with a sentimental idealization of the English countryside; the same emphasis on 'the British tradition of peaceful change' pervades Harold Macmillan's *The Middle Way*. In their assault on Marxist influences on the British labour movement, Tawney, Dalton, and Gaitskell sound an equally strong patriotic note, which also resounds through Durbin's *Politics of Democratic Socialism* down to its concluding paragraph: 'those of us who believe in democracy, have faith in moderation, and search for agreement in the field of politics, have behind us the long and splendid tradition of British political thought and practice'.[81]

---

[80] Trevelyan in R. L. Schuyler and H. Ausubel (eds.), *The Making of English History* (New York, 1952), p. 500; *Biographies of Eminent Persons Reprinted from The Times*, ii (1893), p. 107.

[81] H. Macmillan, *Middle Way*, p. 373; E. F. M. Durbin, *Politics of Democratic Socialism*, p. 321; see also pp. 279, 332, 334.

III

So our initial paradox can be resolved; centrist tendencies are strong in Britain despite her lack of overtly centrist structures because of the centrist tendency of the two-party system, reinforced as it is by centrist influences within other British political institutions. But this only throws up a second paradox: how is it that so prominent a feature of British political life receives so little discussion from political scientists and historians? This neglect is at first sight surprising when one recalls the similarity between the historian's professional (though not necessarily political) outlook and the centrist's scepticism towards political partisanship. For Macaulay, Halifax always saw passing events 'not in the point of view in which they commonly appear to one who bears a part in them, but in the point of view in which, after the lapse of many years, they appear to the philosophic historian'. Through the many controversies Halifax witnessed, Macaulay continues, 'he almost invariably took that view of the great questions of his time which history has finally adopted'.[82]

The recent historians of modern British politics often seem distant in mood from Halifax, or even from the enthusiasm for British consensus politics that permeates G. M. Trevelyan's mature works. British political history is dominated by volumes published in blue or red covers; by biographies of parties and of their leaders, usually written by party members. This rarely leads to overt bias; few of these works display the defects of 'official history', and many are admirably fair-minded. The problem lies rather in the bias unintentionally introduced by the consequent neglect of topics that do not fall neatly within the party framework. Instead we have party histories (the latest, Conservative, in four projected volumes), dictionaries of party activists (the latest, of labour leaders, in five, and still growing), and even a journal of socialist historians—as though comprehension of the British left requires some distinctive historical method. Between these groups there has been a dialogue only of the deaf; one suspects that the historians of Conservatism keep

---

[82] T. B. Macaulay, *Works*, i, p. 191; iv, p. 127.

a weather eye on the writings of Marxist historians, but there is little evidence of intellectual curiosity in the reverse direction.

Two reasons for the neglect of centrist history are the unobtrusive way in which centrism operates in Britain, and the sheer complexity of the subject. But four further disincentives to its discussion deserve more detailed consideration here: the absence of an institutionalized centre that can inspire and sponsor comment; the centrist's lack of appeal to the historians of party; his lack of attraction as a biographical subject; and his weak representation among political theorists. Each of these can now be discussed in turn.

If the Liberal Party had survived as a major force in British politics, the centrist theme might have been sounded more loudly by historians—especially if electoral reform had enabled the Liberals after 1918 to assume the formal role of centre party. As it is, Whigs and Liberals have suffered more than most by British historiographical trends; they are difficult to accommodate within the modern two-party historiography, and are often cast up by party historians on a centrist sandbank which is seen as being continuously eroded by the tides of class-consciousness. Whiggery tends to be seen as a strange survival, even between 1832 and 1886, rather than as pioneering a political tradition within both political parties which still persists. And the apparent inevitability of the Labour Party's rise often causes the Liberals before 1916 to be seen as far more conservative than they really were; attention is thereby drawn away from the Liberals' partial success before 1914 in absorbing the Labour Party into their progressive coalition, and from the continuing Liberal contribution to the mood and strategy of the modern Labour Party.

Nor does the centrist naturally attract the historian of party. Centrist statesmen, even when they receive biographies, tend to be studied in the context of what they have contributed to an internal party tradition—viewed in a chronological, longitudinal way, so to speak, rather than in a horizontal manner that takes full account of responses right across the political spectrum at any one time. This is to risk obscuring the full complexity of the politician's role. Political parties do not live separate lives of their own; they continuously interact in ideas, situation, and strategy. The centrist perspective is necessary even for comprehending the internal history of the two major parties, let alone the workings of the political system as a whole. Politicians in their daily work, especially when in government, must continuously take full account of centrist, apolitical, and even hostile opinion. Centrists are safely entrenched within the parties of right and left largely because those parties continuously interact, continuously attempt to poach on each other's preserves, continuously seek to attract non-party elements of the electorate. Hence Baldwin's remark that if he was not leader of the Conservative Party he 'should like to be the leader of the people who do not belong to any Party'.[83]

Still more misleading is the linear emphasis of the party histories 'from Peel to Churchill', 'from Earl Grey to Asquith', which are in some ways as Whiggish in their self-directed momentum as those numerous Victorian autobiographies charting the journey of the self-improving artisan 'from stonemason's bench to Treasury bench'. By contrast, a centrist perspective suddenly throws neglected careers into sharp relief—those of Melbourne, Northcote, Hartington, Goschen, Granville, Henderson, Hoare, Dalton, and Durbin, for example—or emphasizes neglected dimensions of well-known careers that have hitherto been seen largely from a party-political viewpoint. Politicians' crossings of the major party divide become easier to explain, and the two great twentieth-century peacetime coalitions, long neglected as mere aberrations, move into focus.

In a political history dominated by parties, centrists tend to be seen either through the eyes of their enemies on right or left, or through the eyes of critics within their own party. The Whigs are seen by labour historians (with Tom Paine) as 'a set of childish thinkers and half-way politicians born in the last century', and (with Cobbett) as the shoy-hoys who doubt the virtues of the parliamentary reform they recommend; the

---

[83] Quot. in J. Barnes and K. Middlemas, *Baldwin. A Biography* (1969), p. 714.

Fabians (with Engels in 1892) as 'wolves in sheep's clothing';
R. A. Butler (with R. H. S. Crossman in 1954) as a man for
whom 'there is no last ditch which is really worth defending
if you can get out of it in time and with good grace'.[84] The
centrist is unlikely to be enshrined in his party's pantheon.
Far from being seen as national saviours, the waverers who
got the third Reform Bill through the House of Lords in
April 1832 are passed over as turncoats, best relegated to
a footnote together with the 'bishops and the rats' who
turned the flanks of die-hard peers in 1911. Curzon's biographer notes how he was seen by many Tories as a Judas,
and L. S. Amery thinks this incident helped deny him the
premiership twelve years later.[85]

Furthermore, producing reform without revolution is a
delicate matter. The centrist is too deeply involved in negotia-
tions aiming at a settlement, too conscious of the other
party's difficulties, for those ringing declarations of principle
that enter into party mythology. Fine rhetoric thrives on
a conviction of total righteousness, a sentiment centrists
seldom experience. The centrist case often rests on complicated and delicate considerations that are not easily discussed
in public; yet half-measures and cautious statements are
viewed by fundamentalists merely as lack of zeal. As Sir
Samuel Hoare pointed out in 1933, when defending the
government's India Bill against opposition from his own
Party, the government's case was 'a complicated case of
detail, whilst the attack is an attack of headlines and platform slogans'.[86]

Conservative historians are bound to look askance at those
who allegedly betray their own class, either deliberately or
more commonly through delaying tactics which in the long
term seem to fail. Yet in the absence of the immediate social
catastrophe that the centrists aim to ward off, it is easy for
Conservative fundamentalists to underestimate the effort and

---

[84] T. Paine, *The Rights of Man* (ed. H. Collins, Penguin Books, Harmondsworth, 1971), p. 176; E. P. Thompson, *Working Class* (2nd ed.), p. 825; F. Engels,
Working Class, p. 364, cf. p. 370; R. H. S. Crossman, *The Charm of Politics and
other Essays in Political Criticism* (1958), p. 59.

[85] Earl of Ronaldshay, *The Life of Lord Curzon* (1928), iii, pp. 56–8; L. S.
Amery, *My Political Life*, i, p. 381.

[86] Quot. in J. A. Cross, *Hoare*, p. 169.

ingenuity required even to slow down its pace and intensity. Gash has of course done full justice to Peel in this respect, but Peel is less favourably regarded in the new Party history, and the Party's memory more readily turns to Disraeli. Baldwin's achievement in re-creating the Conservative Party between 1922 and 1924 is acknowledged, but even a Conservative historian like Lord Blake plays down the importance of centrist political arts by seeing him as a man who 'in the end . . . failed because the wounds on English society were not the result of malice, cruelty or spite, and could not be cured by kindness'.[87]

Because of the subtlety of their party allegiance—unquestioned in the case of many centrists (Granville, Northcote, Asquith, Grey, Henderson, Morrison, Butler, Callaghan), but suspect in others—centrists like Peel and Ramsay MacDonald do not evoke enthusiasm from subsequent party activists. The political process is not solely about policies, ideas, and opinions; it is also concerned with loyalties, and although on close investigation many centrists often seem courageous and consistent in their ideas, party activists attach less importance to these qualities than to consistency of personal connection and vigour of party utterance. They suspect that in a crisis, when forced to choose between party interest and what they see as the national interest, centrists will choose the latter, though usually their efforts succeed in reconciling the two.

If the centrist often speaks for a majority within the community as a whole, therefore, he often finds himself fighting his way out of a minority within his own party; for if the two-party system divides the fundamentalists, it also cuts through the centre. Party activists may often regard centrist policies as timid, but the centrist politician is often required to be 'a daring pilot in extremity'; rebutting right-wing Tory criticism of his proposed trade-union legislation in February 1980, Prior commented that 'I sometimes believe there is courage in standing against a stream.' The centrist politician is in constant danger of running up against his party machine

---

[87] R. Blake, *The Conservative Party from Peel to Churchill* (1970), p. 218; cf. R. R. James, *Churchill. A Study in Failure*, p. 192; R. Skidelsky, *Mosley*, p. 20.

and being broken in the process: Peel and the Peelites after 1846, Rosebery by 1905, Edwardian free-trade Conservatives. A centrist dissident from his party's policy is far more likely than the fundamentalist dissident to become embroiled with his constituency party, as Nigel Nicolson found at Bournemouth in 1957 after opposing the Suez venture. 'In London society the idea of a middle party can be understood', wrote Bagehot in 1874, 'but in the country, in the constituencies which are the ultimate source of power, it would be an unintelligible nondescript.'[88] There is no big machine behind centrism as such, and a politician forsakes his party at his peril unless he can count on a personal or regional following. The centrist has no future except to hitch the fundamentalist wagon to his own destination.

The neglect of centrists is accentuated by the more traumatic of the centrist schisms—1846, 1886, 1931—because the leadership of the party they have left cannot openly avow its continuing adherence to the policies of the departed and despised. Disraeli went into full retreat from protection almost immediately after 1846, yet it did not seem decent to avow the fact too soon, and only recently could his subsequent courtship of the middle classes be presented as continuing Peel's strategy for the Party. The aftermath of 1846 made the need for a centrist strategy all the more patent, yet all the more difficult to carry out. Centrists could never be allowed to depart *en masse* from the Party again, yet Peel's actions made it difficult to re-create let alone to champion, a broad church view of the Tory Party. It is often stressed that Peel was 'in a fundamental sense never a party politician',[89] and that he preferred to think of himself as the King's minister; but his pursuit of the centre also stemmed from continuing electoral and parliamentary necessity, as the careers of his successors testify. While they shared his aims, the memory of 1846 injected caution into their tactics (Salisbury in 1885, Balfour after 1903). Likewise the direct avowal of centrist leanings within the Labour Party became virtually impossible after 1931; though

[88] R. Peel, *Memoirs*, i, p. 366; Prior, *Guardian*, 21 Feb. 1980, p. 2; W. Bagehot, *Works*, vii (1974), p. 198.
[89] N. Gash, *Mr. Secretary Peel*, p. 13.

MacDonald has had several successors in strategy, none dares acknowledge the debt.

There are now some signs of a decline in the party orientation of historical writing on British politics. Donald Southgate's substantial *The Passing of the Whigs 1832-1886* (1962) might have been expected to focus on the centrist theme, but his aim was to clarify the careers of a group of men, not to analyse a political tendency, and his emphasis on the importance of landed connections in nineteenth-century Whiggery causes him to locate Whig decline in the 1880s. 'Between Whiggery and democracy', he writes, 'there was fundamental antithesis',[90] and his final chapter says very little about the persistence of the Whig political style into later generations. Arthur Marwick's well-known article of 1964 on 'Middle Opinion in the Thirties' discussed centrist or non-party pressure groups, but the theme was not followed up in his later work. There have been biographies of centrists such as Rosebery (1963), Palmerston (1966 and 1970), Lord John Russell (1972), Goschen (1973), Macleod (1973), and Aberdeen (1978), but these have not focused at all directly on centrism as a theme. The interesting book of an American, Vincent Starzinger, whose *Middlingness. 'Juste Milieu' Political Theory in France and England 1815-48* (1965) discusses nineteenth-century centrist traditions in British and French political theory—focusing on Brougham, Macaulay, Royer-Collard, and Guizot—is little known. Sam Brittan's challenging and original *Left or Right. The Bogus Dilemma* (1968) came from outside the academic profession and, perhaps for that reason, has not provoked extensive academic discussion.

On the other hand, Colin Matthew's *The Liberal Imperialists* (1973) related its theme to what was seen as 'a continuing argument within the British party of progress': should it move towards the centre or towards the left? Kenneth Morgan's important *Consensus and Disunity* (1979) at last does justice to the centrist origins and early aims of the Lloyd George coalition, and as early as 1958 Reginald

---

[90] D. Southgate, *The Passing of the Whigs 1832-1886* (1962), p. 322; cf. pp. 76-7.

Bassett's *1931. Political Crisis* prepared the way for that revaluation of the National Government's record which must now surely be impending, and which is foreshadowed in David Marquand's *Ramsay MacDonald* (1977). Paul Addison's *The Road to 1945* (1975) perceptively acknowledges that 'the history of consensus is more fundamental in politics (though less discussed) than the record of party strife',[91] though its wartime preoccupations have concealed its full significance for peacetime history. J. D. Fair emphasizes the two-party system's restraints on party conflict in his valuable *British Interparty Conferences* (1980).[92]

Centrists are neglected for a third reason: they seldom make a good biographical subject. Their personalities either lack obvious biographical appeal, or the biographer has difficulty in penetrating the sources of their influence, or both. 'Commitment' in politics is by no means confined to fundamentalists. But commitment to centrism inhibits self-advertisement; despite Peel and Gaitskell, the centre is not normally the place to find dramatic renunciations, uncompromising affirmations, or altruistic sacrifices of life, property, or power. The subject therefore lacks romance; indeed, Whigs, Fabians, centrist Conservatives, and social democrats deliberately repudiate extra-parliamentary politics-as-theatre. By contrast, historical research is lavished upon a fundamentalism too extreme even to feature on the parliamentary spectrum—on British Fascism, for example, or on faction-fighting within the left of the inter-war Labour Party—rather than on those aspects of British politics which frustrated both. 'For all the studies of revolution and reaction in modern Western political development', writes Starzinger, 'there has been surprisingly little depth analysis of middlingness.'[93]

There can be no distinct centrist personality-type where the routes to centrism are so multifarious. Besides, centrists sometimes school themselves to display qualities that do not

---

[91] H. C. G. Matthew, *Liberal Imperialists*, p. x (preface); P. Addison, *The Road to 1945*, p. 13 (introduction).

[92] J. D. Fair, *Interparty Conferences*, p. 3.

[93] V. E. Starzinger, *Middlingness. 'Juste Milieu' Political Theory in France and England, 1815–48* (Charlottesville, 1965), p. viii (preface).

come naturally; centrist qualities can also be developed, or occasionally even shed, in later life. But certain qualities are highly valued and developed with relative ease at the centre, though they are not invariably found there and are sometimes found among fundamentalists; the centre simply nourishes with special care the skills that are central to the politician's profession. They are qualities more readily savoured in relatively private gatherings where the guests are few but select—qualities cultivated in those rigorous schools of character, the cabinet and the House of Commons.

For centrists are *par excellence* men of government, and in some cases—Canning, Curzon, and the Whigs generally, for example, though not Hartington or Austen Chamberlain —are frequently accused of undue ambition, whether for financial or other personal reasons. Huskisson's followers lent invaluable official experience to the Whigs' popular following after 1830, just as Peelite executive talents were courted by both parties after 1846. In that year the Conservative Party saw the departure of Peel and almost the whole of the cabinet and the official men; in the Protectionist government of 1852 only two of the forty-five officeholders apart from Stanley had held office under Peel.[94] Almost as indispensable to their Party were the Liberal Imperialists, who (unlike the Peelites) never burned their boats.[95] The Peelite parallel was acknowledged by another centrist governmental grouping, the Conservative ministers in Lloyd George's coalition,[96] and the Gaitskellites played a similar role in the Labour Party after 1964.

Governmental experience mutes the fundamentalist's idealism and demands an intense application that is sometimes accompanied by a certain austerity of public demeanour (Graham, Simon, and Stewart, for example) and does not make for popularity. To take an extreme case, there is Reginald McKenna, of whom *The Dictionary of National*

[94] R. Stewart, *The Foundation of the Conservative Party 1830–1867* (1978), p. 212, cf. N. Gash, *Sir Robert Peel*, p. 708.

[95] H. C. G. Matthew, *The Liberal Imperialists. The Ideas and Politics of a Post-Gladstonian Élite* (1973), p. 290, see also pp. 126, 295.

[96] Earl of Birkenhead, *F.E. The Life of F. E. Smith, First Earl of Birkenhead* (1965), p. 483; cf. R. Blake, *The Unknown Prime Minister. The Life and Times of Andrew Bonar Law 1858–1923* (1955), p. 504.

Biography declares 'his cold businesslike approach to questions about which his audience felt with passion brought him no following in the country and made him more respected than liked in his party'.[97] The Peelites' administrative prestige owed much to the formidable appetite for work, or at least to the concentration of effort on politics, displayed by Peel's close colleague Sir James Graham, but the pace was set by the master himself. Developing this appetite for political work often required a spurning of the temptations abundant in aristocratic universities and still more abundant in the working-class community. In 1828, rejecting the idea of a purely Protestant government, Peel said its supporters would be 'prosperous country gentlemen, fox-hunters, &c. &c., most excellent men, who will attend one night, but who will not leave their favourite pursuits to sit up till two or three o'clock fighting questions of detail'.[98] It is hardly surprising that Peel felt he had little to fear, nearly twenty years later, from a Lord George Bentinck who regularly entered the House of Commons at a late hour with a white greatcoat over his scarlet hunting-coat. Even Disraeli, at moments of depression in the 1850s, grew weary of supporters to whom in a parliamentary division, as he told Stanley in 1853, 'a sharp frost would make a difference of 20 men'.[99]

The centrist's habitat—the governmental office, the cabinet, the parliamentary committee—is either impenetrable or unexciting for the historian, and activity there proceeds in a mood of public service which it is difficult for him to capture, let alone to savour. Rare indeed is the biographer interested in, and capable of, describing in detail his subject's methods of work as did R. T. Davidson and W. Benham in the remarkable thirty-third chapter of their biography of Archbishop Tait. These centrists drive themselves through the detailed paperwork they regard as essential to political achievement. Peel almost drove himself into a nervous breakdown by 1846, Clarendon died with his dispatch boxes beside him, and ill health among leading members of the

---

[97] *Dictionary of National Biography 1941–50* (1959), p. 554.
[98] R. Peel, *Memoirs*, i, pp. 17–18.
[99] R. Stewart, *Foundation of the Conservative Party*, p. 294; see also B. Disraeli, *Lord George Bentinck. A Political Biography* (5th ed., 1852), p. 38.

Attlee government by 1950 may stem partly from the intense strain involved in holding cabinet office continuously through a decade of crises. Only immense stamina (Gladstone, Simon, Heath, Healey), or the deliberate, wise, and in some ways misleading adoption of a certain nonchalance in high office (Melbourne, Palmerston, and Baldwin) could protect centrists against such dangers. It is not just long hours that are involved here, but the close attention to detail required when government measures have to be got through parliament—the preparation of practicable and enforceable schemes, the persuasion of colleagues to support them, and the powers of concentration lying behind Samuel Hoare's *tour de force* when facing 10,000 questions during nineteen committee sessions as a witness before the joint select committee on the India Bill.[1]

Hard work alone is by no means sufficient; centrists need to work well with others—as a matter of day-to-day procedure, and even at the level of political theory, though Russell's conduct during the Aberdeen coalition illustrates the occasional absence of this quality from centrist ranks. 'The great art of government', Peel told his cabinet in 1844, 'is to work by such instruments as the world supplies.'[2] Despite Mosley's centrist pretensions (and he would certainly qualify on the score of hard work), he still held in later life the decidedly uncentrist conviction that he could have done it all on his own. In 1968 he tells us that in 1929 'after eleven years' experience of politics I had complete confidence in my own capacity to solve any problem confronting the nation; that confidence has not diminished but has grown with the years'. In reality, the qualities of self-suppression, conciliation, and mutual tolerance are unobtrusive but essential accompaniments of democratic executive achievement. Democracy, wrote E. M. Forster approvingly, does not tend to produce the Great Man: 'it produces instead different kinds of small men—a much finer achievement'.[3]

---

[1] J. A. Cross, *Hoare*, p. 167, cf. pp. 176, 234, 264.

[2] N. Gash, *Sir Robert Peel*, p. 717.

[3] O. Mosley, *My Life*, p. 229; E. M. Forster, *Two Cheers for Democracy* (Penguin ed., Harmondsworth, 1970), p. 80.

Centrist collaborativeness does not mean that easy-going *bonhomie* which generates the affectionate anecdote (though Melbourne, Palmerston, and Baldwin are exceptions here); pressure of time makes that difficult for them. Nor is the conciliatory temperament necessarily natural to centrists. Macaulay's collaborativeness, for instance, stemmed more from policy than from personality; he admired Halifax as 'a trimmer both by intellect and by constitution', and showed both surprise and respect for the fact that amid such troubled times Halifax could discuss politics in so balanced and abstract a way.[4] Goschen described himself as 'a violent moderate man', and Gaitskell's career illustrates how the centrist politician's commitment can, when given the right occasion, emerge in memorable passion.[5]

With Aberdeen, Granville, and Monckton, the art of conciliation was carried almost to the point of genius, and was crucial to party fortunes. 'As a mediator and conciliator he stood unrivalled', writes Aberdeen's son, 'slow to act, distrustful of his own judgment, and totally devoid of party spirit or personal ambition', he seemed the obvious man to lead the coalition of 1852.[6] Granville's collaborativeness seems to have been innate; everybody commented upon it, and he played as essential a part in the delicate business of creating the Aberdeen coalition in 1852 as in smoothing relations between Gladstone and the Queen in the 1880s. 'In the midst of these troubles', Gladstone told him in December 1885, 'I look to you as the great feud-composer.'[7] Granville was ideal for presenting the Liberal case attractively in the House of Lords, ideal for hosting party receptions at Carlton House Terrace which would hold the party together, the inevitable man for after-dinner speeches on non-political occasions like the Literary Fund Dinner or the annual banquet of the Royal Academy.[8]

[4] [T. B. Macaulay], 'The Life and Writings of Sir William Temple', *Edinburgh Review*, Oct. 1838, p. 169, cf. p. 170; see also J. Hamburger, *Macaulay and the Whig Tradition* (Chicago, 1976), p. 157.

[5] Hon. A. D. Elliott, *Goschen*, ii, p. 275; P. M. Williams, *Gaitskell*, pp. 775, 777.   [6] Quot. in L. Iremonger, *Lord Aberdeen* (1978), p. 199.

[7] A. Ramm (ed.), *The Political Correspondence of Mr Gladstone and Lord Granville 1876–1886* (Oxford, 1962), ii, p. 418, cf. i, pp. xxxiv–xxxv; ii, p. 401; Lord E. Fitzmaurice, *Granville*, i, pp. 80–1; ii, pp. 505–6.

[8] Fitzmaurice, *Granville*, i, pp. 236, 238, 438; ii, pp. 123–4, 128, 505–6.

Samuel Wilberforce, a master of the art of pleasing others with the *ars celare artem*, was the Granville of the episcopal bench, and often mixed socially with Granville in the social life of the Victorian country house. Hartington is another instance of the natural diplomat among centrists—less polished, of course, but often arbiter in delicate private social matters. 'I don't know why it is', he once complained, 'but whenever a man is caught cheating at cards the case is referred to me.'[9] Ramsay MacDonald's skill at finding common ground with others enabled the Labour Party actually to come into existence.[10] It is no accident that of the thirty-six foreign secretaries holding office between 1830 and 1975, only three—Wellington, Salisbury, and Lansdowne—can be definitely ruled out of the centrist category; twenty-three of them feature in the list of centrist politicians presented above, and several others were entrusted with important diplomatic missions. Their personal qualities lead to their selection, but their selection then cultivates their personal qualities.

Skill at detecting and handling shifts in public opinion is collaborativeness displayed on a broader canvas and integral to governmental achievement in a pluralist society. Centrists must often cultivate company they do not find congenial. Whigs incorporated skill at handling public opinion into their innermost creed, but they never relished their radical contacts. Indeed in October 1819, referring to Hunt and the radical leaders, Grey asked 'is there one among them with whom you would trust yourself in the dark?'[11] Yet radical contacts via Place, Parkes, and Attwood were invaluable to Grey in 1831-2, and in later years the Whigs established prudent connections with O'Connell, Cobden, Bright, Chamberlain, and other potential hazards. When Chamberlain entered the cabinet in 1880, Granville told the Queen that 'it was much safer to have the advanced Radicals in office than out, detached from all their surroundings'.[12] If the

---

[9] B. Holland, *The Life of Spencer Compton, Eighth Duke of Devonshire* (1911), ii, p. 211, n. 1.

[10] D. Marquand, *MacDonald*, p. 71.

[11] G. M. Trevelyan, *Lord Grey of the Reform Bill* (1920), p. 188.

[12] Queen Victoria, *Letters, Second Series* (ed. G. E. Buckle, 1928), iii, p. 89.

Liberal Party had survived as a leading party of the left after 1914, the Labour Party's leaders would probably have entered the cabinet which the dockers' leader John Burns had joined in 1905; nor would Liberals have had much to fear from their doing so. Labour itself soon espoused Liberal strategies of co-option—nor is the Grey who 'loved the people, but . . . loved them at a distance' without parallel among Labour's twentieth-century leaders.[13] Authoritarian instincts and traditions made strategies of co-option more difficult for nineteenth-century Conservatives; yet for skill at handling public opinion, Peel could hardly be bettered, and in later years a concessionary form of Conservatism came into full operation on franchise reform, Irish independence, and imperial devolution; some had even expected to see it impinging on Home Rule as early as 1885. For agility in handling public opinion in the twentieth century there is no need to look further than Baldwin and Macmillan.

Coercive policies on the left often flow from benevolent intentions and optimistic views, from an eagerness for a short cut to the social transformation that seems so nearly within grasp; coercive policies on the right often stem from impatience and pessimism. By contrast, the centrist seeks agreement without coercion, and this requires a well-developed sense of timing. Grey postponed till 1830 implementing the parliamentary reform in which he had so long believed, and Gladstone postponed till 1869 the Irish Church disestablishment he was free to adopt after 1845. Fitzmaurice sees patience as 'the essential quality of Lord Granville's mind',[14] and Bernard Holland says that throughout Hartington's political career 'his attitude was that of a man refusing to be hurried'.[15] Contrast this with the rather unexpectedly candid admission in Mosley's autobiography that 'I was always in too much of a hurry', and contrast that again with the quality praised in Mosley's most effective opponent, Baldwin, by one of his disciples, R. A. Butler: 'from him I learned both "the patience of politics"—the importance of

---

[13] J. R. M. Butler, *The Passing of the Great Reform Bill* (1914), p. 54; cf. C. Mayhew, *Party Games* (1969), p. 24.

[14] Fitzmaurice, *Granville*, ii, p. 309.

[15] Holland, *Hartington*, ii, p. 241.

biding one's time before action'.[16] Centrist alertness to public opinion, caution, distaste for confrontation, and capacity for understanding an opponent's point of view—are seen by some critics as merely timid (in Curzon, Baldwin, Macmillan, or Monckton, for example), or even as congenitally inclined to fear the worst (Graham, J. H. Thomas). The seventeenth-century Halifax was himself too alert to the drawbacks of every course, and traces of the same difficulty appear in the careers of Halifax the foreign secretary, together with the fifteenth Earl of Derby, Hartington, Rosebery, Curzon, Asquith, MacDonald, Hoare, and Callaghan.

Some fundamentalists see centrist tactics as conspiratorial and even as involving malign manipulation. For the *Chartist Circular* in May 1840, the Whig was 'a political shuffler, without honour, integrity or patriotism. Dissimulation, selfishness and baseness are his prime moving principles.'[17] A measure of insincerity is of course involved when colleagues need to be co-ordinated and public opinion marshalled, and the politician's situation makes candour more difficult for him than for the ordinary citizen. There is always the danger that this need for indirectness will prove corrupting; hence the need for institutional safeguards against governmental power and for a political system that keeps fundamentalists and centrists in continuous contact. But the centrist's indirectness is closer to tact than to amorality, and is inevitable in any civilized relationship between human beings. Centrist insincerity usually has objectives rather larger than the saving of political skins—the preservation of political continuity for instance, the avoidance of violence, and the extension of political participation. It is rooted in the need to pursue reconciliation, and differs totally from the amoral power-lust that ruthlessly sacrifices human beings to ideals.

In so far as centrists aim at inclining their parties towards centrist views, they might be accused of gaining or retaining power on false pretences; the classic fundamentalist formulation of this view is Disraeli's attack on Peel as 'a man who bamboozles one party and plunders the other', and who thereby deprives parliament of 'the legitimate influence and

[16] O. Mosley, *My Life*, p. 24; R. A. Butler, *Art of the Possible*, p. 29.
[17] *The Chartist Circular*, 2 May 1840, p. 3.

salutary check of a constitutional Opposition'.[18] Yet in 1867 the Adullamites could well have applied the same criticism to Disraeli himself, and the centrist who uses governmental necessity to shift his party towards the centre is no more justly accused of retaining power on false pretences than the fundamentalist who attains power with the aid of his party's centrist clothing.

Centrists' preoccupation with political tactics has perhaps caused them to suffer more than most politicians by the historiographical shift away from political history since 1945—by the tendency to regard non-political influences as paramount, an outlook often rather unexpectedly combined in the same individual with a decidedly uncentrist propensity for a conspiratorial explanation of historical events. Such an outlook plays down the independent influence exerted on a social situation by political tactics and mobilization. The rise of the Labour Party, for instance, was inevitable, Ramsay MacDonald or no; 'the vacuous goodwill of MacDonald and Baldwin' was useless during the economic dislocation of the thirties.[19] This leaves little room for centrists in a situation of social conflict, and Starzinger pessimistically concludes that 'the center is least realistic where it is most relevant, and most realistic where it is least relevant'.[20] By contrast, centrists think that social developments can be profoundly influenced by the way they are perceived, and that perception can be substantially moulded by the actions (often purely symbolic) of political leaders. With skill and self-confidence, centrists can pre-empt even the emergence of a situation where the centre seems 'unrealistic', and can certainly deal with it once it has arrived, as Whig handling of events in 1831-2 amply testifies.

Some British centrists have elevated the pursuit of mutual conciliation to the level of political theory. Many political activists, including Marx, are motivated by an ideal of a harmonious society free from conflict, however conflict-ridden the journey towards it may be; but whereas the fundamentalist pursues uniformity (with or without coercion),

[18] R. Blake, *Disraeli*, p. 189.
[19] R. Skidelsky, *Mosley*, p. 20.
[20] V. E. Starzinger, *Middlingness*, p. 16.

the centrist acquiesces in diversity (with or without enthusiasm), and builds his political structures round the assumption that human beings will disagree. The revisionist social
democrats whose conversations of the late 1930s collectively
produced Durbin's *Politics of Democratic Socialism* elevated
collaborativeness to the level of political theory. Their assault
on the twin demons of Fascism and Communism flowed
naturally from the pursuit of tolerance, conciliation, and
compromise within their private relationships. It is a background very different from Mosley's army-trained aversion
to 'politicking'.[21]

Though seldom formulated in an academic way, the
centrist's collaborativeness simultaneously rejects the abstract
'reason' of the fundamentalist left and the repudiation of
reason widespread on the fundamentalist right. Instead he
espouses 'reasonableness' in human relations—the Trimmer's
recognition that if you abandon persuasion of your opponent
for coercion, he is thereby justified in using the same
methods against you.[22] Centrists enthusiastically join those
who repudiate force in matters of opinion, and vigorously
champion civil liberties—whether they are Portland Whigs
shocked at September Massacres, Liberals repudiating Black
and Tans, or Labour revisionists after the 1930s conducting
strongly ethical assaults on the totalitarianism of right and
left. Social democrats deplored what Tawney regarded as
communist chicanery on questions of personal morality, and
shared Orwell's conviction in 1940 that a better society could
rest only on the prevalence of decent values among individuals.[23] Their acquiescence in compromise, and their
respect for civil rights and political democracy, stem from
a desire to avoid obstructing socialist advance by driving their
anti-socialist opponents to extremes—from a recognition
that unless society moves together, it cannot ultimately hope

[21] R. Skidelsky, 'Great Britain', in S. J. Woolf (ed.), *European Fascism* (1968),
pp. 233, 235–6; see also S. Haseler, *Gaitskellites*, p. 98.
[22] Halifax, *Works* (ed. Kenyon), p. 58.
[23] G. Orwell, *Collected Essays, Journalism and Letters*, i, p. 583; cf, i, p. 582;
see also i, p. 387; E. F. M. Durbin, *Politics of Democratic Socialism*, p. 165;
R. H. Tawney, 'British Socialism Today', in R. Hinden (ed.), *The Radical Tradition* (1964), p. 178.

to move forward either fast or far.[24] Compromise was built into their view of Socialism, which they saw as intermediate between Communism and *laissez-faire* capitalism, and which emerged from a pooling of ideas among a number of friends. Powerfully assisted by trade-union leaders, by the democratic forms so deeply embedded in the British Labour Party's structure, by Labour MPs' consolidation of those forms at Westminster, and by the serious tactical errors committed by the Marxists themselves, the revisionists' ideals prevailed so completely that their next major text after Durbin— Crosland's *The Future of Socialism* (1956)—takes libertarian institutions for granted and abandons exhortation for a purely administrative and technical argument.

Some centrists were thought by contemporaries to possess integrity, a quality which has less to do with any single personal characteristic than with possessing several qualities in combination. Centrist requirements in matters of character are stringent, and its importance is perhaps best clarified by studying the careers of those who have not been thought to possess it. It is not compatible, for instance, with Disraeli's preparedness so rapidly to abandon protection after 1846, or with his willingness in the 1850s (imitated by Lord Randolph Churchill between 1880 and 1885) to use any expedient or political combination to get his party into power. Disraeli gained political prominence only by exploiting, not always scrupulously, an extraordinary political situation; Peelites did their utmost throughout the 1850s to prevent any refurbishment of his character. The centrist Goschen played a crucial role in destroying Lord Randolph Churchill, and centrists after 1922 were nourished by distaste for the political morality of the Lloyd George coalition and for Mosley's overweening conceit and ambition; the air of studied amorality which pervades Mosley's career, and which even his biographer seems occasionally to adopt,[25] would be inconceivable for the centrists under discussion.

Peel thought that Althorp's possession of integrity would

[24] S. Haseler, *Gaitskellites*, p. 44, cf. M. Oakeshott, *Rationalism in Politics and Other Essays* (1967 ed.), p. 49.

[25] G. Peele, review of Skidelsky's *Mosley*, in *Government and Opposition*, xi (1976), p. 121.

have enabled him merely to get up, take off his hat, and shake his head to satisfy the House of Commons that the arguments he rejected were fallacious.[26] Centrists of this type are not necessarily men of intellectual distinction, nor are they always men of great practical achievement; but they are men who at certain crises are looked to for a lead.[27] Integrity of the centrist kind is perhaps more easily cultivated by the aristocrat whose income does not depend on political success, but it is also found among many twentieth-century labour leaders. It differs completely from the fundamentalist's principled adherence to long-held doctrines or loyalties regardless of changing circumstances; 'nobody ever did anything very foolish except from some strong principle', said Melbourne.[28] It survives contact with practical problems and braves hostile audiences. Both Althorp and Hartington won respect through their scrupulous fairness in stating an opponent's case before trying to answer it; their speeches carried weight not from skill in composition or delivery, but from the character of the speaker.[29]

The centrist preoccupation with practical achievement can foster a certain anti-intellectualism in matters of policy— a distaste for the theoretical and the doctrinaire which unites Palmerston to Baldwin, MacDonald to Attlee, Gaitskell to Macmillan. Sir James Graham in 1855 was 'very much opposed to the discussion of abstract questions of extreme right', which he thought merely obstructed the workings of the British political system; 'more than half of the matters of state', he thought, 'as well as of society, are best adjusted by compromise and mutual forbearance'.[30] At the general election of 1922 Lord Robert Cecil rebuked Birkenhead for depreciating the intellect of Bonar Law's ministers by saying that England, if forced to choose between men of second-class brains and men of second-class character, would prefer the former. Bonar Law told the Party conference in December

---

[26] Sir D. Le Marchant, *Memoir of John Charles Viscount Althorp* (1876), p. 566, cf. p. 272.

[27] Cf. L. Iremonger, *Lord Aberdeen*, p. 204.

[28] Quot. in Lord D. Cecil, *Melbourne* (Reprint Society ed., 1955), p. 149.

[29] Le Marchant, *Althorp*, p. 566; B. Holland, *Hartington*, ii, pp. 415, 418; cf. i, pp. 66, 288, 292.

[30] J. T. Ward, *Sir James Graham* (1967), p. 312.

that although the Party might not at present enjoy a monopoly of first-class brains, his ministers were at least men of good judgement and of first-class loyalty,[31] and Baldwin during the 1920s persistently elevated English common sense above 'following at the tail 'of exploded Continental theorists'.[32] Nor was this pragmatic mood confined to Whigs and Conservatives; Gaitskell recalled it as the mood of Durbin's circle in the late 1930s,[33] and in the late 1950s himself repudiated a doctrinaire zeal for nationalization among Labour's fundamentalists. With trade-union help, Labour's revisionists carried forward the Fabian assault on Marxist intellectualism.

Mosley's rejoinder to this—that between the wars, 'all the dull people combined to get Lloyd George down'[34]—fails to recognize that political intelligence is a complex quality with several ingredients. The centrist's political skills can be formidable, his appreciation of character penetrating; his anti-intellectualism consists mainly of keeping intellectualism in its proper place. His need for discretion makes him seem duller than he really is; he must avoid frequent deliverances on his own political inclinations, for these might frustrate his political purposes. 'Judgement' rather than intellect is the quality he prizes. Skidelsky's *Oswald Mosley* tries to have things both ways by simultaneously endorsing Mosley's attacks on the inaction and incompetence of 'the old gang', yet confessing their complete triumph over Mosley in the one arena that mattered for his influence, the House of Commons.

Centrist anti-intellectualism combines with their governmental preoccupation to ensure that they seldom engage in trenchant general reflection, let alone in abstraction and political theory. Centrists are usually in positions of power, whereas memorable prose is the weapon of the powerless. 'A correct arrangement of a few prominent and leading facts is the best foundation for future measures', Peel declared in 1830;[35] his formidable cabinet memoranda left him little

---

[31] J. Ramsden, *Age of Balfour and Baldwin*, pp. 169, 171.

[32] S. Baldwin, *On England and Other Addresses* (1926), p. 154; cf. A. W. Baldwin, *My Father. The True Story* (1955), pp. 162, 163, 200, 208.

[33] E. F. M. Durbin, *Politics of Democratic Socialism*, p. 9.

[34] O. Mosley, *My Life*, p. 276.

[35] N. Gash, *Sir Robert Peel*, p. 717; cf. *Mr. Secretary Peel*, p. 226; W. Bagehot, *Works*, iii (1968), p. 256; R. Peel, *Memoirs*, ii, p. 99.

time or energy for competing with his antagonist Disraeli in producing works of wider range. Governmental experience accustoms the mind to reticence, gives limited scope for imagination, and perhaps eventually limits the imagination itself. Centrists' sometimes oppressive consciousness of responsibility curbs their epistolary freedom and reins in their spontaneity. Their autobiographies can at times (Halifax, Simon, Attlee, Morrison) be memorably uninformative and bland.

'The person who is preoccupied with trimming', Starzinger writes, 'is seldom an original or exciting theorist'—a final reason for historians' neglect of the centrist. Lord John Russell's intellectualism is unusual here, for the centrist is preoccupied as much with governmental strategy as with political ideas. Starzinger (using Huntington's terminology) claims that the 'middling' mind is 'positional' rather than 'inherent' in its ideas—that is, its ideas are not usually generated internally; its policy is primarily concerned with a strategic relationship to ideas generated elsewhere, usually by fundamentalists to right and to left.[36] Starzinger's analysis will not exactly fit the modern British situation. While close empirical knowledge of political institutions and their social context is integral to centrist achievement, imagination and originality were also required for those major centrist policy innovations—the nineteenth-century evolution of the civil service and police force, the twentieth century's liberal concept of empire and the Fabian–Keynesian 'middle way' between *laissez-faire* capitalism and Socialism. Yet the British centrist does to some extent operate on a plane somewhat different from the right–left policy continuum, and pays special attention to questions of strategy and tactics. Centrist abstraction seldom extends beyond the sort of political maxim that is stored away in Melbourne's commonplace-books or collected at the end of Gash's *Peel*—encapsulating the shrewd insight into human nature that is acquired in the course of conducting practical affairs. A distaste for abstraction also extends to other British institutions—to those centrists of the Victorian Church Bishop Wilberforce

---

[36] V. E. Starzinger, *Middlingness*, pp. 150–1; S. P. Huntington, 'Conservatism as an Ideology', *American Political Science Review*, June 1957, pp. 467–8.

and Archbishop Tait, for instance, neither of whom had much time for 'intellectualism' in religious belief.[37]

The weakness of centrist political theory has a root still deeper than this. Duverger argued some time ago that there is no 'centre tendency' in doctrine; 'the dream of the Centre is to achieve a synthesis of contradictory aspirations; but synthesis is a power only of the mind. Action involves choice and politics involve action.'[38] Tactical skill and shrewdness in practical matters the centrist may display, but his policies cannot possess the symmetry and even the internal coherence of those on right and left. The problem is accentuated by the two-party system, where those who cluster in the centre are usually drawn from divergent party traditions and have little opportunity to formulate an independent tradition of their own. It would be as difficult to unite Huskissonites and Whigs behind a general philosophical statement in the 1830s as to unite Whigs and Peelites in the 1850s, or Conservative and Liberal coalitionists in the 1920s. Lord John Russell might insist in 1852 that the title 'Whig' 'has the convenience of expressing in one syllable what Conservative Liberal expresses in seven'——but this did not make the label any more acceptable to his Peelite allies.[39] It is not just that the centre is intellectually fragmented; it is politically fragmented as well. The centrist operating within a pluralist society cannot select his legislative programme from a single fundamentalist tradition; a balance of pressures will determine his priorities when selecting from the programmes of right and left. Centrist policies have therefore been attacked from one direction as 'a rag-bag' which 'could stand for nothing positive. It would exploit grievances and fall apart when it sought to remedy them';[40] or from the other direction as being 'not related to any vision of society', but as

[37] A. R. Ashwell and R. G. Wilberforce, *Life of the Rt. Revd. Samuel Wilberforce. D.D.*, i (1880), p. 53; cf. R. T. Davidson and W. Benham, *Life of Archibald Campbell Tait. Archbishop of Canterbury* (3rd ed., 1891), i. pp. 275-6.

[38] M. Duverger, *Political Parties. Their Organisation and Activity in the Modern State* (Tr. B. and R. North, 1954), p. 215.

[39] J. B. Conacher, *Peelites*, p. 136, cf. p. 138 and W. S. Churchill, *Lord Randolph Churchill*, p. 376.

[40] Jenkins, *The Times*, 10 Mar. 1973, p. 4.

'simply the lowest common denominator obtained from a calculus of assumed electoral expediency'.[41]

Centrist and fundamentalist qualities are therefore complementary, and it is important for any democratic political system to secure an effective interaction between the two. In a memorable discussion, Alexis de Tocqueville regrets the lack of such interaction in France before 1789; discussing the *philosophes*, he points out that 'living as they did, quite out of touch with practical politics, they lacked the experience which might have tempered their enthusiasms. Thus they completely failed to perceive the very real obstacles in the way of even the most praiseworthy reforms.' He emphasizes also that 'political freedom is no less indispensable to the ruling classes to enable them to realise their perils than to the rank and file to enable them to safeguard their rights'.[42] But an interaction between centrists and fundamentalists is desirable for reasons other than political stability. Politics without fundamentalists would be insipid, and would fail to cater adequately for important ideas and sentiments. To take only the area of British foreign policy, A. J. P. Taylor's *The Trouble Makers* (1957) has shown how the fundamentalists in one generation often pioneer the orthodoxy of the next. Centrists lack many talents that are important in politics; sparkle, brilliance, originality, colour, and imagination are all qualities difficult to cultivate while coping with the pressing daily requirements of government. On the other hand, a political system dominated by fundamentalists would be unworkable. The two-party system in Britain has usually ensured a judicious mixture between the two.

Centrists make an essential contribution towards implementing policy through possessing scarce administrative skills. They profoundly influence the drafting and timing of legislation, and prepare public opinion for its reception. Their sensitivity to opinion ranges well beyond the bounds of their own party, and enables them profoundly to influence crucial matters of legislative priority and presentation. Policy

[41] Sir K. Joseph, *Middle Ground*, p. 21.
[42] A. de Tocqueville, *The Ancien Regime and the French Revolution* (Tr. S. Gilbert, Fontana paperback ed., 1966), pp. 162, 164.

in politics is not good or bad in some abstract way; it has no existence separately from its attendant circumstances, and of these the centrist is master. Without centrist political skills, political and social stability would be at risk, governmental achievement would be small, and the two-party system would become unworkable.

Nor is the centrist a mere midwife for delivering the policies conceived by others. True, he has not reversed the over-all leftward drift of British politics since the industrial revolution; but it would be wrong to see his role as merely slowing down this tendency. Sometimes he has accelerated it, sometimes he has helped to halt it, sometimes (in 1792, 1886, 1931, and 1951) he has even helped to send it into reverse. Major political transformations were effected in 1886 and 1931 when centrist politicians totally rejected the fundamentalism of the left, and in 1846 when they repudiated the fundamentalism of the right; in two of these three instances (1846 and 1931) it is doubtful whether the defeated fundamentalists possessed a viable policy at all. At other times it becomes accepted that the national interest has nothing to gain from a compromise solution in a particular area of policy, and the fundamentalist remedy (whether of right or left) is adopted in undiluted form.

It is easy in retrospect to gain the illusion that a simple set of policies is generated by fundamentalists on right or left and then gradually and ineluctably implemented. In reality, fundamentalists generate a wide range of policies, and centrists help to make a selection between them—eliminating some and postponing others until they can be enacted more safely. Not only have some general fundamentalist tendencies on right and left been frustrated in Britain—such as Fascism, militarism, anticlericalism, syndicalism, Communism, and coercive variants of imperialism—but also specific fundamentalist policies such as the capital levy, open diplomacy, disestablishment of the English Church, Black-and-Tan policies in Ireland, prohibition, annual parliaments, Home Rulers' coercion of Ulster, and tariff reform in its initial shape. Other fundamentalist policies—repatriation of coloured immigrants, abolition of the House of Lords, the restoration of hanging, unilateral nuclear disarmament, compulsory peacetime military service, nationalization without compensation and for reasons other than efficiency —have at least been postponed.

The purpose of historical investigation is not to constrict the range of political options open to any one generation, but to extend it. Historical situations never exactly recur, and if the British two-party system has successfully promoted political stability in the past, it will not necessarily do so in the future. And although the two-party system has in the past frustrated the emergence of a distinct and lasting centrist grouping, we may yet see the peculiar mix of circumstances necessary for its healthy· growth. If electoral reform is then secured, centrists may even avoid their predecessors' fate of eventual gravitation to one or other side of the political spectrum. For the historian, as for the politician, the future is unclear. Still, in the present-day climate of opinion, political choice is more likely to be broadened by stressing three things: the difficulty of getting a centre party launched within a simple-majority single-ballot electoral system, the difficulty of perpetuating its centrist flavour once launched, and its drawbacks (if perpetuated, with or without the aid of electoral reform) as a mechanism for upholding social stability and political continuity. Though the virtues of the British two-party system in these respects have long been obvious to those who run the British political system and have therefore been relatively secure, they have never been readily appreciated by the bystander; as they have now also come under attack from some of the professionals, they should now receive the attention they undoubtedly deserve.

VIII

The Rhetoric of Reform in Modern Britain: 1780 – 1918[1]

'It is what men think that determines how they act'; 'one person with a belief is a social power equal to ninety-nine who have only interests.'[2] John Stuart Mill's two assertions epitomize the vigorous Liberal individualism which inspired so many nineteenth-century reforming movements. Such primacy is seldom nowadays assigned to the political role of ideas and beliefs—as emerges clearly from two recent collections of essays on nineteenth-century pressure groups; though several of these campaigns were aimed at Westminster, the authors virtually ignore the parliamentary debates which resulted.[3] The emphasis nowadays often given to a movement's organizational structure and basis of support does of course increase understanding; but the study of rhetoric, language, and communication is worthwhile in its own right, if only because the political process needs to be seen as a whole, and not solely through the reformer's eyes. The discussion which follows will therefore assume that, at least for some historical purposes, it is worth taking Mill the rationalist and social scientist at his world, at two levels: by taking what is said in the reforming debates seriously, and by seeking regularities and interactions in their shape and scope. Evidence from at least five movements active between 1780 and 1918 will be drawn upon: the anti-slave-trade and anti-slavery movements; prohibitionism, launched in 1853; the women's suffrage campaign mounted in 1866; and the ancillary attack between 1869 and 1886 on the Contagious

---

[1] This chapter originated as an unpublished paper prepared for the conference on the history of anti-slavery at Bellagio, 10–15 July 1978; hence the special emphasis given to that topic in the over-all argument. Stylistic and other alterations of this paper, especially in its third section, have been incorporated here.

[2] J. S. Mill, *Representative Government*, pp. 183–4.

[3] J. T. Ward (ed.), *Popular Movements c.1830–1850* (1970); P. Hollis (ed.), *Pressure from Without in Early Victorian England* (1974).

Diseases [CD] Acts which regulated and lent implicit state approval to prostitution in garrison towns. But reference will also be made to the movements to restrict factory hours, Bulgarian atrocities, and animal cruelty, to the Anti-Corn-Law League, and to the campaigns for disestablishment and peace.

I

Several objections can be raised against such an approach. The first of these—that there are no close affinities between these movements—can be quickly dismissed. The attacks on the slave trade and on slavery merged into one another, attracting very much the same people, and even used similar arguments, because the planter somewhat imprudently defended slavery with arguments resembling those he had unsuccessfully employed earlier. The anti-slavery movement's influence on all later reforming campaigns was profound. The factory-hours movement originated with Oastler's letters to the *Leeds Mercury* on 'Slavery in Yorkshire', and in 1832 Sadler pinpointed the affinity between his opponents' arguments and those of the planters.[4] Subsequent reformers often likened the condition of their beneficiaries to that of the slaves before emancipation—partly to stimulate concern, and partly to goad the anti-slavery veterans into extending their range. This was a recurrent theme in Engels's *Condition of the Working Class*, for instance,[5] in J. S. Mill's writing on women, and in Josephine Butler's on prostitution; both Josephine Butler and Emmeline Pankhurst had family links with anti-slavery activity.[6] Libertarian ideals also lay behind the Anti-Corn-Law League, whose parliamentary persistence was the model for the United Kingdom Alliance. Even more important was inspiration and tactical precedent. When ill in 1875, Josephine Butler had a book on the anti-slavery campaign read out to her because she wanted to

---

[4] B. L. Hutchins and A. Harrison, *Factory Legislation* (3rd ed., 1926), pp. 44-6.

[5] F. Engels, *Working Class*, pp. 93, 208.

[6] E. M. Bell, *Josephine Butler*, pp. 18, 22-3; E. Pankhurst, *My Own Story* (1914), pp. 1-3.

hear 'how those people had to see the slaves suffering so long a time such evils while they were not strong enough yet to relieve them'.[7] There were also many personal links and attitudes held in common between the prohibitionist, anti-slavery, anti-Corn-Law, and feminist movements.[8]

These movements do of course differ in many respects. The compensation issue, of major importance in the anti-slavery and prohibitionist campaigns, could hardly arise with women's suffrage. Anti-slavery libertarianism reappears in Josephine Butler's crusade and women's suffrage, but prohibitionism can be seen as libertarian only in a very different sense. Furthermore social reform was largely non-governmental and non-party in flavour during these years, and so reformers came from very diverse backgrounds. The terms 'conservative' and 'reformer' when used here are not synonyms for 'Conservative' and 'Liberal', respectively, and reforming leaders could include an arch-Conservative like Shaftesbury or a radical like Cobden. Again, the lapse of time must be allowed for when comparing movements over so long a time-span; motives and conditions changed. Yet the usefulness of the over-all framework is actually enhanced if applicable to a wide range of movements, provided that its generalizations are not so broad as to dissolve into vacuity. It should clarify what is distinctive about any particular movement, and place in perspective the individual reformer, whose personality and career need to be seen in contexts supplementary to the biographical.

A second objector might see these reforming debates as in a sense irrelevant. The reforms have been won; why bother with historical backwaters? 'The same arguments . . . have been urged again and again in opposition to every measure of enfranchisement', said the feminist Jacob Bright in 1877, 'but, when public opinion became ripe for those measures . . . those arguments disappeared like vapour, and they who employed them had forgotten that they ever made use of

---

[7] City of London Polytechnic: Josephine Butler Papers, Box 1, Envelope 7D.

[8] United Kingdom Alliance, *23rd A.R., 1874–5*, pp. 120–1; Lawson, *H. C. Deb.*, 14 June 1876, c.1857; Ray Strachey, *'The Cause'. A Short History of the Women's Movement in Great Britain* (1928), p. 33; A. Rosen, *Rise Up Women!*, p. 8; Jacob Bright, *H. C. Deb.*, 30 Apr. 1873, c.1195.

them.'[9] For this reason, we possess good histories of the movements promoting Roman Catholic emancipation, free trade, and repeal of the CD Acts, but nothing comparable for their opponents. Yet the ease and inevitability of reform will be exaggerated if the focus rests only on reforming triumphs. The historian will not content himself merely with pinning medals on to the successful. Besides, at least one of these causes (prohibitionism) failed; the peace, disestablishment, and anti-CD Act movements never completely won over the public, and even the successful reforms disappointed their advocates in some ways. The arguments of the defeated and the outdated are valuable if only because they lead the historian towards those contrasts between past and present which are his speciality.

Marx and Freud would lead other objectors to see arguments merely as masks to conceal economic interest or psychological need. 'It was not by any change in the distribution of material interests', wrote J. S. Mill, 'but by the spread of moral convictions, that negro slavery has been put an end to in the British Empire and elsewhere';[10] few would now show his confidence in the primacy of the reformer's role. Instead we are seduced by Eric Williams's brilliantly simplistic erosion of abolitionist altruism in his *Capitalism and Slavery* or by Harold Laski's exhilaratingly misleading analysis of the women's suffrage debate, where he insists that reason makes no impact on public opinion 'until men are driven by the circumstances in which reason presents itself to pay attention to the causes that reason seeks to promote'. Yet by neglecting the parliamentary dimensions of a reform, analyses of this type are undeniably incomplete and in some ways unreal. The faith in slavery, says A. V. Dicey, 'was a delusion; but a delusion, however largely the result of self-interest, is still an intellectual error, and a different thing from callous selfishness. It is at any rate an opinion.'[11]

The psychological approach rightly stresses the underlying

---

[9] *H. C. Deb.*, 6 June 1877, c.1403.

[10] J. S. Mill, *Representative Government*, p. 184.

[11] H. Laski, *The Militant Temper in Politics. Fifth Suffragette Lecture, 18 November 1932* (London Museum, typescript Z 6061), p. 9; A. V. Dicey, *Law and Public Opinion*, p. 16.

personal needs catered for by reforming movements. Conservatives—particularly those with an academic turn of mind —tend to focus quite unreasonably on how skilfully a reforming argument is formulated rather than on the needs it struggles to express. 'Poor little Miniver!' says H. G. Wells, when discussing the suffragette leader in his *Ann Veronica*, '. . . because she states her case in a tangle, drags it through swamps of nonsense, it doesn't alter the fact that she is right.' Her gospel 'meant something, something different from its phrases, something elusive, and yet something that in spite of the superficial incoherence of its phrasing, was largely essentially true'.[12] The psychological approach brings out the complexity of human motivation, and emphasizes the limited sphere of reason in public argument, but it seldom has sufficient evidence at its disposal, and it can do little to explain why the reformer chooses this cause rather than that, or why he uses this argument rather than that; nor can it say much about his over-all political and economic situation. For these wider inquiries, his public statements have some value.

Then there is the objection founded on the worldly-wise recognition that politicians do not say what they think. They certainly do make code statements to one another, and by no means fully clarify their full range of motives in public. To analyse a reforming debate merely through the printed word in *Hansard* would be to ignore crucial matters such as who is speaking, in what tone, and on what occasion—even setting aside whether the report itself is accurate;[13] the earlier parliamentary debates are not even reported verbatim, and are sometimes tendentious. Yet this is only to say that the historian must display as much caution here as elsewhere. Besides, the objection would carry more weight if the aim was to rely on *Hansard* for the precise views of any one individual; here the aim is to detect over-all patterns in the shape and scope of reforming argument. Again, however

---

[12] H. G. Wells, *Ann Veronica* (George Newnes ed., n.d.), pp. 198, 204.

[13] e.g. Gladstone, *Autobiographical Memoranda 1832–1845* (ed. J. Brooke and M. Sorensen, 1972), p. 124; Hon. L. A. Tollemache, *Talks with Mr Gladstone*, p. 55; R. R. James, *Lord Randolph Churchill*, p. 243, n. 1; K. Rose, *Superior Person. A Portrait of Curzon and his Circle in Late Victorian England* (1969), p. 129; J. Ehrman, *The Younger Pitt* (1969), p. 53.

insincere politicians may be, the historian will be very interested in how they set about convincing their contemporaries. Their speeches are events in their own right, and employ only arguments with contemporary resonance; they should therefore illuminate contemporary situations and attitudes. 'Politicians rarely alter people's opinions', Enoch Powell has said: 'politicians articulate, crystallise, dramatise if you like, render intelligible and therefore render capable of being turned into action, legislative or administrative, something which is present already in people's minds'.[14]

The worldly-wise objection is often supplemented by saying that politicians' speeches cannot be important because they rarely influence opinion in parliament. True, party or personal loyalties often predetermine parliamentary divisions, though party discipline was relatively loose before the 1880s and was looser on social reform than in some other areas. But it would be regrettable if experienced men were regularly swayed by a single speech; parliamentary votes should perhaps normally express a politician's long experience and over-all cast of mind, rather than reflect a sudden impulse or conversion. Besides, a speech can articulate ideas which have already been brought privately to the attention of government, whose dispositions have been modified accordingly; the threat of a speech can often be as effective on policy as its actual delivery. Even in the debate, a speech can have influence without necessarily altering opinion; it can boost or undermine morale, for instance. In 1913 Lord Curzon could look back on many parliamentary occasions where speeches had influenced a vote 'in this sense, that a policy which was regarded with grave doubt or suspicion has been acclaimed, either with or without a division, owing to the adroit or powerful defence of a Minister; that a successful attack on a policy or a plan has led to its abandonment, sooner than face the risks of the division lobby; or even . . . that anticipated defeat has been converted into overwhelming victory'. On several occasions politicians do privately or publicly admit that a speech has influenced their vote. In the slave-trade debate of 1791, some MPs publicly admitted to

[14] *Guardian*, 22 Feb. 1971, p. 11.

changing their mind as a result of it, and we know that in 1867 admiration for the speech, or at least for the person, of J. S. Mill caused John Bright and Labouchere, among others, to support the women's suffrage which they later strongly opposed.[15]

Besides, a parliamentary speech often has other functions: it is an important way of influencing extra-parliamentary opinion. By repeatedly launching debates on women's suffrage, said Jacob Bright in 1873, 'we have taken the best means in our power to instruct the people upon a great public question. The substance of this debate will be carefully reported in the newspapers . . . and therefore we shall secure that, for at least one day in the year there will be a general discussion on a question so deeply affecting the interests and privileges of a large portion of Her Majesty's subjects.'[16] The fate of the Corn Laws was profoundly influenced by parliamentary debates, a fact which helped determine the strategy of several later reforming movements.

But this provokes a rather different objection: that a reforming movement's over-all rhetorical flavour is not fully conveyed by speeches in parliament, which contrast markedly with speeches addressed to enthusiastic extra-parliamentary gatherings. The prudent reforming leader cultivates a judicious moderation in parliament, but allows himself more vigour in the public meeting. In campaigning for franchise reform in 1867, said one periodical, John Bright's position was 'undeniably a difficult one; for he is expected to talk moderation in one place and violence in another, and yet preserve some show of consistency'.[17] If the *Hansard* debates could be compared with press reports of British anti-slavery meetings, or of planter meetings and opinion in Jamaica, major contrasts in mood would no doubt emerge. The sheer status of parliament restrained its speakers, whose comments on slavery bore in mind the twin necessities of discouraging a slave insurrection and preventing

---

[15] Earl Curzon of Kedleston, *Modern Parliamentary Eloquence. Rede Lecture, Cambridge, 1913* (1913), p. 22; *H. C. Deb.*, 19 Apr. 1791, c.358.
[16] *H. C. Deb.*, 30 Apr. 1873, c.1196; cf. John Bright in the local option debate, *H. C. Deb.*, 14 June 1881, c.556; Samuel Smith, *My Life-Work*, p. 477.
[17] [H. W. Cole], 'The Four Reform Orators', *Quarterly Review*, Apr. 1867, p. 569.

the planters from losing faith in British government and its aspirations. Likewise prohibitionist attacks on the brewer and publican were far less inhibited outside parliament than inside. Still, the parliamentary debate was important in itself, and was seen as such by the reformers, whose efforts were oriented towards it, and so long as its limitations as a guide to reforming mood and opinion are borne in mind, the inquiry can continue.

Four broad dimensions of the parliamentary debate can be detected in relation to the five reforming movements under discussion—dimensions which logically, and to some extent also actually, make their appearance during the run-up to legislation in the following order. There is first the matter of principle to be debated, the view that is taken of human personality and its potential; when the old principle is challenged by the new, there follows the process of inquiry; when the old principle has been discredited, the opposition attempt diversions from the main line of argument, and the reformers respond with countermoves; lastly there is the attempt through legislation to apply the newly evolved principle to a particular political and social situation.

II

An ideal of the human personality and its potential lies behind all five movements, and owes much to the long-standing British tradition of upholding civil liberties against the executive. This ideal was championed after the 1780s by a series of movements under the leadership of the British middle classes, defined not in any narrowly economic sense but simply as those groupings located between the two extremes of the social spectrum. The individual human being, whether black or white, male or female, young or old, rich or poor, moral or immoral, is seen as either actually or potentially capable of rationality, if freed to make choices for himself. If unconstrained by pressures from convention or tradition, from the state or from other human beings, he will grow morally and educationally. Even the lunatic and the animal will be tamed if approached in the right way.

These reformers detested the extreme subordination

entailed by slavery, but disliked patronizing feudal relationships almost as much. Few reformers were as uncompromisingly and openly hostile to aristocracy as Josephine Butler,[18] but all sought to supplant traditional relationships entailing deference and superstition by instrumental and contractual relationships entailing rational calculation. Middle-class people did the real work in all these movements, though aristocratic sympathizers were welcome as figure-heads; the House of Lords constituted a major legislative obstacle in every case. In presiding over such movements Shaftesbury hoped to validate traditional aristocratic relationships, but this aim—even in the factory movement—was probably not widely shared among the rank and file. As for the Anti-Corn-Law League, Cobden privately told Villiers in 1841 that 'henceforth we will grapple with the religious feelings of the people. Their veneration for God shall be our leverage to upset their reverence for the aristocracy.'[19] The temperance and feminist movements worked for an opportunity society where people find their own level in a free market;. if this entails for some a humble destination, at least their self-respect will not be insulted by any formal exclusion from political influence or social respectability.

Humane principles had become so powerful by the late eighteenth century that they went uncontested in parliamentary debates. Nobody at Westminster publicly denied the basic humanity of the slave, whatever might have been said privately there or in the West Indies. The public argument was simply on whether it was at present practicable to alter his condition and (in the later stages) whether this could be done compatibly with humanity to the planters. The planters' parliamentary spokesmen quite often stressed the uncivilized state of African society, but claimed that the slave trade benefited the African by removing him from it. Anti-slavery spokesmen replied that the slave trade had itself produced the barbarism of Africa, and that interior districts unaffected by the trade were peaceable kingdoms. In 1792 Pitt argued that even if it were conceded that Africa

---

[18] See e.g. *C.D. Acts Commission, Parl. Papers*, 1871 (C.408), XIX, Q.12932.

[19] BL Add. MS 43662 (Cobden Papers) f. 27; Cobden to C. P. Villiers, 'Sunday', n.d. [endorsed 6 June 1841].

was at present uncivilized, so also had Britain once been.[20] The same vigorous assertion of human equality was made by Whitbread in 1792 ('Had not Africans organs, dimensions, senses, affections, passions?') as by Earl Russell when, like Whitbread, he quoted Shakespeare in the House of Lords debate of 1917 on women's suffrage ('If you prick us, do we not bleed? if you tickle us, do we not laugh?').[21] All these reformers were collaborating to broaden out the concept of citizenship; 'grant that a woman who trades in her person is the meanest of citizens', the opponents of the CD Acts protested in 1871, 'yet she does not cease to be a citizen, much less to be a woman'.[22]

In 1792 Wilberforce took pleasure in the fact that the planters 'had been beat out of all chance of defending the trade itself, or the abuses of it'. The promoters of the trade, said Fox in the debate of 1797, 'finding they could not defend it upon its own principle, hypocritically canted against the principle, but still continued the practice'.[23] Likewise in the run-up to 1833, the planters' spokesmen argued only about the methods and timing of emancipation. Claiming humane purposes for their trade, they argued that the slaves would suffer by its abrupt ending, and pleaded for humanity also to the planters themselves. Here—as with factory hours, women's suffrage, state-regulated prostitution, and prohibition—the two sides competed for the humane label, and the reformers were accused of merely complicating an agreed pursuit of humanitarian objectives. Assuming that there must be a remedy for every evil, the reformer (wrote Lord Salisbury) makes two hardships for the purpose of curing one.[24] In parliamentary debates on prohibition, the drink interest never denied the need to curb drunkenness, but claimed that the supposed cure for it could succeed only through perpetrating inhumanities of a worse kind. As for the campaign over state-regulated prostitution, it became

---

[20] Pitt, *H. C. Deb.*, 2 Apr. 1792, c.1155; Wilberforce, ibid., c.1072.

[21] Whitbread, *H. C. Deb.*, 2 Apr. 1792, c.1104; *H. L. Deb.*, 17 Dec. 1917, c.216 (Russell).

[22] *CD Acts Commission, Parl. Papers*, 1871 (C.408), XIX, appx. D, p. 835.

[23] Wilberforce, *H. C. Deb.*, 2 Apr. 1792, c.1058; cf. Pitt, ibid., c.1134; Fox, *H. C. Deb.*, 15 May 1797, c.575.

[24] Lady G. Cecil, *Salisbury*, ii (1921), p. 38.

a contest between those whose humanity led them to invoke state power against disease, and those whose humanity led them to repudiate the consequent assaults on the liberties and equal status of women.

The planters' defensive stance is the more remarkable because parliamentary attacks on slavery were so vigorous— often citing peculiarly shocking instances of brutality, and even verging on that radical tendency described by Coleridge (in his analysis of radical rhetoric in 1817) as 'the display of defects without the accompanying advantages, or vice versa'.[25] Yet the planters made no attempt to adduce counter-examples of benevolent master/slave relationships, or to conduct a generalized defence of slavery as an institution. There is a contrast here with women's suffrage; J. S. Mill made much of wife-beating in his *Subjection of Women*, and the anti-suffragist, like the parliamentary planter, had to repudiate such brutalities as untypical. But unlike the planter, the anti-suffragist vindicated the protective relationship under attack, which he said reflected nothing more sinister than a differentiation of social role, justifiable in terms of woman's personal qualities. Her relatively emotional but sympathetic temperament and her illogical but imaginative intellect allegedly equipped her for family and philanthropic as opposed to political, professional, and war-making roles. The planters produced no such investigation of the African's personal qualities. One further contrast: whereas the anti-suffragist, a conservative, assigned superiority to the allegedly deprived group, enlarging upon woman's idealism and moral sensibility, it was the anti-slave-trade spokesman, a reformer, who idealized the African, though in 1804 Wilberforce explicitly dissociated himself from such notions.[26]

The opponents of slavery were more ready to compromise than later reforming movements, which argued that the welfare of women, drunkards, or prostitutes required immediate women's suffrage, prohibition, or CD Act repeal; all but the most radical abolitionists publicly conceded the need to move slowly. They were much preoccupied with

[25] R. J. White (ed.), *Political Tracts of Wordsworth, Coleridge and Shelley* (Cambridge, 1953), p. 71.
[26] *H. C. Deb.*, 30 May 1804, c.444.

precisely how to move from the evils of the old world into the blessings of the new—through apprenticeship and educational schemes, religious instruction and the like. They and the planters' parliamentary spokesmen remained vague, however, on how long the educational process must be, and how readiness for freedom could be assessed. By contrast, the more radical reformer here, as in campaigns to extend the franchise, thought women, working men, or slaves could mature only through actually enjoying liberty. This argument was heard rather more often during women's suffrage debates (perhaps partly because in the early suffragist campaign only a limited, property-based franchise was at issue); 'the way to teach people politics', said the prohibitionist Sir Wilfrid Lawson, in the women's suffrage debate of 1897, 'was to let them take part in politics, else it was to act on the principle of the old lady who would not allow her son to go into the water until he had learned to swim'.[27]

Slaves, it was argued, must first acquire the taste for material accumulation which alone could deter them from lying in the sun once immediate wants had been supplied; only then could their emancipation be made complete. 'The bitterest reproach that can be uttered against the system of slavery', said Buxton in 1823, is that 'it debases the man . . . it enfeebles his powers.' Genetic inferiority was not of course being alleged here, but the degrading impact of environment. 'We make the man worthless', said Buxton, 'and, because he is worthless, we retain him as a slave.' Suffragists also admitted that the relationship they attacked distorted human personality, yet this did not lead them publicly to espouse gradualism; 'the enervating habits we have imposed on her have impaired her physical powers', said the enthusiastic radical feminist Joseph Cowen in 1884, 'and then we cite to her detriment the weakness which our customs have created'.[28] But the contrast may stem from nothing more than the fact that the anti-slavery movement

[27] Lawson, *H. C. Deb.*, 3 Feb. 1897, c.1212; cf. Buckingham, *H. C. Deb.*, 7 June 1833, c.475.
[28] Buxton, *H. C. Deb.*, 15 May 1823, c.271, cf. *H. C. Deb.*, 6 Mar 1828, c.1044, Canning *H. C. Deb.*, 16 Mar. 1824, c. 1103, Cowen, *H. C. Deb.*, 12 June 1884, c.165.

was closer to its goal than the suffragists, who in 1884 were still at the stage of seeking to shift opinion by voicing an uncompromising demand. As for the champions of the prostitute and the drunkard, they admitted the moral decline but claimed that the remedy must be applied at once—not simply because the evil was serious, but because they thought the evil was directly stimulated by legislation which failed to embody their principle.

A powerful driving-force behind this ideal of human equality and dignity—originating as it did in the fourfold influences of evangelical theology, literary sensibility, industrial entrepreneurship, and Enlightenment rationalism—was the liberal's faith in progress through liberty and participation. 'The proper sphere for all human beings is the largest and the loftiest which they are able to attain', said Cowen in the women's suffrage debate of 1884: 'and this can only be ascertained by complete liberty of choice'.[29] Emancipate blacks, women, and working men from the shackles of slavery, tradition, superstition, and drink, it was argued, and who could set a limit to their attainments? The very process of agitating helped to emancipate, by stirring up stagnant communities and encrusted habits of mind. Nineteenth-century liberalism was a bold and exhilarating experiment, powered by dynamic movements in religion, politics, and the economy. The attack on the slave trade aimed, among other things (as Henry Thornton put it in 1792) 'to vindicate the honour of commerce, and rescue it from the disgraceful imputation, that it had, or could have, any thing in common with the slave trade, which was a scandalous traffic in human flesh'.[30] The label 'traffic' was useful, both here and in relation to the sale of drink, to distinguish illegitimate from legitimate trading; both crusades wanted moral boundaries set here to the complete freedom of trade which they favoured elsewhere.[31] If only a healthy trade could be established, then civilization—through abolishing slavery, the Corn Laws, religious discrimination, ignorance, drunkenness, and the

    [29] Cowen, *H. C. Deb.*, 12 June 1884, c.163; cf. Mill, *H. C. Deb.*, 20 May 1867, c.821.   [30] *H. C. Deb.*, 2 Apr. 1792, c.1088.
    [31] Cf. T. Clarkson, *Slave Trade*, p. 613; Ayrton, *H. C. Deb.*, 7 May 1860, c.785; Lawson, *H. C. Deb.*, 14 June 1876, c.1866.

ascription of social and political roles—would rapidly spread throughout the globe. It was hardly a cause to feel moderate about; indeed, in the slave-trade debate of 1792, Fox admitted that 'he neither felt nor wished to feel any thing like moderation upon this subject'.[32]

Burke might dismiss a spirit of innovation as 'generally the result of a selfish temper and confined views'[33] but the reformers saw their efforts as decidedly broad and altruistic —defending deprived groups not only in their own society but in other societies, not only for their own time but for posterity. Tom Paine distinguished between the English people, with their arts and manufactures, who were looking towards the future—and their governments, who looked only towards mere precedent and the past. 'As for novelty', said J. S. Mill in the women's suffrage debate of 1867, 'we live in a world of novelties; the despotism of custom is on the wane.'[34] Except for Oastler in the factory·movement, these reformers displayed few of the modern radical's doubts about the future. Like Wilfrid Lawson moving his local option resolution in 1879, they thought time was on their side.[35] Inventions for them bring, not disruption of established habits and pollution of the environment, but liberty, affluence, and the avoidance of pain; railways, the penny post, and mechanization of trades involving animals seemed harbingers of the new society.[36] The thought of posterity brought courage when resisting heavy odds. When the going was difficult in her suffrage work, Dora Montefiore always bore her children's welfare in mind: 'I felt I was working, not for the present, but for the future, when he and she, and those of their generation would be the inheritors of a better world.'[37] Such breathless enthusiasm was greeted by conservatives with scepticism, and with the belief that well-intentioned but hasty reforms can do more harm than good; the new society therefore arrived rather more slowly than the reformers hoped.

[32] *H. C. Deb.*, 2 Apr. 1792, c.1114.
[33] E. Burke, *French Revolution*, p. 119.
[34] Mill, *H. C. Deb.*, 20 May 1867, c.819; T. Paine, *Rights of Man*, p. 219.
[35] *H. C. Deb.*, 11 Mar. 1879, c.651.   [36] See pp. 229–30.
[37] D. Montefiore, *From a Victorian to a Modern* (1927), p. 197.

The reformer gained optimism and energy from his belief that relatively straightforward issues of principle were involved; the advantage did not in those days seem to lie with experts and administrators. The reformer's intense consciousness of personal responsibility reflected the widespread conviction that the ordinary citizen can, by taking pains, transform the world; it was a philanthropic and reforming attitude that mirrored the thrusting entrepreneurship which was then producing such wonders in commerce and industry. Furthermore, government was at that time only slowly assuming responsibility for introducing legislative reforms; there was still plenty of scope for the private MP. Wide differentials in wealth and a scarcity of government agencies also gave many openings to the initiative of the private citizen. Like one of their twentieth-century descendants, Eleanor Rathbone, these reformers were motivated by 'a stubborn Victorian belief in the reality of individual responsibility and the efficacy of individual attack'.[38]

III

The next stage in the reforming sequence—preliminary inquiry into the evil—offered infinite excuses for delay. Reformers might have been expected to welcome every opportunity for vindicating their cause through outside inquiry, for this could easily outweigh the risk of giving the conservative another opportunity for a diversionary move. Yet they were surprisingly impatient with empirical inquiry, even anti-empirical, in several dimensions: in initial motivation, in the unimportance for them of direct personal observation, in their equivocal attitude to collecting favourable factual information, and in their over-all approach to the particular political situation they faced. Each of these dimensions deserves exploration.

Information about the evil under attack does of course help to launch the reformer on his crusade. Noteworthy are his distress, his dreamings at night, his illness, even his

---

[38] M. Stocks, *Eleanor Rathbone. A Biography* (1949), p. 315, cf. p. 327; see also F. Parkin, *Middle Class Radicalism. The Social Bases of the British Campaign for Nuclear Disarmament* (Manchester, 1968), pp. 20-1.

obsession with the evil he is attacking. Of his lunacy legislation during June 1845 Shaftesbury complained, 'I dream every night, and pass, in my visions, through every clause, and confuse the whole in one great mass.' About to throw himself fully into agitating against Bulgarian atrocities, W. T. Stead says, 'I had a terrible afternoon. It was like a Divine possession that shook me almost to pieces, wrung me and left me shuddering.'[39] The oppressed and mutilated bodies were thought to contain immortal souls: 'to one class of persons these women appear like devils', said Josephine Butler of prostitutes in 1871, but 'to another class they are their true selves; the image of God may be marred, but it never is wholly blotted out'.[40]

None the less empirical inquiry was only one of several factors launching the reformer on his crusade. Their day-to-day experience of living was enough for some. Victorian urban Lancashire seemed squalid enough for the crusade against drunkenness to seem urgent, nor did Mid-Victorian feminists need much formal instruction on the disabilities of women. Reforming zeal rarely originates in the study and the library, and the more closely the reformer was brought into contact with his problem, the more he felt that indignation was a mood more suitable than inquiry. The cause, though always important for its own sake, sometimes seems to acquire a higher purpose for the reformer which could in theory be as readily attained by reforming movements of any kind. Chance is largely the explanation why one cause is preferred at any particular time, and once one cause has been satisfactorily dealt with the reformer moves on to another.

The reformers were anti-empirical in a second sense. Rare indeed was the opponent of slavery who actually visited slave territories. It was dangerous in the 1780s even for an inhabitant of Bristol to give evidence against slavery, let alone for abolitionists to go further afield. But lack of

---

[39] E. Hodder, *Shaftesbury*, ii, p. 112; cf. p. 190; R. T. Shannon, *Bulgarian Atrocities Agitation*, p. 71; see also R. I. and S. Wilberforce, *William Wilberforce*, iii, pp. 213, 215; C. Buxton, *Fowell Buxton*, pp. 191–2; Livesey, in W. Logan, *The Early Heroes of the Temperance Reformation* (Glasgow, 1873), pp. 94–5; Dunlop, in *Weekly Record of the Temperance Movement*, 22 Mar. 1862, p. 98.

[40] *C.D. Acts Commission, Parl. Papers*, 1871 (C.408), XIX, Q.12943.

courage is not the explanation; more relevant is the fact that the reformer's mind was usually made up, and did not require reinforcing by personal investigation, nor were his perceptions so blunt as to require visual stimulus. Temperance reformers sought even to insulate themselves from the evil under attack. They knew that drunkenness occurred in pubs and slum areas but wanted to keep it at a distance, and huddled in temperance halls and teetotal communities to uphold a higher standard of life. When it comes to prohibition, there is even an inverse correlation between the areas ready to enact the reform (largely rural in nature), and the areas where the problem was most serious (largely urban)—one of several reasons why prohibition eventually seemed defective as a panacea.[41] The leaders of Mid-Victorian feminism were middle-class, educated, and often unmarried women who were not primarily preoccupied with the overburdened working-class housewife, or with her twin burdens of poverty and excessive child-bearing. She plays her part in Victorian feminist rhetoric, of course, but she had little to gain in the short term from the reforms the pioneer feminists took up: work, education, and personal security for unmarried or widowed middle-class women.

Josephine Butler's movement seems at first sight an exception, if only because she personally reclaimed prostitutes. Yet she too kept her distance from the garrison towns which the CD Acts sought to benefit. Osborne Morgan, leading off for the Acts' defenders in 1883, enlarged upon the repealers' ignorance of the districts where the Acts applied, though his arguments did not prevail with the House. 'Of the operation of the Acts', Josephine told the 1871 royal commission, 'I neither can nor will speak, and I must decline to do so because I have no interest in the operation of the Acts. It is nothing to me whether they operate well or ill, but I will tell you what you wish to know as to my view of the principle of the Acts.'[42] She thought a person ignorant of the areas affected was as good a judge of a wrong principle as anyone else, saying that

[41] B. Harrison, *Drink and the Victorians*, p. 377.

[42] *CD Acts Commission, Parl. Papers*, 1871 (C.408), XIX, Q.12863; cf. Morgan, *H. C. Deb.*, 20 Apr. 1883, c.797; O'Shaughnessy, c.818.

'negro slavery was abolished in our British possessions by a body of persons in England who had never seen a negro slave'.[43]

The reformer shows himself anti-empirical also in his tone and mood when publicly presenting his case. Wilberforce often employed public arguments which had not influenced his own outlook; in his parliamentary speech of 1789 he presented an abundance of empirical information on the slave trade, as did Cobden on the impact of the Corn Laws in the 1840s. Wilberforce even carefully documented his belief that slavery held back both the population and the prosperity of the West Indies. Yet one suspects that such documentation is, for him personally at least, rather beside the point, and that the recitation of it goes somewhat against the grain. Still more was this so for some of the less politically minded rank and file in his and other reforming movements. In the debate of 1883 which got the CD Acts suspended, James Stansfeld, parliamentary leader of the attack on the Acts, regretted that he had been 'obliged to speak largely and mainly of hygiene' and went on, 'I revolt against the task . . . What I have done I have done for conviction and for duty's sake.' Like Wilberforce, Stansfeld would stoop to factual discussion in the hope of winning over opponents, for he was a practical reformer; but in the debate of 1886 which secured the Acts' abolition, he abandoned the hygienic argument altogether 'because hon. Members had come to their own conclusion upon the matter on different and higher grounds'.[44]

The reformers were anti-empirical in a fourth respect: they disliked adjusting their arguments to the practical political needs of the day. 'Policy . . . Sir, is not my principle', Wilberforce told parliament in 1789, 'and I am not ashamed to say it.' In the debate of 1791, he could not restrain himself from wondering 'whether it was not almost an act of unbecoming condescension to stoop to discuss the question in the view of commercial interest'.[45] His objection to slavery was absolute, and arguments founded on expediency were for

[43] SCHC CD Acts, *Parl. Papers*, 1882 (340), IX, QQ.5431–2.
[44] *H. C. Deb.*, 20 Apr. 1883, c.772; *H. C. Deb.*, 16 Mar. 1886, c.983.
[45] *H. C. Deb.*, 12 May 1789, c.62; 18 Apr. 1791, c.277.

him irrelevant. The reformer fled into principle and emotion partly from repugnance at the earthbound approach adopted by his opponents; Whitbread in 1807 thought that the slave trade 'had been made almost intirely [*sic*] a matter of cold calculations of profit and loss between English money and African blood'.[46] The 'breeches pocket' arguments (as fastidious opponents contemptuously called them) which Chadwick and Cobden regularly used in the 1840s reflect more on their audience and on the reformers' shrewdness in manipulating it, than on their own motives.

The role of empirical inquiry in accelerating reform is now so central, the process of its collection through government agencies so continuous—that the reasons for this fourth dimension of reforming anti-empiricism deserve more extended discussion. It was partly a matter of the reformer's lack of time and tranquillity. Eulogy and haste, short-term pressures and bitter disputes—these tended to fill the horizon of all but the most philosophical among them. Still more was this so in militant organizations like Mrs Pankhurst's. 'Facts and figures, serious investigation, considerations of principle and consistency', Mrs Billington-Greig complained in 1911, 'these are all foreign to the atmosphere of hurry. The future law-maker would be the better for a period of calm.'[47] The politician's working conditions were not dissimilar, but he derived balance and proportion from the fact that he was beset by a multitude of miscellaneous questions pressing for settlement.

Furthermore, on venturing into the world of politics, the reformer entered an arena where (as Darwin often complained) the scientific outlook was not much in evidence. Peel's oratory was only beginning to alter this mood in the 1840s, and Shaftesbury grumbled in his diary in 1842 at Peel's 'perpetual talk of "imports and exports" (his mind and heart never entertain higher projects in the responsibilities of Government)'.[48] Slavery debates never adduced physiological or anthropometric evidence on the qualities of the African.

---

[46] *H. C. Deb.*, 23 Feb. 1807, c.1052.
[47] T. Billington-Greig, *The Militant Suffrage Movement. Emancipation in a Hurry* (n.d.), p. 173; see also pp. 242-3.
[48] Quot. in E. Hodder, *Shaftesbury*, i, p. 434, cp. p. 408.

Temperance debates were never informed by research into the social and medical role of drink and of publicans in slum areas; the prohibitionist's remedy for drunkenness sprang fully armed from the conscience. Women's suffrage debates often enlarged upon women's characteristics, but in a most impressionistic and anecdotal manner; there is not a hint of that attention to brain size and weight which aroused discussion in the equivalent debates of South Australia. British feminists felt no need to engage in systematic inquiry; they were grappling with disabilities that seemed self-evident.

But even if a firmly empirical and scientific mode of argument had been common at Westminster, it would hardly have suited those who were pioneering new perceptions of the world. Whatever rhetorical styles might become appropriate later, a new sensitivity had first to be created by shock tactics. The reformers therefore took the risk of emotionalism, sentimentality, and exaggeration; nor was this a serious risk in a society so much more publicly emotional than our own. Emotionalism was not of course universally acceptable. 'If you want to drive John Bull mad', said Fitzjames Stephen of the Bulgarian atrocities agitation, 'the plan is to tickle (rather delicately—yet not too delicately) his prurience with good circumstantial accounts of "insults worse than death" inflicted on women.'[49] But the reformer needed to adapt his argument to his audience, and the general public was unlikely to be roused by the detailed and systematic inquiry that would impress a government. Wilberforce in 1789 therefore tried to get his fellow MPs to imagine themselves into the situation of a slave being transported across the Atlantic, just as M. T. Sadler in the 1830s tried to make them feel what it was actually like to be a factory child. 'I often think, when fatigued, how much less my weariness must be than that of the wretched factory women', wrote Shaftesbury in 1844.[50] Likewise the opponents of animal cruelty in the 1840s invited readers to imagine the agonies they would endure if placed in the animal's situation.

[49] R. T. Shannon, *Bulgarian Atrocities Agitation*, p. 66.
[50] E. Hodder, *Shaftesbury*, ii, p. 40, cf. E. Halévy, *Victorian Years 1841-1895* (Tr. E. I. Watkin, Benn paperback ed., 1961), p. 104; Wilberforce, *H. C. Deb.*, 12 May 1789, c.45; Kydd, *Factory Movement*, i, p. 172.

Reinforcing this note of emotion was the fact that many of the reformers were—as women, nonconformists, respectable working men, or radical members of the middle class—largely excluded from exercising political power at the national level where a male-dominated and predominantly Anglican and aristocratic political system seemed actually to be promoting immorality. The reformers lacked familiarity with the compromises involved in government, yet were unable to obtain legislative changes that would relieve them of their correspondingly heavy load of guilt. Hence the gnawing anguish, the strong language, and the strange tactics they sometimes adopted. 'My mind was confined to one gloomy and heart-breaking subject for months', wrote Clarkson. 'It had no respite, and my health began now materially to suffer.' Even the Anglican and aristocratic Shaftesbury felt intensely frustrated by his powerlessness to redress social evils, when briefly out of parliament in 1846-7.[51] If the state either will not intervene against the evil, or cannot be trusted to do so in the proper way, only two courses remain for the reformer: the personal protest which evades complicity through abstinence (from slave-grown sugar, from drink, from meat, from political activity, or office-holding), or the campaign for national self-exculpation through prohibitory measures which will somehow avoid increasing the power of the untrustworthy politicians who run the state machine. Local and national bureaucracy, nowadays central to social-reform processes, were therefore either bypassed altogether, or employed in a way which did little to foster empirical inquiry.

Abstinence was particularly welcome as an outlet. 'The ladies who now heard him', said Mr Sykes, MP, at the annual anti-slavery meeting of 1825, 'would hardly believe him when he told them that for every cup of tea they sweetened, they had to pay a premium on Slavery.'[52] Abstinence, voluntary or compulsory, lay at the heart of the temperance movement, and was also central to the outlook of Josephine Butler's movement, which argued that vice would be encouraged if the

[51] T. Clarkson, *Slave Trade*, p. 333, cf. E. Hodder, *Shaftesbury*, ii, p. 168; Kydd, *Factory Movement*, i, pp. 233-4.
[52] *Anti-Slavery Monthly Reporter*, 30 June 1825, p. 6.

state tried to protect the individual against the ill health which resulted from it; venereal disease would decline with the spread of chastity.[53] By contrast, the CD Acts seemed to legitimize the prostitute's trade, and to assume its permanence; as George Russell pointed out in 1883, the Acts 'all but close the paths of regeneration against these women. We efface the divine stamp upon them; we stamp them with the signet of the State, which marks them as the common prey of animal desire.'[54] Whereas the regulationists were prepared to sacrifice individual liberty to the public good, Josephine Butler's crusaders were eager to give full play to the individual moral decision, and were horrified at the prospect of police, doctors, and bureaucrats combining against morality and popular rights. Here, as elsewhere, abstinence required no state interference or inspection, and so did nothing to extend the collection of systematic information on the problem in question.

The same could be said of the second strategy for evading complicity—national self-exculpation, for this involved no more than a reluctant half-entry into politics. It produced a variant of state intervention which carried into the very process of legislation much of that shrinking from complicity, that evasion of responsibility, that unconcern with practical considerations of enforcement, which might be anticipated from politically inexperienced groups.[55] The reformer often expressed alarm, in the process of reform, at the churches' lack of impact. Collaborating across denominational boundaries, he subordinated liturgical and theological considerations to his awareness of society's pressing problems,[56] and so accelerated the nineteenth century's transfer of concern from a heavenly to an earthly Utopia. He thereby became a conscious pioneer of ecumenicalism, an unconscious pathbreaker for secularization.

His variant of state intervention was of a peculiar type. His

[53] Cf. William Shaen, in *Parl. Papers*, 1881 (351), VIII, Q.7172.

[54] *H. C. Deb.*, 20 Apr. 1883, c.820.

[55] For further discussion on this point, see my 'State Intervention and Moral Reform in Nineteenth-Century England', in P. Hollis (ed.), *Pressure from Without*, pp. 310–15.

[56] See e.g. Josephine Butler, *The Dawn*, Mar. 1893, pp. 9–10; cf. F. Parkin, *Middle Class Radicalism*, pp. 63–4.

indignant repudiation of Liberal individualism did not reflect enthusiasm for bureaucratized state welfare, but conviction that the state must play some role in elevating morality.[57] He wanted legislation which took the form of a secularized Decalogue, and saw law primarily as 'the most powerful national schoolmaster'. Like A. V. Dicey he disliked the bureaucratization associated with public welfare but acknowledged the educational impact of law.[58] Moral reformers were fond of quoting Mr Gladstone's dictum that 'Government ought to make it easy to do right and difficult to do wrong.'[59] For them, law must embody correct moral principles, and must at all costs avoid condoning slavery, drunkenness, or adultery through descending from its high estate to regulating or licensing these evils. Nor did they expect the state to punish the sinner: the drunkard, the prostitute, and her client. They pitied such people as victims of those who traded in vice—of the retailer and manufacturer of drink, and the brothelkeeper.

But moral reformers diverged on how far the state might go in its promotion of morality; should it legislate to ensure that the individual made the correct choice (thus inhibiting his moral self-development) or should it content itself with creating a climate within which the individual would voluntarily make the correct choice? T. H. Green and many 'constructive' Late-Victorian Liberals favoured local prohibition of drink sales because they took the first of these views, and the United Kingdom Alliance did its best to advertise his *Liberal Legislation and Freedom of Contract*.[60] But a Whig like Bishop Magee favoured the second view, arguing that 'it would be better that England should be free than that England should be compulsorily sober. I would distinctly

---

[57] e.g. Pope, in *Alliance News*, 28 Oct. 1865, p. 337; Josephine Butler in *The Shield*, 3 Dec. 1870, p. 316.

[58] William Shaen, *Suggestions on the Limits of Legitimate Legislation on the Subject of Prostitution* (1877), p. 7; see also A. V. Dicey, *Law and Public Opinion*, pp. 42-3. See also Mrs Butler, in *The Shield*, 29 June 1872, p. 990.

[59] Quot. in W. Hoyle, *Our National Resources and How They Are Wasted* (cheap ed., 1871), p. 110, cf. W. Ellison, in *CD Acts Commission, Parl. Papers*, 1871 (C.408), XIX, Q.20275.

[60] See *Alliance News*, 29 Jan. 1881, pp. 66-8, and advertisements, ibid., 12 Mar. 1881, p. 161; 19 Mar. 1881, p. 184, etc., and cf. T. H. Green, *Works* (ed. R. L. Nettleship, 3rd ed., 1891), ii, pp. 345-6, 514-15; iii, p. 374.

prefer freedom to sobriety, because with freedom we might in the end attain sobriety; but in the other alternative we should eventually lose both freedom and sobriety.'[61] On this issue, Mill the agnostic agreed with the bishop; his enthusiasm for morality led him actually to repudiate prohibition. Pre-occupied—almost, at times, obsessed—with the miseries of slum life, the prohibitionist was impatient with such finicking arguments, but the politician had to bear in mind the threat to the authority of the law in the event of prohibitionist enactments failing to gain public acquiescence, particularly as the moral reformers disliked the regulatory legislation and official inspection which would have founded legislation on a secure factual basis. The politician has always to con-cern himself with society in its existing state, and with problems of enforcement when it comes to legislating for its improvement. He could never indulge in the luxury of turning a blind eye either to the evil itself or to the con-sequences of legislating to reduce it.[62]

Behind this unfamiliar attitude to legislation is the nineteenth-century moral reformer's profoundly religious outlook on the world; religion and politics were only begin-ning to draw apart, and the reformers under discussion were inspired by two broad views of the way God impinges on human affairs—views not always clearly distinct in the mind of any single individual. The first of these sees God in the role of the severely just father-figure whose methods of promoting national and individual morality are capricious and frequently drastic in the Old Testament manner. For us the Victorians sometimes epitomize faith in the future; yet this optimism was combined, sometimes even in the same person, with a fear of impending national catastrophe, and Babylon was often used as a symbol to denote a corrupt modern civilization, and was regularly applied to London. Both the French Revolution and the collapse of the ancient empires were invoked in support of the view that moral decline prepares the way for national decay. Macaulay's vision of the New Zealand traveller taking his stand on a

[61] *H. L. Deb.*, 2 May 1872, c.86.
[62] Morgan, *H. C. Deb.*, 20 Apr. 1883, c.791, cf. Mill, in *C.D. Acts Commission*, Q.20033.

broken arch of London Bridge to sketch the ruins of St. Paul's caught the Victorian imagination.[63] For many, progress seemed a blessing only precariously grasped, and material prosperity potentially corrupting; and since economic prosperity seemed to depend on moral stamina, even the prosperity seemed insecure. 'We bear upon us but too plainly the marks of a declining empire', Wilberforce announced in his *Practical View*, blaming the decline in religion and morality.[64] Divine retribution could strike the nation through natural catastrophes, plagues, wars, or revolutions, and the individual through misfortune, disease, and death. The moral reformer therefore saw himself as a sort of national coastguard, simultaneously protecting himself and warning his fellow-citizens of their impending fate.

Such visions were likely to meet cold scepticism from the House of Commons; Gladstone told Shaftesbury in 1837 that the House would readily accept a secular argument, but to assert the highest religious principle as a motive for action there was 'incomparably more delicate and difficult'.[65] Still, Wilberforce and other anti-slavery MPs quite often produced the possibility of divine retribution as a weapon,[66] and the dangers involved in doing so became apparent in 1807, when the anti-abolitionist General Gascoyne pointed out that the war seemed to be going remarkably well for a slave-trading nation; still more surprising, wartime victories seemed to come by the hand of men who vigorously upheld that trade. Mr Hibbert in the same year dwelt upon the arbitrariness of a divine hurricane which for twenty years had left in peace the slave-trading Jamaica, and had then for four years devastated areas there which bore no special responsibility for the trade, and had sunk British ships which were 'in nowise participating in the slave

---

[63] G. O. Trevelyan, *The Life and Letters of Lord Macaulay* (2nd ed., 1883), p. 359, cf. Lord Macaulay, *Life and Works*, vi, p. 455.

[64] W. Wilberforce, *A Practical View of the Prevailing System of Professed Christians* (6th ed., 1798), p. 498; cf. R. K. Webb, *Harriet Martineau. A Radical Victorian* (1960), pp. 275–6.

[65] D. C. Lathbury (ed.), *Correspondence on Church and Religion of William Ewart Gladstone* (1910), ii, p. 346, cf. p. 235.

[66] *H. C. Deb*., 1 Mar. 1799, c.526; 6 Apr. 1797, c.278; 15 May 1797, c.570; 18 Apr. 1791, c.277.

trade'.[67] Objections of this type did not prevent the divine-retribution argument from recurring in all the reforming movements under discussion except for women's suffrage. Furthermore the private correspondence of Josephine Butler shows that for her, at least, this consciousness of national guilt was by no means a mere figure of speech.

Opponents of reform were shocked at the alleged capriciousness of divine intervention; according to Osborne Morgan in the debate of 1883 on the CD Acts, the abolitionists always assumed 'that these diseases only prey upon the guilty parties; but we all know that this is essentially a case in which the sins of the fathers are visited on the children to the third and fourth generation'.[68] The moral economy which lies behind the reforming outlook seems to centre upon groups rather than individuals; a family, a city, or a nation is seen as being punished collectively for the sins of individuals within the group. To the modern mind, Josephine Butler and her supporters seem curiously acquiescent in such a capricious deity; when questioned in 1871 about the plight of the innocent victims of venereal disease, she seemed content with the idea that 'it is the law of nature that children should suffer for the sins of their parents', and that legislation could not infringe it.[69] The unpredictability of the Old Testament deity who manifested himself only through disrupting natural regularities required reformers to ascertain the divine will, intuitively and apprehensively, as best they could.

It is hardly surprising that reformers gradually turned to a divine mechanism more compatible with empirical inquiry—the idea that God works through regular and predictable laws, and that human suffering results only from the failure of human beings to act in accordance with them. The reformer's duty then becomes to discover these laws and propagate knowledge of them, thereby promoting justice in this world as well as in the next. Whereas to the twentieth-century

---

[67] Gascoyne, *H. C. Deb.*, 10 Feb. 1807, c.719; Hibbert, *H. C. Deb.*, 16 Mar. 1807, c.115.

[68] *H. C. Deb.*, 20 Apr. 1883, c.777.

[69] *C.D. Acts Commission*, QQ. 13108–9; cf. Samuel Solly, in Committee . . . to inquire into . . . Venereal Disease, *Parl. Papers*, 1867-8 (4031), XXXVII, QQ. 3897-8, 3912-13.

eye Wilberforce's catastrophic deity seems intolerably capricious—the rational, predictable deity of Cobden, Chadwick, Florence Nightingale, and George Combe seems merely redundant. Still, the idea of a rational deity is intimately bound up with social reform and with the origins of social science, if only because it is so eminently compatible with systematic statistical observation. By observing the uniformities of the divine pattern—most notably in relation to trade and health—the legislator could devise reforms which would inevitably succeed because they are harmonious with the divine plan. Such a view would not now be linked with religious attitudes at all, but in its early years the new outlook needed (whether consciously or unconsciously) to seek credence and respectability by sheltering under religion's umbrella. Once safely established, it could brave the elements alone.

To take some illustrations. Pitt's idea that 'the labour of a man is always more productive than that of a mere brute' rests on the belief that in economic relationships effect predictably follows cause.[70] On such a view, the slave economy faces, not divine intervention in catastrophic form, but all the drawbacks resulting from failure to act in accordance with an entirely rational and observable divine plan. Even if slavery keeps labour artificially cheap, and if slave-grown products are artificially protected through differential tariffs, the slave economy will still languish because the slave lacks enthusiasm for his work, the land is unscientifically cultivated, the slave's purchasing-power is depressed, and state mechanisms of coercion are inflated in a vain attempt to keep the slave subordinated. The very institution of slavery, by making labour so cheap, 'put an extinguisher on inventive genius and mental effort, and on every hope of elevation from such a cause', said Mr James Whitmore in 1825. James Cropper in the following year stressed that when referring to the damage done by slavery to the soil, he was 'not speaking of any *miraculous* interposition of Divine Providence, for the operation of this principle can be easily

[70] *H. C. Deb.*, 2 Apr. 1792, c.1139; cf. Society for the Mitigation and Gradual Abolition of Slavery, [First] *A.R.*, p. 28; see also Milbank, in *H. C. Deb.*, 2 Apr. 1792, c.1104.

seen and understood; our own soils would become barren, if they were constantly cultivated with the *same* crop'.[71]

Likewise the factory reformer claims that prosperity cannot come through overworking mill-hands; parallels were regularly drawn between them and the slaves, and arguments were no doubt transferred from the one crusade to the other. The Anti-Corn-Law League repeatedly emphasized the damage done by superstitious and medieval tariff systems which obstructed the divine ordering of the economy. Cobden's prescriptions for personal conduct, legislation, and international diplomacy emerge from as comprehensive and systematic a view of the world as those of Marx; if only clumsy and uninstructed mankind will allow trade to flow freely between nations in accordance with the divine plan, prosperity will result. The links are obvious between such a position and a women's suffrage movement which repudiated ascribed social roles and wanted talent to reach its own level. Josephine Butler's movement, the temperance movement (whose arguments always had their physiological dimension), and the Chadwickian campaign for public health all argued that health would flow naturally from moral and rational conduct. The energy Stansfeld put into the statistical attack on the CD Acts owed much to tactical considerations, but much also to his conviction that—in William Fowler's words—'health will follow upon morality, and only upon morality'.[72]

The two views of divine action are not always separated in the reformer's mind. In Shaftesbury's diary, for instance, the social catastrophe which results from selfish government makes its appearance as a sort of plague or judgement. The mob is always about to erupt into the streets, and is restrained only by the divine pleasure. Revolution here, as quite often among nineteenth-century reformers, becomes a sort of reckoning; it has social and observable causes, but it is also the instrument of the Almighty, and unpredictable in its

[71] Society for the Mitigation and Gradual Abolition of Slavery, *2nd A.R., 1825*, p. 62; James Cropper, in *Anti-Slavery Monthly Reporter*, 31 May 1826, p. 186, cf. Whitmore, ibid., 30 June 1825, p. 6.

[72] SC on CD Acts, *Parl. Papers*, 1882 (340), IX, Q.5434; Stansfeld, in Social Purity Alliance, *A.R. 1883-4*, p. 15; *The Shield*, Nov. 1874, p. 211; *H. C. Deb.*, 20 Apr. 1883, c.773.

timing and effects. The two views of divine action are, even when held separately, similar in some respects. Both leave rather a small role for legislative action; whereas the catastrophic deity puts a high premium on religious and moral effort and makes any kind of social planning both futile and presumptuous, the mechanistic deity is self-acting and requires human beings to refrain from interfering with a delicate mechanism. Neither approach therefore assists in accumulating empirical information on social problems through the civil service, because in neither scheme can man fully control his own destiny.

In both views of the deity, nuance is lacking on the effects of legislative change; the choice lies only between paradise and purgatory, with legislation producing rather abrupt shifts from the one to the other. The catastrophic deity is either appeased or angered; the mechanistic deity is either assisted or obstructed. For the reformer beleaguered within a hostile society, this ever-present possibility of transformation is energizing, even exhilarating, as is the associated notion of the small-scale earthly paradise. A miniature 'heaven below' can be rapidly conjured up if divine precepts are scrupulously followed within any locality, whether local or national. The anti-slavery movement seeks to demonstrate the African's capacity for civilization through the model settlement in Sierra Leone, and holds out high hopes of emancipated slaves in the French West Indian colonies. Likewise the temperance movement advertises the sobriety of prohibitionist estates like Bessbrook and Saltaire,[73] and the women's suffrage movement expects wonders from the American frontier states, Utah and Wyoming, and later New Zealand and Australia. Conversely unprincipled localities— Liverpool, for instance, with its policy of free trade in drink in the 1860s, or the garrison towns where the CD Acts apply —become hells in miniature. When Sir Wilfrid Lawson referred to Liverpool in the debate of 1871 as 'next door to a very hell upon earth',[74] he was called to order and had to

---

[73] For Bessbrook, see *H. C. Deb.*, 27 Apr. 1883, c.1356; for Saltaire, P. T. Winskill, *The Temperance Movement and its Workers*, iii (1892), p. 110.

[74] Lawson, *H. C. Deb.*, 17 May 1871, c.952; cf. my *Separate Spheres*, pp. 135, 150-1.

climb down. Conservatives could enlarge upon the imperfection of these alleged Utopias; temperance Utopias always encountered a boundary problem, and statistical complexities bedevilled any comparison between the incidence of venereal disease in the garrison towns and in the allegedly comparable towns exempt from the CD Acts. Even if the pleasantness of the Utopia were conceded, one could easily argue—as did anti-suffragists in relation to the overseas adoption of women's suffrage—that it could not usefully be applied more widely; anti-suffragists felt that Britain had nothing to learn from reforms applied in immature colonial societies exempt from 'imperial' responsibilities.

The success of a reform at home often required or inspired the reformer to extend it overseas. British anti-slavery became more international after 1833, Josephine Butler's movement more international after 1874. 'We English must conquer our insular spirit', she wrote in 1875, 'and learn to regard the human family as one, and our cause as one all over the world.'[75] The reformer felt ashamed if other nations preceded his own, exhilarated at the thought of his own nation coming first in this holy competition. In abolishing slavery, precedents set by France, Denmark, and republics in Spanish America became important at various stages in the British campaign, particularly towards the end when parliament was actively considering methods of emancipation. But in other areas, British humanitarians felt they had cause for national pride, and the RSPCA approached Europe with the same missionary zeal as Cobden with his free-trade doctrines after 1846.

The temperance movement was perennially distressed that Europe excelled Britain in sobriety;[76] surprise that sobriety could be so prevalent in a Catholic nation during his visit to France in 1828 helped to make a temperance pioneer out of the Scottish evangelical John Dunlop.[77] Nor could British

---

[75] Josephine Butler Papers, Box 1, Envelope 9: Josephine Butler to Mr Edmondson, 13 Feb. 1875 (copy); cf. her speech at Leeds, in *The Shield*, 4 July 1870, p. 153.

[76] e.g. Samuel Smith, *H. C. Deb.*, 27 Apr. 1883, cc.1323-4; cf. Gladstone, *H. C. Deb.*, 5 Mar. 1880, c.47.

[77] John Dunlop, *Autobiography* (ed. J.G.D., 1932), p. 59.

temperance reformers claim to have pioneered prohibitionism, which arrived in Britain in 1853 as an attempt to promote the 'Maine Law' which had already been introduced
in an American state; the fortunes of the United Kingdom
Alliance in British politics always hung heavily on prohibitionist success in America. Plimsoll seriously damaged British
prohibitionism in 1872 when he drew upon personal observation of its ineffectiveness there. By 1883, Australian precedents for local option were being cited in the House,[78] and
Australasia featured prominently in many women's suffrage
speeches; suffragette cries of 'New Zealand, Australia' were
heard from the gallery during the women's suffrage debate
in 1906.[79] These overseas developments gave self-confidence
to the British reformer, but it would have been nicer still to
set the trend, and this yearning for national moral leadership
frequently reappears—among free traders in the 1840s,
among enthusiasts for the welfare state a century later, and
even among advocates of unilateral nuclear disarmament
in the 1950s.[80]

The overriding concern among these reformers is with
moral, not social, reform—a preoccupation which encouraged protest rather than investigation, certainty rather than
doubt. This preoccupation deserves some emphasis because
now so unfamiliar. Hope had not yet been abandoned that
material progress would be associated with, and accompanied by, moral progress; this is the key to priorities and
strategies that might otherwise be puzzling. Empirical
inquiry, for instance, gains low priority because on matters
of moral principle there is no need for inquiry—the reformers
already know. Listing the gains accruing from abolitionism,
Thomas Clarkson stressed that these were largely moral in
nature; the virtuous had been separated from the vicious,
moral boundaries had been set to the activities of trade and
commerce, and a load of guilt had been shed. The trade's
defenders 'virtually denied that man was a moral being; they

---

[78] For Bruce's comments on Plimsoll, see *H. C. Deb.*, 11 July 1872, c.958; for
Harcourt on Australia, *H. C. Deb.*, 27 Apr. 1883, cc.1312-13.

[79] *H. C. Deb.*, 25 Apr. 1906, c.1584.

[80] e.g. *Parl. Papers*, 1840 (601), V, p. vii, and Q.1153; F. Parkin, *Middle Class
Radicalism*, p. 106.

substituted the law of force for the law of reason', whereas now the reformers had 'restored the rational creature to his moral rights'. Human suffering may be shocking, he argues, but its effects are at least confined to this world, whereas assaults on morality affect the next. 'When the moral springs of the mind are poisoned, we lose the most excellent part of the constitution of our nature, and the divine image is no longer perceptible in us.'[81]

Even free trade became a moralistic crusade: 'we have always considered the moral evils of the corn laws even more to be deprecated than their direct physical influence', declared the League's periodical in 1843.[82] Cobden was pre-occupied with the selfishness, slackness, national jealousies, and political corruption which protection seemed to encourage, and the aged Gladstone became a free trader 'on moral no less than on economic grounds', believing that 'human greed and selfishness are interwoven with every thread of the protective system'.[83] Pushing the first Labour budget through the House of Commons in 1924, Philip Snowden was confirmed in his distaste for protection's corrupting influence on politics by the sight of vested interests crowding the lobbies in their eagerness to preserve the duties on their goods.[84] As for the factory-hours movement, early in his speech on the Ten Hours Bill, Shaftesbury set aside the economic dimension of the question, wishing to remain 'within the bounds that I have always hitherto observed in the discussion of this matter, and touch only the consideration of the moral and physical effects' of the factory system on working people.[85]

The slave trade was attacked with such passion partly because it made Christianity impossible to blacks on both sides of the Atlantic. Moral growth could hardly emerge from a system of coerced labour, or from observing white masters setting so pernicious an example. In the late 1820s the anti-slavery movement conducted a vendetta against the Society

[81] T. Clarkson, *Slave Trade*, pp. 613-14.
[82] *Anti-Bread Tax Circular*, 11 Apr. 1843, p. 116.
[83] W. E. Gladstone, *Autobiographica* (ed. J. Brooke and M. Sorensen, 1971), p. 74.   [84] P. Snowden, *Autobiography*, ii (1934), pp. 650, 652.
[85] *H. C. Deb.*, 15 Mar. 1844, c.1075.

for the Conversion . . . of Negro Slaves for ignoring the fact that conversion and slavery could never go together.[86] There was some parliamentary argument on whether the Bible condoned slavery—though biblical arguments were not prominent at Westminster. Here, as with the so-called 'Bible wine question' in the temperance movement or St. Paul's views on women, the Bible was plundered primarily for mere debating points. Wilberforce in 1823 contented himself with saying that West Indian slavery was far less humane than slavery in the ancient world.[87] The slaves could not be civilized, it was argued, under a coercive social system; for the emancipated slave, as for the British working man, the radical abolitionist J. S. Buckingham envisaged leisure 'devoted to the acquisition of knowledge', so that 'religious and moral, as well as entertaining and useful instruction, would teach them that the wants of man could be best satisfied by industry and prudence'.[88] To the planters' claim that the slave merchants removed the African to a relatively civilized milieu, Fox in 1791 had a short answer which later helped build up the Liberal ideal of empire: 'what right had we to be the judges of this, or to force upon them a new condition?'[89]

The same ideal of self-directed moral improvement lay behind the other movements under discussion. Indeed, one of the side-benefits even of the movements to abolish the slave trade, slavery, and animal cruelty was to set up new standards of humanity for the British population as a whole, and thus indirectly to civilize them too.[90] Cobden always hoped that what the working man gained from free trade he would use for self-improvement; it was partly this hope that led him into the freehold land movement in the late 1840s.[91] The factory-hours movement, shocked as it was by the factory system's threat to the integrity of working-class home life, had similar objectives. 'With your success have

---

[86] *Anti-Slavery Monthly Reporter*, 30 Nov. 1831, p. 471.

[87] Wilberforce, *H. C. Deb.*, 15 May 1823, c.294; cf. Bishop of Rochester, *H. L. Deb.*, 5 July 1799, c.1133.

[88] *H. C. Deb.*, 31 May 1833, c.234.

[89] Fox, *H. C. Deb.*, 19 Apr. 1791, c.353; cf. Holland, *H. L. Deb.*, 5 July 1799, c.1118.   [90] See pp. 116, 127, 252.

[91] See his speech at Leeds, in *Freeholder*, 1 Jan. 1851, pp. 4–5.

commenced new duties', Shaftesbury told the short-time committees after Ten Hours had been enacted in 1847— urging them to spend their hard-won leisure on religion, moral improvement, and education.[92] Likewise the temperance society—together with the co-op movement and the friendly society—cultivated the moral fibre among working men that was necessary to uphold respectability.

Considerations of morality were central to Josephine Butler's attack on the CD Acts; for her, this was very much a symbolic issue in the crusade by the high-minded for moral progress. It was primarily the vice, and not the disease, which she wished to arrest, and she felt that the state must not protect from venereal disease the individual who deliberately risked getting it.[93] State-regulated prostitution, she thought, promoted in both sexes the false idea that sin is inevitable, and in concerning herself with prostitution she was as much concerned with the morality of the customer as with that of the prostitute. There was no room for expediency when resisting Acts which committed what Josephine saw as 'the greatest crime of which earth can be witness, the crime of blotting out the soul by depriving God's creatures of free-will, of choice and of responsibility, and by reducing the human being to the condition of a passive, suffering minister to the basest passions'.[94] By contrast, the doctor's preoccupation only with the disease seemed to ride roughshod over morality. There were 'loud shouts of "Oh, oh", and "Stop, stop" ' in 1872 when Dr Peacock interrupted a Gloucestershire meeting against the CD Acts with the claim that 'it was the duty of the medical man to alleviate human suffering irrespective of moral considerations'.[95] Questions of morality were also involved in the related campaign for women's suffrage, which often claimed that emancipated women would aid moral reform, whether in sexual or international relations. Hence the strength of antisuffragism within the drink interest, in London's clubland,

[92] E. Hodder, *Shaftesbury*, ii, p. 195; cf. Kydd, *Factory Movement*, i, p. 342; E. Hodder, *Shaftesbury*, i, p. 437.

[93] *C.D. Acts Commission*, QQ.13104, 13106.

[94] J. Butler, *Letter to the Members of the Ladies National Association, Aug. 1875*, p. 19 (in City of London Polytechnic, Josephine Butler Collection).

[95] *The Shield*, 4 Jan. 1873, p. 6.

in military circles, and among traditionalists of every class. Women's suffrage would remove woman from her protective cocoon and encourage her to make political choices for herself; it owed much to J. S. Mill's belief in the moral benefits of political participation. The moralistic approach to social reform persisted into the Campaign for Nuclear Disarmament in the 1950s, whose analysts see its apparently altruistic concern with moral issues as typical of British middle-class radicalism;[96] it is a tradition in British life which continues to offer a somewhat muted political alternative to the twentieth-century preoccupation with material progress.

Preoccupation with morality encouraged the reformer in his concern for principle, and often lent him the appearance of Pharisaism. For Fox in June 1789, 'the question of the abolition of the slave trade, was a question between humanity on the one side, and interest on the other'; for Fielden in 1844, the Ten Hours Bill was 'a question between mammon and mercy'.[97] Yet this was grossly to over-simplify the issue; Peel was quick to resent Fielden's claim to a monopoly of good feeling, and prohibitionists were accused of employing methods which stiffened the drink interest in its resistance to improvement of any type.[98] A conviction of divine inspiration was almost necessary to the reformer if he was to nerve himself to embark on his crusade. 'As I stood at the table', wrote Shaftesbury of his speech on the Colliery Bill in 1842, 'and just before I opened my mouth, the words of God came forcibly to my mind, "Only be strong and of a good courage"—praised be His Holy Name, I was as easy from that moment as though I had been sitting in an armchair.' Opponents often found the reformer's tone almost as offensive as his content; Mr Frankland Lewis, for instance, who spoke immediately after Buxton's attack on the apprenticeship scheme on 10 June 1833, complained of his adopting 'an *ex-cathedra* tone which only accident had given him'.[99]

[96] F. Parkin, *Middle Class Radicalism*, p. 2.

[97] Fox, *H. C. Deb.*, 23 June 1789, c.100; N. Gash, *Sir Robert Peel* (1972), p. 441.

[98] e.g. Henley, *H. C. Deb.*, 8 May 1872, c.472.

[99] Ashley's diary, 9 June 1842, quot. in E. Hodder, *Shaftesbury*, i, p. 421; Lewis, *H. C. Deb.*, 10 June 1833, c.524.

The conservative must have found it offensive to know that reform was being promoted for his own moral self-development as well as for the sake of the slave, working man, woman, or prostitute. 'It was the quality of despotism to corrupt the heart', said Whitbread in 1792; the continuous exercise of unrestricted authority allegedly corrupted master and trader as well as slave.[1] It gradually inured him to the brutality he so commonly witnessed, either on his estate or on the transatlantic passage. Almost as distasteful to the conservative was the mutual congratulation at reforming meetings, where reformers nerved themselves for the perilous assault, and well-tried and much-loved performers orated from the platform; Wilberforce was greatly fussed over on announcing his retirement from public life at the anti-slavery society's annual meeting of 1825. 'I seem to feel, that the humanity and justice of the people of England are represented in your persons', Mr Denman told the annual anti-slavery meeting in 1828: 'I am proud of the assemblage before me.'[2] A planter petition of 1826 referred to the 'canting pretenders of the day to religion', and an 'affected religion and bastard morality' was attacked in Mr Bernal's parliamentary speech of 1830.[3] Planters in the West Indies loathed the abolitionist Methodist missionaries championed by the anti-slavery movement at home, and enlarged upon the selectiveness of the anti-slavery party's humanity which so cavalierly neglected their own legitimate claims.[4] Birmingham temperance reformers in 1873 appealed to their MP P. H. Muntz to vote for the Permissive Bill 'as he valued his immortal soul'; the CD Acts' defenders had to endure a running fire of insult in the 1870s and 1880s, and in the last women's suffrage parliamentary debate before the first world war, Lord Charnwood wished that the suffragettes 'were not quite so sure that theirs is the liberal, the humane, the progressive, the chivalrous view upon this question'.[5]

[1] Whitbread, *H. C. Deb.*, 2 Apr. 1792, c.1101; cf. Fox, in *H. C. Deb.*, 3 Apr. 1798, c.1405; Society for the Mitigation and Gradual Abolition of Slavery, *1st A.R.*, p. 90.   [2] *Anti-Slavery Monthly Reporter*, May 1828, p. 225.
[3] *H. C. Deb.*, 20 Apr. 1826, c.491; Bernal, *H. C. Deb.*, 23 Nov. 1830, c.651.
[4] e.g. Molineux, *H. C. Deb.*, 21 May 1789, c.98; Sandon, *H. C. Deb.*, 3 June 1833, c.320.
[5] Muntz, *H. C. Deb.*, 7 May 1873, c.1652; Charnwood, *H. L. Deb.*, 6 May

Given the reformer's overriding preoccupation with moral principle, empirical inquiry's role was limited to reinforcing views already held, and to winning broader support for those views. Describing his inquiry headed 'Propositions to be proved by extracts from African travellers', Wilberforce tells us that his method of investigation was 'commonly . . . to mark with the letter which belongs to each proposition, each passage which proves it as I go along, and then to extract and bring together all the extracts which belong to each head'.[6] Likewise *The Anti-Slavery Reporter* was stuffed with information on the iniquitous conditions and legislative situation of the slaves—evidence adduced only in support of a preconceived position.

As for the public inquiry, the reformer saw this as redundant; principle had launched him on his reform and this could hardly be affected by empirical information. Opponents of slavery in 1832 had no more need of a House of Lords inquiry into iniquities which sprang from false principle than the factory movement required the royal commission of 1833. Josephine Butler did not hesitate to inform the royal commission on the CD Acts that 'we hold that the practical working of an Act, which is vicious in principle, is no fit subject for an inquiry, and therefore we do not require your verdict any more than if it were to tell us if there is a God or not'.[7] The need for reform is, to the reformer, self-evident; it is only the desire to propagate his beliefs that induces him reluctantly to supplement his case with statistics and pepper it with footnotes. But in the end he is usually pushed into an inquiry by a combination of the conservative's eagerness for delay and the more practical reformer's realization that only through inquiry can recruits be won. Inquiry usually reinforces the case for action, though often with the aid of arguments which the crusader does not find congenial; at last he seems on the threshold of success.

1914, c.105. See also Osborne Morgan, *H. C. Deb.*, 20 Apr. 1883, cc.775, 780, and Roebuck's appeal to temperance reformers in *H. C. Deb.*, 8 June 1864, c.1413.

[6] R. I. and S. Wilberforce, *William Wilberforce*, iii, pp. 203-4.

[7] *C.D. Acts Commission*, Q.12932; cf. Lord Suffield, *H. L. Deb.*, 24 May 1832, c.7; Buxton, *Anti-Slavery Reporter*, May 1832, p. 144; E. P. Thompson, *Working Class* (2nd ed.), p. 372; Hutchins and Harrison, *Factory Legislation*, p. 54.

IV

Yet he is deceived. The conservative has an experience, initiative, organization, and even moral advantage which the reformer can dislodge only with difficulty. Superiority in physical strength, property, and intelligence is not sufficient to bestow political power; 'to make these various elements of power politically influencial', wrote Mill, 'they must be organised; and the advantage in organisation is necessarily with those who are in possession of the government'.[8] Even today the reformer needs all his processions, demonstrations, and protests to countermine the continuous validation of existing institutions through formal and informal routines, ceremonials, and functions.[9] Still more was this so between 1780 and 1918, when the reformers' ways of influencing public opinion were so much more limited, the prestige of government so much greater, and habits of deference and tradition so well entrenched. Nowadays 'we regard the crusade as morally more legitimate than the lobby', whereas for the Victorians the reverse would have been true.[10] But once the reformer had won the moral advantage by mobilizing the conscience of the religious public and rousing the humanitarian's wrath, the conservative might consider it prudent to concede, however tacitly, the main point.

But his resources of resistance were by no means exhausted; he could then engage in the prolonged pursuit of the diversionary move. A war of attrition through a flourish of side-issues, together with the reformer's countermoves, offers some hope of submerging the substantive question, and so of regaining the moral advantage. It can first be claimed that the time is not ripe; to cite Laski's formulation, 'declare, in the first place, that the demand is impossible; insist when it has been proved to be possible that the time for its translation into statute has not yet come . . .'. The slave trade gained a new lease of life after 1793, for example, from the argument that energies should now focus on winning the

[8] J. S. Mill, *Representative Government*, p. 183.
[9] F. Parkin, *Middle Class Radicalism*, p. 38; F. Parkin, 'Working-class Conservatives: A Theory of Political Deviance', *British Journal of Sociology*, Sept. 1967, pp. 285 ff.
[10] P. Hollis, preface to *Pressure from Without*, p. vii.

war.[11] The time is usually so unusual—whether from wars, economic dislocation, changes of government, and so on— that this weapon is almost continuously to hand. Yet the reformer has a counter-weapon: the seizing of a temporary crisis to justify a permanent change, often without adequate foundation in the evidence available at the time. This is the story of the slave trade's abolition in 1806-7, the repeal of the Corn Laws during the Irish famine, the introduction of women's suffrage during the first world war and of family allowances in the second.

But if the time should at last turn out to be ripe there is the conservative game of pursuing logical consequences or resisting thin ends of the wedge. In F. M. Cornford's words, 'the *Principle of the Wedge* is that you should not act justly now for fear of raising expectations that you may act still more justly in the future'.[12] Defending church rates in 1861, Lord Robert Cecil could unashamedly block the smallest of reforms in order to postpone or perhaps even prevent the larger: 'at the pass to which things have come', he confessed (indiscreetly, perhaps, for his cause), 'it is better to defend the outworks at once than to let the enemy advance further . . . We have kept Church Rates alive thirty years and with our present numbers we can keep them alive ten years longer. At that rate we may keep tithes twenty years after that, and endowments twenty years longer still . . . Who can tell what changes may have passed over England and the world when fifty years shall have elapsed? Supposing every other hope gone then, there is still the hope of delay.'[13] A conservative strategy more subtle, because concealed under the guise of reform, was to act as did Gladstone towards the Irish Church in 1869: to lop off the diseased branches in the hope of preserving the tree.

Planters portrayed opponents of the slave-trade as paving the way for abolishing slavery, or at least as risking a confusion

---

[11] H. Laski, *Militant Temper*, p. 18; cf. Tarleton, *H. C. Deb.*, 30 May 1804, cc.469-70; *H. C. Deb.*, 16 Mar. 1807, c.137.

[12] F. M. Cornford, *Microcosmographia Academica. Being a Guide for the Young Academic Politician* (6th ed., 1966), p. 23.

[13] Cecil, *Salisbury*, i, p. 320.

in the slave's mind between the two.[14] The humanitarians
did indeed want slavery ended, but thought that the abolition
of the trade would cause slavery to 'gradually wear out
without the immediate intervention of any positive law'.
When a Bill for gradually abolishing slavery was introduced
in 1807, Wilberforce therefore opposed it as untimely.[15]
Yet slavery survived, and humanitarians later had to nerve
themselves for a new and more direct assault. The two
phases of the campaign were intimately linked—by personnel,
by technique, and in other ways—but the planters' argument
in defence of the trade would have been retrospectively
justified only if this logical consequence (that is, the campaign to abolish slavery) had been greatly accelerated, and
they were wrong to imply that conceding the first reform
rendered the second inevitable; a decade elapsed between
the mounting of the anti-slavery campaign and its triumph
in 1833. Likewise with anti-suffragist fears about the consequences of women's suffrage; this reform was indeed
followed by adult suffrage, which did indeed put women
in a majority in the electorate; and women did indeed enter
parliament and the cabinet.[16] But these developments were
implemented in such a way as to produce a minimum of
social or political disruption; nor did earlier concessions to
the feminists prevent anti-suffragists from offering strenuous
resistance to these further changes on their merits. A decade
intervened between the enactment of women's suffrage and
adult suffrage; nor has the advent of women into politics
even now begun to effect the political and social transformation the anti-suffragists feared.

Logical consequences could be followed up by advertising
the reformer's ugly associations—either with extremists in
his own movement, or with other unpopular movements. The
parliamentary humanitarians were forced into distancing
themselves from their enthusiasts, and into insisting that
the abolition they favoured was only gradual. 'Far from

[14] e.g. Pulteney, *H. C. Deb.*, 28 Feb. 1805, c.660; Hawkesbury, *H. C. Deb.*,
24 June 1806, c.805.
[15] Howick, *H. C. Deb.*, 23 Feb. 1807, c.954; Wilberforce, *H. C. Deb.*, 17 Mar.
1807, c.143.
[16] For anti-suffragist predictions, see Leatham, in *H. C. Deb.*, 30 Apr. 1873,
c.1226; Asquith, *H. C. Deb.*, 12 July 1910, cc.249–50.

meaning to attempt to cut down slavery in the full maturity of its vigour', said Fowell Buxton in 1823, 'we rather shall leave it gently to decay—slowly, silently, almost imperceptibly, to die away, and to be forgotten.'[17] He proposed to begin by emancipating the slaves' children at birth—a provision which had already been adopted successfully elsewhere. As for the reformer's ugly associations with other reformers, the integration between reforming causes is not always a fiction of the distorted conservative mind. The reforming temperament often encourages simultaneous involvement in several causes, just as conservatives on one issue often turn out to be conservative also on many others. The symbolic nature of many reforming crusades often mobilizes those who are restive for other reasons.[18] Furthermore, when faced by some common enemy reformers in several causes often incorrectly assume that, in Cobden's phrase, 'all good things pull together'[19]—that their present unity springs from the compatibility between their aims rather than from the tactical or psychological needs of the immediate situation.

Ugly associations were perhaps most effectively dwelt upon by conservatives when they advertised the anti-slave-trade movement's links with French revolutionaries in the 1790s. 'Gentlemen ought to be on their guard against a spirit of innovation', R. J. Buxton warned parliament in February 1793: 'liberty was not now in danger from its arch enemy despotism, but from those, who under the appearance of erecting a temple to liberty, were actually endeavouring to destroy it, to overturn all government, and establish anarchy upon its ruins'.[20] Roebuck adopted similar tactics in 1864, when stressing the affinities between prohibitionism and sabbatarianism; in support of the Sunday Closing Bill, he pointed out, 'those two muddy streams of sentiment had united. Running side by side for a long time, they had at last united their waters, and now they formed one foaming,

---

[17] *H. C. Deb.*, 15 May 1823, c.266.

[18] Cf. F. Parkin, *Middle Class Radicalism*, pp. 3, 5, 32, 41.

[19] Cobden quot. in P. Hollis (ed.), *Pressure from Without*, p. 142; see also p. 151.

[20] Buxton, *H. C. Deb.*, 26 Feb. 1793, c.515; cf. *H. L. Deb.*, 11 Apr. 1793, cc.653 (Abingdon), 659 (Clarence); *H. C. Deb.*, 28 Feb. 1805, c.655 (Tarleton).

muddy river, which it was difficult to stem, and very disagreeable to see. (An hon. *Member*: And to smell.) Aye, and to smell.'[21]

Suffragists tried in vain to forestall this conservative tactic by clearly distinguishing their movement from Josephine Butler's attack on the CD Acts. That bitter opponent of Josephine Butler's movement, Cavendish Bentinck, pointed out in 1883 that the Acts' opponents consisted of three groups, all of them unpleasant: those who saw venereal disease as a divine punishment for vice, those who held exaggerated notions on women's rights, and 'the ultra-revolutionary party, the followers of the late Mr Mazzini'.[22] Anti-suffragists did their utmost to associate their opponents with unorthodox ideas on the family,[23] and later with Socialism—claiming that both were egalitarian movements running their heads against nature.

But there was an equally effective and almost contradictory conservative device: to ridicule the selectivity of the reforming· conscience. 'The Young Man in a Hurry', wrote Cornford, 'is afflicted with a conscience, which is apt to break out, like measles, in patches.'[24] No objection was more frequent than the claim in 1833 from William Cobbett (rather more conservative than radical on this issue) that the slaves were fed and clothed 'a good deal better than the working people in England, Ireland, and Scotland'.[25] Baring in 1824 pointed out that the whip was used not only against West Indian slaves but also to maintain discipline in the British armed services, and 'nothing, he was aware, offended the abolitionists so much, as to assimilate the condition of the slaves . . . with that of any portion of the subjects of our own, or of any other country'.[26] Conservatives were attracted by this device because it enabled them to seize the moral

[21] *H. C. Deb.*, 6 May 1864, c.171.
[22] Bentinck, *H. C. Deb.*, 20 Apr. 1883, c.827, cf. Osborne Morgan, *H. C. Deb.*, 1 May 1872, c.56; cf. Fawcett, *H. C. Deb.*, 30 Apr. 1873, c.1247.
[23] e.g. Bouverie, *H. C. Deb.*, 3 May 1871, c.83.
[24] F. M. Cornford, *Microcosmographia*, p. 13; cf. leader in *The Times*, 30 May 1970, p. 9.
[25] Cobbett, *H. C. Deb.*, 18 Mar. 1833, c.730; cf. Col. Tarleton, *H. C. Deb.*, 4 Feb. 1791, c.1208; Bryan Edwards, *H. C. Deb.*, 15 May 1797, c.574; James Wilson, *H. C. Deb.*, 6 Mar. 1828, c.1047.
[26] *H. C. Deb.*, 16 Mar. 1824, c.1162.

advantage from the reformer. But the humanitarians could make several rejoinders. They could argue, with Burke in 1791, that a reform once embarked upon should be completed before others are attempted[27] and that reformers should not be deterred from attacking one evil by claims that other evils also require attack; with Brougham in 1830 (responding to Orator Hunt's disruption of the anti-slavery movement's annual meeting) that opponents of slavery tended also to be active in many other causes; and with J. S. Buckingham in 1833 (rebutting Gladstone's reference to the plight of Sheffield steel-grinders) that their occupation was at least voluntary within a free labour market where dangerous work fetched a higher price.[28]

This branch of the conservative attack had the effect of pressing the reformer in any one cause to embrace a number of others. The social problem was progressively revealed in its full ramifications and complexity as a result of facts and impressions conveyed to reformers in the course of their work, but conservative reproaches increased the incentives towards widened perspectives. Nowhere was this more so than with the factory-hours movement; 'we speak with execration of the cart-whip of the West Indies', said Sadler in his speech of 1832, 'but let us see this night an equal feeling rise against the factory-thong of England'.[29] Fellow reformers sometimes appropriated this conservative device, so that Late-Victorian piecemeal reformers were simultaneously beset by conservatives reproaching them for their selective conscience and by Socialists whose integrated critique of capitalist society led them to repudiate the idea of single-issue 'causes' altogether. Edwardian feminists faced not only the conservative objection to women's suffrage

---

[27] *H. C. Deb.*, 4 Feb. 1791, c.1209.

[28] Wilberforce, *H. C. Deb.*, 23 Feb. 1807, c.994; Brougham, *Anti-Slavery Monthly Reporter*, iii, p. 255; Brougham used this argument with some justification—see C. Bolt, *The Anti-Slavery Movement and Reconstruction. A Study in Anglo-American Co-operation 1833–77* (1969), p. 112; Buckingham, *H. C. Deb.*, 7 June 1833, c.478, cf. Gladstone, in *H. C. Deb.*, 3 June 1833, c.333.

[29] Sadler in Kydd, *Factory Movement*, i, p. 183; cf. Vyvyan, *H. C. Deb.*, 30 May 1833, c.127; J. T. Ward, *The Factory Movement 1830–1855*, p. 109. See also my article, 'A Genealogy of Reform in Modern Britain', in C. Bolt and S. Drescher (eds.), *Anti-Slavery, Religion, and Reform. Essays in Memory of Roger Anstey* (Folkestone, 1980), pp. 119–48.

as such, but also the progressive Liberal and socialist objection to enacting women's suffrage only on the existing restricted property basis. Furthermore, in their competition for public attention, reformers engaged in mutual reproach; the anti-slavery and factory-hours movements, for instance, argued about whose form of slavery was the worst. For similar reasons the RSPCA in the 1880s felt bound to assist the foundation of the .NSPCC. The libertarian ideals of nineteenth-century Liberalism caused it to ramify into wider and wider areas of life—into the family, via the feminist and temperance movements; into rural areas, through the movements for free speech, educational reform, and free trade in land; into religious worship, through the movements for religious equality and equal opportunity; and, in its Edwardian phase, into working-class life generally through its espousal of liberty in its economic dimension.

A humane sensibility which had begun with the slaves in the West Indies gradually radiated outwards towards the labouring masses at home. 'Slavery' was a word which came trippingly to the pens of Marx and Engels when discussing British industrial populations, and anti-slavery meetings in the 1840s were occasionally disrupted by reproachful Chartists.[30] Social reform during the 1840s advanced through the reformers' mutual recrimination. The Anti-Corn-Law League sniped at the anti-slavery, factory-hours, and public-health movements; Chartists sniped at all four, together with Owenism; and Shaftesbury complained in February 1845, when proposing restrictions of child labour in calico print-works, that his opponents 'on the first introduction of the Ten Hours Bill, sent me to the collieries; when I invaded the collieries, I was referred to the Print-works; from the Print-works I know not where I shall be sent, for can anything be worse?'[31] The dynamic of nineteenth-century reform processes was accelerating well before the appointment of government inspectors, who speeded its pace still further.[32]

[30] e.g. *Scottish Patriot*, 28 Mar. 1840, p. 203; *Northern Star*, 28 Nov. 1840, p. 6; cf. pp. 138, 254.

[31] E. Hodder, *Shaftesbury*, ii, p. 88, cf. G. M. Trevelyan, *The Life of John Bright* (1925 ed.), p. 105; Cobden, in *H. C. Deb.*, 12 Mar. 1844, c.887.

[32] Cf. O. MacDonagh, 'The Nineteenth Century Revolution in Government: A Reappraisal', *Historical Journal*, 1958, p. 58.

One powerful diversionary move yet remains for the conservative. In the later stages of the discussion he can focus
upon means rather than ends—not yet on how the reform
is to be implemented, but on the arguments and methods
used by reformers in the course of agitation. The reformer
at first has difficulty even in getting argument off the ground,
so powerful is society's inertia; the initial quality of reforming argument therefore needs to be high. G. H. Francis,
the Early-Victorian analyst of political oratory, argued
that speeches decline in quality the nearer to legislation
the reformer approaches, and cited the anti-slavery and
parliamentary-reform movements in support.[33] At this
early stage, one of the Liberal Party's several distinguished
nineteenth-century politician-intellectuals would elaborate a
convincing case for reform; he possessed the imagination,
intelligence, and distance from the here-and-now to pioneer
new perceptions. But audiences are not necessarily influenced
by arguments according to their intrinsic merit; they are not
necessarily influenced by argument at all. A vein of anti-
intellectualism runs through the conservative case—among
planters and anti-suffragists, for example. 'Although they
might not be able to give a single argument for their opinion',
said Mr Laing, opposing Mill on women's suffrage in its first
parliamentary debate, 'he would back their instinct against
the logic of the hon. Member.'[34]

For the effective presentation of the reforming case, the
opposition must therefore first be got into the lists. Discussing the campaign to reform the law on married women's
property, James Bryce in 1880 said 'it is to some extent
more difficult to deal with a question where you have got
no opponents, and where your enemy conceals himself in
sullen silence behind earthworks, than when he boldly comes
out into the open to confront you'.[35] The reformer's case is
not always at first as clearly articulated or even as firmly based
as he imagines; many clever objections can be formulated,

[33] G. H. Francis, *Orators of the Age* (1847), p. 20.
[34] *H. C. Deb.*, 20 May 1867, c.839; cf. *H. C. Deb.*, 1 May 1872, c.54; 28 Feb.
1805, c.658.
[35] Married Women's Property Committee, *Report of the Proceedings at the
Annual Meeting, 4th Feb. 1880* (Manchester, 1880), p. 16.

many amusing asides presented, many reforming inconsistencies and illogicalities dwelt upon—before he can in argument meet all comers. Once the reforming case has been set up, it must be constantly repeated to overcome the initial presumption against change. But this opens up an opposite danger—that of boring people with arguments that have become painfully familiar, as in the annual parliamentary debates on prohibition during the 1870s. Once beaten out of the field of argument on the substantive issue, the conservative can turn to the nature and extent of the support for the proposed reform, and can take pleasure in pursuing three profitable courses: he can emphasize that the reformers are nasty people, saying nasty things, and using deceitful and unfair tactics. Each of these conservative devices must now be considered in turn.

The reformer's contemporaries filter his words through their perception of all the defects and oddities of his personality. Among the most startling of the reformer's oddities is of course the fact that he has espoused his cause at all. The discovery of a new and humane cause constitutes in itself an implied reproach upon all those dull people who failed themselves to discover it; reforming innovators encounter as much initial hostility from colleagues as scientific inventors. This unpleasantness can be shaken off by enlarging upon the reformer's eccentricity, or by burrowing beneath his apparently altruistic surface—to argue that the grievance is in some sense artificial, and that its agitation merely serves the reformer's personal purposes. 'A party whose mission it is to live entirely upon the discovery of grievances', said Salisbury of the radicals in the 1880s, 'are apt to manufacture the element upon which they subsist.'[36]

Whereas the conservative deplores reformers' destruction of the better society his ancestors enjoyed, the reformer seems perpetually discontented not only with society as it is, but even (often correctly) with the results of his own reforms once enacted. They never seem to produce the outcome he

---

[36] Cecil, *Salisbury*, iii (1931), p. 65; cf. Paul Smith (ed.), *Lord Salisbury on Politics*, pp. 318-19; Second Earl of Birkenhead, *F.E.*, p. 488. See also T. S. Kuhn, *The Structure of Scientific Revolutions* (2nd ed., Chicago, 1970), pp. 7, 24, 35.

desires, nor does legislative success deter him from ever restlessly moving on to further disruptions of established habit. In 1874 the radical John Morley pointed out that most of the reforming aspirations from two generations before had been implemented, 'but the results of their fulfilment have been so disappointing as to make us wonder whether it is really worth while to pray, when to have our prayers granted carries the world so very slight a way forward'.[37] The reformer can readily be made to seem a discontented and sour person, unable to accept the necessities of the human condition, unable to live with the imperfections of his fellow human beings, unable to recognize that existing institutions function tolerably well if worked in the right spirit. 'Feminist women are merely crying for the moon', said the anti-feminist Lord Ampthill in 1925: 'they are revolting . . . not against the tyranny of man, but against the tyranny of Nature'.[38]

The reformer's nastiness for the conservative often also lay in his social class or status. His reforming zeal seemed (and to some extent was) an outcrop of his low social status. Humanitarians attacked feudal relationships and interests powerful at the highest social level, and the unrespectable character of their witnesses was often dwelt upon.[39] Opponents often capitalized on women's prominence in humanitarian campaigning; O'Connell in 1833 denounced attacks of this kind on anti-slavery petitions as showing 'bad taste and . . . bad feeling'.[40] T. F. Buxton in May rejoiced that his supporters' triumph would at last preserve them from being 'stigmatized by the grossest epithets which could be extracted from the vocabulary of abuse'.[41]

Crusaders whose beneficiaries themselves agitated for the reform—nonconformists, women, and working men—were particularly vulnerable to this objection. Reforming movements often performed in themselves an emancipating

[37] J. Morley, *On Compromise* (1921 ed.), p. 4.
[38] *Morning Post*, 10 July 1925, p. 12.
[39] e.g. *H. C. Deb.*, 2 Apr. 1792, cc.1092, 1117; T. Clarkson, *Slave Trade*, pp. 414, 422.
[40] *H. C. Deb.*, 3 June 1833, c.309.
[41] *H. C. Deb.*, 30 May 1833, c.157, cf. Ker Seymer's defence of temperance reformers at *H. C. Deb.*, 3 June 1863, c.290.

purpose, by encouraging their beneficiaries into political life. Anti-suffragists were even more likely to be disgusted than planters at the sight of women agitators, and their defects were energetically canvassed in parliamentary debates and popular postcards. 'A few restless itinerant ladies—my Lady A here, Miss B there—pass from town to town', said the prominent anti-suffragist Henry James in 1871, 'delivering their often-repeated and well learnt speeches. But what support do they receive from those they address?' The very process of agitation could render the reformer unattractive in appearance. The Edwardian suffragette in militant incidents was by no means alone in offering the conservative one of his most effective arguments; as Ibsen's reformer-hero points out, 'a man should never put on his best trousers when he goes out to battle for freedom and truth'.[42]

For the conservative, the reformer is not only a nasty person, he also says nasty things. The edge of his reforming oratory is sharpened by his consciousness of social or personal inferiority. His righteous indignation and his social situation combine to render his opponents villains in his eyes. To embody evil in particular individuals is exhilarating, and lends the reforming campaign a focus convenient at the branch level, though such an outlook is too shrill to carry conviction in parliament. The conservative can thereby capitalize upon invaluable lapses of taste and sensibility, amidst an audience drawn from his own class. Wilberforce's parliamentary speech of 1789 ably refuted the opposition's arguments, and he took care always to attack only the system of slavery and slave trading rather than the individuals enmeshed in it.[43] He saw the whole British society as being implicated in the trade, and wished that the more enlightened slave-owners could reside on their estates and so influence West Indian opinion directly instead of remaining in Britain as absentees.[44] But for the more enthusiastic humanitarians, as for the more zealous disciples of Marx, it was always difficult in practice

[42] James, *H. C. Deb.*, 3 May 1871, c.112; Ibsen, *An Enemy of the People* (Tr. Eleanor Marx, Heinemann Drama Library ed., 1951), p. 63.

[43] Wilberforce, *H. C. Deb.*, 2 Apr. 1792, c.1055; cf. Whitbread, *H. C. Deb.*, 27 Feb. 1807, c.1051, and cf. Ashley in the factory-hours movement, *H. C. Deb.*, 15 Mar. 1844, c.1074.

[44] *H. C. Deb.*, 12 May 1789, c.42; *H. C. Deb.*, 16 Mar. 1824, c.1146.

to act on the Master's recognition that oppressor and oppressed were alike victims of a social situation. Descriptions of brutal individual incidents towards slaves featured even in parliamentary speeches against the slave trade, and the planters could justifiably claim that these misrepresented the master/slave relationship. A recurrent refrain in Peel's speeches towards 1833 became the need to avoid antagonizing the planters through inflammatory language, and even T. F. Buxton in 1831 admitted that such citing of individual instances had probably hindered the cause.[45]

Yet this did not prevent Buxton from engaging in a more generalized dramatization of his cause. In 1832 he shocked MPs with his calculation that 2,200,000 strokes of the cartwhip must be annually inflicted on the slaves;[46] in the country at large, the whip came to symbolize the system under attack, just as the strap was used as a rhetorical device (even in parliament) by the factory-hours movement,[47] and the speculum by Josephine Butler—though she strongly criticized Dr Hooppell for actually exhibiting such instruments at public meetings. 'Sir James Mackintosh called the anger of the West Indian planters against the English anti slavery party "a rebellion for the whip" ', she wrote in 1872, 'but really we may truly say the rage of these medical legislators now is a "rebellion for the speculum" that hideous instrument of hell.'[48] The temperance reformer's verbal assault on the publican could be counter-productive, as when a placard entitled 'The Publican's Prayer' and beginning 'Our father which art in hell' was produced during the parliamentary debate of 1871 on the Permissive Bill.[49] The pursuit of villains reached its apogee, or nadir, when Edwardian suffragettes gave up the attempt to convert the elector and identified individual politicians—Asquith, Loulou Harcourt, Winston Churchill—as their real obstacles to success. From

---

[45] *H. C. Deb.*, 15 Apr. 1831, c.1417, cf. cc.1408-9.

[46] *H. C. Deb.*, 24 May 1832, c.45, cf. Lord Calthorpe, in Society for the Mitigation and Gradual Abolition of Slavery, *2nd A.R.*, 1825, p. 50.

[47] S. Kydd, *Factory Movement*, i, pp. 183, 226, 279.

[48] City of London Polytechnic, Josephine Butler Papers, Box 1, envelope 6: Josephine Butler to Mr Edmondson, 30 Jan. 1872, cf. her letter to Mrs Wilson, dated '26 August' (in Box 1).

[49] *H. C. Deb.*, 17 May 1871, c.927.

this there followed physical assaults on opponents and their property which did more harm than good.

Coleridge attacked reformers in 1817 for producing 'startling particular facts, which, dissevered from their context, enable a man to convey falsehood while he says truth', and for 'concealment of the general and ultimate result behind the scenery of local and particular consequences'.[50] Temperance reformers often tried to browbeat audiences into accepting their remedy by prolonged and vigorous emphasis on the evils of drunkenness without concurrent reference to the major social services the publican provided in the slum. With such denunciations, said Hartington in 1879, the temperance reformer was merely worsening the evil by discouraging respectable people from entering the trade; in the following year the temperance leader Sir Wilfrid Lawson conceded the point.[51] Some temperance leaders eventually came to see that their energies would be better spent on depicting the pleasures of teetotalism.[52]

There is of course another side to this story; through championing unpopular ideas the reformers were crusading for free speech in at least two dimensions. Not only did they frequently brave country-wide and often violent opposition in press and public meeting; they were also broadening out the range of topics which could be publicly discussed in polite society. There was always a tension here between eroding established humanitarian standards by filling one's speech with accounts of brutality, and risking the continuance of inhumane conduct by choosing to remain silent about its details. MPs often deplored the detailed discussion in parliament of cruelty to slaves by anti-slavery leaders like William Smith, and attacked the libellous propaganda distributed through the anti-slavery machine. But Fox in 1791 had an effective rejoinder: 'let them remember that humanity consisted not in a squeamish ear. It consisted not in starting

---

[50] In R. J. White (ed.), *Political Tracts*, p. 71.

[51] Hartington, *H. C. Deb.*, 11 Mar. 1879, c.739; Lawson, *H. C. Deb.*, 5 Mar. 1880, c.445.

[52] e.g. J. Livesey, quot. in J. Pearce (ed.), *Joseph Livesey as Reformer and Teacher* (1885), p. cxxxvi; cf. T. Whittaker, *Life's Battles*, pp. 133-4.

or shrinking at such tales as these, but in a disposition of heart to relieve misery.'[53]

Josephine Butler's movement was perhaps the most daring in its outspokenness; L. S. Amery recalled his nervousness even in 1911 at the thought of mentioning syphilis in the House of Commons,[54] and Josephine's movement had to out-flank press and parliamentary censorship by creating its own periodicals, and by using public meetings to generate public discussion. Here, as with vivisection, the doctors disliked the public meeting; the subject was 'one which it is impossible to treat fairly in all its bearings before a mixed and un-instructed audience in the compass of a speech'.[55] Josephine Butler, by contrast, saw publicity as her major weapon. On women's suffrage, the objection was not so much to the topic itself as to women's involvement in publicly debating it. As one suffragist complained in 1876: 'if women are silent on this subject, they are said to be hostile or indifferent, and if they speak they are said to be unfeminine'.[56] The anti-suffragist's dilemma was, by contrast, to encourage women into speaking in public about the need for their sex to be reticent and retiring; like Josephine Butler's medical opponents, the anti-suffragists felt that some of their weightiest arguments 'do not lend themselves to the atmo-sphere of a public meeting, and when clothed in the words of a tactless or unskilful speaker, are apt to arouse animosity, and even to excite derision'.[57]

The reformer's pursuit of publicity seemed almost to involve stealing an unfair advantage. Indeed, conservative

---

[53] Fox, in *H. C. Deb.*, 19 Apr. 1791, c.352; cf. Col. Tarleton, *H. C. Deb.*, 2 Apr. 1792, c.1093; Mr Bernal, *H. C. Deb.*, 19 May 1826, c.1339; Baring, *H. C. Deb.*, 16 Mar. 1824, c.1159.

[54] L. S. Amery, *My Political Life*, i, p. 375; cf. M. Vicinus (ed.), *Suffer and be Still. Women in the Victorian Age* (Bloomington, Indiana, 1972), p. 97.

[55] Association for Promoting the Extension of the Contagious Diseases Act, *4th A.R., 1872*, p. 9; for vivisection, see Sir T. Watson, in *R. C. Vivisection, Parl. Papers*, 1876 (C.1397), XLI, Q.112; R. D. French, 'Medical Science and Victorian Society', p. 58.

[56] Forsyth, *H. C. Deb.*, 26 Apr. 1876, c.1668, cf. *H. C. Deb.*, 6 June 1877, c.1374; Sir A. Rollitt, *H. C. Deb.*, 27 Apr. 1892, cc.1458-9; Attwood in 1832, quot. in P. Hollis (ed.), *Pressure from Without*, p. 1.

[57] *Anti-Suffrage Review*, May 1909, p. 4, cf. Curzon, ibid., July 1914, p. 110, and G. L. Mosse, 'The Anti-League: 1844-1846', *Economic History Review*, xvii (1947), pp. 135, 141. See also my *Separate Spheres*, pp. 111-13.

distaste rested as much on the reformer's allegedly deceitful and unfair tactics as on his unpleasant personality and remarks. Even the systematic agitation of the country seemed to some early nineteenth-century MPs barely legal as a strategy. The planters wanted parliament to consider questions on their merits, and disliked their opponents' pledging of MPs and mounting of election propaganda.[58] Baring complained that when Brougham stood for Yorkshire in 1830 'there were persons led about in chains, with blackened faces, in order to rouse the feelings of the people'.[59] Sir James Graham, prime enemy of the factory-hours movement in the 1840s, seems to have been haunted by the fear of being hustled into legislation by the movement's pressure from without, and many were the complaints in temperance debates of the early 1870s about the pressures being exerted on MPs from both sides.[60] Similar complaints were made by Edwardian anti-suffragists,[61] but from the reformer's point of view such pressure was essential to galvanize their few and often lukewarm supporters at Westminster into resisting the well-entrenched vested interests so powerful there.

Politicians rightly asked whether the reformer's energetic methods reflected or distorted public opinion; politicians not only wanted to be popular—they knew that legislation without public support might well fail. Referenda and systematic opinion–sampling were not yet available, and general elections were only gradually being transformed into polls of opinion on national policy; could the politician even assume that if the reformers were more numerous or zealous than the conservatives, their cause should prevail, especially when the view of the apathetic might turn out to be crucial? The reformer was probably not deliberately trying to mislead, but his whole situation insulated him psychologically and even socially from any objective view of public opinion. The anti-slavery movement for instance made much

[58] e.g. *H. C. Deb.*, 18 Feb. 1796, c.742; *H. C. Deb.*, 10 Feb. 1807, cf. 718–19; *H. C. Deb.*, 16 Mar. 1824, c.1159; *H. C. Deb.*, 30 May 1833, c.131.

[59] *H. C. Deb.*, 15 Apr. 1831, c.1464.

[60] For Graham, see E. Hodder, *Shaftesbury*, ii, p. 40; see also Viscount Bury, *H. C. Deb.*, 8 May 1872, c.497; Muntz, *H. C. Deb.*, 5 Mar. 1880, c.492; Lawson, *H. C. Deb.*, 28 Apr. 1875, c.1779; Samuelson, *H. C. Deb.*, 7 May 1873, c.1636.

[61] e.g. Cremer, *H. C. Deb.*, 16 Mar. 1904, c.1351.

of its huge petitions: 'there could not be a more complete expression of public opinion than those petitions presented', said O'Connell in June 1833.[62] But the planters, like conservatives throughout the century, took leave to doubt it, and enlarged upon the emotional or intimidating methods used to get signatures, the low or bogus quality of the signatories, and the over-all fallibility of the petition as an index to opinion. Debates on all these reforms became arguments about whether the reformers' methods accurately displayed public opinion. Chartism carried the petition to its apogee, yet in the licensing debate of 1862 it was noted that despite this 'they heard very little about the Charter now'.[63] Anti-suffragists even savoured the delights of delving into subscription lists and pressure-group propaganda for evidence on the reformers' small following or discreditable connections.[64]

Preoccupation with the reformer's methods, as distinct from his formal objectives, became particularly intense on the subject of violence. Both conservatives and reformers had been sufficiently influenced by humanitarian values to seek a reputation for superiority in this respect. For the reformers, physical force was very much a last resort. Their movements built on new storeys and outworks to the Victorian humanitarian edifice. They struggled to eliminate violence directly through their attacks on slavery, on drunkenness, on shocking industrial conditions, and on callousness towards women; but they also saw their agitations as a civilizing influence in themselves, because they warded off revolutionary dangers by enlisting wider and wider groups in the political process. Reformers frequently spoke of the violence which might result if statesmen ignored their demands, but their aim was always to ward off that danger. On the other hand, the conservative made his own bid for humanitarian credit by accusing the reformer of stirring up discontent among dangerous groups (slaves, working people, Irishmen); of unsettling the political framework generally by his agitation;

[62] O'Connell, *H. C. Deb.*, 3 June 1833, c.309; cf. *Anti-Slavery Monthly Reporter*, 31 July 1826, p. 198.
[63] Ker Seymer, *H. C. Deb.*, 27 June 1862, c.1185.
[64] Cf. my *Separate Spheres*, pp. 176, 184.

and of risking violence by trying to move too rapidly in humane directions. In the debates on slavery and the slave-trade, for example, both sides adduced St. Domingo in support of their case. Humanitarians presented themselves as defending the planters against the violent demise which (in a characteristic blend of sociological and prophetic explanation) they foresaw as their destiny.[65] Here, as with Roman Catholic emancipation shortly before, the reforming debate virtually ended in a choice between what Peel would have called 'different kinds and different degrees of evil'—between the disruption which the planters felt would flow from emancipation and the insurrection which the anti-slavery movement predicted would flow from its post-ponement.[66]

The reforming leaders' relationship to violence was therefore very delicate, and its dimensions can be illustrated through consecutively analysing its impact on the several movements under discussion. T. F. Buxton in 1833, for instance, needed simultaneously to warn the government of the danger from insurrection while doing his best to damp it down through direct appeals to the beneficiaries of his reforming effort.[67] The situation of Chartist, Anti-Corn-Law League, and factory-movement leaders was rather different, in that the danger of insurrection came from their own following, whereas nobody had predicted insurrection from the British anti-slavery movement. 'You will some day see and confess the service I have been able to render', Shaftesbury told Peel in 1841, when refusing a post in the Queen's household for the sake of the factory-hours movement.[68] Here, as with the movements for parliamentary reform, Roman Catholic emancipation, Chartism, and free trade, reforming leaders were simultaneously wielding the threat of violence as a public weapon while privately trying to damp it

[65] e.g. Noel, in *Anti-Slavery Monthly Reporter*, May 1828, p. 231; cf. Sir J. Mackintosh, ibid., 9 May 1831, p. 258.

[66] Sir R. Peel, *Memoirs*, i, p. 182 (letter to Wellington, 11 Aug. 1828); cf. *H. C. Deb.*, 3 June 1833, cc.343–4.

[67] See *H. C. Deb.*, 30 May 1833, c.161; 24 July 1833, c.1218.

[68] E. Hodder, *Shaftesbury*, i, p. 356, cf. ii, p. 115; B. Harrison and P. Hollis, 'Chartism, Liberalism and the Life of Robert Lowery', *English Historical Review*, July 1967, pp. 513–14.

down. The situation of the temperance reformer and the opponent of the CD Acts was in important respects different again, for efforts to represent respectable working men as on the verge of rebellion at the offence being given to their moral ideals were never very convincing;[69] the violence being warded off in this area was the traditional and routine violence, often occurring in family situations, which was then commonplace in the slum. By contrast the temperance reformer's opponent could claim credit for warding off an interference with traditional comforts which might spark off a conflagration.[70]

Like the attacks on drink and the CD Acts, feminists could not convincingly present themselves as restraining their supporters from resorting to revolution, and at first they resembled their predecessors in uniting humanitarian objectives with humanitarian methods. But in 1908 Herbert Gladstone correctly pointed out that 'predominance of argument alone . . . is not enough to win the political day' and that 'there comes a time when political dynamics are far more important than political argument'. This encouraged the Pankhursts to draw the wrong conclusion and assume that violence of any kind would suit the purpose, and to diverge from earlier reformers by developing a militant offshoot which tried to coerce politicians with simulated mass violence. This was a gift to the anti-suffragists, who tried to tar the non-militants with the suffragette brush.[71] In a lecture to ageing suffragettes in 1932, Laski tried to expose the hypocrisies of politicians who wished to respond to violence without appearing to do so: 'when an angry clamour surrounds the demand, insist that you cannot yield to violence; and when finally, you are driven to yield, say that it is because you have been intellectually convinced that the perspective of events has changed'.[72] Yet this argument falls into the trap the suffragettes had themselves

[69] *The Shield*, 31 May 1870, p. 119; Samuel Smith, *H. C. Deb.*, 27 Apr. 1883, c.1324.

[70] See Ker Seymer, *H. C. Deb.*, 3 June 1863, cc.292-3; cf. my 'The Sunday Trading Riots of 1855', *Historical Journal*, 1965, pp. 238, 242.

[71] Gladstone, *H. C. Deb.*, 28 Feb. 1908, cc.242-3; see also Arnold Ward, *H. C. Deb.*, 28 Mar. 1912, cc.715-16.

[72] H. Laski, *Militant Temper*, p. 18.

designed for the politicians, for it fails to distinguish between political violence of different types, and presents the political system as responding in an almost mechanistic way to its incidence. In reality, in all the movements under discussion, the politicians were shrewd enough to ward off any threat from mass violence, and in the case of the suffragettes they called the bluff of those whose militancy attempted to simulate it. Violence did indeed assist the enactment of women's suffrage in 1917-18—not Mrs Pankhurst's letter-bombs, smashed windows, and burned buildings, but the potential threat of an aroused working class of both sexes on the Russian revolutionary model.[73] Women's enfranchise- ment on an age-restricted basis as part of an adult suffrage measure—something the suffragettes had never demanded —seemed the safest way of moderating present and impend-ing popular discontents and channelling them towards parliament. Still, there are limits even to the conservative's capacity for initiating diversionary moves; the time eventually comes when the politician has been pushed to the point of legislating.

V

Yet here the extra-parliamentary reformer is at his most vulnerable, for the experienced politician excels him in three areas: he has a wider understanding of human nature, a fuller knowledge of the over-all political situation, and greater experience in framing legislation. In the final stages of the reforming process, therefore, the extra-parliamentary movement is very much in the hands of its leaders, who are themselves in thrall to sympathetic statesmen. The reformer may have a more lively appreciation than the politician of the altruistic and idealistic side of human nature, but the politician will have a firmer grasp of human nature as it is than of human nature as it should be. 'Life is nothing without enthusiasms'. Richard Pankhurst was fond of telling his family,[74] yet enthusiasms survive only with difficulty

---

[73] See my *Separate Spheres*, pp. 186, 217-20.
[74] E. S. Pankhurst, *The Suffragette Movement*, p. 67; cf. Josephine Butler, in *The Shield*, 31 Jan. 1874, p. 37.

amidst the politician's necessary preoccupation with established fact.

The aged Gladstone, who was in a position to know, told
Tollemache that 'nowhere does the ideal enter so little as
into politics; nowhere does human conduct fall so far below
the highest ethical standard' than in parliament.[75] Not the
least of parliament's nineteenth-century integrating functions
lay in its supplying a school of realism and compromise to
the politically inexperienced groups that were being incorporated into the governmental system. Samuel Smith was
by no means the only Victorian philanthropist to find his
arrival at Westminster a broadening experience; looking back
in his autobiography he described the House of Commons
as 'a wonderfully educating institution . . . No man can long
sit there and be an extreme dogmatist, or can fail to perceive
that political truth is many sided.'[76] There, extremists of
right and left were compelled to hear the arguments used by
their opponents; there the theorist was either forced to take
account of practical considerations or risk being ignored.

Principles at first sight appear to offer the reformer a
shield to protect him from the need for thought when faced
by practical situations within the politician's murky world.
The man of principle and the rationalistic reformer—or, in
C. W. R. Cooke's parlance, the prigs and the professors—
shun the smoking-room and refuse compromise.[77] But as
soon as legislation is nigh, the reformer finds an intruder on
the scene who, unlike the reformer, is accustomed to grappling
closely with the arguments of those who disagree and who is
not a specialist in the area but a jack of all trades—the
statesman who aims to settle the matter. Whereas Shaftesbury could refer to 'my especial questions' in 1846,[78] whereas
John Bright could reserve himself for the occasional set-piece
oration on a chosen theme,[79] the statesman must resign

[75] L. A. Tollemache, *Talks with Mr. Gladstone*, p. 168, cf. Lord Robert Cecil
in *Saturday Review*, 17 Sept. 1864, p. 358.

[76] S. Smith, *My Life-Work*, p. 146, cf. p. 145.

[77] C. W. R. Cooke, *Four Years in Parliament*, pp. 17–18, 54.

[78] E. Hodder, *Shaftesbury*, ii, p. 168.

[79] S. H. Harris, *Auberon Herbert. Crusader for Liberty* (1943), p. 78; see also
Balfour's forceful attack on Bright's parliamentary rhetoric in *H. C. Deb.*, 12 Aug.
1880, cc.1043–4.

himself to speaking imperfectly and impromptu, often on all manner of topics. He gains in width of perspective what he loses in formal consistency, which is the luxury of those who are free from conflicting governmental responsibilities; Canning did not hesitate to point this out in 1826 when taunted on that score by Buxton.[80]

When legislation is nigh, the full ramifications of the proposed change need to be considered, and attention has to move to practical topics such as the likely impact of abolition on slavery in other countries, on prosperity and public order in the West Indies, and on relationships between the British parliament and the colonial assemblies. These were all considerations raised after 1788 by the planters' and traders' spokesmen at Westminster. Perhaps most important of all considerations was the need to conciliate the planter interest since, as statesmen from 1823 onwards realized, slavery could not be effectively abolished without full co-operation from the planters. Far from firing shots at the planters across an abyss, the statesman needed to grapple with their immediate concerns and devise a scheme for compensation. A similar breadth of range had to be displayed when considering the other reforms under discussion: the impact of shorter factory hours on levels of employment for example, the implications of parliamentary reform for governmental stability, the bearing of women's suffrage on Britain's international standing, and so on. In his tussle with the factory-hours movement during 1844, Sir James Graham tried to impress on his hearers the sheer fragility of the legislative process: 'the subject is delicate', he declared on one occasion, 'it is like a house built of cards, from which one can not be removed without danger to the whole fabric'.[81]

The politician's knowledge of human nature and of the over-all political situation, then, enable him to frame legislation; but this, in its final form, often differs markedly from the reformer's original proposals. The emancipation of the slaves is accompanied by an apprenticeship scheme; restriction of factory hours is enforced by inspectors; the Corn Laws are repealed only after delay; the CD Acts are at first

---

[80] *H. C. Deb.*, 1 Mar. 1826, c.980.   [81] *H. C. Deb.*, 18 Mar. 1844, c.1215.

only suspended, not abolished; the women are enfranchised initially only under an age restriction and in company with newly-enfranchised men. The reformer may sometimes privately envisage making some of these concessions, but for tactical reasons he refrains from advocating them in public. The campaign against capital punishment shows how badly such a strategy may misfire; its uncompromising assaults on the demoralization resulting from public executions merely caused politicians to remove them behind prison walls— thus making it possible to perpetuate capital punishment itself for another century.[82] But the reformer will sometimes oppose concessions both publicly and privately to the end— as did Sylvia Pankhurst on women's suffrage in 1917-18—if only because he too displays that 'fatal tendency to under-estimate difficulties and to neglect mechanisms' which has been detected in American social-gospel leaders.[83]

An effective political system needs to bring those who discover and expose evils into regular contact with specialists who devise remedies for them, and to break down the barrier between the idealistic reformer and the statesman experienced in running the governmental machine. For the simplicity of outlook associated with the deeply religious mind frequently encourages contentment with the registering of a protest; the anti-slavery, temperance, and peace movements often took on this flavour, and sometimes even advertised their contempt for any attempt at palliation. Challenged by the royal commission in 1871 to show how voluntary effort could curb venereal disease, Josephine Butler had no solution other than increasing efforts at voluntary reclamation.[84] The old opponent of slavery George Thompson told a prohibitionist meeting in the same year that 'he had never gone for half measures', and that the drink trade was 'not an evil to be regulated, but a gigantic crime to be abolished'.[85]

In so far as the reformers recognized their defect, they were not necessarily unduly concerned. Their role was to

---

[82] D. D. Cooper, *The Lesson of the Scaffold* (1974), pp. 47, 51, 175-6.

[83] H. F. May, *Protestant Churches and Industrial America* (New York, 1949), p. 233.

[84] *C.D. Acts Commission*, Q.13052.

[85] Thompson, *Alliance News*, 14 Oct. 1871, p. 661; cf. Fox, *H. C. Deb.*, 18 Feb. 1796, c.760; A. C. F. Beales, *The History of Peace* (1931), p. 98.

compel the statesman to find a way through administrative and other complexities; for them, government was not an extraordinarily difficult business provided that one embarked upon it with the right character and principles.[86] Some reforming leaders—Shaftesbury and Cobden perhaps, certainly Wilberforce—had a sneaking admiration for the statesman; others professed to despise his role, and pointed to the unprincipled inconsistency allegedly associated with it. Policy, for them, consisted merely in choosing the good and rejecting the bad. Outlining the misery he would feel in wearing court dress, John Bright in 1858 consoled himself by saying 'better teach the people something good for the future than resign oneself to work institutions already in existence. Few men can do the former; the latter is but a matter of routine.'[87] Perhaps after his own (scarcely successful) experience in government later, he would have modified this view.

In dealing with slavery and drink, one last-minute obstacle proved particularly intractable: the problem of compensation. When collecting evidence against the slave trade, Clarkson was struck by the sudden sight of Bristol when he first saw it a mile off: 'I began . . . to tremble, for the first time, at the arduous task I had undertaken, of attempting to subvert one of the branches of the commerce of the great place which was then before me.'[88] The planters tried to frighten their opponents by stressing the antiquity of their trade and the immense amount of capital invested in it; Wilberforce and others countered with figures on its small proportion even of Bristol's and Liverpool's trade.[89] But many reformers denied the need for, or the justice of, paying compensation at all. Why should the exploiter be compensated if his profits had already been so huge? And if he himself had so much to gain, spiritually and even materially, by the change? And if the exploited received nothing at all?

Here was another opportunity for conservative diversion,

---

[86] Cf. E. Burke, *French Revolution*, p. 151; J. W. Osborne, *William Cobbett. His Thought and his Times* (New Brunswick, 1966), p. 251.

[87] J. Bright, *The Diaries* (1930), pp. 241-2.

[88] T. Clarkson, *Slave Trade*, p. 180.

[89] Wilberforce, *H. C. Deb.*, 18 Apr. 1791, cc.271-2; 2 Apr. 1792, c.1065; Howick, *H. C. Deb.*, 23 Feb. 1807, c.948.

and even for recruiting new allies. For if compensation were not paid in this instance, would any property be safe?[90] Baring in 1823 even taunted Buxton himself, as a brewer, with favouring compensation when it came to free trade in beer; to judge from the heat of Buxton's rejoinder, Baring drew blood.[91] The Whig government in 1833 decided to conciliate all interests by tying its emancipationist measure to specific compensation proposals, and the precedent was cited approvingly by Gladstone in the local option debate of 1880.[92] Compensation became a major issue in temperance controversy during the 1880s, but it was not of course relevant in every reforming cause. Compensation was not paid to the slave-traders in 1807; indeed, Pitt had argued in 1792 that compensation in the latter case would render all government regulation of commerce impossible.[93] Lawson in 1877 pointed out that compensation had been paid neither to the factory owners when working hours were cut, nor to the landlords when the Corn Laws were repealed;[94] feminism did not even give rise to the issue.

The reformer's failure to compromise at the denouement might be defended by pointing to a clear division of labour, fully recognized in reforming circles, between the politician and the reformer; the reformer pushes the axis of discussion leftwards, knowing that the politician will eventually effect a compromise settlement, and that the settlement will be the more radical for his publicly uncompromising stance.[95] With the shrewder reforming leader this may indeed be so, but such a theory will not fit all the movements under discussion here. The reformer's relationship with the history of reform between 1780 and 1918 is rather more paradoxical than the historiography of reforming movements often leads us to expect. He undoubtedly stirs up new sensitivities,

---

[90] See e.g. Earl of Westmoreland on the slave trade, *H. L. Deb.*, 5 Feb. 1807, c.667; cf. Muntz on the drink trade, *H. C. Deb.*, 7 May 1873, c.1652.

[91] *H. C. Deb.*, 15 May 1823, cc.348, 352.

[92] *H. C. Deb.*, 5 Mar. 1880, cc.469–70.

[93] *H. C. Deb.*, 2 Apr. 1792, c.1146.

[94] *H. C. Deb.*, 13 Mar. 1877, cc.1888–9.

[95] Cf. H. Zinn, 'Abolitionists, Freedom-Riders, and the Tactics of Agitation', in M. Duberman (ed.), *The Antislavery Vanguard: New Essays on the Abolitionists* (Princeton, 1965), pp. 433–4.

pioneers new attitudes, but in the later stages he sometimes hinders more than he helps, sometimes gets much less than he had hoped for, and sometimes gets no reform at all. This is partly because his aims usually extend beyond any particular legislative reform; his grandiose perspective both hinders compromise when his campaign reaches its denouement, and leads him to resist the indignity of having his reform tacked on to another measure—prohibition on to a licensing measure, women's suffrage on to an adult-suffrage measure, and so on.[96] The reformer's victory needs to be striking, and enacted in such a way that the children of darkness can be clearly distinguished from the children of light. Listing the benefits introduced by the agitation against the slave trade, Clarkson includes the fact that 'in private life it has enabled us to distinguish the virtuous from the more vicious part of the community' and that in public life 'it has separated the moral statesman from the wicked politician'.[97]

Such an outlook views the politician's proposals merely as attempts to divide the reformers, or as tricks to put them off the scent. 'My soul was deeply troubled at the sight of so many men with so base and low a moral standard as you seem to have, and such utter scepticism both about God and human nature', Josephine Butler told one of the royal commissioners in 1871.[98] In 1872 H. A. Bruce's compromise proposals were dismissed by her movement simply as a wily plot,[99] and in 1898 she still saw government as preparing to throw 'a great net of medical tyranny . . . craftily planned, and cautiously begun' over the civil population.[1] While the opponents of any reform are indeed eager to split its advocates, the politician usually aims in reality simply to settle a tiresome question to the moderate satisfaction of middle opinion.

[96] See my *Drink and the Victorians*, pp. 269, 374; C. Pankhurst, *Unshackled*, p. 187; R. Fulford, *Votes for Women. The Story of a Struggle* (1958 ed.), p. 214.
[97] T. Clarkson, *Slave Trade*, p. 613; cf. H. Temperley, *British Antislavery 1833-1870* (1972), p. 138; J. Butler in *The Storm-Bell*, Apr. 1899, p. 162, July 1898, p. 73. [98] Quot. in G. Petrie, *A Singular Iniquity*, p. 116.
[99] *The Shield*, 7 Sept. 1872, p. 1067.
[1] *Storm-Bell*, Feb. 1898, p. 19, cf. *The Dawn*, 1 Aug. 1888, p. 11, and cf. P. A. Taylor's stance on vaccination, *H. C. Deb.*, 19 June 1883, cc.994, 996.

But the politician compounds his sin in the eyes of the reformer by trying to build up a centre tendency in public opinion which will enable him to enact compromise legislation. This is difficult because the reformer has often provoked an equal and opposite reaction among those he attacks, nor has the moderate position much dramatic appeal. Dundas in trying to build up a regulationist grouping in parliament was but the earliest in a chain of moderates—from Charles Ellis in 1797 to Canning in 1823 to Gladstone in 1860 to H. A. Bruce in 1871-2 to Joseph Chamberlain in 1877 (to take examples from only the anti-slavery, CD Act, and temperance questions)—who found themselves stranded midway between two apparently irreconcilable groupings. Stanley's concessions to both sides in 1833 eventually got emancipation through the House, but his description of the legislator's plight when beset by two rival interests is almost as eloquent as Gladstone's when trying to get his wine-licence scheme through the House in 1860: 'we are, in regard to this Bill', said Gladstone, 'much in the position of Hercules, as we are encountered by two figures of Virtue and Vice. But instead of Virtue soliciting us to go one way, and Vice pressing us to go another, we have both Virtue and Vice leagued against us, both standing across the road and refusing to allow us to proceed.'[2] Gladstone was not alone among nineteenth-century statesmen in identifying the reformer himself as a major obstacle to reform; Dundas said the same of the abolitionists in 1796, Bruce of the prohibitionists in 1871, and numerous politicians of the suffragettes between 1906 and 1914.[3]

At the point of legislation, the reformer faces his most severe test, and he quite often utters cries of pain as a result.[4] It is difficult for a single individual to combine in his own person a recognition of the compromises necessary to hold

---

[2] Gladstone, *H. C. Deb.*, 7 May 1860, c.828; Stanley, *H. C. Deb.*, 11 June 1833, c.584; cf. Grey, *H. L. Deb.*, 25 June 1833, c.1202.

[3] Dundas, *H. C. Deb.*, 18 Feb. 1796, c.751; cf. Stanley, *H. C. Deb.*, 24 July 1833, c.1194; Bruce, *H. C. Deb.*, 17 May 1871, c.949; cf. Fowler's remark quot. in D. A. Hamer, *Liberal Politics in the Age of Gladstone and Rosebery. A Study in Leadership and Policy* (Oxford, 1972), pp. 212-13; Ramsay MacDonald on the suffragettes in *H. C. Deb.*, May 1913, c.1983.

[4] e.g. Buxton, *H. C. Deb.*, 10 June 1833, c.546.

the government on course with a continuing indignation against the evil which will stoke up the fires of the reforming movement up till the end. It is also difficult to survive as leader of a righteously indignant movement after accepting the statesman's compromise offer. Nineteenth-century reforming leaders were seldom in complete control of their movements,[5] and in accepting compromise offers as the best which could be got, Buxton in 1833, Cobden in 1846, Shaftesbury in 1850-3, Stansfeld in 1883, and Mrs Fawcett in 1917 reveal themselves retrospectively in a better light than the fiery impossibilist Josephine Butler, the jovially ineffectual Wilfrid Lawson, and the disastrously courageous Emmeline Pankhurst.

No notion of any one-to-one relationship between reforming effort and reforming legislation can therefore survive a close analysis of nineteenth-century reform movements. Indeed, of the United Kingdom Alliance it has been argued that 'failure was too often regarded as proof of steadfast adherence to principle'.[6] The agitation against Bulgarian atrocities achieved no more than a temporary and small-scale alteration in British foreign policy, and did not free Russia from needing to resort to arms, as W. T. Stead apologetically explained to the Tsar twelve years later.[7] With slave-trade abolition and women's emancipation, the reform was won only when, and perhaps partly because, the agitation had fallen well below its peak strength.

The pioneer woman doctor Elizabeth Garrett Anderson claimed in 1884 that the arguments used by the opponents of reform have always been wrong.[8] It is of course true that many of the conservative's fears proved exaggerated, and that many of the consequences of reform that he correctly predicted were longer delayed and more safely implemented than he expected. But conservatives often themselves helped to ward off the disastrous consequences which they had

---

[5] On this problem, see e.g. C. Buxton, *T. F. Buxton*, pp. 325, 331; N. McCord, *The Anti-Corn Law League 1838-1846* (1958), pp. 200-3; E. Hodder, *Shaftesbury*, ii, pp. 201-2.

[6] J. R. Greenaway, 'The Local Option Question and British Politics 1864-1914' (unpublished Ph.D. thesis, Leeds, 1974), p. 66.

[7] R. T. Shannon, *Bulgarian Atrocities Agitation*, pp. 264-6.

[8] *Women's Suffrage Journal*, 1 July 1884, p. 184.

predicted; Peel, for instance, set out in his political practice after 1832 to prevent the Reform Act from accomplishing the social and political disruption which the Act's opponents had anticipated. Furthermore, the conservative's warnings were often at the time salutary for reformers rushing too breathlessly forward into change. Even when successful, reformers were often disappointed at the outcome of their reforms. The planters were entirely correct in predicting disaster to the economy of the West Indies if slavery were abolished. The economic problems of the West Indies did not precede but followed the abolition of the trade, with its consequent shortage of labour and catastrophic decline in sugar production.[9] And if protectionist fears for the landed interest and for British national security were in the short term misplaced, the free-trade case was severely weakened in the longer term by the agricultural depression of the late 1870s and virtually destroyed by the submarine threat to the national food supply during the first world war.

The analysis conducted here cannot of course specify any exact time-span between the four stages of reforming debate, or even whether those four stages will ever be completed. It may also lose validity if it is extended to cover other movements (especially interest groups, as distinct from cause groups) and other cultures. On the other hand, the analysis may actually be improved and refined by such extension. The vitality of the Anglo-American philanthropic connection between 1780 and 1918, the tendency for British reform movements to grow an international dimension—both suggest that parallels in other cultures are likely to be found. But if attempts are made to apply the analysis to Britain outside the period between 1780 and 1918, major adjustments will be required, for those years were in many ways distinctive; reforming movements were profoundly influenced in their rhetoric by the advent of new and inexperienced groups, often with millennial expectations, on to a political scene which was not yet democratic, and which favoured the minimum of government intervention.

---

[9] H. Temperley, 'Capitalism, Slavery, and Ideology', *Past and Present*, no. 75 (May 1977), pp. 103–4.

Yet there is also something timeless about the situation which has been analysed. Belief that present sufferings are not inevitable, suspicion of the corruptions associated with the wielding of power, a yearning for the harmony which could result from getting one's own ideas and values universally accepted, impatience with the half-measures and untidiness inevitable in a political system where all do not agree—these are rather more permanent features of the human experience. So also are the fear that a new society will be less humane, less stable, less congenial than the old; the belief that changes, if they must be introduced at all, can safely be introduced only slowly; the suspicion that those who wish to move faster have consciously or unconsciously some sinister interest to promote; and the conviction that social institutions and attitudes are toughly resistant to change, and can rarely be substantially modified by legislation. Britain since 1918 has certainly witnessed many of the situations and responses so far discussed; indeed, elements of the nineteenth-century rhetoric of reform can still be seen and heard all around us.

Whether this analysis can be applied more widely or not, it may help to modify the somewhat jaundiced portraits of the conservative temperament in Laski's lecture and in Cornford's *Microcosmographia Academica*, while at the same time sketching a radical temperament somewhat more congenial than Coleridge portrays in his *Lay Sermon* of 1817. It also clothes with concrete incidents some of the shrewd perceptions which these authors, for different reasons, were unable to illustrate at the time of writing. The analysis perhaps lends some support to A. V. Dicey's view of the conservative as 'in reality . . . in most cases . . . an honest man of average ability, who has opposed a beneficial change not through exceptional selfishness, but through some intellectual delusion unconsciously created by the bias of a sinister interest'.[10] But this perception should not be purchased at the price of totally repudiating John Stuart Mill's view that 'nothing is more certain than that improvement in human affairs is wholly the work of the uncontented characters'.[11]

[10] A. V. Dicey, *Law and Public Opinion*, p. 16.
[11] J. S. Mill, *Representative Government*, p. 211.

Index

Where several entries appear under one heading, the most important of them feature in heavy type. Individuals appear under the name by which they are best known (thus 'Disraeli', not 'Beaconsfield').